Collins
Junior
illustrated
Dictionary

HarperCollins Publishers
Westerhill Road
Bishopbriggs
Glasgow
G64 2QT

Second Edition 2014

10 9 8 7 6 5 4 3 2 1

© HarperCollins Publishers 2010, 2014

ISBN 978-0-00-755305-1

Collins® is a registered trademark of
HarperCollins Publishers Limited

www.collinsdictionary.com
www.collins.co.uk

A catalogue record for this book is
available from the British Library

Typeset by Davidson Publishing Solutions, Glasgow

Design by Q2A Media Services Private Limited

Printed by Martins the Printers, Berwick-upon-Tweed

MIX
Paper from
responsible sources
FSC™ C007454
www.fsc.org

FSC™ is a non-profit international organisation established to promote the
responsible management of the world's forests. Products carrying the FSC
label are independently certified to assure consumers that they come from
forests that are managed to meet the social, economic and ecological needs
of present and future generations, and other controlled sources.

Find out more about HarperCollins and the environment at
www.harpercollins.co.uk/green

Entered words that we have reason to believe
constitute trademarks have been designated as
such. However, neither the presence nor absence of
such designation should be regarded as affecting
the legal status of any trademark.

HarperCollins does not warrant that any
website mentioned in this title will be provided
uninterrupted, that any website will be error free,
that defects will be corrected, or that the website or
the server that makes it available are free of viruses
or bugs. For full terms and conditions please refer to
the site terms provided on the website.

Editors
Jennifer Baird
Ian Brookes

Computing Support
Thomas Callan

For the Publisher
Gerry Breslin
Kerry Ferguson

Contents

Using this dictionary

A dictionary tells you what a word means and how to spell it. The words in a dictionary are listed in alphabetical order.

How to find a word

Look up the word **fruit**. What letter does it begin with? Use the **alphabet line** at the side of the page. The blue box tells you that the blue words on this page (called **headwords**) start with **f**.

Think about the next letter or letters of the word. You are looking for a word beginning with **fru**. Use the **guide words** at the top of the page. These tell you the first headword and the last headword to appear on that page. The guide words for this page are **from - funnel**. Does **fru** come after **fro**? Does **fru** come before **fun**?

When you think you have the right page, look at the headwords. These are in alphabetical order. If you run your finger down the headwords on this page, you will see more than one that begins with **fr**, so look for a headword that begins with **fru**.

Keep looking until you find the word **fruit**.

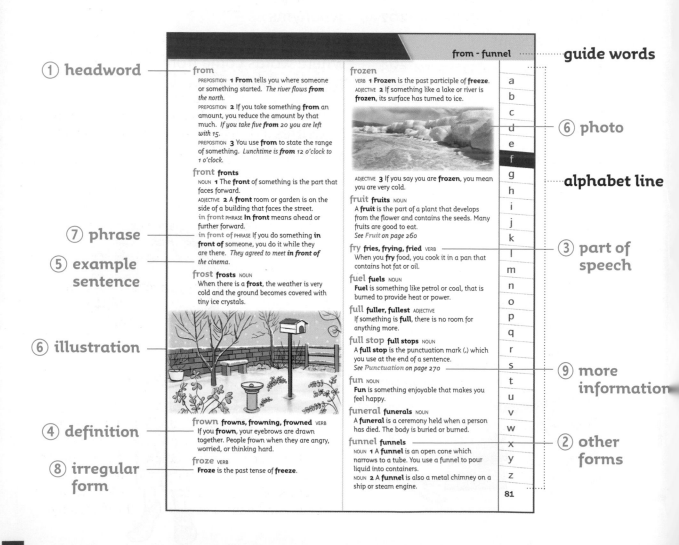

① **headword**

⑥ **photo**

guide words

alphabet line

③ **part of speech**

⑦ **phrase**

⑤ **example sentence**

⑥ **illustration**

⑨ **more information**

④ **definition**

② **other forms**

⑧ **irregular form**

from - funnel

from
PREPOSITION **1 From** tells you where someone or something started. *The river flows from the north.*
PREPOSITION **2** If you take something **from** an amount, you reduce the amount by that much. *If you take five from 20 you are left with 15.*
PREPOSITION **3** You use **from** to state the range of something. *Lunchtime is from 12 o'clock to 1 o'clock.*

front fronts
NOUN **1** The **front** of something is the part that faces forward.
ADJECTIVE **2** A **front** room or garden is on the side of a building that faces the street.
in front PHRASE **In front** means ahead or further forward.
in front of PHRASE If you do something **in front of** someone, you do it while they are there. *They agreed to meet in front of the cinema.*

frost frosts NOUN
When there is a **frost**, the weather is very cold and the ground becomes covered with tiny ice crystals.

frown frowns, frowning, frowned VERB
If you **frown**, your eyebrows are drawn together. People frown when they are angry, worried, or thinking hard.

froze VERB
Froze is the past tense of **freeze**.

frozen
VERB **1 Frozen** is the past participle of **freeze**.
ADJECTIVE **2** If something like a lake or river is **frozen**, its surface has turned to ice.

ADJECTIVE **3** If you say you are **frozen**, you mean you are very cold.

fruit fruits NOUN
A **fruit** is the part of a plant that develops from the flower and contains the seeds. Many fruits are good to eat.
See *Fruit* on page 260

fry fries, frying, fried VERB
When you **fry** food, you cook it in a pan that contains hot fat or oil.

fuel fuels NOUN
Fuel is something like petrol or coal, that is burned to provide heat or power.

full fuller, fullest ADJECTIVE
If something is **full**, there is no room for anything more.

full stop full stops NOUN
A **full stop** is the punctuation mark (.) which you use at the end of a sentence.
See *Punctuation* on page 270

fun NOUN
Fun is something enjoyable that makes you feel happy.

funeral funerals NOUN
A **funeral** is a ceremony held when a person has died. The body is buried or burned.

funnel funnels
NOUN **1** A **funnel** is an open cone which narrows to a tube. You use a funnel to pour liquid into containers.
NOUN **2** A **funnel** is also a metal chimney on a ship or steam engine.

a b c d e f g h i j k l m n o p q r s t u v w x y z

81

Using this dictionary

Finding out about a word

1. The **headword** is the word you are looking up.

2. On the same line as the headword, you will see how to spell **other forms** of the word, such as plural nouns, verb tenses or other adjective forms, called comparatives and superlatives.

3. Next you will see the **part of speech**. This tells you what type of word the headword is, such as a noun, verb, adjective, adverb or pronoun.

4. After the part of speech, you will find the **definition**. The definition tells you what the word means. The definitions are numbered if there is more than one. Each definition has its own part of speech.

5. Some words have an **example sentence** in *italics*. This shows you how the word might be used in speech or writing.

6. Some words have a **photo** or other **illustration** to help you read the word and understand its meaning.

7. A **phrase** may also be included. Under the word **front**, you will also find the definition of the phrases **in front** and **in front of**.

8. An **irregular form** of a word is a plural noun or verb tense which does not follow the usual spelling rules. You can find many irregular forms in this dictionary.

9. Some definitions tell you where to look for **more information**, such as another headword, or the pages at the back of the dictionary.

Other dictionary features

Pronunciation is how you say a word. Some words can be spelled the same, but sound different and mean different things – these words are called homographs. This dictionary gives you pronunciation help for some words, including homographs. For example:

> **tear** **tears, tearing, tore, torn**
> (*rhymes with* **fear**) NOUN **1** Tears are the drops of liquid that come out of your eyes when you cry.
> (*rhymes with* **fair**) VERB **2** If you **tear** something, such as paper or fabric, you pull it apart.

Some definitions include a **label**, such as FORMAL, INFORMAL or TRADEMARK. This tells you a little more about the word or how it is used:

> **Rollerblade** **Rollerblades**
> NOUN; TRADEMARK **Rollerblades** are roller skates which have the wheels set in one straight line on the bottom of the boot.

Related words are given at the end of some entries, with their parts of speech. These tell you other forms of the word, such as the noun or adverb form. For example:

> **blur** **blurs** NOUN
> A **blur** is a shape that you cannot see clearly. *The car went past so fast it was just a blur.*
> **blurred** ADJECTIVE **blurry** ADJECTIVE

Collins Word Wizard

Collins Word Wizard (pages 255 – 279) gives you extra help with vocabulary, grammar and spelling. It has pages to help you understand parts of speech, punctuation, and prefixes and suffixes, as well as handy hints for learning tricky spellings. Look out for the themed picture pages and games to play with the dictionary.

A
B
C
D
E
F
G
H
I
J
K
L
M
N
O
P
Q
R
S
T
U
V
W
X
Y
Z

Aa

a or **an** ADJECTIVE
A and **an** are used when you talk about one of something. **A** is used when the next sound is a consonant; **an** is used when the next sound is a vowel (a, e, i, o or u). *a car... **an** apple*

abandon **abandons, abandoning, abandoned**
VERB **1** If you **abandon** something, you leave it and do not return. *The cub had been **abandoned** by its mother.*
VERB **2** If you **abandon** a piece of work, you stop doing it before it is finished.

abbreviation **abbreviations** NOUN
An **abbreviation** is a short form of a word or phrase. *The **abbreviation** for compact disc is CD.*

ability **abilities** NOUN
If you have the **ability** to do something, you are able to do it.

able **abler, ablest** ADJECTIVE
If you are **able** to do something, you can do it.

aboard PREPOSITION
If you are **aboard** a ship or plane, you are on or in it.

about
ADVERB **1** You say **about** in front of a number to show it is not exact. *I'll be home at **about** five o'clock.*
PREPOSITION **2** If you talk or write **about** something, you say things to do with that subject. *He is talking **about** boats.*

above PREPOSITION
If something is **above** something else, it is over it, or higher up. *He held the ball **above** his head.*

abroad ADVERB
When you go **abroad**, you go to a different country.

absent ADJECTIVE
If someone is **absent**, they are not here.

absolutely ADVERB
You can use **absolutely** to make what you are saying sound stronger. *You must stay **absolutely** still.*

absorb **absorbs, absorbing, absorbed**
VERB
If something **absorbs** a liquid, it soaks it up or takes it in.

absurd ADJECTIVE
Something that is **absurd** seems silly, because it is quite different from what you would expect. *It's **absurd** to wear your jumper in this heat.*

abuse NOUN
Abuse is cruel treatment of someone.

accelerate **accelerates, accelerating, accelerated** VERB
When someone **accelerates**, they speed up.

accept **accepts, accepting, accepted** VERB
If you **accept** something you have been offered, you say yes to it.

accident **accidents** NOUN
An **accident** is something nasty that happens by chance. *He broke his leg in a climbing **accident**.*
accidentally ADVERB

account **accounts**
NOUN **1** An **account** is something written or spoken that tells you what has happened.
NOUN **2** An **account** is also money that you keep at a bank.

accurate ADJECTIVE
An **accurate** measurement or description is exactly right.

ache **aches** NOUN
An **ache** is a dull, lasting pain.

achieve **achieves, achieving, achieved**
VERB
If you **achieve** something, you usually get it by hard work.
achievement NOUN

acid **acids** NOUN
Some **acids** give food a sharp, sour taste. Lemons and vinegar contain acid. Strong acid can burn your skin.

acid rain NOUN
Acid rain is rain that is mixed with dirty gases in the air. It can damage buildings, trees and fish.

acrobat **acrobats** NOUN
An **acrobat** is someone who does difficult and exciting tricks, like balancing on a high wire.

across PREPOSITION
If you go **across** something, you go from one side to the other.

act **acts, acting, acted**
VERB **1** When you **act**, you do something. *He had to act quickly to put out the fire.*
VERB **2** If you **act** in a play or film, you have a part in it.
NOUN **3** An **act** is something that you do.

action **actions** NOUN
An **action** is a movement of part of your body.

active
ADJECTIVE **1** Someone who is **active** moves about a lot, or is very busy.
ADJECTIVE **2** In grammar, a verb in the **active** voice is one where the subject does the action, rather than having it done to them.
See **voice**

activity **activities** NOUN
Activity is when there are a lot of things happening.

actor **actors** NOUN
An **actor** is a man or woman whose job is to act in plays or films.

actress **actresses** NOUN
A female actor is sometimes called an **actress**.
See **actor**

actual ADJECTIVE
You describe something as **actual** when you mean it is real. *The shop said the paint was red, but the actual colour was pink.*
actually ADVERB

adapt **adapts, adapting, adapted**
VERB **1** If you **adapt** to something new, you change in some way that helps you.
VERB **2** If you **adapt** something, you change it to suit your needs. *The book was adapted to make a film.*

adaptable ADJECTIVE
Someone who is **adaptable** can change to deal with new situations.

add **adds, adding, added**
VERB **1** If you **add** something, you put it with whatever you have already. *Put flour in the bowl and add an egg.*
VERB **2** If you **add** numbers of things together, you find out how many you have. The sign + means add. *2 + 3 = 5. I have two marbles in the bag. If I add these three, it makes five altogether.*

addition NOUN
Addition is adding numbers or things together.

address **addresses** NOUN
Your **address** is the name or number of your house, and the street and town where you live.

adjective **adjectives** NOUN
An **adjective** is a word that describes someone or something. "Beautiful" and "green" are adjectives.
See Adjective on page 269

admire **admires, admiring, admired**
VERB **1** When you **admire** someone, you think very highly of them.
VERB **2** When you **admire** something, you enjoy looking at it. *They stopped the car to admire the view.*

a
b
c
d
e
f
g
h
i
j
k
l
m
n
o
p
q
r
s
t
u
v
w
x
y
z

admit admits, admitting, admitted
VERB **1** If you **admit** something, you agree that it is true.
VERB **2** If people are **admitted** to a place, they are allowed to go in.

adopt adopts, adopting, adopted VERB
If a person **adopts** a child, they make the child their own by law.

adore adores, adoring, adored VERB
If you **adore** someone, you love them very much.

adult adults NOUN
An **adult** is a grown-up person or animal.

advance advances, advancing, **advanced** VERB
If someone **advances**, they move forward. *The army advanced nine miles in one day.*

advantage advantages NOUN
An **advantage** is something that helps you do better than other people. *His long legs gave him an advantage in the race.*

adventure adventures NOUN
If you are having an **adventure**, you are doing something exciting.

adverb adverbs NOUN
An **adverb** is a word that answers questions like how, when, where and why. In the sentence "The girl came quietly into the room", the word "quietly" is an adverb telling you how the girl came in.
See Adverb on page 269

advertise advertises, advertising, **advertised** VERB
If you **advertise** something, you tell people about it through newspapers, posters or TV.

advertisement advertisements NOUN
An **advertisement** is a notice in the paper, or on a poster or TV, about a job or things for sale.

advice NOUN
If you give someone **advice**, you say what you think they should do.

advise advises, advising, advised VERB
When you **advise** someone, you tell them what you think they should do.

aerial aerials NOUN
An **aerial** is a wire that sends or receives radio or television signals.

aeroplane aeroplanes NOUN
An **aeroplane** is a flying vehicle with wings and one or more engines.

affect affects, affecting, affected VERB
When something **affects** someone or something else, it changes them in some way.

affection NOUN
Affection is a feeling of caring for someone.

afford affords, affording, afforded VERB
If you can **afford** something, you have enough money to buy it or do it.

afraid ADJECTIVE
Someone who is **afraid** thinks that something nasty might happen.

after PREPOSITION
If something happens **after** something else, it happens at a later time. *We'll watch television after supper.*

afternoon afternoons NOUN
The **afternoon** is the time of day between 12 o'clock (noon) and about six o'clock in the evening.

afterwards ADVERB
If something happens **afterwards**, it happens after another event or time. *We went swimming, and afterwards we had an ice cream.*

again ADVERB
If you do something **again**, you do it once more.

against
PREPOSITION **1** If you play **against** someone, you are not on their side.
PREPOSITION **2** If you are **against** something, you are touching it and leaning on it. *She felt tired and leaned **against** the tree.*

age **ages**
NOUN **1** Your **age** is how old you are.
NOUN **2** An **age** is a special period in history, like the Stone Age.

ago ADVERB
If something happened four days **ago**, it is four days since it happened.

agree **agrees, agreeing, agreed**
VERB **1** If you **agree** with someone, you think the same about something.
VERB **2** If you **agree** to do something, you say you will do it.
agreement NOUN

ahead ADVERB
Something or someone who is **ahead** of you is in front of you.
*My brother ran **ahead** of us.*

aim **aims, aiming, aimed**
VERB **1** If you **aim** at something, you point a weapon at it.
VERB **2** If you **aim** to do something, you plan to do it.

air NOUN
Air is the mixture of gases that we breathe.

aircraft NOUN
An **aircraft** is a vehicle that flies. Helicopters and aeroplanes are aircraft.

airport **airports** NOUN
An **airport** is a place where aircraft land and take off.

alarm **alarms**
NOUN **1** An **alarm** is something like a bell or flashing light that warns you of something.
NOUN **2 Alarm** is a feeling of fear.
*He looked at the hungry bear in **alarm**.*

album **albums** NOUN
An **album** is a book that you put things like stamps or photographs in.

alien **aliens** NOUN
In science fiction, an **alien** is a creature from outer space.

alight ADJECTIVE
If something is **alight**, it is burning.

alike ADJECTIVE
If two or more things are **alike**, they are the same in some way.

alive ADJECTIVE
If a person, animal or plant is **alive**, they are living now.

all ADJECTIVE
You say **all** when you mean the whole of a particular group or thing. *Put **all** your toys away.*

Allah NOUN
Allah is the Muslim name for God.

allergy **allergies** NOUN
If you have an **allergy** to something, it makes you ill. *Tom has an **allergy** to nuts, so he must not eat them.*

alley **alleys** NOUN
An **alley** is a narrow path with buildings or walls on both sides.

a
b
c
d
e
f
g
h
i
j
k
l
m
n
o
p
q
r
s
t
u
v
w
x
y
z

alligator **alligators** NOUN
An **alligator** is a reptile. It is of the same family as a crocodile, but smaller.
See Reptiles on page 264

alliteration NOUN
Alliteration is the use of words close together which begin with the same sound, for example "hundreds of huge hairy horses".

allow **allows, allowing, allowed** VERB
If someone **allows** you to do something, they let you do it.

all right
ADJECTIVE **1** If someone is **all right**, they are well or safe. *See if the baby's **all right**.*
INTERJECTION **2** You say **all right** if you agree to something.

almost ADVERB
Almost means very nearly, but not quite. *He tripped and **almost** fell.*

alone ADJECTIVE
If you are **alone**, there is nobody with you.

along PREPOSITION
If you go **along** something, you move towards the end of it.

aloud ADVERB
If you read something **aloud**, you read it so that people can hear you.

alphabet **alphabets** NOUN
An **alphabet** is all the letters used to write words, written in a special order.

alphabetical ADJECTIVE
Alphabetical means arranged in the order of the letters of the alphabet. *She read out the names on the register in **alphabetical** order.*

already ADVERB
If you have done something **already**, you did it earlier.

also ADVERB
You say **also** when you want to add to something you have just said.

alter **alters, altering, altered** VERB
When you **alter** something, you change it in some way.

alternate **alternates, alternating, alternated** VERB
When two things **alternate**, they regularly happen one after the other. *He **alternates** between being friendly and completely ignoring me.*

although CONJUNCTION
You say **although** when you expected something different. ***Although** my dad was cross, he still gave me my pocket money.*

altogether ADVERB
If you say there are a number of things **altogether**, you are counting all of them. *I've picked four apples and you've picked two, so that's six **altogether**.*

aluminium NOUN
Aluminium is a light, silver-coloured metal. It is used for making rolls of foil and containers like cans and pie dishes.

always
ADVERB **1** If you **always** do something, you do it every time. *He **always** puts his things away when he has used them.*
ADVERB **2** If something has **always** been so, it has been that way at all times. *They have **always** been good friends.*

a.m. ADVERB
a.m. is the time between midnight and noon. *I get up at 7 **a.m.***
See **p.m.**

am VERB

Am is a present tense form of **be** used when you are talking about yourself. *I **am** six years old.*
See **be**

amaze amazes, amazing, amazed VERB

If something **amazes** you, it surprises you very much.
amazement NOUN

amazing ADJECTIVE

Something that is **amazing** is very surprising or wonderful.

ambition ambitions NOUN

If you have an **ambition** to do something, you want to do it very much.

ambulance ambulances NOUN

An **ambulance** is a vehicle that is used to take people to hospital.

among

PREPOSITION **1** If something is **among** a number of things, it is surrounded by them. *He sat **among** piles of books.*
PREPOSITION **2** If something is divided **among** several people, they all have a share.

amount amounts NOUN

An **amount** of something is how much there is of it.

amphibian amphibians NOUN

An **amphibian** is an animal that is able to live on land and in water.
amphibious ADJECTIVE
See Amphibians on page 264

amuse amuses, amusing, amused VERB

If you **amuse** somebody, you make them smile or stop them feeling bored.

an ADJECTIVE

An is a form of "a" used when the next sound is a vowel.
See **a**

analogue ADJECTIVE

An **analogue** watch or clock shows the time with hands that move round a dial.
See **digital**

anchor anchors NOUN

An **anchor** is a heavy metal hook on a long chain. It is dropped over the side of a boat to stop it moving.

ancient ADJECTIVE

If something is **ancient**, it is very old.

and CONJUNCTION

You use **and** to join two or more words or phrases together. *I like chocolate, **and** my brother does too.*

angel angels NOUN

Angels are beings some people believe act as messengers for God.

anger NOUN

Anger is the strong feeling you have about something that is unfair.

angle angles NOUN

An **angle** is the shape that is made when two lines or surfaces join. The size of an angle is measured in degrees.

angry angrier, angriest ADJECTIVE

If you feel **angry**, you are very cross.
angrily ADVERB

animal animals NOUN

Animals are living things which are not plants. Humans, dogs, birds, fish, reptiles and insects are all animals.

a
b
c
d
e
f
g
h
i
j
k
l
m
n
o
p
q
r
s
t
u
v
w
x
y
z

A
B
C
D
E
F
G
H
I
J
K
L
M
N
O
P
Q
R
S
T
U
V
W
X
Y
Z

ankle **ankles** NOUN
Your **ankle** is the joint between your foot and your leg.

anniversary **anniversaries** NOUN
An **anniversary** is a day when you remember something special which happened on that date in an earlier year.

announce **announces, announcing, announced** VERB
If you **announce** something important, you tell people about it publicly. *My sister's engagement was **announced** last week.*

annoy **annoys, annoying, annoyed** VERB
If you do something which **annoys** someone, you make them cross.

annual **annuals**
ADJECTIVE **1** Something that is **annual** happens once a year, like a birthday.
NOUN **2** An **annual** is a book that comes out once a year.

another ADJECTIVE
Another means one more. *Amy finished her chocolate and took **another** one immediately.*

answer **answers, answering, answered**
VERB **1** When you **answer**, you say or write something to someone who has asked you a question.
NOUN **2** Your **answer** is what you say or write to a question.

ant **ants** NOUN
Ants are small insects which live in large groups called colonies.
See Insects on page 264

antelope **antelopes** NOUN
Antelopes are animals that look like deer, but their horns are not branch-shaped. They live in Africa and Asia.

anticlockwise ADVERB
If something goes **anticlockwise**, it moves in the opposite direction to the hands of a clock.

antique **antiques** NOUN
An **antique** is an old object which is valuable because it is beautiful or rare.

antiseptic **antiseptics** NOUN
An **antiseptic** is a substance that prevents infection by killing germs.

antonym **antonyms** NOUN
An **antonym** is a word that means the opposite of another word.
See Antonyms on page 273

anxious ADJECTIVE
Someone who is **anxious** is nervous or worried about something.

any
ADJECTIVE **1 Any** means one, some, or several. *Do you have **any** milk?*
ADJECTIVE **2 Any** can also mean even the smallest amount. *I mustn't eat **any** nuts.*

anybody PRONOUN
Anybody is any person.

anyone PRONOUN
Anyone is any person.

anything PRONOUN
Anything means any object, event, situation or action.

anywhere ADVERB
Anywhere means in, at or to any place. *Just put it down **anywhere**.*

apart ADJECTIVE
If something is **apart** from something else, there is a space between them. *He stood with his feet **apart**.*

ape **apes** NOUN
Apes are like monkeys but are larger and have no tails. Chimpanzees and gorillas are apes.

apologize apologizes, apologizing, apologized; also spelt **apologise** VERB
When you **apologize**, you say you are sorry for something you have done.

apology apologies NOUN
An **apology** is something you say or write to tell someone you are sorry.

apostrophe apostrophes NOUN
An **apostrophe** is a punctuation mark (') used in contractions and to show belonging.
See Punctuation on page 270

apparatus NOUN
The **apparatus** for a particular task is the equipment you use for it.

appear appears, appearing, appeared
VERB **1** When something **appears**, it moves into a place where you can see it.
VERB **2** If something **appears** to be a certain way, that is how it seems.

appearance appearances
NOUN **1** Someone's **appearance** in a place is their sudden arrival there.
NOUN **2** Your **appearance** is the way you look to other people.

appetite appetites NOUN
If you have an **appetite**, you are looking forward to eating something.

applause NOUN
Applause is clapping your hands to show that you liked something.

apple apples NOUN
An **apple** is a round crisp fruit which grows on a tree.
See Fruit on page 260

apply applies, applying, applied VERB
If you **apply** for something, like a job, you usually ask for it in writing.

appreciate appreciates, appreciating, appreciated VERB
If you **appreciate** something, you feel grateful for it.

approach approaches, approaching, approached VERB
When someone **approaches** you, they get nearer to you.

approve approves, approving, approved VERB
If you **approve** of something, you think it is good.
approval NOUN

approximate ADJECTIVE
An **approximate** answer may not be exactly right. *What is the **approximate** distance between those trees?*

approximately ADVERB
If you say **approximately**, you mean about. *It is **approximately** 5 metres long.*

apricot apricots NOUN
An **apricot** is a small, round yellow-orange fruit with a large stone in the centre.

April NOUN
April is the fourth month of the year. It has 30 days.

apron aprons NOUN
An **apron** is a piece of material that you wear to keep your clothes clean.

aquarium aquaria or aquariums NOUN
An **aquarium** is a glass tank for fish and other underwater animals.

arch arches NOUN
An **arch** is a curved part of a bridge, wall or building.

a
b
c
d
e
f
g
h
i
j
k
l
m
n
o
p
q
r
s
t
u
v
w
x
y
z

13

archery NOUN

Archery is a sport in which people shoot at a target with a bow and arrow.

architect architects NOUN

An **architect** is a person who designs buildings.

are VERB

Are is a present tense form of **be**. *They are both in my class.*

See **be**

area areas

NOUN **1** The **area** of something is the size of its surface. To find the area of a rectangle, you multiply the length by the breadth.

NOUN **2** You use the word **area** to mean in or around a place. *There are lots of shops in this area.*

argue argues, arguing, argued VERB

If you **argue** with someone, you say that you do not agree with them, and give your reasons.

argument arguments NOUN

An **argument** is a talk between people who do not agree. In some arguments, people shout angrily.

arithmetic NOUN

Arithmetic is about adding, subtracting, multiplying and dividing numbers.

arm arms NOUN

Your **arm** is the part of your body between the shoulder and the hand.

arm

armchair armchairs NOUN

An **armchair** is a chair with a support on each side for your arms.

armour NOUN

Armour is metal clothing that soldiers used to wear in battle.

army armies NOUN

An **army** is a large organized group of people who are trained to fight in case of war.

around

PREPOSITION **1** You say **around** when things are in various places. *There are lots of cupboards around the house.*

PREPOSITION **2** You can use **around** when something is on all sides of something else. *The Earth's atmosphere is the air around it.*

arrange arranges, arranging, arranged

VERB **1** If you **arrange** something like a party, you make plans and organize it.

VERB **2** If you **arrange** things like flowers, you group them in a special way.

array arrays

NOUN **1** An **array** is a group of things set out neatly in columns and rows.

NOUN **2** An **array** is also a large number of things displayed together. *Ben's mouth watered at the array of cakes.*

arrest arrests, arresting, arrested VERB

If the police **arrest** someone, they take them to the police station.

arrive arrives, arriving, arrived VERB

When you **arrive** at a place, you reach it at the end of your journey.

arrival NOUN

arrow arrows

NOUN **1** An **arrow** is a thin stick with a pointed end, which is shot from a bow.

NOUN **2** An **arrow** can also be a sign which shows people which way to go.

art NOUN

Art is something like painting or sculpture, which is beautiful or has a special meaning.

artery **arteries** NOUN
An **artery** is a tube which carries blood from your heart to the rest of your body.

article **articles**
NOUN **1** An **article** is a piece of writing in a magazine or newspaper.
NOUN **2** An **article** can also be an object. *What is this strange article?*

artificial ADJECTIVE
Artificial things are made by people. They do not occur naturally.

artist **artists** NOUN
An **artist** is a person who does things like painting or sculpture.

as
CONJUNCTION **1** If one thing happens **as** something else happens, it happens at the same time as the second thing. *We watched television as we ate our sandwiches.*
CONJUNCTION **2** You say **as** when you are going to give a reason for something. *As I like school I get there early.*

ascend **ascends, ascending, ascended**
VERB
When you **ascend**, you move upwards. *He ascended the stairs to his room.*

ascending ADJECTIVE
When things are arranged in **ascending** order, each thing is higher than the one before it. *The numbers 21, 37 and 49 are in ascending order.*

ash **ashes**
NOUN **1** **Ash** is the dust left after a fire.
NOUN **2** An **ash** is a large tree.

ashamed ADJECTIVE
If you are **ashamed**, you feel sorry about something you have done.

ask **asks, asking, asked**
VERB **1** If you **ask** someone a question, you are trying to find something out.
VERB **2** If you **ask** someone for something, you want them to give it to you.

asleep ADJECTIVE
If you are **asleep**, your eyes are closed and your body is resting.

aspirin **aspirins** NOUN
Aspirin is a drug which you take to help you if you have a pain, fever or cold. An **aspirin** is a tablet of this drug.

ass **asses** NOUN
An **ass** is an animal like a horse but smaller and with longer ears.

assemble **assembles, assembling, assembled**
VERB **1** If you **assemble** something, you fit the parts of it together.
VERB **2** When people **assemble**, they come together in a group.

assembly **assemblies** NOUN
Assembly is a gathering of all the teachers and pupils in a school.

assistant **assistants**
NOUN **1** A person's **assistant** is someone whose job is to help them.
NOUN **2** A shop **assistant** is a person who works in a shop selling things.

asthma NOUN
Asthma is a disease of the chest. It causes wheezing and makes it difficult for you to breathe properly.

astonish **astonishes, astonishing, astonished** VERB
If you are **astonished** by something or someone, you are very surprised.

astronaut **astronauts** NOUN
An **astronaut** is a person who travels in space.

a
b
c
d
e
f
g
h
i
j
k
l
m
n
o
p
q
r
s
t
u
v
w
x
y
z

A B C D E F G H I J K L M N O P Q R S T U V W X Y Z

astronomer astronomers NOUN
An **astronomer** is a scientist who studies the stars and planets.

at
PREPOSITION **1** You use **at** to say where someone or something is. *Rajeev waited for me **at** the bus stop.*
PREPOSITION **2** You use **at** to show the direction something is going in. *I threw the snowball **at** my brother.*
PREPOSITION **3** You use **at** to say when something happens. *The party starts **at** six o'clock.*

ate VERB
Ate is the past tense of **eat**.

atlas atlases NOUN
An **atlas** is a book of maps.

atmosphere atmospheres
NOUN **1** A planet's **atmosphere** is the layer of air or other gas around it.
NOUN **2** You can use **atmosphere** to talk about the general mood of a place. *In the classroom the **atmosphere** was relaxed.*

atom atoms NOUN
An **atom** is the smallest part of any substance.

attach attaches, attaching, attached VERB
When you **attach** something to an object, you join the two things together.

attachment attachments NOUN
An **attachment** is a computer file that is attached to an e-mail or text message.

attack attacks, attacking, attacked VERB
If a person **attacks** somebody, they try to hurt them.

attempt attempts, attempting, attempted VERB
If you **attempt** something difficult, you try to do it.

attend attends, attending, attended VERB
If someone **attends** something like a meeting, they are present at it.

attention
NOUN **1** If something attracts your **attention**, you notice it suddenly.
NOUN **2** If you pay **attention** to someone, you listen carefully to them.

attic attics NOUN
An **attic** is a room at the top of a house, just under the roof.

attract attracts, attracting, attracted
VERB **1** If something or somebody **attracts** you, you find them interesting. *Joe was **attracted** to the display by the flashing lights.*
VERB **2** If something like a magnet **attracts** an object, it makes it move towards it.

attractive ADJECTIVE
If something is **attractive**, it is nice to look at.

audience audiences NOUN
An **audience** is a group of people watching or listening to something like a play, film, talk or piece of music.

August NOUN
August is the eighth month of the year. It has 31 days.

aunt aunts NOUN
Your **aunt** is the sister of one of your parents, or the wife of your uncle.

author authors NOUN
The **author** of a book is the person who wrote it.

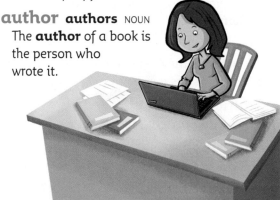

authority authorities
NOUN **1 Authority** is a quality that someone has that makes people take notice of what they say.

NOUN **2** The **authorities** are people like the police who have a lot of power.

autograph **autographs** NOUN
An **autograph** is the signature of a famous person.

automatic ADJECTIVE
An **automatic** machine is one that can do things on its own.
automatically ADVERB

autumn **autumns** NOUN
Autumn is the season between summer and winter. The weather cools and many trees lose their leaves.

available ADJECTIVE
If something is **available**, you can get it. *Tickets are **available** now.*

avalanche **avalanches** NOUN
An **avalanche** is a huge mass of snow and ice that falls down a mountain.

avenue **avenues** NOUN
An **avenue** is a wide road with trees on either side.

average **averages**
NOUN **1** An **average** is a result obtained by adding several amounts together and then dividing the total by the number of different amounts. *If four children have a total of 36 sweets, the **average** is nine sweets per child.*
ADJECTIVE **2** If something is **average**, it is the standard or usual thing.

avoid **avoids, avoiding, avoided** VERB
If you **avoid** someone or something, you keep away from them.

awake ADJECTIVE
If you are **awake**, you are not sleeping.

award **awards** NOUN
An **award** is a prize that you are given for doing something well.

aware ADJECTIVE
If you are **aware** of something, you know about it.

away
ADVERB **1** If you move **away** from somewhere, you move so that you are further from that place.
ADVERB **2** If you are **away** from somewhere, you are not in that place. *Katherine is **away** from school today.*

awful ADJECTIVE
Something **awful** is very unpleasant or bad.

awkward
ADJECTIVE **1** If something is **awkward**, it is difficult to do or use.
ADJECTIVE **2** If people are **awkward**, they move in a clumsy way.

axe **axes** NOUN
An **axe** is a tool with a long handle and a heavy sharp blade at one end. It is used for chopping wood.

axis **axes**
NOUN **1** An **axis** is an imaginary line through the centre of something, around which it moves.
NOUN **2** An **axis** is also one of the two sides of a graph. A graph has a horizontal axis and a vertical axis.

a
b
c
d
e
f
g
h
i
j
k
l
m
n
o
p
q
r
s
t
u
v
w
x
y
z

Bb

baby babies NOUN
A **baby** is a very young child.

back backs
NOUN **1** The **back** of something is the part opposite the front.
ADVERB **2** If you go **back** to a place, you go somewhere you have been before.
NOUN **3** Your **back** is the part of your body which is behind you, from your neck to the top of your legs.
NOUN **4** The **back** of an animal is the part on top, between its neck and the beginning of its tail.
back to front PHRASE If you have something on **back to front**, you are wearing it the wrong way round.

background backgrounds NOUN
The **background** of a picture is everything behind the main part.

backwards
ADVERB **1** If you move **backwards**, you move with your back facing in the direction you are going.
ADVERB **2** If you do something **backwards**, you do it in the opposite of the usual way. *Let's try counting* ***backwards*** *from one hundred.*

bacon NOUN
Bacon is salted meat from a pig.

bacteria PLURAL NOUN
Bacteria are very tiny living things which break down waste. They can cause diseases.

bad worse, worst
ADJECTIVE **1** You say somebody is **bad** if they are naughty or wicked.
ADJECTIVE **2** If something is **bad**, it can hurt or upset you in some way.

badge badges NOUN
A **badge** is a sign people wear to show they belong to a school or club.

badger badgers NOUN
A **badger** is a strongly built animal with short legs and neck. It has long grey fur and a striped head.

badly ADVERB
If something is done **badly**, it is done in a way that is not successful or effective.

bag bags NOUN
A **bag** is a soft container for carrying or holding things.

bait NOUN
Bait is food used to trap animals.

bake bakes, baking, baked VERB
When you **bake** food, you cook it in an oven.

baker bakers NOUN
A **baker** makes and sells bread, cakes and pies.

balance balances, balancing, balanced
VERB
When you **balance**, you keep steady. *She tried to balance on one leg.*

balcony balconies NOUN
A **balcony** is a platform on the outside of a building. Balconies have a railing or wall around them.

bald balder, baldest ADJECTIVE
People who are **bald** have no hair on the top of their head.

ball balls NOUN
Anything round can be called a **ball**. You need a ball for lots of games, like tennis and football.

ballet ballets NOUN
A **ballet** is a sort of play where the story is told with dancing and music.

balloon balloons NOUN
A **balloon** is a small rubber bag. If you blow hard into it, it gets bigger and makes a very light toy or decoration.

bamboo NOUN
Bamboo is a kind of grass with strong hollow stems which are useful as garden canes or for making furniture.

ban bans, banning, banned VERB
If someone is **banned** from doing something, they are told by people in charge that they must not do it.

banana bananas NOUN
A **banana** is a long yellow fruit which grows on trees in hot countries.
See Fruit on page 260

band bands
NOUN **1** A **band** is a small number of people, like a gang of robbers or a group of musicians.
NOUN **2** A **band** can also be a strip of material such as iron, cloth or rubber.

bandage bandages NOUN
A **bandage** is a strip of cloth used to cover a wound.

bang bangs, banging, banged
NOUN **1** A **bang** is a sudden loud noise.
VERB **2** If something **bangs**, or you bang it, it makes a loud noise.

bank banks
NOUN **1** A **bank** is a business that looks after people's money.
NOUN **2** The **bank** of a river is the ground either side of the water.

banner banners NOUN
A **banner** is a long strip of cloth or paper with a message written on it.

bar bars
NOUN **1** A **bar** is a long piece of something hard, like metal or wood.
NOUN **2** A **bar** can also be a counter where people can buy drink.

barbecue barbecues NOUN
A **barbecue** is a grill on which food is cooked outdoors over hot charcoal.

barber barbers NOUN
A **barber** is someone who cuts men's hair.

bar code bar codes NOUN
A **bar code** is a pattern of numbers and lines printed on something that is for sale, so that the price can be read by a machine.

bare barer, barest
ADJECTIVE **1** If part of your body is **bare**, it is not covered by clothes.
ADJECTIVE **2** If something is **bare**, it has nothing in it or on it. *It was winter and the trees were bare.*

bargain bargains NOUN
A **bargain** is something which is sold at a low price, and which you think is good value.

a
b
c
d
e
f
g
h
i
j
k
l
m
n
o
p
q
r
s
t
u
v
w
x
y
z

19

A
B
C
D
E
F
G
H
I
J
K
L
M
N
O
P
Q
R
S
T
U
V
W
X
Y
Z

bark **barks, barking, barked**
VERB **1** When a dog **barks**, it makes a sudden rough, loud noise.
NOUN **2 Bark** is the outside covering of a tree.

barley NOUN
Barley is a cereal that is grown for food and drink.

bar mitzvah NOUN
A Jewish boy's **bar mitzvah** is a ceremony that takes place on his 13th birthday. After this he is regarded as an adult.

barn **barns** NOUN
A **barn** is a large building where a farmer stores hay and other crops.

barrel **barrels** NOUN
A **barrel** is a large wooden, metal or plastic container for holding liquids.

barrier **barriers** NOUN
A **barrier** is something like a fence or wall, that stops people getting past.

base **bases**
NOUN **1** The **base** is the bottom of something.
NOUN **2** Number **bases** are a whole pattern of counting. A base ten counting system uses units, tens and hundreds.

basement **basements** NOUN
The **basement** of a building is a floor below ground level.

basic
ADJECTIVE **1 Basic** is used to describe things like the food and equipment that people really need in their lives.
ADJECTIVE **2 Basic** also means the simplest things you need to know about a subject. *I'm not good at this yet, but I've got the **basic** idea.*
basically ADVERB

basin **basins** NOUN
A **basin** is a wide round container which is open at the top.

basket **baskets** NOUN
A **basket** is used for holding or carrying things. It is usually made from strips of thin wood or cane.

basketball NOUN
Basketball is a game between two teams of five players. Each team tries to score by throwing a ball through a circular net fixed to a high board.

bat **bats, batting, batted**
NOUN **1** In some games, like table tennis, you use a wooden **bat** to hit the ball.
NOUN **2** A **bat** is also a small animal like a mouse with leathery wings. Bats fly at night, and sleep hanging upside down.
VERB **3** If you are **batting**, you are having a turn at hitting the ball with a bat in cricket, baseball or rounders.

bath **baths** NOUN
A **bath** is a container for water. It is big enough to sit or lie in, so that you can wash yourself all over.

bathroom **bathrooms** NOUN
The **bathroom** is the room where the bath or shower is.

battery **batteries** NOUN
A **battery** is an object which stores electric power. There are tiny batteries for things like watches, and larger batteries for torches.

battle **battles** NOUN
A **battle** is a fight between enemy forces, on land, at sea or in the air.

bawl **bawls, bawling, bawled** VERB
If a child is **bawling**, it is crying very loudly and angrily.

bay **bays** NOUN
A **bay** is a deep curve in a coastline.

be **am, is, are, being, was, were, been**
VERB **1** You use **be** to say what a person or thing is like. *She **is** very young.*
VERB **2** You also use **be** to say that something is there. *There **is** a tree in the garden.*

beach **beaches** NOUN
The **beach** is the land covered with sand or pebbles that is next to the sea.

bead beads NOUN
A **bead** is a small piece of glass or plastic with a hole through it. Beads can be threaded together to make a necklace or bracelet.

beak beaks NOUN
A **beak** is the hard outside part of a bird's mouth.

beam beams, beaming, beamed
NOUN **1** A **beam** is a long thick bar of wood, metal or concrete, used to support part of a building.
NOUN **2** A **beam** is also a line of light from an object such as a torch or the sun.
VERB **3** If you **beam**, you give a big smile.

bean beans NOUN
A **bean** is a vegetable. Its outer covering is called a pod, and inside it has large seeds, also called beans.
See *Vegetables* on page 260

bear bears, bearing, bore
NOUN **1** A **bear** is a large, strong animal with thick fur and sharp claws.
VERB **2** If you **bear** something, you put up with it. *I can't bear all this homework.*

beard beards NOUN
A **beard** is the hair which grows on the lower part of a man's face.

beat beats, beating, beat, beaten
VERB **1** If you **beat** someone in a race or competition, you do better than they do.
VERB **2** If someone **beats** another person or an animal, they hit them hard.
VERB **3** If you **beat** eggs, you stir them very fast.
VERB **4** Your heart **beats** with a regular rhythm all the time.

beautiful
ADJECTIVE **1** You say something is **beautiful** if it gives you great pleasure to look at it or listen to it.
ADJECTIVE **2** You say someone is **beautiful** if they are lovely to look at.

beaver beavers NOUN
A **beaver** is a furry animal which lives in or near water.

because CONJUNCTION
You say **because** when you are going to give a reason for something. *I left the party because they were playing silly games.*

become becomes, becoming, became, become VERB
To **become** means to start being different in some way. *The smell became stronger.*

bed beds
NOUN **1** A **bed** is a piece of furniture to lie down on when you rest or sleep.
NOUN **2** The **bed** of the sea or of a river is the ground beneath it.

bedroom bedrooms NOUN
Your **bedroom** is the room where you sleep.

bee bees NOUN
A **bee** is a flying insect. People keep bees for the honey that they make.
See **beehive**
See also *Insects* on page 264

beech beeches NOUN
A **beech** is a large tree.

beef NOUN **Beef** is the meat from a cow.

beehive beehives NOUN
A **beehive** is a house for bees, where a beekeeper collects the honey.

been VERB
Been is the past participle of **be**. *We have always been good friends.*
See **be**

A
B
C
D
E
F
G
H
I
J
K
L
M
N
O
P
Q
R
S
T
U
V
W
X
Y
Z

beer **beers** NOUN
Beer is a drink made from grain.

beetle **beetles** NOUN
A **beetle** is an insect with four wings.
The front two act as hard covers to the body
when the beetle is not flying.
See Insects on page 264

beetroot **beetroots** NOUN
Beetroot is a dark red root vegetable.
See Vegetables on page 260

before
PREPOSITION **1** If something happens **before**
something else, it happens earlier. *Can I see
you before lunch?*
ADVERB **2** If you have done something **before**,
it is not the first time.

beg **begs, begging, begged** VERB
If you **beg** someone to do something, you ask
them very anxiously to do it. *Krishna begged
his dad to take him to the football match.*

begin **begins, beginning, began, begun**
VERB
When you **begin**, you start. *I began school
on Thursday.*

beginner **beginners** NOUN
A **beginner** is someone who has just started
to learn something.

beginning **beginnings** NOUN
The **beginning** of something is the first
part of it.

begun VERB
Begun is the past participle of **begin**.

behave **behaves, behaving, behaved** VERB
The way you **behave** is the way you act.
behaviour NOUN

behind
PREPOSITION **1** **Behind** means on the other side
of something. *She was behind the counter.*
PREPOSITION **2** If you are **behind** someone, you
are at the back of them.

beige ADJECTIVE
Something that is **beige** is a pale creamy-
brown colour.
See Colours and shapes on page 266

believe **believes, believing, believed** VERB
If you **believe** something or someone, you
think what is said is true.

bell **bells** NOUN
A **bell** is a piece of metal shaped like a cup,
which rings when something hits it.

belong **belongs, belonging, belonged**
VERB **1** If something **belongs** to you, it is your
own.
VERB **2** If you **belong** to something, like a club,
you are a member of it.

below PREPOSITION
If something is **below** something else, it is
underneath it.

belt **belts** NOUN
A **belt** is a strip of leather or other material
that you put round your waist.

bench **benches** NOUN
A **bench** is a long seat, usually made of wood.

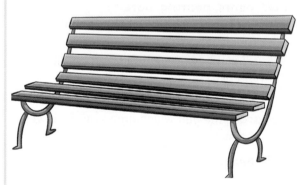

bend **bends, bending, bent** VERB
When something **bends**, it becomes curved or
crooked.

beneath PREPOSITION
If something is **beneath** something else, it is
below it.

bent ADJECTIVE
If something is **bent**, it has become curved or
crooked.
See **bend**

berry **berries** NOUN
A **berry** is a small round soft fruit that grows
on a bush or a tree.

beside PREPOSITION
If something is **beside** something else, it is at the side of it.

best ADJECTIVE
Best means the "most good", or better than anything else. *That's the **best** programme I've seen.*

better
ADJECTIVE **1** Something that is **better** than something else is of a higher standard or quality. *Your bicycle is **better** than mine.*
ADJECTIVE **2 Better** can also mean more sensible. *It would be **better** to go home.*
ADJECTIVE **3** If you are feeling **better** after an illness, you are not feeling so ill.

between PREPOSITION
If something is **between** two other things, it is in the space or time that separates them. *The toyshop is **between** the bank and the library.*

beware VERB
You tell people to **beware** if there is danger of some kind. ***Beware** of the bull.*

Bible **Bibles** NOUN
The **Bible** is the sacred book of the Christian religion.

bicycle **bicycles** NOUN
A **bicycle** is a vehicle with two wheels. You sit on it and turn pedals with your feet to make it go.

big **bigger, biggest** ADJECTIVE
Something or somebody **big** is large in size or importance.

bike **bikes** NOUN
Bike is an abbreviation of **bicycle**.

bill **bills**
NOUN **1** A **bill** is a piece of paper saying how much money you owe. *Mum's just had the electricity **bill**.*
NOUN **2** A bird's **bill** is its beak.

bin **bins** NOUN
A **bin** is a container, usually with a lid, for putting rubbish in.

bind **binds, binding, bound** VERB
If you **bind** something, you tie something like string or cloth tightly round it so that it is held in place.

biology NOUN
Biology is the study of living things.

bird **birds** NOUN
A **bird** is an animal with two legs, two wings and feathers.

birth **births** NOUN
The **birth** of a baby is when it comes out of its mother's body.

birthday **birthdays** NOUN
Your **birthday** is a special date that is remembered every year, because it was the day you were born.

biscuit **biscuits** NOUN
A **biscuit** is a small, flat, crisp kind of cake.
*See **Other foods** on page 261*

bit **bits**
NOUN **1** A **bit** of something is a small piece of it.
NOUN **2** A **bit** is a piece of metal that goes in a horse's mouth.
VERB **3 Bit** is also the past tense of **bite**.

bite **bites, biting, bit, bitten** VERB
If you **bite** something, you use your teeth to hold, cut or tear it.

bitter
ADJECTIVE **1** If something has a **bitter** taste, it tastes sharp and unpleasant.
ADJECTIVE **2** Someone who is **bitter** feels angry and disappointed.

a
b
c
d
e
f
g
h
i
j
k
l
m
n
o
p
q
r
s
t
u
v
w
x
y
z

black blacker, blackest
ADJECTIVE
If the colour of something is **black**, it is the colour of these letters.
See Colours and shapes on page 266

blackberry blackberries NOUN
Blackberries are small, soft, dark purple fruits that grow on brambles.

blackbird blackbirds NOUN
A **blackbird** is a European songbird.

blackboard blackboards NOUN
A **blackboard** is a dark board that people can write on in chalk.

blackcurrant blackcurrants NOUN
Blackcurrants are very small, dark purple fruits.

blade blades
NOUN **1** A **blade** is the sharp edge of a knife or sword.
NOUN **2** A single piece of grass is a **blade**.

blame blames, blaming, blamed VERB
If somebody **blames** a person for something bad that happened, they say that person made it happen.

blank blanker, blankest ADJECTIVE
If something is **blank**, it has nothing written or drawn on it.

blanket blankets NOUN
A **blanket** is a large warm cloth, often used to cover people in bed.

blaze blazes NOUN
A **blaze** is a strong bright fire.

blazer blazers NOUN
A **blazer** is a kind of jacket, often in the colours of a school or sports team.

bleed bleeds, bleeding, bled VERB
If part of your body **bleeds**, blood comes out of it.

blend blends, blending, blended VERB
When you **blend** two or more things together, they become a smooth mixture.

blew VERB
Blew is the past tense of **blow**.

blind blinds
NOUN **1** A **blind** is rolled material that you pull down to cover a window.
ADJECTIVE **2** Someone who is **blind** cannot see.
blindness NOUN

blindfold blindfolds NOUN
A **blindfold** is a strip of cloth tied over someone's eyes so that they cannot see.

blink blinks, blinking, blinked VERB
When you **blink**, you shut your eyes and open them again quickly.

blister blisters NOUN
A **blister** is a small bubble on your skin, containing watery liquid. Blisters are caused by a burn or rubbing.

blizzard blizzards NOUN
A **blizzard** is a bad snowstorm with strong winds.

block blocks, blocking, blocked
NOUN **1** A **block** of flats or offices is a large tall building.
NOUN **2** A **block** of something like stone or wood is a large rectangular piece of it.
VERB **3** To **block** means to get in the way.

blog blogs NOUN
A **blog** is a website that describes the daily life of the person who writes it.

blonde or blond ADJECTIVE
Blonde hair is pale yellow in colour. The spelling **blond** is used when referring to men.

blood NOUN
Blood is the red liquid that your heart pumps round inside your body.

A B C D E F G H I J K L M N O P Q R S T U V W X Y Z

bloom blooms, blooming, bloomed VERB
When a plant **blooms**, its flowers open.

blossom NOUN
Blossom is the flowers that appear on a tree or bush.

blot blots NOUN
A **blot** is a mark made by a drop of liquid, especially ink.

blouse blouses NOUN
A **blouse** is a kind of shirt worn by a girl or a woman.

blow blows, blowing, blew, blown
VERB **1** When the wind **blows**, the air moves faster.
VERB **2** If you **blow**, you send out a stream of air from your mouth.
NOUN **3** A **blow** is a hard hit.

blue bluer, bluest ADJECTIVE
Something that is **blue** is the colour of the sky on a sunny day.
See *Colours and shapes* on page 266

bluebell bluebells NOUN
A **bluebell** is a flower that often grows wild in woods in Europe.

blunt blunter, bluntest
ADJECTIVE **1** A **blunt** knife is not sharp.
ADJECTIVE **2** Something that is **blunt** has a rounded, rather than pointed, end.
*My pencil's **blunt**.*

blur blurs NOUN
A **blur** is a shape that you cannot see clearly.
*The car went past so fast it was just a **blur**.*
blurred ADJECTIVE **blurry** ADJECTIVE

blush blushes, blushing, blushed VERB
When you **blush** you become red in the face, usually because you are embarrassed.

board boards NOUN
A **board** is a flat, thin piece of wood.

boast boasts, boasting, boasted VERB
If you **boast**, you talk too proudly about something.

boat boats NOUN
A **boat** is a small vessel for travelling on water.
See **ship**

body bodies
NOUN **1** Your **body** is every part of you. Some animals, like elephants, have very large bodies.
See *The body* on page 256
NOUN **2** You can say **body** when you mean just the main part of a person, not counting head, arms and legs.
NOUN **3** A **body** is a dead person.

bog bogs NOUN
A **bog** is an area of land that is always wet and spongy.

boil boils, boiling, boiled
VERB **1** When liquid **boils** it gets very hot. It bubbles and steam rises from it.
VERB **2** If you **boil** food, you cook it in boiling water.
NOUN **3** A **boil** is a painful red swelling on the skin.

bold bolder, boldest
ADJECTIVE **1** Someone who is **bold** is not afraid of risk or danger.
ADJECTIVE **2** Letters that are in **bold** type are thicker than ordinary printed letters.

a b c d e f g h i j k l m n o p q r s t u v w x y z

A
B
C
D
E
F
G
H
I
J
K
L
M
N
O
P
Q
R
S
T
U
V
W
X
Y
Z

bolt bolts, bolting, bolted

NOUN **1** A **bolt** is a long round metal pin with a flat end. It screws into a nut to fasten things.

NOUN **2** A **bolt** is a metal bar that you can slide across to keep a door shut.

VERB **3** If you **bolt** a door or window, you lock it with a bolt.

VERB **4** When a person or animal **bolts**, they suddenly run very fast.

bomb bombs NOUN

A **bomb** is a weapon which explodes and damages a large area.

bone bones NOUN

Your **bones** are the hard parts inside your body which make up your skeleton.

bonfire bonfires NOUN

A **bonfire** is a fire lit outdoors, usually to burn garden rubbish.

bonnet bonnets

NOUN **1** A **bonnet** is the metal cover over a car's engine.

NOUN **2** A **bonnet** is also a baby's or woman's hat tied under the chin.

book books, booking, booked

NOUN **1** A **book** is a number of pages held together inside a cover.

VERB **2** If you **book** something, you ask someone to keep it for you. *We booked seats at the cinema.*

boot boots

NOUN **1 Boots** are strong shoes that cover your ankle and sometimes your calf.

NOUN **2** The **boot** of a car is a space for luggage.

border borders

NOUN **1** A **border** is the line dividing two countries.

NOUN **2** A **border** is a strip along the edge of something, usually as a decoration.

bore bores, boring, bored

VERB **1** If somebody **bores** you, you do not find them interesting.

VERB **2** If you **bore** a hole in something,

you make a hole with a drill.

VERB **3 Bore** is the past tense of **bear**.

bored ADJECTIVE

When you are **bored**, you feel tired and impatient because you have nothing interesting to do.

boredom NOUN

boring ADJECTIVE

Something **boring** is so dull that you have no interest in it.

born VERB

When a baby is **born**, it comes out of its mother's body.

borrow borrows, borrowing, borrowed
VERB

When you **borrow** something, someone lets you have it for a while but they expect you to give it back later.

boss bosses NOUN

Someone's **boss** is the head of the place where they work.

bossy ADJECTIVE

A **bossy** person likes to tell others what to do.

both ADJECTIVE OR PRONOUN

You use **both** when you are talking about two things or people. *He put both books in the drawer.*

bother bothers, bothering, bothered

VERB **1** If something **bothers** you, it annoys you or makes you feel worried.

VERB **2** If you **bother** about something, you care about it and take trouble over it.

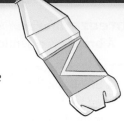

bottle **bottles** NOUN
A **bottle** is a container for keeping liquids in. Bottles are usually made of glass or plastic.

bottom **bottoms**
NOUN **1** The **bottom** of something is the lowest part of it.
NOUN **2** Your **bottom** is the part of your body that you sit on.

bought VERB
Bought is the past tense of **buy**.

boulder **boulders** NOUN
A **boulder** is a big rounded rock.

bounce **bounces, bouncing, bounced**
VERB
When something **bounces**, it springs back in the opposite direction as soon as it hits something hard.

bound **bounds, bounding, bounded**
VERB **1** When animals or people **bound**, they move quickly with large leaps.
ADJECTIVE **2** If something is **bound to** happen, it is sure to happen.

boundary **boundaries** NOUN
The **boundary** of an area of land is its outer limit.

bow **bows, bowing, bowed**
(*rhymes with* **low**) NOUN **1** A **bow** is a kind of knot with two loops used to tie laces and ribbons.
NOUN **2** A **bow** is also a weapon used for shooting arrows.
NOUN **3** The **bow** for a stringed musical instrument is a long piece of wood with horsehair stretched along it.
(*rhymes with* **now**)
VERB **4** When you **bow**, you bend your body forward.

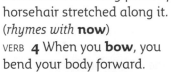

bowl **bowls** NOUN
A **bowl** is an open container used for holding liquid or serving food.

box **boxes** NOUN
A **box** is a container with straight sides, made from something stiff, like cardboard, wood or plastic.

boy **boys** NOUN
A **boy** is a male child.

bracelet **bracelets** NOUN
A **bracelet** is a band or chain which is worn round the wrist or arm as an ornament.

bracket **brackets** NOUN
Brackets are a pair of written marks **( )** placed round words that are not part of the main text.
See **Punctuation** *on page 270*

Braille NOUN
Braille is a form of writing using raised dots that blind people can read by touching the dots with their fingers.

brain **brains** NOUN
Your **brain** is inside your head and controls your whole body. It lets you think, feel and remember.

brainy **brainier, brainiest** ADJECTIVE
Someone who is **brainy** is clever and good at learning things.

brake **brakes** NOUN
The **brake** is the part of a vehicle that slows it down or stops it.

bramble **brambles** NOUN
A **bramble** is a wild bush with thorns. The fruit are called blackberries.

a
b
c
d
e
f
g
h
i
j
k
l
m
n
o
p
q
r
s
t
u
v
w
x
y
z

A
B
C
D
E
F
G
H
I
J
K
L
M
N
O
P
Q
R
S
T
U
V
W
X
Y
Z

branch branches NOUN
A **branch** is part of a tree that grows out from the trunk.

brass NOUN
Brass is a yellow metal made from copper and zinc. It is used for making things like ornaments and some musical instruments.

brave braver, bravest ADJECTIVE
If you are **brave**, you show you can do something even if it is frightening.
bravely ADVERB **bravery** NOUN

bread NOUN
Bread is a very common food, made with flour and baked in an oven.
See *Other foods* on page 261

breadth NOUN
The **breadth** of something is the distance that it measures from one side to the other.

break breaks, breaking, broke, broken
VERB **1** If you **break** something, it splits into pieces or stops working.
VERB **2** If you **break** a rule or a promise, you fail to keep it.

breakdown breakdowns NOUN
If someone's car has a **breakdown**, it stops working during a journey.

breakfast breakfasts NOUN
Breakfast is the first meal of the day.

breast breasts NOUN
Breasts are the two round parts on the front of a woman's body, which can produce milk to feed a baby.

breath NOUN
Your **breath** is the air that you take into and let out of your lungs.

breathe breathes, breathing, breathed
VERB
When you **breathe**, you take air into your lungs through your nose or mouth, and then let it out again.

breed breeds NOUN
A **breed** of an animal is a particular kind. For example, a labrador is a breed of dog.

breeze breezes NOUN
A **breeze** is a gentle wind.

brick bricks NOUN
A **brick** is a block used for building. It is made of baked clay.

bride brides NOUN
A **bride** is a woman on or near her wedding day.

bridge bridges NOUN
A **bridge** is something built over things like rivers, railways or roads, so that people or vehicles can get across.

brief briefer, briefest ADJECTIVE
Something that is **brief** lasts only a short time.
briefly ADVERB

briefcase briefcases NOUN
A **briefcase** is a flat case used for carrying papers.

bright brighter, brightest
ADJECTIVE **1 Bright** colours are clear and easy to see.
ADJECTIVE **2** A light that is **bright** shines strongly.
ADJECTIVE **3** Someone who is **bright** is quick at learning or noticing things.

brilliant
ADJECTIVE **1** A **brilliant** colour or light is extremely bright.
ADJECTIVE **2** Someone who is **brilliant** is extremely clever or skilful.

brim brims
NOUN **1** If you fill a cup to the **brim**, you fill it right up to the top.
NOUN **2** The **brim** of a hat is the part that sticks outwards from the head.

bring brings, bringing, brought
VERB **1** If you **bring** someone on a visit, they come with you.
VERB **2** If you **bring** something, you have it with you when you arrive.

bristle bristles NOUN
The **bristles** of a brush are the thick hairs or thin pieces of plastic which are fixed to the main part of it.

brittle ADJECTIVE
If something is **brittle**, it is hard but easily broken.

broad broader, broadest ADJECTIVE
Something such as a road or river that is **broad** is very wide.

broadcast broadcasts NOUN
A **broadcast** is a programme or announcement on radio or television.

broke VERB
Broke is the past tense of **break**.

broken VERB
Broken is the past participle of **break**.

brooch brooches NOUN
A **brooch** is a small piece of jewellery which is worn pinned to a dress, blouse or coat.

broom brooms NOUN
A **broom** is a kind of brush with a long handle.

brother brothers NOUN
Someone's **brother** is a boy or man who has the same parents as they have.

brought VERB
Brought is the past tense of **bring**.

brown browner, brownest ADJECTIVE
Something that is **brown** is the colour of earth or of wood.
See Colours and shapes on page 266

bruise bruises NOUN
A **bruise** is a purple mark on your skin where something has hit it.

brush brushes NOUN
A **brush** is a lot of bristles fixed to a handle. Different brushes are used for jobs like cleaning your teeth or painting.

bubble bubbles NOUN
A **bubble** is a ball of air or gas. You can make bubbles with soapy water. Fizzy lemonade has bubbles, too.

bucket buckets NOUN
A **bucket** is a container with a handle, often used for carrying water.

buckle buckles NOUN
A **buckle** is a fastening on the end of a belt or strap.

bud buds NOUN
A **bud** is a small lump on a plant which will open into a leaf or flower.

Buddhist Buddhists NOUN
A **Buddhist** is someone who follows the teachings of Buddha.

budgerigar budgerigars NOUN
Budgerigars are small brightly-coloured birds, often kept as pets.

buffalo buffaloes NOUN
A **buffalo** is an animal like a large cow with long curved horns.

bug bugs
NOUN **1** A **bug** is an insect.
NOUN **2** A **bug** is also an illness, such as a flu bug or a stomach bug.

a
b
c
d
e
f
g
h
i
j
k
l
m
n
o
p
q
r
s
t
u
v
w
x
y
z

A
B
C
D
E
F
G
H
I
J
K
L
M
N
O
P
Q
R
S
T
U
V
W
X
Y
Z

build **builds, building, built** VERB
If you **build** something, you make it by joining things together.

builder **builders** NOUN
A **builder** is a person whose job is to build houses and other buildings.

building **buildings** NOUN
A **building** is a place like a house that has walls and a roof.

bulb **bulbs**
NOUN **1** A **bulb** is the glass part of a lamp that gives out light.
NOUN **2** A **bulb** is also a root shaped like an onion. Many spring flowers such as daffodils and tulips grow from bulbs.

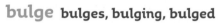

bulge **bulges, bulging, bulged**
VERB
If something **bulges**, it sticks out in a lump. *His pockets **bulged** with conkers.*

bull **bulls** NOUN
A **bull** is a male cow, elephant or whale.

bulldozer **bulldozers** NOUN
A **bulldozer** is a tractor with a steel blade on the front. It is used for moving large amounts of earth or stone.

bullet **bullets**
NOUN **1** A **bullet** is a small piece of metal fired from a gun.
NOUN **2** A **bullet point** is a heavy dot used to draw attention to a piece of text.

bully **bullies** NOUN
A **bully** is someone who hurts or frightens other people.

bump **bumps, bumping, bumped**
VERB **1** If you **bump** into something, you hit it while you are moving.
NOUN **2** If you hear a **bump**, it sounds like something falling to the ground.
NOUN **3** A **bump** is a raised uneven part on a surface such as a road.

bumper **bumpers** NOUN
Bumpers are bars on the front and back of a vehicle that protect it if there is an accident.

bun **buns** NOUN
A **bun** is a small round cake.

bunch **bunches** NOUN
A **bunch** is a group of things together, like flowers or grapes.
See Collective nouns on page 268

bundle **bundles** NOUN
A **bundle** is a number of small things that have been tied together.

bungalow **bungalows** NOUN
A **bungalow** is a house with all its rooms on one floor.

burger **burgers** NOUN
A **burger** is a flat piece of minced meat. It is often eaten in a bread roll.

burglar **burglars** NOUN
A **burglar** is someone who breaks into buildings to steal things.

burn **burns, burning, burned** or **burnt**
VERB **1** If something is **burning**, it is being spoiled or destroyed by fire.
VERB **2** People often **burn** fuel, such as coal, to keep warm.
NOUN **3** A **burn** is an injury caused by heat or fire.

burrow **burrows** NOUN
A **burrow** is a hole in the ground that an animal lives in.

burst **bursts, bursting, burst** VERB
When something like a balloon or tyre **bursts**, it splits open suddenly.

bury **buries, burying, buried** VERB
If you **bury** something, you put it in a hole in the ground and cover it.

bus **buses** NOUN
A **bus** is a large motor vehicle. People pay to go on buses.

bush **bushes** NOUN
A **bush** is a large woody plant with lots of branches. It is smaller than a tree.

business **businesses**
NOUN **1 Business** is the work of making, buying and selling things or services.
NOUN **2** A **business** is a group of people who make and sell things.

bus stop **bus stops** NOUN
A **bus stop** is a place where people can get on or off buses.

busy **busier, busiest**
ADJECTIVE **1** When you are **busy**, you are working hard on something.
ADJECTIVE **2** A place that is **busy** is full of people doing things or moving about.

but CONJUNCTION
You use **but** to join two parts of a sentence when the second part is unexpected. *Megan likes most green vegetables, **but** she won't eat broccoli.*

butcher **butchers** NOUN
A **butcher** is a shopkeeper who cuts up meat and sells it.

butter NOUN
Butter is a yellow fat made from cream. You spread it on bread or use it for cooking.
*See **Other foods** on page 261*

butterfly **butterflies** NOUN
A **butterfly** is an insect with four large wings which flies during the day.
*See **Insects** on page 264*

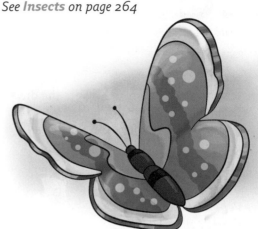

button **buttons**
NOUN **1** A **button** is a small disc used to fasten clothes.
NOUN **2** A **button** is also a part of a machine that you press to make it work.

buy **buys, buying, bought** VERB
When you **buy** something, you get it by paying money for it.

buzz **buzzes, buzzing, buzzed** VERB
If something **buzzes**, it makes a "zzz" sound like a bee.

by
PREPOSITION **1** You use **by** to show who or what has done something. *The announcement was made **by** the head teacher.*
PREPOSITION **2** You use **by** to show how something is done. *He cheered us up **by** taking us to the cinema.*
PREPOSITION **3** You use **by** to talk about being next to or near to another thing. *They live **by** the park.*
PREPOSITION **4** If something happens **by** a particular time, it happens before that time. *We should finish **by** tea time.*
PREPOSITION OR ADVERB **5** You use **by** to talk about going past something. *We drove **by** her house.*

a
b
c
d
e
f
g
h
i
j
k
l
m
n
o
p
q
r
s
t
u
v
w
x
y
z

Cc

cab cabs
NOUN **1** The **cab** is the place where the driver sits in a bus, truck or train.
NOUN **2** A **cab** is another word for a taxi.

cabbage cabbages NOUN
A **cabbage** is a vegetable that looks like a large ball of leaves.
See Vegetables on page 260

cabin cabins
NOUN **1** A **cabin** is a room in a ship, boat or aeroplane for passengers or crew.
NOUN **2** A **cabin** is also a small house in a wild place such as a forest.

cable cables
NOUN **1** A **cable** is a thick rope or chain.
NOUN **2** A **cable** is also a bundle of wires with a rubber covering, which carries electricity.
NOUN **3** **Cable television** is a system in which the signals are sent along wires.

cactus cactuses or cacti NOUN
A **cactus** is a plant with spines. It can grow in hot, dry places like deserts.

café cafés NOUN
A **café** is a place with tables and chairs where you buy drinks and snacks.

cage cages NOUN
A **cage** is a box or room with bars in which birds or animals are kept.

cake cakes NOUN
A **cake** is a sweet food made with flour, sugar, fat and eggs, and baked in an oven.
See Other foods on page 261

calculate calculates, calculating, calculated VERB
If you **calculate** something in maths, you work it out.

calculation calculations NOUN
A **calculation** is something you work out in maths.

calculator calculators NOUN
A **calculator** is a small electronic machine which you can use to give you the answer to different calculations.

calendar calendars NOUN
A **calendar** is a list of the months, weeks and days in a year.

calf calves
NOUN **1** **Calves** are young cows, elephants and whales.
See Young animals on page 265
NOUN **2** Your **calf** is the part at the back of your leg between the knee and ankle.

call calls, calling, called
VERB **1** If you **call** someone, you shout for them, or telephone them.
VERB **2** If you **call** someone something, you give them a name.
VERB **3** If an animal or thing is **called** something, that is their name.

calm calmer, calmest
ADJECTIVE **1** If you are **calm**, you do not seem worried or excited.
ADJECTIVE **2** If the sea is **calm**, it is smooth and still because there is no wind.

came VERB
Came is the past tense of **come**.

camel camels NOUN
A **camel** is a large animal which carries people and things in the desert.

camera cameras NOUN
A **camera** is a piece of equipment you use to take pictures.

camouflage camouflages, camouflaging, camouflaged VERB
To **camouflage** something is to hide it by giving it the same colour or appearance as its surroundings.

camp camps NOUN
A **camp** is a place where people stay in tents.

can could; cans
VERB **1** If you **can** do something, you are able to do it. *I can swim.*
NOUN **2** A **can** is a metal container for something like food, drink or paint.

canal canals NOUN
A **canal** is a narrow stretch of water made for boats to travel along.

cancel cancels, cancelling, cancelled
VERB
If you **cancel** something that has been planned, you stop it from happening.

candle candles NOUN
A **candle** is a wax stick with a string called a wick inside. You light the wick and it burns to give light.

cane canes
NOUN **1** A **cane** is the long hollow stem of a plant such as bamboo.
NOUN **2** A **cane** is a tall narrow stick used to support things.

cannot VERB
Cannot is the same as **can not**.

canoe canoes NOUN
A **canoe** is a small light boat, moved with a paddle.

can't VERB
Can't is a contraction of **cannot**.

canvas NOUN
Canvas is strong cloth, used for making things like tents and sails.

canyon canyons NOUN
A **canyon** is a narrow valley with very steep sides, often with a river.

cap caps
NOUN **1** A **cap** is a soft flat hat with a peak at the front.
NOUN **2** A **cap** is also a small flat lid on a bottle or container.

capable ADJECTIVE
If a person is **capable** of doing something, they are able to do it. *He's capable of doing better.*

capacity capacities NOUN
The **capacity** of something is the largest amount it can hold, produce or carry. *The capacity of this jug is one litre.*

capital capitals
NOUN **1** The **capital** is the main city in a country. *Paris is the capital of France.*
NOUN **2** A **capital** is a big letter of the alphabet, such as A, B and C. Capital letters are also called upper-case letters.
See **lower-case**
See also Punctuation on page 270

captain captains
NOUN **1** A **captain** is the person in charge of a ship or an aeroplane.
NOUN **2** A **captain** is the person who leads a team in sports like football.

caption captions NOUN
A **caption** is the words printed underneath a picture which explain what the picture is about.

capture captures, capturing, captured
VERB
If you **capture** somebody, you take them prisoner.

car cars NOUN
A **car** is a road vehicle with wheels and an engine. It needs a driver and has room for passengers.

a b c d e f g h i j k l m n o p q r s t u v w x y z

33

A B C D E F G H I J K L M N O P Q R S T U V W X Y Z

caravan **caravans** NOUN
A **caravan** is a vehicle pulled by a car in which people live or spend their holidays.

carbon NOUN
Carbon is a chemical found in coal and diamonds. All living things contain carbon.

carbon footprint **carbon footprints** NOUN
Your **carbon footprint** is the amount of pollution released into the atmosphere by the things you do.

card **cards**
NOUN **1** **Card** is strong, stiff paper.
NOUN **2** A greetings **card** usually has a picture on the front and is sent to people on special days such as birthdays.
NOUN **3** Playing **cards** are small pieces of card with numbers or pictures on them. They are used for card games.

cardboard NOUN
Cardboard is thick, stiff paper.

cardigan **cardigans** NOUN
A **cardigan** is a knitted jacket. You fasten it at the front with buttons.

care **cares, caring, cared**
VERB **1** If you **care** about something or someone, you think they are important.
VERB **2** If you **care** for a person or animal, you look after them.
NOUN **3** If you do something with **care**, you take trouble over it.

career **careers** NOUN
Someone's **career** is the work they do, which they hope to do for a long time. *John wants a career in teaching.*

careful ADJECTIVE
If someone is **careful**, they try to do things safely and well.

careless ADJECTIVE
If you are **careless**, you do not pay attention to what you are doing.

caretaker **caretakers** NOUN
A **caretaker** is a person who looks after a large building such as a school.

cargo **cargoes** NOUN
Cargo is the goods carried on a ship or plane.

carnival **carnivals** NOUN
A **carnival** is a sort of party in the streets. There is usually music and dancing, and people dress up and decorate cars and trucks.

carpenter **carpenters** NOUN
A **carpenter** is a person who works with wood, usually for furniture.

carpet **carpets** NOUN
A **carpet** is a thick covering for a floor, often made of wool.

carriage **carriages**
NOUN **1** A **carriage** is one of the vehicles that make up a passenger train.
NOUN **2** A **carriage** is also a vehicle with wheels, pulled by horses.

carrot **carrots** NOUN
A **carrot** is a long thin orange vegetable that grows under the ground.
*See **Vegetables** on page 260*

carry **carries, carrying, carried** VERB
When you **carry** something, you pick it up and take it with you.

cart **carts** NOUN
A **cart** is a heavy wooden vehicle pulled by horses or cattle on farms.

carton **cartons** NOUN
A **carton** is a strong cardboard or plastic box for holding food or drink.

cartoon **cartoons**
NOUN **1** A **cartoon** is a film where the characters are drawn instead of being real people.
NOUN **2** A **cartoon** is also a funny drawing in a magazine, newspaper or book.

cartwheel **cartwheels** NOUN
A **cartwheel** is a movement. You put your hands on the floor and move your legs round in a circle until you land on your feet again.

carve carves, carving, carved
VERB **1** If you **carve** an object, you cut it out of something like stone or wood.
VERB **2** If someone **carves** a piece of meat, they cut slices from it.

case cases NOUN
A **case** is a box for keeping or carrying things in.

cash NOUN
Cash is coins and paper money.

cast casts, casting, cast
NOUN **1** The **cast** of a play or film is all the people who act in it.
NOUN **2** A **cast** is an object made by pouring liquid plaster or metal into a container and leaving it to harden.
VERB **3** If something **casts** a shadow onto a place, it makes a shadow fall there.
VERB **4** If someone like a witch **casts** a spell on someone or something, they do magic that affects that person or thing.

castle castles NOUN
A **castle** is a large building with thick walls or ditches round it to protect it from attack.

cat cats NOUN
A **cat** is a small furry animal, often kept as a pet. There are also larger, wild cats, such as lions and tigers.

catalogue catalogues NOUN
A **catalogue** is a list of things for sale or for looking at.

catch catches, catching, caught
VERB **1** If you **catch** something, you take hold of it while it is moving.
VERB **2** If you **catch** a bus or train, you get on it to go somewhere.
VERB **3** If you **catch** something like measles, you get that illness.

catching ADJECTIVE
An illness that is **catching** can spread very quickly.

category categories NOUN
A **category** is a set of things with a particular feature or quality in common.

caterpillar caterpillars NOUN
A **caterpillar** is a very small animal like a worm with legs, that will change into a butterfly or moth.

cathedral cathedrals NOUN
A **cathedral** is a large, important church.

cattle NOUN
Bulls and cows are called **cattle**.

caught VERB
Caught is the past tense of **catch**.

cauliflower cauliflowers NOUN
A **cauliflower** is a round white vegetable with green leaves on the outside.
See Vegetables on page 260

cause causes, causing, caused VERB
To **cause** something means to make it happen.

cautious ADJECTIVE
Someone who is **cautious** acts carefully to avoid possible danger.

cave caves NOUN
A **cave** is a large hole in the side of a hill or cliff, or under the ground.

CD CDs NOUN
CD is an abbreviation of **compact disc**.

a
b
c
d
e
f
g
h
i
j
k
l
m
n
o
p
q
r
s
t
u
v
w
x
y
z

35

CD-ROM **CD-ROMs** NOUN
CD-ROM is an abbreviation of **compact disc read-only memory**. It is a disc which can be played on a computer to show sounds and pictures.

ceiling **ceilings** NOUN
The **ceiling** is the inside roof of a room.

celebrate **celebrates, celebrating, celebrated** VERB
If you **celebrate** something, you do something enjoyable like having a party, to show it is a special occasion.

celebrity **celebrities** NOUN
A **celebrity** is a famous person.

celery NOUN
Celery is a vegetable with long, pale green stalks.
See Vegetables on page 260

cell **cells**
NOUN **1** Animals and plants are made from tiny parts called **cells**.
NOUN **2** A **cell** is also a small room where a prisoner lives.

cellar **cellars** NOUN
A **cellar** is a room under a house where you can store things.

cement NOUN
Cement is a grey powder which is mixed with sand and water and used to make bricks stick together.

cemetery **cemeteries** NOUN
A **cemetery** is a place where dead people are buried.

centimetre **centimetres** NOUN
A **centimetre** (cm) is a measure length. It is the same as 10 millimetres.

centipede **centipedes** NOUN
A **centipede** is a tiny animal like a worm, but with lots of legs.

central ADJECTIVE
Something that is **central** is in the middle of an object or an area.

centre **centres**
NOUN **1** The **centre** of anything is the middle of it.
NOUN **2** A **centre** is a place where people can go for a particular purpose, for example sports.

century **centuries** NOUN
A **century** is a period of 100 years. The 21st century is the time between 2000 and 2099.

cereal **cereals**
NOUN **1 Cereal** is a plant which has seeds called grain that can be used for food.
NOUN **2 Cereal** is also a food made from grain that is often eaten for breakfast.
See Other foods on page 261

ceremony **ceremonies** NOUN
A **ceremony** is a set of formal actions performed at a special occasion such as a wedding.

certain ADJECTIVE
If you are **certain** of something, you are sure it is true.

certificate **certificates** NOUN
A **certificate** is a piece of paper which says that something important like a birth or marriage took place.

chain **chains** NOUN
A **chain** is made from rings of metal joined together in a line.

chair **chairs** NOUN
A **chair** is a seat with a back, for one person.

chalk NOUN

Chalk is a soft white rock. It can be made into sticks for writing on blackboards.

challenge challenges, challenging, challenged

NOUN **1** A **challenge** is something new and exciting that needs a lot of effort. *Learning how to cook is a new **challenge** for me.*

VERB **2** If someone **challenges** you, they ask you to have a competition with them.

champion champions NOUN

A **champion** is a person who has beaten everyone else in a contest.

chance chances

NOUN **1** If there is a **chance** that something will happen, it might happen.

NOUN **2** If you are given a **chance** to do something, you are allowed to do it if you want to.

by chance PHRASE If something happens **by chance**, it has not been planned.

change changes, changing, changed

VERB **1** When something **changes**, it becomes different.

VERB **2** When you **change** your clothes, you put on different ones.

NOUN **3** If there is a **change** in something, it is different in some way.

NOUN **4 Change** is the money you are given when you pay more than the right amount for something.

channel channels

NOUN **1** A **channel** is a passage for water or other liquid.

NOUN **2** Television companies use **channels** to broadcast programmes.

chaos NOUN

Chaos is a state of complete confusion, where nothing is organized.

chapter chapters NOUN

A **chapter** is a part of a book.

character characters

NOUN **1** The **characters** of a book, film or play are the people it is about.

NOUN **2** Someone's **character** is the sort of person they are. *She has a kind **character**.*

charge charges, charging, charged

VERB **1** If someone **charges** you money, they ask you to pay for something.

VERB **2** If something or someone **charges** towards you, they rush forward.

in charge PHRASE If you are **in charge** of something, you are the person looking after it.

charity charities NOUN

A **charity** is an organization which raises money for a particular cause, such as people in need.

charm charms

NOUN **1** A **charm** is a small ornament that is fixed to a bracelet or necklace.

NOUN **2** A **charm** is also a magical spell or an object that is supposed to bring good luck.

chart charts

NOUN **1** A **chart** is a sheet of paper that shows things like dates or numbers.

NOUN **2** A **chart** can also be a map of the sea or of the stars.

chase chases, chasing, chased VERB

If you **chase** someone, you run after them to try and catch them.

chat chats NOUN

A **chat** is a friendly talk about things that are not very important.

A
B
C
D
E
F
G
H
I
J
K
L
M
N
O
P
Q
R
S
T
U
V
W
X
Y
Z

chatroom chatrooms NOUN
A **chatroom** is a site on a computer network where people discuss a particular subject.

chatter chatters, chattering, chattered VERB
When people **chatter**, they talk about unimportant things.

cheap cheaper, cheapest ADJECTIVE
Something **cheap** costs very little, or less than you might expect.

cheat cheats, cheating, cheated VERB
When someone **cheats**, they lie or do unfair things to get what they want.

check checks, checking, checked
VERB **1** If you **check** something, you make sure it is correct or safe.
NOUN **2** A **check** is a pattern of squares.

checkout checkouts NOUN
A **checkout** is the place in a supermarket where you pay.

cheek cheeks NOUN
Your **cheeks** are the sides of your face below your eyes.

cheeky cheekier, cheekiest ADJECTIVE
Cheeky speech or behaviour is rude and disrespectful.

cheer cheers, cheering, cheered VERB
When you **cheer**, you shout to show you are pleased about something or to encourage a person or team.

cheerful ADJECTIVE
Someone who is **cheerful** shows they are feeling happy.

cheese cheeses NOUN
Cheese is a food made from milk. Some cheeses have a strong flavour.
See Other foods on page 261

cheetah cheetahs NOUN
A **cheetah** is a large wild animal of the cat family, with black spots.

chef chefs NOUN
A **chef** is the head cook in a restaurant or hotel.

chemist chemists
NOUN **1** A **chemist** is a person who makes up medicine.
NOUN **2** The **chemist** is a shop where you can buy medicine and things like soap and toothpaste.
NOUN **3** A **chemist** can be a scientist trained in chemistry.

chemistry NOUN
Chemistry is the scientific study of how substances are made up and how they work together.

cheque cheques NOUN
A **cheque** is a piece of paper that people use to pay for things.

cherry cherries NOUN
A **cherry** is a small round red or black fruit with a hard seed called a stone in the middle.
See Fruit on page 260

chess NOUN
Chess is a game for two people. It is played on a board marked in black and white squares.

chest chests
NOUN **1** Your **chest** is the top part of the front of your body, between your neck and your waist.
NOUN **2** A **chest** is a large heavy box, usually made of wood.

chestnut chestnuts
NOUN **1** A **chestnut** is a large tree.
NOUN **2** A **chestnut** is also a shiny brown nut that grows on a chestnut tree.

chew chews, chewing, chewed VERB
When you **chew** food, you bite it several times.

chick chicks NOUN
A **chick** is a baby bird.
See Young animals on page 265

chicken
chickens NOUN
A **chicken** is a bird kept on a farm for its eggs and meat.

chickenpox NOUN
Chickenpox is an illness that gives you itchy spots.

chief **chiefs** NOUN
A **chief** is a person in charge of other people.

child **children** NOUN
A **child** is a young boy or girl.

childhood NOUN
A person's **childhood** is the time of life when they are a child.

childish ADJECTIVE
You call a person **childish** if they are not acting like an adult is expected to act.

children PLURAL NOUN
Children is the plural of **child**.

chilly **chillier, chilliest** ADJECTIVE
If you feel **chilly**, you are not quite warm enough to be comfortable.

chime **chimes** NOUN
A **chime** is the musical sound made by a bell or a clock.

chimney **chimneys** NOUN
A **chimney** is a pipe which takes smoke from a fire up into the air.

chimpanzee **chimpanzees** NOUN
A **chimpanzee** is a small ape with dark fur that lives in forests in Africa.

chin **chins** NOUN
Your **chin** is the part of your face below your mouth.

chip **chips, chipping, chipped**
NOUN **1** A **chip** is a long thin fried piece of potato.
See Other foods on page 261
NOUN **2** A silicon **chip** is a tiny piece of special material used in computers.

VERB **3** When you **chip** something, you break a small piece off it.

chisel **chisels** NOUN
A **chisel** is a tool with a long thin blade and a sharp end, which is used for cutting wood or stone.

chocolate **chocolates**
NOUN **1 Chocolate** is a brown sweet or drink made from cocoa.
NOUN **2** A **chocolate** is a sweet covered with a layer of chocolate.

choice **choices**
NOUN **1** A **choice** is the different things that you can choose from.
NOUN **2** A **choice** can also be someone or something that you choose. *If you need a captain, Jessica would be a good **choice**.*

choir **choirs** NOUN
A **choir** is a group of people who sing together.

choke **chokes, choking, choked** VERB
If you **choke**, you cannot breathe because not enough air can get to your lungs. *He **choked** on a chicken bone.*

choose **chooses, choosing, chose, chosen** VERB
To **choose** something is to decide which thing you want to have or do.

chop **chops, chopping, chopped**
VERB **1** When someone **chops** something like wood, they cut it with an axe.
NOUN **2** A **chop** is a slice of meat on a bone.

chorus **choruses** NOUN
A **chorus** is a part of a song which is repeated after each verse.

chose VERB
Chose is the past tense of **choose**.

chosen VERB
Chosen is the past participle of **choose**.

a
b
c
d
e
f
g
h
i
j
k
l
m
n
o
p
q
r
s
t
u
v
w
x
y
z

Christian **Christians** NOUN
A **Christian** is someone who follows the teachings of Jesus Christ.

Christmas **Christmases** NOUN
Christmas is a Christian festival held on December 25, when the birth of Jesus Christ is celebrated.

chuckle **chuckles, chuckling, chuckled**
VERB
When you **chuckle**, you laugh quietly.

church **churches** NOUN
A **church** is a building where Christians worship.

cigarette **cigarettes** NOUN
A **cigarette** is a thin roll of paper with tobacco in, which people smoke.

cinema **cinemas** NOUN
A **cinema** is a place where people watch films.

circle **circles** NOUN
A **circle** is a perfect round shape.
circular ADJECTIVE
See Colours and shapes on page 266

circuit **circuits** NOUN
A **circuit** is the complete path that an electric current flows through. You can make a simple circuit with a battery, a bulb and wires.

circumference **circumferences** NOUN
The **circumference** of a circle is the distance around its edge.

circus **circuses** NOUN
A **circus** is a travelling group of people such as clowns and acrobats.

city **cities** NOUN
A **city** is a large busy town.

claim **claims, claiming, claimed**
VERB **1** If someone **claims** something, they ask for it because it is theirs.
VERB **2** If you **claim** something is the case, you say it is the case. *Amy **claims** she was the first to finish.*

clap **claps, clapping, clapped** VERB
When you **clap**, you make a noise by hitting your hands together.

class **classes**
NOUN **1** A **class** is a group of people who are taught together.
NOUN **2** A **class** is also a group of people or things that are alike in some way.

classify **classifies, classifying, classified**
VERB
To **classify** things is to arrange them in groups with similar features. *These books are **classified** as non-fiction.*

classroom **classrooms** NOUN
A **classroom** is a room in a school where children have lessons.

clause **clauses** NOUN
In grammar, a **clause** is a group of words with a subject and a verb. It may be a complete sentence or one part of a sentence. For example, "the girl laughed" is a clause because it has a subject (the girl) and a verb (laughed).

claw **claws** NOUN
The **claws** of a bird or animal are the hard curved nails at the end of its feet.

clay NOUN
Clay is a type of sticky earth that goes hard when it is dry. It is used to make bricks and pots.

clean **cleaner, cleanest** ADJECTIVE
If something is **clean**, it is free from dirt.

clear **clearer, clearest; clears, clearing, cleared**
ADJECTIVE **1** If a thing is **clear**, you can see through it.
ADJECTIVE **2** If something you say or write is **clear**, it is easy to understand.
VERB **3** If you **clear** an area, you move things that are not wanted out of the way.

clever **cleverer, cleverest** ADJECTIVE
Someone who is **clever** is able to learn and understand things easily.

click **clicks, clicking, clicked** VERB
When you **click** something, it makes a short snapping sound.

cliff **cliffs** NOUN
A **cliff** is a steep hill by the sea.

climate **climates** NOUN
The **climate** of a place is the sort of weather it usually has.

climb **climbs, climbing, climbed** VERB
When you **climb** something, you move upwards using your hands and feet.

cling **clings, clinging, clung** VERB
If you **cling** to someone or something, you hold onto them tightly.

clinic **clinics** NOUN
A **clinic** is where people go to get help from a doctor or nurse.

clip **clips, clipping, clipped**
NOUN **1** A **clip** is something small and springy which holds things in place.
VERB **2** If you **clip** something like a hedge, you cut small pieces off it.

cloak **cloaks** NOUN
A **cloak** is a loose coat without sleeves that fastens at the neck.

cloakroom **cloakrooms** NOUN
A **cloakroom** is a room where coats can be left.

clock **clocks** NOUN
A **clock** is an instrument that measures and shows the time.

clockwise ADVERB
If something goes **clockwise**, it moves in the same direction as the hands on a clock.

clockwork
ADJECTIVE
Clockwork toys move when they are wound up with a key.

close **closer, closest; closes, closing, closed**
(*rhymes with* **dose**) ADJECTIVE **1** If something is **close**, it is very near.
(*rhymes with* **doze**) VERB **2** When you **close** something like a door, you shut it.

closed ADJECTIVE
If something is **closed**, it is not open.

cloth **cloths**
NOUN **1** **Cloth** is material made from something like cotton or wool.
NOUN **2** A **cloth** is a piece of cloth used for cleaning.

clothes PLURAL NOUN
Clothes are the things people wear, such as shirts, trousers and dresses.
See *Clothes* on page 257

cloud **clouds**
NOUN **1** A **cloud** is a patch of white or grey mist that floats in the sky.
NOUN **2** You can use **cloud** to describe a lot of smoke, steam or dust.
cloudy ADJECTIVE

clover NOUN
Clover is a small wild plant. It has white or purple flowers, and leaves divided into three parts.

clown **clowns** NOUN
A **clown** is someone in a circus who wears funny clothes and does silly things to make people laugh.

club **clubs** NOUN
A **club** is an organization joined by people who are interested in the same thing, such as chess or riding.

a
b
c
d
e
f
g
h
i
j
k
l
m
n
o
p
q
r
s
t
u
v
w
x
y
z

clue clues NOUN
A **clue** is something that helps to solve a problem or mystery.

clump clumps NOUN
A **clump** is a small group of plants growing together.

clumsy clumsier, clumsiest ADJECTIVE
Someone who is **clumsy** moves awkwardly and carelessly.
clumsily ADVERB

clung VERB
Clung is the past tense of **cling**.

cluster clusters NOUN
A **cluster** is a number of things close together in a small group.

clutch clutches, clutching, clutched VERB
If you **clutch** something, you hold it tightly with your hand.

clutter NOUN
Clutter is an untidy mess.

coach coaches
NOUN **1** A **coach** is a long motor vehicle used for taking passengers on long journeys.
NOUN **2** A **coach** is also a section of a train that carries passengers.
NOUN **3** A **coach** is someone who trains you for a sport or gives you extra lessons.

coal NOUN
Coal is a hard black rock which is dug out of the ground and burned to give heat.

coarse coarser, coarsest ADJECTIVE
Anything that is **coarse** looks and feels rough.

coast coasts NOUN
The **coast** is the place where the land meets the sea.

coat coats
NOUN **1** A **coat** is a piece of clothing with long sleeves, that you wear over other clothes when you go out.
NOUN **2** An animal's **coat** is its fur.
NOUN **3** A layer of paint is called a **coat**.

cobweb cobwebs NOUN
A **cobweb** is a net made by a spider to trap insects.

cock cocks NOUN
A **cock** is any male bird.

cocoa NOUN
Cocoa is a brown powder made from the seeds of the cacao tree, and also a hot drink made from this powder.

coconut coconuts NOUN
A **coconut** is a large nut with white flesh, milky juice, and a hard hairy shell.

cocoon cocoons NOUN
A **cocoon** is a covering of silky threads that some young insects make for themselves before they grow into adults.

cod NOUN
A **cod** is a large sea fish which is caught for food.

code codes
NOUN **1** A **code** is a system of changing letters in a message for other letters or symbols, so that only people who know the code can read it.
NOUN **2** A **code** is also a group of letters and numbers that identify something. *Do you know the telephone **code** for York?*
NOUN **3** A **code** is also a set of rules.

coffee NOUN
Coffee is a coarse powder made by grinding roasted coffee beans, and also a hot drink made from this powder.

See Other foods on page 261

cog cogs NOUN
A **cog** is a wheel with teeth which turns another part of a machine.

coil coils NOUN
A **coil** is a series of loops into which something has been wound.

coin **coins** NOUN
A **coin** is a small piece of metal used as money.

cold **colder, coldest; colds**
ADJECTIVE **1** If the weather is **cold**, the temperature outside is low.

NOUN **2** A **cold** is a common illness. You sneeze and your nose feels blocked.

collage **collages** NOUN
A **collage** is a picture made by sticking pieces of paper or cloth onto a surface.

collapse **collapses, collapsing, collapsed** VERB
If someone or something **collapses**, they suddenly fall down.

collar **collars**
NOUN **1** The **collar** of a shirt or jacket is the part that fits round your neck.
NOUN **2** A **collar** is also a leather band round the neck of a dog or cat.

collect **collects, collecting, collected**
VERB **1** If you **collect** a number of things, you bring them together for a special reason. *She **collected** sticks for firewood.*
VERB **2** If you **collect** someone or something from a place, you call there and take them away. *We had to **collect** her from school.*

collection **collections** NOUN
A **collection** is a group of things brought together over a period of time. *My dad's got a huge stamp **collection**.*

collective noun **collective nouns** NOUN
In grammar, a **collective noun** refers to a group of things. For example, a group of sheep is called a "flock".
See Collective nouns on page 268

college **colleges** NOUN
A **college** is where people go to study after they have left school.

collide **collides, colliding, collided** VERB
If a moving object **collides** with something, it hits it.
collision NOUN

colon **colons** NOUN
The punctuation mark **:** is a **colon**. You can use it in several ways, for example in front of a list of things.
See Punctuation on page 270

colour **colours** NOUN
The **colour** of something is the way it looks in daylight. *The **colour** of grass is green.*
See Colours and shapes on page 266

colt **colts** NOUN
A **colt** is a young male horse.

column **columns**
NOUN **1** A **column** is a tall stone post which supports part of a building.
NOUN **2** A **column** is also a vertical strip of print in a newspaper or magazine.
NOUN **3** If numbers are arranged in vertical lists, these are called **columns**.

comb **combs** NOUN
A **comb** is a flat piece plastic or metal with narrow teeth on one edge. You use it to tidy your hair.

combine **combines, combining, combined** VERB
If you **combine** things, you mix them together.

come **comes, coming, came, come**
VERB **1** To **come** to a place is to move there or arrive there.
VERB **2** If you **come** from a place, you were born there, or it is your home.

comedy **comedies** NOUN
A **comedy** is a play or film that makes people laugh.

comet **comets** NOUN
A **comet** is an object which travels around the sun, leaving a long bright trail behind it.

comfort **comforts, comforting, comforted** VERB
If you **comfort** someone, you make them feel less worried or unhappy.

comfortable ADJECTIVE
If something is **comfortable**, it is easy to wear or use.

comic **comics**
NOUN
A **comic** is a magazine that tells stories in pictures.

comma **commas** NOUN
A **comma** is a punctuation mark (,) which is used to separate parts of a sentence or items on a list.
See Punctuation on page 270

command **commands, commanding, commanded** VERB
If you **command** someone to do something, you order them to do it.

commercial **commercials** NOUN
A **commercial** is an advertisement on television or radio.

common ADJECTIVE
If something is **common**, you often see it or it often happens.

common noun **common nouns** NOUN
Common nouns name things in general. For example, "boy", "dog" and "computer" are all common nouns.
See Noun on page 268

common sense NOUN
If you have **common sense**, you usually act sensibly and do the right thing.

commotion NOUN
A **commotion** is a lot of noise, confusion and excitement.

communicate **communicates, communicating, communicated** VERB
If you **communicate** with someone, you give them information by talking or writing to them.

compact disc **compact discs** NOUN
A **compact disc** is a round flat silver-coloured object which can store information. It is called a **CD** for short.

company **companies**
NOUN **1 Company** is being with others so you are not lonely.
NOUN **2** A **company** is a group of people who work together to make or sell things.

comparative **comparatives** NOUN
In grammar, the **comparative** is the form of an adjective which has "more" of that adjective. For example, "happier" is the comparative of "happy".
See Adjective on page 269

compare **compares, comparing, compared** VERB
When you **compare** two or more things, you look at them to see in what ways they are the same or different.

compass **compasses**
NOUN **1** A **compass** is an instrument with a needle that always points to north.
NOUN **2** A **pair of compasses** is an instrument used for drawing circles.

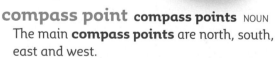

compass point **compass points** NOUN
The main **compass points** are north, south, east and west.

competition **competitions** NOUN
A **competition** is an event to find out who is best at doing something.

complain **complains, complaining, complained** VERB
If you **complain**, you say that you are not happy about something.

A B C D E F G H I J K L M N O P Q R S T U V W X Y Z

complete

ADJECTIVE **1** If something is **complete**, it has been finished.

ADJECTIVE **2** If you talk about a **complete** thing, you mean all of it. *I need a complete change of clothes.*

complicated ADJECTIVE

Something **complicated** is made up of so many parts that it is difficult to understand or deal with.

compose composes, composing, composed VERB

If you **compose** something, like a poem or a piece of music, you write it.

compound compounds NOUN

In language, a **compound** is a word that is made up of two or more words. "Playground", "armchair" and "toothache" are all compounds.

computer computers NOUN

A **computer** is a machine that stores information and works things out according to instructions in a program.

conceal conceals, concealing, concealed VERB

If you **conceal** something, you hide it carefully.

concentrate concentrates, concentrating, concentrated VERB

If you **concentrate** on something, you give it all your attention.

concerned ADJECTIVE

If you are **concerned** about something, it worries you.

concert concerts NOUN

A **concert** is a performance by musicians, usually in a big hall.

conclusion conclusions

NOUN **1** A **conclusion** is something you decide is true after you have thought carefully.

NOUN **2** The **conclusion** of something is its ending.

concrete NOUN

Concrete is a building material made of cement, sand and water, which goes hard when it is set.

condition conditions

NOUN **1** The **condition** of something is the state it is in.

NOUN **2** A **condition** is a rule you must agree to before you are allowed to do something. *You can go out on one condition – you must be home by five.*

conductor conductors NOUN

A **conductor** is someone who controls the way musicians play together.

cone cones NOUN

A **cone** is a solid curved shape with a flat circular base and a pointed top.
See Solid shapes on page 266

confess confesses, confessing, confessed VERB

If you **confess**, you say that you have done something wrong.

confident

ADJECTIVE **1** If you are **confident** about something, you are sure about it.

ADJECTIVE **2** People who are **confident** know that they can do something well.

confuse confuses, confusing, confused

VERB **1** To **confuse** someone means to make them unsure what to do. *The new road layout confused everyone.*

VERB **2** If you **confuse** two things, you mix them up by mistake. *I always confuse the twins because they are so alike.*

congratulate congratulates, congratulating, congratulated VERB

If you **congratulate** someone, you say you are pleased that something special has happened to them.

conjunction conjunctions NOUN

In grammar, a **conjunction** is a word that joins two other words or parts of a sentence. "And", "but", "while" and "although" are all conjunctions.

a
b
c
d
e
f
g
h
i
j
k
l
m
n
o
p
q
r
s
t
u
v
w
x
y
z

connect connects, connecting, connected VERB
If you **connect** two things, you join them together.

connective connectives NOUN
In grammar, a **connective** is a word or phrase that joins parts of a text. For example, "and", "at last" and "because" are connectives.

conquer conquers, conquering, conquered VERB
To **conquer** people is to take control of their country by force.

conscious ADJECTIVE
If you are **conscious**, you are awake and know what is happening.

consecutive ADJECTIVE
If things are **consecutive**, they happen one after the other. *October, November and December are consecutive months.*

conservation NOUN
Conservation is the protection of the environment.

consider considers, considering, considered VERB
If you **consider** something, you think about it carefully.

consist consists, consisting, consisted VERB
Something that **consists** of particular things is made up of them. *The book consists of an introduction, ten chapters and an index.*

consonant consonants NOUN
A **consonant** is any letter of the alphabet except a, e, i, o and u. See **vowel**

constant ADJECTIVE
Something that is **constant** happens all the time. *My friend Elizabeth complains of a constant headache.*

construct constructs, constructing, constructed VERB
If you **construct** something, you build it or make it.

consume consumes, consuming, consumed VERB
If you **consume** something, you eat or drink it, or use it up.

contain contains, containing, contained VERB
The things that something **contains** are the things in it.

container containers NOUN
A **container** is something you put things in.

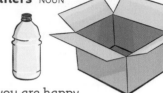

content ADJECTIVE
If you are **content**, you are happy and satisfied with your life.

contents PLURAL NOUN
The **contents** of something like a box or cake are the things in it. The **contents page** of a book tells you what is in it.

contest contests NOUN
A **contest** is a competition or game which you try to win.

continent continents NOUN
A **continent** is a very large area of land, such as Africa or Asia.

continue continues, continuing, continued VERB
If you **continue** to do something, you go on doing it.

continuous ADJECTIVE
Something that is **continuous** goes on without stopping.

contraction contractions NOUN
A **contraction** is a shortened form of a word or of words. For example, "I'm" is a contraction of "I am".

contradict contradicts, contradicting, contradicted VERB
If you **contradict** someone, you say the opposite of what they have just said.

control controls, controlling, controlled VERB **1** If you **control** something, you make it behave exactly as you want it to.

NOUN **2** The **controls** on a machine are knobs or other things used to work it.

convenient ADJECTIVE
If something is **convenient**, it is easy to use or do.

conversation conversations NOUN
If you have a **conversation** with someone, you talk to each other.

convince convinces, convincing, convinced VERB
If someone or something **convinces** you, they make you believe that something is true.

cook cooks, cooking, cooked VERB
When you **cook** food, you prepare it for eating by heating it.

cooker cookers NOUN
A **cooker** is a piece of equipment for cooking food.

cookie cookies NOUN
A **cookie** is another word for a biscuit.

cool cooler, coolest ADJECTIVE
If something is **cool**, its temperature is low but it is not cold.

coordinates NOUN
Coordinates are two numbers or letters which help you find the exact position of something. They are often used on maps, graphs and charts.

cope copes, coping, coped VERB
If you **cope** with a task or problem, you deal with it successfully.

copper NOUN
Copper is a reddish-brown metal.

copy copies, copying, copied
NOUN **1** A **copy** is something made to look exactly like something else.
VERB **2** If you **copy** something, you make a copy of it.
VERB **3** If you **copy** what someone does, you do the same thing.

coral corals NOUN
Coral is a hard substance that forms in the sea from the skeletons of tiny animals called corals.

cord cords NOUN
Cord is thick, strong string.

core cores NOUN
The **core** of a fruit is the hard part in the middle that contains seeds.

cork corks
NOUN **1 Cork** is the light bark of the cork oak tree.
NOUN **2** A **cork** is a piece of cork used to block the open end of a bottle.

corn NOUN
Corn is a cereal crop, such as wheat or sweet corn.

corner corners NOUN
A **corner** is the place where two edges or roads join.

correct corrects, correcting, corrected
ADJECTIVE **1** Something that is **correct** is true and has no mistakes.
VERB **2** If you **correct** your work, you put right any mistakes you made.

corridor corridors NOUN
A **corridor** is a long passage in a building or train.

cost costs, costing, cost VERB
If something **costs** an amount of money, you can buy it for that amount.

costume costumes NOUN
A **costume** is the clothes worn by an actor, or that people wear for special events.

a
b
c
d
e
f
g
h
i
j
k
l
m
n
o
p
q
r
s
t
u
v
w
x
y
z

cosy **cosier, cosiest** ADJECTIVE
A house or room that is **cosy** is comfortable and warm, and not too big.

cot **cots** NOUN
A **cot** is a bed with high sides for a baby or a young child.

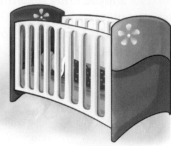

cottage **cottages** NOUN
A **cottage** is a small house, usually in the country.

cotton
NOUN **1** **Cotton** is cloth made from the soft fibres of the cotton plant.
NOUN **2** **Cotton** is also a thread used for sewing.
NOUN **3** **Cotton wool** is soft fluffy cotton, often used for cleaning the skin.

cough **coughs** NOUN
A **cough** is a noise made by someone forcing air out of their throat.

could
VERB **1** **Could** is part of the verb **can**. You use **could** to say that something might happen. *It could rain tomorrow.*
VERB **2** You also say **could** when you are asking for something politely. *Could you please tell me the way to the station?*

council **councils** NOUN
The **council** is a group of people who look after the affairs of a town, district or county.

count **counts, counting, counted**
VERB **1** When you **count**, you say numbers in order. *Count up to a hundred.*
VERB **2** If you **count** a number of things, you are finding out how many there are.

counter **counters**
NOUN **1** A **counter** is a long narrow table in a shop, where things are sold.
NOUN **2** A **counter** is also a small round flat object, usually made of plastic, that is used in board games.

country **countries**
NOUN **1** A **country** is a land that has its own government and often its own language.
NOUN **2** The **country** is land away from towns and cities.

couple **couples**
NOUN **1** A **couple** of things or people means two of them. *It should only take a couple of days.*
NOUN **2** Two people are sometimes called a **couple**, especially if they are married or having a relationship.

coupon **coupons** NOUN
A **coupon** is a piece of printed paper that allows you to pay less than usual for something.

courage NOUN
Courage is not showing that you are afraid of something.

course **courses**
NOUN **1** A **course** is a series of lessons.
NOUN **2** A **course** can also be one part of a meal.
of course PHRASE You use **of course** to make something you are saying stronger. *Of course I still want to go.*

court **courts**
NOUN **1** A **court** is an area marked out for a game like tennis or badminton.
NOUN **2** A **court** is also a place where things to do with the law are decided.
NOUN **3** The **court** of a king or queen is where they live with their family.

courtyard **courtyards** NOUN
A **courtyard** is an open flat area of ground with walls all round it.

cousin cousins NOUN
Your **cousin** is a child of your uncle or aunt.

cover covers, covering, covered
VERB **1** If you **cover** something, you put something over it to protect or hide it.
NOUN **2** The **covers** on a bed are the blankets or duvet that you have over you to keep you warm.
NOUN **3** The **cover** of a book or magazine is the outside of it.

cow cows NOUN
A **cow** is a large farm animal that gives milk.

coward cowards NOUN
A **coward** is someone who avoids anything dangerous, painful or difficult.

cowboy cowboys NOUN
A **cowboy** is a man whose job is to look after cattle.

crab crabs NOUN
A **crab** is a sea animal. It has four pairs of legs, two pincers, and a flat round body covered by a shell.

crack cracks, cracking, cracked
VERB **1** If you **crack** something, or it cracks, it has a small split in it but does not quite break.
NOUN **2** A **crack** is the line on something that shows it is nearly broken.
NOUN **3** A **crack** is also a sudden loud noise.

cracker crackers
NOUN **1** A **cracker** is a thin crisp biscuit, often slightly salty.
NOUN **2** A **cracker** can be a cardboard tube covered in coloured paper, that people have at parties. It makes a sharp sound when you pull the ends apart.

cradle cradles NOUN
A **cradle** is a small box-shaped bed for a baby.

crane cranes
NOUN **1** A **crane** is a machine that moves heavy things by lifting them.
NOUN **2** A **crane** is also a large water bird with long legs and a long neck.

crash crashes, crashing, crashed
NOUN **1** A **crash** is a traffic accident.
NOUN **2** A **crash** is also a sudden loud noise like something breaking.
VERB **3** If something **crashes**, it hits something else and makes a loud noise.

crate crates NOUN
A **crate** is a large box used for transporting or storing things.

crawl crawls, crawling, crawled VERB
When you **crawl**, you move forward on your hands and knees.

crayon crayons NOUN
A **crayon** is a coloured pencil.

craze crazes NOUN
A **craze** is something that is very popular for a short time.

crazy crazier, craziest
ADJECTIVE **1** Someone or something **crazy** is very strange or foolish.
ADJECTIVE **2** If you are **crazy** about something, you are very keen on it.

creak creaks, creaking, creaked VERB
If something **creaks**, it makes an odd squeaking sound.

cream
ADJECTIVE **1** Something that is **cream** in colour is yellowish-white.
NOUN **2 Cream** is the pale yellow liquid taken from the top of milk.

crease creases, creasing, creased
NOUN **1** A **crease** is a line made by folding or wrinkling something.
VERB **2** If you **crease** something, you make lines appear on it.

create creates, creating, created VERB
To **create** something means to cause it to happen, or exist.

creature creatures NOUN
A **creature** is any animal, such as a bird, fish or insect.

a
b
c
d
e
f
g
h
i
j
k
l
m
n
o
p
q
r
s
t
u
v
w
x
y
z

credit card credit cards NOUN
A **credit card** is a plastic card that allows someone to buy goods and pay for them later.

creep creeps, creeping, crept VERB
If you **creep** somewhere, you move quietly and slowly.

crescent crescents NOUN
A **crescent** is a curved shape that is wider in the middle than at the ends, like a new moon.

crew crews NOUN
A **crew** is the people who work on a ship, aircraft or spaceship.

cricket crickets
NOUN **1 Cricket** is an outdoor game between two teams of eleven players.
NOUN **2** A **cricket** is a small jumping insect that makes a chirping sound by rubbing its wings together.

cried VERB
Cried is the past tense of **cry**.

cries VERB
Cries is a present tense form of **cry**.

crime crimes NOUN
A **crime** is something which is against the law.

criminal criminals NOUN
A **criminal** is someone who has done something that is against the law.

crimson ADJECTIVE
Something that is **crimson** is a dark red colour.

crinkle crinkles, crinkling, crinkled VERB
When something **crinkles**, it becomes slightly creased.

crisp crisper, crispest; crisps
ADJECTIVE **1** Things like fruit and biscuits that are **crisp** are fresh and firm.
NOUN **2** A **crisp** is a crunchy, thinly sliced piece of fried potato.
See Other foods on page 261

criticize criticizes, criticizing, criticized; also spelt **criticise** VERB
If you **criticize** someone, you say what you think is wrong with them.

crocodile crocodiles NOUN
A **crocodile** is a large reptile, about five metres long.
See Reptiles on page 264

crooked ADJECTIVE
Something that is **crooked** is bent or twisted.

crop crops NOUN
A **crop** is plants grown for food.

cross crosser, crossest; crosses, crossing, crossed
ADJECTIVE **1** Someone who is **cross** is angry about something.
NOUN **2** A **cross** is a mark like + or ×.
VERB **3** If you **cross** something like a road, you go from one side to the other.

crossing crossings NOUN
A **crossing** is a place where you can cross the road safely.

crouch crouches, crouching, crouched VERB
If you **crouch** down, you bend your legs under you so that you are close to the ground.

crow crows NOUN
A **crow** is a large black bird.

crowd crowds NOUN
A **crowd** is a large number of people together in one place.

crowded ADJECTIVE
A place that is **crowded** is full of people.

crown crowns NOUN
A **crown** is an ornament that kings and queens sometimes wear on their heads.

A B C D E F G H I J K L M N O P Q R S T U V W X Y Z

cruel **crueller, cruellest** ADJECTIVE
Someone who is **cruel** hurts people or animals without caring.

cruise **cruises** NOUN
A **cruise** is a holiday on a ship that travels to different places.

crumb **crumbs** NOUN
A **crumb** is a very small piece of dry food such as bread or biscuit.

crumble **crumbles, crumbling, crumbled** VERB
If you **crumble** something that is soft, it breaks into lots of little pieces.

crunch **crunches, crunching, crunched** VERB
If you **crunch** something, you crush it noisily, for example between your teeth or under your feet.

crush **crushes, crushing, crushed** VERB
To **crush** something is to destroy its shape by squeezing it.

crust **crusts** NOUN
The **crust** is a hard layer on the outside of something such as bread.

cry **cries, crying, cried**
VERB **1** When you **cry**, tears come from your eyes.
NOUN **2** A **cry** is a sudden sound that you make when you are surprised or hurt.

crystal **crystals** NOUN
A **crystal** is a mineral that has formed into a regular shape.

cub **cubs** NOUN
A **cub** is a young wild animal such as a lion, fox or bear.
See **Young animals** on page 265

cube **cubes** NOUN
A **cube** is a solid shape with six square faces all the same size.
See **Solid shapes** on page 266

cuckoo **cuckoos** NOUN
A **cuckoo** is a grey bird. Cuckoos lay their eggs in other birds' nests.

cucumber **cucumbers** NOUN
A **cucumber** is a long, thin, dark green vegetable, eaten raw.
See **Vegetables** on page 260

cuddle **cuddles, cuddling, cuddled** VERB
When you **cuddle** someone, you put your arms round them.

culprit **culprits** NOUN
A **culprit** is someone who has done something harmful or wrong.

cunning ADJECTIVE
Someone who is **cunning** plans to get what they want, often by tricking other people.

cup **cups**
NOUN **1** A **cup** is a small container with a handle, which you drink out of.
NOUN **2** A **cup** is also a prize for the winner of a game or competition.

cupboard **cupboards** NOUN
A **cupboard** is a piece of furniture with doors and shelves.

a b c d e f g h i j k l m n o p q r s t u v w x y z

51

A
B
C
D
E
F
G
H
I
J
K
L
M
N
O
P
Q
R
S
T
U
V
W
X
Y
Z

cure cures, curing, cured

NOUN **1** A **cure** is something that makes people better when they have been ill.

VERB **2** If someone or something **cures** a person, they make them well again.

curiosity NOUN

Curiosity is wanting to know about things.

curious

ADJECTIVE **1** Someone who is **curious** wants to know more about something.

ADJECTIVE **2** Something that is **curious** is unusual and hard to explain.

curl curls, curling, curled

VERB **1** If an animal **curls** up, it makes itself into a rounded shape.

NOUN **2 Curls** are pieces of hair shaped in curves and circles.

curly ADJECTIVE

currant currants NOUN

Currants are small dried grapes.

current currents

NOUN **1** A **current** is a steady movement of water or air.

NOUN **2** A **current** is also the movement of electricity through a wire.

curriculum curriculums or curricula

NOUN

A **curriculum** is the different courses taught at a school or college.

curry curries NOUN

Curry is an Indian dish made with spices.

cursor cursors NOUN

A **cursor** is a small sign on a computer screen that shows where the next letter or number will appear.

curtain curtains

NOUN

A **curtain** is a large piece of material that you pull across a window to cover it.

curve curves NOUN

A **curve** is a smooth, gradually bending line.

curved ADJECTIVE

cushion cushions NOUN

A **cushion** is a soft object put on a seat to make it more comfortable.

custom customs NOUN

A **custom** is something that people usually do. *It's his custom to take the dog for a walk after supper.*

customer customers NOUN

A **customer** is a person who buys something, especially from a shop.

cut cuts, cutting, cut

VERB **1** If you **cut** yourself, you hurt yourself by accident on something sharp.

VERB **2** If you **cut** something, you use a knife or scissors to remove parts of it.

cutlery NOUN

Cutlery is the knives, forks and spoons that you eat your food with.

cycle cycles, cycling, cycled

NOUN **1** A **cycle** is a bicycle.

VERB **2** If you **cycle**, you ride a bicycle.

cyclist NOUN

cylinder cylinders NOUN

A **cylinder** is a three-dimensional shape like a tube with flat circular ends.

cylindrical ADJECTIVE

See Solid shapes on page 266

Dd

dad **dads** NOUN
Your **dad** is your father.

daddy **daddies** NOUN
INFORMAL Your **daddy** is your father.

daffodil **daffodils** NOUN
A **daffodil** is a yellow trumpet-shaped flower that blooms in the spring.

dagger **daggers** NOUN
A **dagger** is a weapon like a knife.

daily ADJECTIVE
Something that is **daily** happens every day.

dairy **dairies** NOUN
A **dairy** is a shop or company that sells milk and food made from milk, such as butter and cheese.

daisy **daisies** NOUN
A **daisy** is a small wild flower with white petals and a yellow centre.

dam **dams** NOUN
A **dam** is a wall built across a river or stream to hold back water.

damage **damages, damaging, damaged**
VERB
To **damage** something means to harm or spoil it.

damp **damper, dampest** ADJECTIVE
Something that is **damp** is slightly wet.

dance **dances, dancing, danced** VERB
When you **dance**, you move your body in time to music.

dandelion **dandelions** NOUN
A **dandelion** is a wild plant with bright yellow flowers.

danger **dangers** NOUN
A **danger** is something that could harm you.

dangerous ADJECTIVE
If something is **dangerous**, it is likely to harm you.

dare **dares, daring, dared** VERB
If you **dare** to do something, you are brave enough to do it.

dark **darker, darkest** ADJECTIVE
When it is **dark**, there is not enough light to see properly. **darkness** NOUN

dart **darts, darting, darted**
VERB **1** If a person or animal **darts**, they move suddenly and quickly.
NOUN **2** A **dart** is a short arrow that you throw in the game of darts.

dash **dashes, dashing, dashed**
VERB **1** If you **dash** somewhere, you run or go there quickly.
NOUN **2** A **dash** is the punctuation mark (–) which shows a change of subject, or which may be used instead of brackets.
See Punctuation on page 270

data NOUN
Data is information, usually in the form of facts or figures.

database databases NOUN
A **database** is a collection of information, often stored in a computer.

date dates
NOUN **1** If someone asks you the **date**, you tell them the day and the month.

NOUN **2** A **date** is a small brown sticky fruit which grows on palm trees.

daughter
daughters
NOUN

A girl is the **daughter** of her parents.

dawn NOUN
Dawn is the time of day when it first begins to get light.

day days NOUN
A **day** is the 24 hours between one midnight and the next.

daylight NOUN
Daylight is the light that there is during the day before it gets dark.

dazzle dazzles, dazzling, dazzled VERB
If a light **dazzles** you, it is so bright that you cannot really see for a while.

dead ADJECTIVE
A person, animal or plant that is **dead** is no longer living.

deaf deafer, deafest ADJECTIVE
Someone who is **deaf** cannot hear very well, or cannot hear at all.

deal deals, dealing, dealt
VERB **1** When you **deal** in a card game, you give cards to the players.

VERB **2** If you **deal** with something, you do what needs to be done with it.

dear dearer, dearest
ADJECTIVE **1** You use **Dear** at the beginning of a letter or message before the name of the person you are writing to.

ADJECTIVE **2** If something is **dear**, it costs a lot of money.

death NOUN
Death is the end of life, when an animal or person dies.

decade decades NOUN
A **decade** is a period of ten years.

decay decays, decaying, decayed VERB
When something like a plant or piece of meat **decays**, it becomes rotten.

deceive deceives, deceiving, deceived
VERB
If someone **deceives** you, they make you believe something untrue.

December NOUN
December is the 12th month of the year. It has 31 days.

decide decides, deciding, decided VERB
If you **decide** to do something, you make up your mind to do it.

decimal decimals
ADJECTIVE **1** A **decimal** system involves counting in units of ten.

NOUN **2** A **decimal** or **decimal fraction** is written with a dot followed by numbers, such as 0·2, 8·35. The numbers after the dot represent tenths, hundredths and so on.

NOUN **3** A **decimal point** is the dot that comes between whole numbers and fractions.

NOUN **4** A **decimal place** is the position of a number after a decimal point.

decision decisions NOUN
A **decision** is a choice you make about what you think should be done.

deck **decks** NOUN
A **deck** is a floor on a ship or bus.

decorate
decorates,
decorating,
decorated

VERB **1** If you
decorate
something, you
add things to
make it more
attractive.
VERB **2** If someone **decorates** a room, they
paper it or paint it.
decorations PLURAL NOUN

decrease **decreases, decreasing,**
decreased VERB
If something **decreases**, or if you decrease it,
it becomes less.

deep **deeper, deepest** ADJECTIVE
If something is **deep**, it goes a long way
down. *The river is very **deep**.*

deer NOUN
A **deer** is a large hoofed
animal. Male deer have
horns called antlers.

defeat **defeats, defeating, defeated** VERB
If you **defeat** someone, you beat them in a
game or battle.

defend **defends, defending, defended**
VERB
If you **defend** someone or something, you do
something to protect them against danger.
defence NOUN

define **defines, defining, defined** VERB
If you **define** something, you say what it is or
what it means.

definite
ADJECTIVE **1** Something that is **definite** is
unlikely to be changed. *We have a **definite**
date for the outing.*

ADJECTIVE **2 Definite** can also mean certain or
true. *Lots of stories were going round, but they
heard nothing **definite**.*
definitely ADVERB

definition **definitions** NOUN
A **definition** explains the meaning of a word.

degree **degrees**
NOUN **1** A **degree** is a unit of measurement of
temperature, for example, 20°C.
NOUN **2** In maths, a **degree** is a unit of
measurement of angles. For example, a right
angle is 90°.

delay **delays, delaying, delayed** VERB
If something **delays** you, it causes you to slow
down or be late.

delete **deletes, deleting, deleted** VERB
If you **delete** some writing, you cross it out or
remove it.

deliberate ADJECTIVE
If you do something that is **deliberate**, you
do it on purpose.
deliberately ADVERB

delicate
ADJECTIVE **1** Something that is **delicate** is small
and graceful.
ADJECTIVE **2** Someone who is **delicate** becomes
ill easily.

delicious ADJECTIVE
Food that is **delicious** tastes or smells very
nice.

delight **delights, delighting, delighted**
VERB
If something **delights** you, it gives you a lot of
pleasure.
delighted ADJECTIVE

deliver **delivers, delivering, delivered**
VERB
If you **deliver** something, you take it to
someone and hand it to them.

demand **demands, demanding,**
demanded VERB
If you **demand** something, you say strongly
that is what you want.

a
b
c
d
e
f
g
h
i
j
k
l
m
n
o
p
q
r
s
t
u
v
w
x
y
z

demonstrate demonstrates, demonstrating, demonstrated
VERB **1** If someone **demonstrates** something, they show you how to do it.
VERB **2** If people **demonstrate**, they hold a public meeting or march to show they are strongly for or against something.
demonstration NOUN

den dens NOUN
A **den** is the home of some wild animals such as lions or foxes.

dense denser, densest ADJECTIVE
Something **dense** is hard to see through. *They were in a **dense** forest.*

dent dents, denting, dented VERB
If somebody **dents** something, they make a dip in it by hitting it.

dentist dentists NOUN
A **dentist** is someone who looks after people's teeth.

deny denies, denying, denied VERB
If you **deny** something, you say that it is untrue.

depart departs, departing, departed VERB
When someone or something **departs** from a place, they leave it.
departure NOUN

depend depends, depending, depended VERB
1 If you **depend** on someone, you need them.
VERB **2** If you can **depend** on someone, you know you can trust them.

depth NOUN
The **depth** of something is how deep it is.

descend descends, descending, descended VERB
To **descend** means to go down.

descending ADJECTIVE
When things are in **descending** order, each thing is lower than the one before it. *The numbers 10, 9, 8 and 7 are in **descending** order.*

describe describes, describing, described VERB
If you **describe** a person or thing, you say what they are like.
description NOUN

desert deserts NOUN
A **desert** is very dry land with very little plant life.

deserted ADJECTIVE
If a place is **deserted**, there are no people there.

deserve deserves, deserving, deserved VERB
If you **deserve** something, you have earned it by what you have done.

design designs, designing, designed
NOUN **1** A **design** is a pattern that is used to decorate something.
VERB **2** If you **design** something, you plan it and make a drawing of it.

desk desks NOUN
A **desk** is a special table that you use for writing or reading.

desktop ADJECTIVE
A **desktop** computer is small enough to be used at a desk.

dessert desserts NOUN
A **dessert** is a sweet food served after the main course of a meal.

destroy destroys, destroying, destroyed VERB
To **destroy** something means to damage it so much it cannot be mended.

detail details NOUN
A **detail** is a small part or thing that you notice when you look at something carefully.

detective detectives NOUN
A **detective** is a person whose job is to find out who did a crime.

determined ADJECTIVE
If you are **determined** to do something, nothing will stop you.

develop develops, developing, developed VERB
When something **develops**, it grows or becomes more advanced.

dew NOUN
Dew is the small drops of water that form on surfaces outdoors at night.

diagonal ADJECTIVE
A **diagonal** line slants from one corner of something to the opposite corner.

diagram diagrams NOUN
A **diagram** is a drawing that explains something.

dial dials NOUN
A **dial** is a numbered disc on an instrument like a clock.

dialogue dialogues NOUN
In a story, play or film, **dialogue** is conversation.

diameter diameters NOUN
A **diameter** is a straight line drawn right through the centre of a circle.

diamond diamonds
NOUN **1** A **diamond** is a very hard, clear jewel which sparkles.
NOUN **2** A **diamond** is also a shape with four straight sides, like a square but slightly flattened.
See *Colours and shapes* on page 266

diary diaries NOUN
A **diary** is a book in which to write about what you have done.

dice NOUN
Dice are small cubes with spots on each of their six sides.

dictionary
dictionaries NOUN
A **dictionary** is a book in which words are listed alphabetically and explained.

did VERB
Did is the past tense of **do**.

didn't VERB
Didn't is a contraction of **did not**.

die dies, dying, died VERB
When a person, animal or plant **dies**, they stop living.

diesel diesels NOUN
A **diesel** is a kind of engine that burns a special oil instead of petrol.

diet diets
NOUN **1** A **diet** is the food that a person or animal normally eats.
NOUN **2** A **diet** is also a special range of foods that a doctor tells someone to eat if they have a health or weight problem.

difference differences
NOUN **1** The **difference** between two things is the way in which they are unlike each other.
NOUN **2** In maths, you can work out the **difference** between two numbers by taking the smaller number away from the larger number.

different ADJECTIVE
Something that is **different** from something else is not like it in one or more ways.

difficult ADJECTIVE
Something that is **difficult** is not easy to do or understand.
difficulty NOUN

dig digs, digging, dug VERB
When people **dig**, they break up soil or sand with a spade or garden fork.

a
b
c
d
e
f
g
h
i
j
k
l
m
n
o
p
q
r
s
t
u
v
w
x
y
z

A
B
C
D
E
F
G
H
I
J
K
L
M
N
O
P
Q
R
S
T
U
V
W
X
Y
Z

digest **digests, digesting, digested** VERB
When you **digest** food, your body breaks it down so that it can be used.
digestion NOUN

digit **digits** NOUN
A **digit** is a written symbol for any of the numbers from o to 9. For example, 384 is a three-digit number.

digital
ADJECTIVE **1 Digital** instruments such as watches have changing numbers instead of a dial with hands.
See **analogue**
NOUN **2 Digital television** is television in which the picture is sent in digital form.

dim **dimmer, dimmest** ADJECTIVE
If the light is **dim**, it is rather dark and it is hard to see things.

din NOUN
A **din** is a loud, annoying noise.

dining room **dining rooms** NOUN
A **dining room** is the room where people have their meals.

dinner **dinners** NOUN
Dinner is the main meal of the day.

dinosaur **dinosaurs** NOUN
A **dinosaur** was a large reptile which lived and became extinct in prehistoric times.

dip **dips, dipping, dipped** VERB
If you **dip** something into a liquid, you put it in quickly.

direct **directs, directing, directed**
VERB **1** If you **direct** someone, you show them the way to go.
VERB **2** A person who **directs** something, like a film, is in charge of it.

ADJECTIVE **3 Direct** means in a straight line without stopping, for example on a journey.
*Is there a **direct** flight to Paris?*

direction **directions**
NOUN **1** A **direction** is the way in which someone or something is moving or pointing.
NOUN **2 Directions** are instructions that tell you what to do or which way to go.

dirt NOUN
Dirt is dust, mud or stains on a surface or fabric.

dirty **dirtier, dirtiest** ADJECTIVE
Something that is **dirty** is marked or covered with mud or stains.

disabled ADJECTIVE
A **disabled** person has a condition or injury that makes it hard or impossible to do some things.
disability NOUN

disagree **disagrees, disagreeing, disagreed** VERB
If you **disagree** with someone, you think what they are saying is wrong.

disappear **disappears, disappearing, disappeared** VERB
If someone **disappears**, they go out of sight.

disappoint **disappoints, disappointing, disappointed** VERB
If something **disappoints** you, it is not as good as you thought it would be.
disappointment NOUN

disapprove VERB
If you **disapprove** of something, you think it is wrong or bad.

disaster **disasters** NOUN
A **disaster** is something very bad that happens, such as an air crash.
disastrous ADJECTIVE

disc **discs** NOUN
A **disc** is a flat round object.

discover **discovers, discovering, discovered** VERB
When you **discover** something, you find it or find out about it.
discovery NOUN

discuss **discusses, discussing, discussed** VERB
When you **discuss** something, you talk about it with someone else.
discussion NOUN

disease **diseases** NOUN
A **disease** is an illness in people, animals or plants.

disguise **disguises** NOUN
A **disguise** is something that changes the way you look, so that people do not recognize you.

disgust NOUN
Disgust is a feeling of strong dislike for someone or something.

dish **dishes** NOUN
A **dish** is a shallow container for cooking or serving meals in.

dishonest ADJECTIVE
If someone is **dishonest**, they are not to be trusted.

dishwasher **dishwashers** NOUN
A **dishwasher** is a machine that washes things like plates.

disk **disks** NOUN
A **disk** is used for storing information in a computer.

dislike **dislikes, disliking, disliked** VERB
If you **dislike** someone or something, you do not like them.

dismiss **dismisses, dismissing, dismissed** VERB
When someone in authority **dismisses** you, they tell you to leave.

display **displays** NOUN
A **display** is an arrangement of things which is done to show to people.

dissolve **dissolves, dissolving, dissolved** VERB
If something **dissolves** in a liquid, it becomes mixed in with it.
See **solution**

distance **distances** NOUN
The **distance** between two things is the amount of space between them.

distant ADJECTIVE
Distant means far away.

distinct ADJECTIVE
If something is **distinct**, you can hear or see it clearly.

distribute **distributes, distributing, distributed** VERB
If you **distribute** things like leaflets, you hand them out to several people.

district **districts** NOUN
A **district** is the area around a place. *He's the only doctor in this **district**.*

disturb **disturbs, disturbing, disturbed** VERB
If you **disturb** someone, you interrupt them or spoil their peace and quiet.

disturbance **disturbances** NOUN
A **disturbance** is something that spoils people's peace and quiet.

a
b
c
d
e
f
g
h
i
j
k
l
m
n
o
p
q
r
s
t
u
v
w
x
y
z

59

ditch ditches NOUN

A **ditch** is a channel dug at the side of a road or field, to drain water.

dive dives, diving, dived VERB

To **dive** is to jump head first into water with your arms above your head.
diver NOUN

divide divides, dividing, divided

VERB **1** When something is **divided**, it is separated into smaller parts.

VERB **2** When you **divide** numbers, you share them into equal groups. For example, 15 can be divided into 3 groups of 5, or 5 groups of 3.
$15 \div 3 = 5$ or $15 \div 5 = 3$

division divisions

NOUN **1 Division** is separating something into two or more parts.

NOUN **2** In maths, **division** is the process of dividing one number by another. The sign $\div$ is used for division.

divorce divorces NOUN

A **divorce** is the legal ending of a marriage.

Diwali NOUN

Diwali is a Hindu festival of light that is celebrated in the autumn.

dizzy dizzier, dizziest ADJECTIVE

If you feel **dizzy**, your head feels funny, as if you are going to fall over.

do does, doing, did, done

VERB **1** If you **do** something, you get on and finish it. *Have you **done** your work?*

VERB **2 Do** can be used with other verbs. *Do you want some more?*

doctor doctors NOUN

A **doctor** is a person who treats people when they are ill.

document documents

NOUN **1** A **document** is a piece of paper which is an official record of something.

NOUN **2** A **document** is also a piece of text stored as a file in a computer.

dodge dodges, dodging, dodged VERB

If you **dodge**, you move suddenly out of the way.

does VERB

Does is a present tense form of **do**.

doesn't VERB

Doesn't is a contraction of **does not**.

dog dogs NOUN

A **dog** is an animal. Dogs bark and are often kept as pets, or used to guard things.

doll dolls NOUN

A **doll** is a child's toy that looks like a baby or a small person.

dollar dollars NOUN

A **dollar** is a unit of money in countries such as the USA and Australia.

dolphin dolphins NOUN

A **dolphin** is a mammal which lives in the sea.

dome domes NOUN

A **dome** is a round roof.

done VERB

Done is the past participle of **do**.

donkey donkeys NOUN

A **donkey** is an animal like a small horse, with longer ears.

don't VERB

Don't is a contraction of **do not**.

door doors NOUN
A **door** swings or slides to open and close the entrance to something.

dose doses NOUN
A **dose** is the amount of a medicine that you have to take.

dot dots NOUN
A **dot** is a small round mark.

double ADJECTIVE
If something is **double** the size or amount of something else, it is twice as big.

doubt doubts NOUN
If you have a **doubt** about something, you are not sure about it.

doubtful
ADJECTIVE **1** If you are **doubtful** about something, you are not sure about it.
ADJECTIVE **2** Something that is **doubtful** seems unlikely or uncertain.

dough NOUN
Dough is the floury mixture used to make things like pastry or bread.

doughnut doughnuts NOUN
A **doughnut** is a ring of sweet dough cooked in hot fat.

dove doves NOUN
A **dove** is a bird like a small pigeon.

down
PREPOSITION **1** If you go **down** a hill, you go to a lower level.
ADVERB **2** If you put something **down**, you put it on a surface.
ADVERB **3** If an amount of something goes **down**, it gets less. *My pocket money's gone down.*
NOUN **4 Down** is soft feathers.

download downloads, downloading, downloaded VERB
When you **download** a program from a disk or from the Internet, you move it into a file on your own computer.

downstairs ADVERB
If you go **downstairs**, you go towards the ground floor.

doze dozes, dozing, dozed VERB
When you **doze**, you sleep lightly.

dozen dozens NOUN
If you have a **dozen** things, you have 12 of them.

draft drafts NOUN
A **draft** is an early rough version of something you are writing.

drag drags, dragging, dragged VERB
If you **drag** a heavy object, you pull it along the ground.

dragon dragons NOUN
In stories, a **dragon** is a fierce animal like a big lizard. It has wings and claws and breathes fire.

dragonfly dragonflies NOUN
A **dragonfly** is a brightly-coloured insect, usually found near water.
See Insects on page 264

drain drains, draining, drained
NOUN **1** A **drain** is a pipe that carries water away.
VERB **2** If a liquid **drains** away, it flows slowly to somewhere else.

drake drakes NOUN
A **drake** is a male duck.

drama dramas
NOUN **1** A **drama** is a serious play for the theatre, television or radio.
NOUN **2 Drama** is exciting and interesting things that happen.

dramatic ADJECTIVE
Something **dramatic** is very exciting and interesting.
dramatically ADVERB

A
B
C
D
E
F
G
H
I
J
K
L
M
N
O
P
Q
R
S
T
U
V
W
X
Y
Z

drank VERB
Drank is the past tense of **drink**.

draught draughts
NOUN **1** A **draught** is a current of cold air coming into a room or vehicle.
PLURAL NOUN **2 Draughts** is a game played with round pieces on a board.

draw draws, drawing, drew, drawn
VERB **1** When you **draw**, you use something like a pencil or crayon to make a picture or a pattern.
VERB **2** When you **draw** the curtains, you pull them across a window.
NOUN **3** A **draw** is the result in a game or competition in which nobody wins.

drawer drawers NOUN
A **drawer** is a box that slides in and out of a piece of furniture.

drawing drawings NOUN
A **drawing** is a picture made with a pencil, pen or crayon.

dread dreads, dreading, dreaded VERB
If you **dread** something, you feel worried and frightened about it.

dreadful ADJECTIVE
Something that is **dreadful** is very bad or unpleasant.

dream dreams, dreaming, dreamed or dreamt
VERB **1** When you **dream**, you see events in your mind while you are asleep.
VERB **2** If you **dream** while you are awake, you think about things you would like to happen.
dream NOUN

dress dresses, dressing, dressed
VERB **1** When you **dress**, you put on your clothes.
NOUN **2** A **dress** is a piece of clothing for women or girls made up of a skirt and top joined together.

drew VERB
Drew is the past tense of **draw**.

dribble dribbles, dribbling, dribbled
VERB **1** When babies **dribble**, water trickles from their mouth.
VERB **2** When players **dribble** the ball in a game like football, they kick it several times quickly to keep it moving.

drift drifts, drifting, drifted
VERB **1** When something **drifts**, it is carried along slowly by wind or water.
NOUN **2** A **drift** is a pile of snow heaped up by the wind.

drill drills NOUN
A **drill** is a tool for making holes.

drink drinks, drinking, drank, drunk
VERB **1** When you **drink**, you take liquid into your mouth and swallow it.
NOUN **2** A **drink** is a liquid which you swallow to stop you being thirsty.

drip drips, dripping, dripped VERB
When something **drips**, drops of liquid fall from it one after the other.

drive drives, driving, drove, driven VERB
If someone **drives** a vehicle, they make it move and control it.

driver drivers NOUN
The **driver** of a vehicle is the person who is driving it.

drop drops, dropping, dropped
VERB **1** If you **drop** something, you let it fall.
NOUN **2** A **drop** is a tiny amount of liquid.

drought **droughts** NOUN
A **drought** is a long period of time when no rain falls.

drove VERB
Drove is the past tense of **drive**.

drown **drowns, drowning, drowned** VERB
If someone **drowns**, they die because they have gone under water and cannot breathe.

drug **drugs** NOUN
A **drug** is a substance that is used to treat or prevent disease, or stop pain. Some drugs can be dangerous.

drum **drums** NOUN
A **drum** is a musical instrument which you hit to make a noise. It has skin stretched tightly over the end.

drunk VERB
Drunk is the past participle of **drink**.

dry **drier** or **dryer, driest** ADJECTIVE
Something that is **dry** has no water in it at all.
dry VERB

duck **ducks** NOUN
A **duck** is a common water bird with short legs and webbed feet.

due ADJECTIVE
If something is **due** at a particular time, it should happen then.

dug VERB
Dug is the past tense of **dig**.

dull **duller, dullest**
ADJECTIVE **1** Something that is **dull** is not interesting.
ADJECTIVE **2** **Dull** means not bright.
ADJECTIVE **3** A **dull** pain is not sharp.

dumb ADJECTIVE
Someone who is **dumb** is unable to speak.

during PREPOSITION
Something that happens **during** a period of time happens in that period. *I worked **during** the holidays.*

dusk NOUN
Dusk is the part of the day when it is beginning to get dark.

dust NOUN
Dust is dry fine powdery material such as particles of earth, dirt or pollen.
dusty ADJECTIVE

dustbin **dustbins** NOUN
A **dustbin** is a large container with a lid, for rubbish.

duty **duties** NOUN
A **duty** is something you feel you should do. *He only went to see his aunt because he felt it was his **duty**.*

duvet **duvets** NOUN
A **duvet** is a bed cover filled with feathers or other light material.

DVD **DVDs** NOUN
DVD is an abbreviation for **digital video disc**. It is a disc on which a film or music is recorded.

dye **dyes, dyeing, dyed** VERB
If you **dye** something such as hair or cloth, you change its colour by soaking it in a special liquid.

dying VERB
Dying is the present participle of **die**.

Ee

each ADJECTIVE
Each means every one taken separately. *She gave **each** child a pencil.*

eager ADJECTIVE
If you are **eager**, you very much want to do or have something.

eagle eagles
NOUN
An **eagle** is a large strong bird with a sharp curved beak and claws.

ear ears NOUN
Your **ears** are the parts of your body that you use for hearing.

early earlier, earliest
ADJECTIVE OR ADVERB **1 Early** means near the beginning of a period of time. *We took the **early** train to school.*
ADJECTIVE OR ADVERB **2** You also use **early** to mean sooner than expected. *I arrived at the party **early**.*

earn earns, earning, earned VERB
If you **earn** something, such as money, you get it by working for it.

earphones PLURAL NOUN
Earphones are a small piece of equipment which you wear over or inside your ears so that you can listen to music or talking without anyone else hearing.

earring earrings NOUN
An **earring** is a piece of jewellery that is fixed to the ear for decoration.

earth
NOUN **1** The **Earth** is the planet we live on.
NOUN **2** The soil that plants grow in is also called **earth**.

earthquake earthquakes NOUN
An **earthquake** is when the ground shakes because of movement beneath the surface.

east NOUN
East is one of the four main points of the compass. It is the direction in which the sun rises.
See **compass point**
eastern ADJECTIVE

Easter NOUN
Easter is a Christian festival that celebrates Christ's return to life.

easy easier, easiest ADJECTIVE
Something that is **easy** can be done without difficulty.
easily ADVERB

eat eats, eating, ate, eaten VERB
When you **eat**, you chew and swallow food.

e-book e-books NOUN
An **e-book** is a book which is produced for reading on a computer screen. E-book is an abbreviation of **electronic book**.

echo echoes NOUN
An **echo** is a sound that bounces back from something like the walls of a cave or building.

eclipse
eclipses NOUN
An **eclipse** of the sun is when the moon comes in front of the sun and hides it for a short time.

edge edges
NOUN **1** An **edge** is the end or side of something.
NOUN **2** An **edge** is where two faces of a three-dimensional shape meet. For example, a cuboid has 12 edges.

edible ADJECTIVE
Something that is **edible** is safe to eat.

edit edits, editing, edited
VERB **1** If you **edit** a piece of writing, you correct it so that it is ready for printing.

VERB **2** When someone **edits** a film or television programme, they select different parts and arrange them in a particular order.

educate **educates, educating, educated**
VERB
To **educate** someone means to teach them over a long period, so that they learn about many different things.

education NOUN
Education is the teaching you receive at school, college or university.

eel **eels** NOUN
An **eel** is a long thin fish that looks like a snake.

effect **effects** NOUN
An **effect** is a change made by something. *I'm still suffering from the **effects** of my cold.*

effort **efforts** NOUN
Effort is the physical or mental energy needed to do something.

egg **eggs**
NOUN **1** An **egg** is an oval object laid by female birds. Reptiles, fish and insects also lay eggs. A baby animal develops inside the egg until it is ready to be born.
NOUN **2** In a female mammal, an **egg** is a cell produced in its body which can develop into a baby.

Eid NOUN
Eid is a Muslim festival where people exchange gifts and eat a meal together.

eight NOUN
Eight is the number 8.

eighteen NOUN
Eighteen is the number 18.

either
ADJECTIVE, PRONOUN OR CONJUNCTION **1** You use **either** to refer to each of two possible things. *You can **either** come with me or stay here.*
ADJECTIVE **2** You use **either** to refer to both of two things. *There were fields on **either** side of the road.*

elastic
ADJECTIVE **1** Something **elastic** is able to stretch easily.
NOUN **2** **Elastic** is a material, like rubber, which stretches and can then return to its original size.

elbow **elbows** NOUN
Your **elbow** is the joint in the middle of your arm where it bends.

elbow

electric ADJECTIVE
A machine or other object that is **electric** works by using electricity.
electrical ADJECTIVE

electricity NOUN
Electricity is a form of energy that is used for heating and lighting, and to work machines. It comes along wires.

electronic ADJECTIVE
Something **electronic** has transistors or silicon chips which control an electric current.
electronically ADVERB

elephant **elephants** NOUN
An **elephant** is a large four-legged mammal with a long trunk, large ears, and ivory tusks.

eleven NOUN
Eleven is the number 11.

else ADVERB
You can use **else** to mean other than this or more than this. *Can you think of anything **else**?*

e-mail or **email** NOUN
E-mail is the sending of messages from one computer to another.

embarrass **embarrasses, embarrassing, embarrassed** VERB
To **embarrass** someone means to make them feel shy, ashamed or guilty about something.

a
b
c
d
e
f
g
h
i
j
k
l
m
n
o
p
q
r
s
t
u
v
w
x
y
z

65

emerald **emeralds** NOUN
An **emerald** is a bright green precious stone.

emerge **emerges, emerging, emerged**
VERB
If someone **emerges** from a place, they come out so that they can be seen.

emergency **emergencies** NOUN
An **emergency** is an unexpected and serious event which needs immediate action to deal with it.

emotion **emotions** NOUN
Emotion is a strong feeling, such a love or fear.

employ **employs, employing, employed**
VERB
If someone **employs** you, they pay you to work for them.

employer **employers** NOUN
Employers are people who pay other people to work for them.

empty **emptier, emptiest; empties, emptying, emptied**
ADJECTIVE **1** Something that is **empty** has no people or things in it.
VERB **2** If you **empty** a container, you pour or take everything out of it.

enchanted ADJECTIVE
In stories, something that is **enchanted** is under a magic spell.

encourage **encourages, encouraging, encouraged** VERB
If you **encourage** someone, you tell them that what they are doing is good and they should go on doing it.

encyclopedia **encyclopedias** NOUN
An **encyclopedia** is a book or set of books giving information about many different subjects.

end **ends, ending, ended**
NOUN **1** The **end** of a period of time or an event is the last part.
NOUN **2** The **end** of something is the farthest point of it. *The bathroom is at the **end** of the passage.*

VERB **3** If something **ends**, it finishes.

ending **endings** NOUN
An **ending** is the last part of a word, story, play or film.

enemy **enemies** NOUN
Your **enemy** is someone who fights or works against you.

energetic ADJECTIVE
Someone who is **energetic** is active and lively.
energetically ADVERB

energy
NOUN **1** **Energy** is the strength you need to do things. You get energy from food.
NOUN **2** **Energy** is also the power that makes things heat up, make a sound, give light or move. Electricity is one kind of energy.

engine **engines**
NOUN **1** An **engine** is a machine that makes things move.
NOUN **2** An **engine** is also a large vehicle that pulls a railway train.

engineer **engineers** NOUN
An **engineer** is a person who designs or builds things such as machinery, instruments or bridges.

enjoy **enjoys, enjoying, enjoyed** VERB
If you **enjoy** doing something, you like doing it very much.
enjoyable ADJECTIVE **enjoyment** NOUN

enormous ADJECTIVE
Something that is **enormous** is extremely large.

enough ADJECTIVE
Enough means as much as you need. *Have you had **enough** to eat?*

enter enters, entering, entered
VERB **1** If you **enter** a place, you go into it.
VERB **2** If you **enter** a competition or examination, you take part in it.

entertain entertains, entertaining, entertained VERB
If you **entertain** somebody, you do something that they enjoy and find amusing.

entertainment NOUN
Entertainment is things that people watch for pleasure, such as shows and films.

enthusiastic ADJECTIVE
If you are **enthusiastic** about something, you are very interested in it, or excited about it.

entire ADJECTIVE
Entire means the whole of something. *The **entire** class came to my party.*

entrance entrances NOUN
An **entrance** is the way into a place.

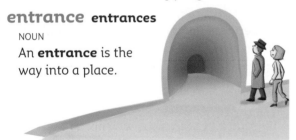

entry entries NOUN
Entry is the act of entering a place. *No **entry** after 11 p.m.*

envelope envelopes NOUN
An **envelope** is a folded paper cover for a letter or card.

envious ADJECTIVE
If you are **envious** of somebody, you wish you could have the same things that they have.

environment environments NOUN
The **environment** is the natural world around us.

envy envies, envying, envied VERB
If you **envy** somebody, you wish you could have the same things that they have.

episode episodes NOUN
An **episode** is one of several parts of a story or drama.

equal ADJECTIVE
If two things are **equal**, they are the same as each other in size, number or amount.

equals VERB
In maths, the symbol = stands for **equals**. The numbers on each side of it have the same value: $2 + 2 = 4$

equation equations NOUN
Equations are sometimes called number sentences. The numbers on the left equal the numbers on the right. For example, $3 + 3 = 2 \times 3$ is an equation.

equator NOUN
The **equator** is an imaginary line drawn round the centre of the earth, lying halfway between the North and South Poles.

equipment NOUN
Equipment is the things that you need to do something. *We need some new kitchen **equipment** – especially a fridge.*

error errors NOUN
An **error** is a mistake, or something that is wrong.

erupt erupts, erupting, erupted VERB
When a volcano **erupts**, it throws out hot molten lava, ash and steam.

escape escapes, escaping, escaped VERB
If a person or animal **escapes**, they get away from somebody or something.

especially ADVERB
You say **especially** to mean most of all. *I like cats, **especially** black ones.*

essay essays NOUN
An **essay** is a short piece of writing on a particular subject.

essential ADJECTIVE
Something that is **essential** is absolutely necessary.

a
b
c
d
e
f
g
h
i
j
k
l
m
n
o
p
q
r
s
t
u
v
w
x
y
z

A B C D E F G H I J K L M N O P Q R S T U V W X Y Z

estate estates
NOUN **1** An **estate** is a large area of land in the country, belonging to one person or group.
NOUN **2** An **estate** is also an area of land with lots of houses on it.

estimate estimates, estimating, estimated VERB
If you **estimate** something, you guess the size or amount of it.

euro euros NOUN
A **euro** is a unit of money used in most countries of the European Union.

European Union NOUN
The **European Union** is an organization of countries in Europe that work together on matters such as trade and agriculture.

even
ADVERB **1** You say **even** when something is rather surprising. *I like to play outside **even** when it is raining.*
ADJECTIVE **2** If something like a path is **even**, it is smooth and flat.
ADJECTIVE **3** An **even** number can be divided by two, with no remainder. *2, 18 and 36 are all **even** numbers.*

evening evenings NOUN
The **evening** is the part of the day between late afternoon and the time you usually go to bed.

event events NOUN
An **event** is something important that happens.

eventually ADVERB
Eventually means in the end, after a lot of delays or problems.

ever ADVERB
Ever means at any time in the past or future. *Have you **ever** seen such a big dog?*

every ADJECTIVE
Every means each one. *I spoke to **every** child in that class.*

every other PHRASE
Every other means one in every two. *I see my friend **every other** week.*

everybody PRONOUN
Everybody means every person. ***Everybody** has to eat.*

everyone PRONOUN
You can use **everyone** instead of **everybody**. ***Everyone** knew who she was.*

everything PRONOUN
Everything means all of something.

everywhere ADVERB
Everywhere means in all places. *Children **everywhere** love stories.*

evidence NOUN
Evidence is anything you see, read or are told which gives you reason to believe something.

evil ADJECTIVE
An **evil** person is extremely wicked.

ewe ewes NOUN
A **ewe** is a female sheep.

exact ADJECTIVE
Something that is **exact** is accurate in every detail.

exactly ADVERB
You say **exactly** when you mean no more and no less. *My father is **exactly** two metres tall.*

exaggerate exaggerates, exaggerating, exaggerated VERB
If you **exaggerate**, you say something is better or worse than it really is.

exam exams NOUN
Exam is an abbreviation of **examination**.

examination examinations
NOUN **1** An **examination** is a test people take to find out how much they have learned.
NOUN **2** A doctor makes a medical **examination** to find out how healthy you are.

examine examines, examining, examined VERB
If you **examine** something, you look at it carefully or closely.

example examples NOUN
An **example** is one thing which shows what the rest of a set is like. *This is an **example** of my work.*

excellent ADJECTIVE
Something that is **excellent** is extremely good.

except PREPOSITION
Except means apart from. *Everyone went outside **except** David.*

exception exceptions NOUN
An **exception** is something that does not fit in with a general rule. *With the **exception** of bats, mammals cannot fly.*

exchange exchanges, exchanging, exchanged VERB
If you **exchange** something, you change it for something else.

excite excites, exciting, excited VERB
If something **excites** you, it makes you feel happy and interested.
exciting ADJECTIVE **excitement** NOUN

excited ADJECTIVE
If you feel **excited**, you feel happy and unable to rest. *Sam was **excited** about going on holiday.*

exclaim exclaims, exclaiming, exclaimed VERB
When you **exclaim**, you speak suddenly or loudly, because you are excited or angry.
exclamation NOUN

exclamation mark exclamation marks NOUN
An **exclamation mark** is a punctuation mark (!) used in writing to express a strong feeling.
*See **Punctuation** on page 270*

excuse excuses NOUN
An **excuse** is a reason you give for doing something, or not doing it.

exercise exercises
NOUN **1 Exercise** is regular movements you make to keep fit.
NOUN **2** An **exercise** is a piece of work that you do to help you learn something.

exhausted ADJECTIVE
When you are **exhausted**, you are so tired you have no energy left.

exhibition exhibitions NOUN
An **exhibition** is a collection of pictures or other things in a public place where people can come to see them.

exist exists, existing, existed VERB
Things that **exist** are present in the world or universe now.
existence NOUN

exit exits NOUN
An **exit** is the way out of a place.

expand expands, expanding, expanded VERB
When something **expands**, it gets bigger.

expect expects, expecting, expected VERB
If you **expect** something, you think it will happen.

expedition expeditions NOUN
An **expedition** is a journey made for a special reason.

expel expels, expelling, expelled VERB
If someone is **expelled** from school, they are told not to come back because their behaviour has been so bad.

A
B
C
D
E
F
G
H
I
J
K
L
M
N
O
P
Q
R
S
T
U
V
W
X
Y
Z

expensive ADJECTIVE
Something that is **expensive** costs a lot of money.

experience experiences
NOUN **1** An **experience** is something that happens to you.
NOUN **2 Experience** is knowing about something because you have been doing it for a long time.

experiment experiments NOUN
An **experiment** is the testing of something, either to find out its effect or to prove something.

expert experts NOUN
An **expert** is someone who is very skilled at doing something or who knows a lot about something.

explain explains, explaining, explained
VERB **1** To **explain** means to say things to help people understand.
VERB **2** When you **explain**, you give reasons for something that happened.

explanation explanations
NOUN **1** An **explanation** is something that helps people understand something. *She gave us a clear **explanation** of the way the machine works.*
NOUN **2** An **explanation** is something that tells you why something happened.

explode
explodes, exploding, exploded VERB
If something such as a firework **explodes**, it bursts with a loud bang.
explosion NOUN

explore explores, exploring, explored
VERB
If you **explore** a place, you travel in it to find out what it is like.
exploration NOUN **explorer** NOUN

explosive explosives NOUN
An **explosive** is a substance that can explode.

express expresses, expressing, expressed VERB
If you **express** an idea or feeling, you put it into words or show it by the way you act. *He could only **express** the way he felt by bursting into tears.*

expression expressions NOUN
Your **expression** is the look on your face that lets people know what you are thinking or feeling.

extinct ADJECTIVE
If an animal or plant family is **extinct**, it no longer has any living members. *The dodo has been **extinct** for more than 300 years.*

extra ADJECTIVE
You use **extra** to mean more than usual. *You'd better take an **extra** jumper – it's going to be cold.*

extraordinary ADJECTIVE
Someone or something that is **extraordinary** is very special or unusual.

extreme ADJECTIVE
Extreme means very great. ***Extreme** cold can cause many problems.*
extremely ADVERB

eye eyes

NOUN **1** Your **eyes** are the part of your body that you use for seeing.
NOUN **2** The **eye** of a needle is the small hole at one end.

eyesight NOUN
Eyesight is the ability to see.

Ff

fabric fabrics NOUN
Fabric is material made in some way such as by weaving or knitting.

face faces, facing, faced
NOUN **1** Your **face** is the front part of your head from your chin to your forehead.
See The body on page 256
VERB **2** If you **face** something, you have your face towards it.
NOUN **3** The **face** of a clock or watch is the part with the numbers on it that show the time.
NOUN **4** A **face** is a surface of a three-dimensional shape.

fact facts NOUN
A **fact** is something that is true.
factual ADJECTIVE

factor factors NOUN
A **factor** is a whole number which will divide exactly into another whole number. For example, 3 is a factor of 12.

factory factories NOUN
A **factory** is a large building where a lot of things are made.

fade fades, fading, faded
VERB **1** If a colour **fades**, it gets paler.
VERB **2** If the light **fades**, it gets darker.

fail fails, failing, failed
VERB **1** If someone **fails** when they try to do something, they cannot do it.
VERB **2** If something **fails**, it stops working. *The brakes **failed**, and the car hit a wall.*

failure failures NOUN
If something is a **failure**, it does not work as planned. *The picnic was a **failure** because it rained all day.*

faint faints, fainting, fainted; fainter, faintest
VERB **1** If someone **faints**, they become unconscious for a short time.
ADJECTIVE **2** Something like a sound or mark that is **faint** is not easy to hear or see.

fair fairer, fairest; fairs
ADJECTIVE **1** Something that is **fair** seems reasonable to most people.
ADJECTIVE **2** People who are **fair** have light-coloured hair.
NOUN **3** A **fair** is a form of entertainment that takes place outside with stalls, sideshows, and machines to ride on.

fairly ADVERB
Fairly means quite or rather.

fairy fairies NOUN
In stories, **fairies** are tiny people with wings, who have magical powers.

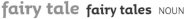

fairy tale fairy tales NOUN
A **fairy tale** is a story in which magical things happen.

faithful ADJECTIVE
If you are **faithful** to someone, you can be trusted and relied on.

fake fakes NOUN
A **fake** is a copy of something made to trick people into thinking that it is genuine.

fall falls, falling, fell, fallen
VERB **1** When someone or something **falls**, they drop towards the ground.
VERB **2** If someone's face **falls**, they suddenly look upset or disappointed.

false
ADJECTIVE **1** If something is **false**, it is not the real thing. *My uncle has a **false** tooth.*
ADJECTIVE **2** If something you say is **false**, it is not true.

familiar ADJECTIVE
Something **familiar** is well-known or easy to recognize. *It was good to see a **familiar** face.*

family **families**

NOUN **1** A **family** is a group of people made up of parents and their children.

See Family on page 258

NOUN **2** A **family** is also a group of animals or plants of the same kind. *Lions and tigers belong to the cat **family**.*

famine **famines** NOUN

A **famine** is a shortage of food which may cause many people to die.

famous ADJECTIVE

Someone or something **famous** is very well known.

fan **fans**

NOUN **1** A **fan** is an object which creates a draught of cool air when it moves.

NOUN **2** If you are a **fan** of something or of someone famous, you are very interested in them.

fantastic ADJECTIVE

Something **fantastic** is wonderful and very pleasing.

fantasy **fantasies**

NOUN **1** A **fantasy** is a story about things that do not exist in the real world.

NOUN **2** **Fantasy** is imagining things.

far **farther** or **further**; **farthest** or **furthest**

ADVERB **1** **Far** means a long way away. *Are you going **far**?*

ADVERB **2** You use **far** to ask questions about distance. *How **far** is the house from here?*

fare **fares** NOUN

A **fare** is the money that you pay to go on something like a plane or a bus.

farm **farms** NOUN

A **farm** is a large area of land together with buildings, used for growing crops or keeping animals.

farmer **farmers** NOUN

A **farmer** is a person who owns or manages a farm.

fascinate **fascinates, fascinating, fascinated** VERB

If something **fascinates** you, it interests you very much.

fashion **fashions** NOUN

A **fashion** is the style of things like clothes that are popular for a time.

fashionable ADJECTIVE

fast **faster, fastest; fasts, fasting, fasted**

ADJECTIVE **1** Someone or something that is **fast** can move very quickly.

ADJECTIVE **2** If a clock is **fast**, it shows a time that is later than the real time.

VERB **3** If someone **fasts**, they eat no food for a period of time.

fasten **fastens, fastening, fastened** VERB

When you **fasten** something, you close it or do it up. *Remember to **fasten** your seat belt.*

fat **fatter, fattest; fats**

ADJECTIVE **1** A **fat** person or animal has a heavy body.

NOUN **2** **Fat** is a solid or liquid substance used in cooking. It comes from animals or vegetables.

father **fathers** NOUN

Your **father** is your male parent.

fault **faults**

NOUN **1** If people say something is your **fault**, they are blaming you for something bad that has happened.

NOUN **2** A **fault** is something wrong with the way something was made.

faulty ADJECTIVE

favour **favours** NOUN

A **favour** is something helpful you do for someone.

favourite **favourites** NOUN

Your **favourite** person or thing is the one you like better than all the others. *This teddy is my **favourite** toy.*

fear fears, fearing, feared
NOUN **1 Fear** is the nasty feeling you have when you think you are in danger.
VERB **2** If you **fear** someone or something, you are frightened of them.

feast feasts NOUN
A **feast** is a large and special meal for many people.

feat feats NOUN
A **feat** is a brave or impressive act.

feather feathers NOUN
A **feather** is one of the very light pieces that make up a bird's coat.

feature features NOUN
A **feature** is a particular part or characteristic of something that is interesting or important.

February NOUN
February is the second month of the year. It has 28 days except in a leap year, when it has 29.

fed VERB
Fed is the past tense of **feed**.

feed feeds, feeding, fed VERB
If you **feed** a person or animal, you give them food.

feel feels, feeling, felt
VERB **1** If you **feel** something, like happy or sad, that is how you are at that time.
VERB **2** If you **feel** an object, you touch it to find out what it is like.

feeling feelings NOUN
A **feeling** is something you feel, like anger or happiness.
See *Feelings* on page 259

feet PLURAL NOUN
Feet is the plural of **foot**.

felt
VERB **1 Felt** is the past tense of **feel**.
NOUN **2 Felt** is a thick cloth made by pressing short threads together.

female females NOUN
A **female** is a person or animal that belongs to the sex that can have babies or young.
female ADJECTIVE

feminine ADJECTIVE
Someone who is **feminine** has the qualities generally expected of a woman, such as gentleness.

fence fences NOUN
A **fence** is a wooden or wire barrier between two areas of land.

ferocious ADJECTIVE
A **ferocious** animal or person is violent and fierce.

ferry ferries NOUN
A **ferry** is a boat that takes passengers and sometimes vehicles across a short stretch of water.

festival festivals
NOUN **1** A **festival** is an organized series of events and performances.
NOUN **2** A **festival** can also be a special day or period of religious celebration.

fetch fetches, fetching, fetched VERB
If you **fetch** something, you go and get it and bring it back.

a
b
c
d
e
f
g
h
i
j
k
l
m
n
o
p
q
r
s
t
u
v
w
x
y
z

fever **fevers** NOUN
If you have a **fever** when you are ill, you have a high temperature.

few **fewer, fewest** ADJECTIVE
Few means a small number of things. *I saw him a few minutes ago.*

fibre **fibres** NOUN
A **fibre** is a thin thread of something such as wool or cotton.

fiction NOUN
Fiction is books or stories about people and events which are made up by the author.
See **non-fiction**

fidget **fidgets, fidgeting, fidgeted** VERB
If you **fidget**, you keep moving about because you are nervous or bored.

field **fields** NOUN
A **field** is a piece of land with a fence around, used to grow crops or keep animals in.

fierce **fiercer, fiercest** ADJECTIVE
An animal that is **fierce** is dangerous.

fifteen NOUN
Fifteen is the number 15.

fifty NOUN
Fifty is the number 50.

fight **fights, fighting, fought** VERB
If you **fight** someone, you try to hurt them.

figure **figures**
NOUN **1** A **figure** is any of the numbers from 0 to 9.
See **digit**
NOUN **2** A **figure** is also the shape of a person. *It was just getting dark when I saw a small figure coming towards me.*

file **files**
NOUN **1** A **file** is a box or folded piece of card that you keep papers in.
NOUN **2** A **file** is also a set of data in a computer, which is stored under a name.
NOUN **3** A **file** is also a metal tool with rough surfaces which is used to smooth things like wood or metal.

fill **fills, filling, filled** VERB
If you **fill** something, you put so much into it there is no room for any more.

film
films
NOUN **1** A **film** is moving pictures shown on a screen.
NOUN **2** **Film** is a long narrow piece of plastic that is used in a camera to take photographs.

filthy **filthier, filthiest** ADJECTIVE
Something that is **filthy** is very dirty.

fin **fins** NOUN
A fish's **fins** are like small wings that stick out of its body. They help the fish to swim and to keep its balance.

final ADJECTIVE
In a series of any kind, the **final** one is the last one.
finally ADVERB

find **finds, finding, found** VERB
When you **find** someone or something, you see the person or thing you have been looking for.

fine **finer, finest; fines**
ADJECTIVE **1** Something that is **fine** is extremely good.
ADJECTIVE **2** Something like a thread or nib that is **fine** is very thin.
ADJECTIVE **3** If you say you are **fine**, you mean you are well and happy.
ADJECTIVE **4** When the weather is **fine**, it is dry and sunny.
NOUN **5** A **fine** is money that is paid as a punishment.

finger **fingers** NOUN
Your **fingers** are the four long jointed parts at the end of your hand.

fingernail **fingernails** NOUN
Your **fingernails** are the thin hard areas that cover the ends of your fingers.

fingerprint **fingerprints** NOUN
A **fingerprint** is a mark that shows the skin pattern at the tip of a finger.

finish **finishes, finishing, finished** VERB
When you **finish** something, like a meal or a book, you reach the end of it.

fir **firs** NOUN
A **fir** is a tall pointed evergreen tree with cones, and leaves like needles.

fire **fires, firing, fired**
NOUN **1 Fire** is the flames produced when something burns.
NOUN **2** A **fire** is also something powered by coal, gas or electricity that gives out heat.
VERB **3** If someone **fires** a gun, a bullet is sent from the gun they are using.

fire engine **fire engines** NOUN
A **fire engine** is a large vehicle that carries firefighters and equipment for putting out fires.

firefighter **firefighters** NOUN
A **firefighter** is a person whose job is to put out fires and rescue trapped people and animals.

fireplace **fireplaces** NOUN
A **fireplace** is the opening beneath a chimney where a fire can be lit.

firework **fireworks** NOUN
A **firework** is a thing that burns with coloured sparks when you light it. Some fireworks make a loud noise.

firm **firmer, firmest**
ADJECTIVE **1** Something that is **firm** does not move easily when you press or push it. *This pear isn't ripe – it is too* ***firm****!*
ADJECTIVE **2** If someone is **firm** with you about something, you know they will not change their mind.

first ADJECTIVE OR ADVERB
If something is **first** or happens first, it is number one and comes before anything else.

first aid NOUN
First aid is simple treatment given as soon as possible to a person who is injured or who suddenly becomes ill.

first person NOUN
The **first person** refers to yourself when you are speaking or writing. It is expressed as "I" or "we".

fish **fishes, fishing, fished**
NOUN **1** A **fish** is an animal that lives in water. It has gills, fins and a scaly skin.

VERB **2** To **fish** is to try and catch fish for food or sport.

fisherman **fishermen** NOUN
A **fisherman** is a person who catches fish as a job or for sport.

fist **fists** NOUN
You make a **fist** by tucking your fingers into the palm of your hand.

fit **fitter, fittest; fits, fitting, fitted**
ADJECTIVE **1** Someone who is **fit** is healthy.
VERB **2** If something such as clothing **fits** you, it is the right size for you.
VERB **3** If something **fits** something else, it is the right size to go with it. *This is the lid that* ***fits*** *that box.*

five NOUN
Five is the number 5.

a
b
c
d
e
f
g
h
i
j
k
l
m
n
o
p
q
r
s
t
u
v
w
x
y
z

A
B
C
D
E
F
G
H
I
J
K
L
M
N
O
P
Q
R
S
T
U
V
W
X
Y
Z

fix fixes, fixing, fixed
VERB **1** If you **fix** something that has broken, you make it work again.
VERB **2** If you **fix** something somewhere, you put it there firmly so that it cannot be moved. *She **fixed** a lamp to the wall.*

fizzy fizzier, fizziest ADJECTIVE
A **fizzy** drink is full of little bubbles of gas.

flag flags NOUN
A **flag** is a piece of cloth that can be fixed to a pole as a symbol of a nation, or as a signal.

flake flakes NOUN
A **flake** is a small thin piece of something.

flame flames NOUN
A **flame** is a flickering tongue or blaze of fire.

flannel flannels NOUN
A **flannel** is a small square of towelling, used for washing yourself.

flap flaps, flapping, flapped
NOUN **1** A **flap** is something flat that is fixed along one edge so that the rest of it can move freely.
VERB **2** When a bird **flaps** its wings, it moves them up and down quickly.

flash flashes, flashing, flashed
NOUN **1** A **flash** is a bright light which comes suddenly
and only lasts a moment, like lightning in a storm.
VERB **2** If something **flashes** past, it moves so fast that you cannot see
it properly.

flask flasks NOUN
A **flask** is a bottle for carrying drinks. It keeps hot drinks hot and cold drinks cold.

flat flats; flatter, flattest
NOUN **1** A **flat** is a set of rooms, usually on one level, for living in.
ADJECTIVE **2** Something that is **flat** is level and smooth.
ADJECTIVE **3** A battery that is **flat** has lost its electrical power.
ADJECTIVE **4** A **flat** shape is one like a circle, that is two-dimensional.

flavour flavours NOUN
The **flavour** of food is its taste.

flea fleas NOUN
A **flea** is a small jumping insect that feeds on blood.

fleece fleeces
NOUN **1** A sheep's **fleece** is its woollen coat.
NOUN **2** A **fleece** is a kind of warm jacket or pullover.

flesh
NOUN **1** Flesh is the soft part of your body.
NOUN **2** The **flesh** of a fruit or vegetable is the soft inner part that you eat.

flew VERB
Flew is the past tense of **fly**.

flick flicks, flicking, flicked VERB
If you **flick** something, you move it sharply with your finger.

flies
VERB **1** **Flies** is a present tense form of **fly**.
NOUN **2** **Flies** is also the plural of **fly**.

flight flights
NOUN **1** A **flight** is a journey through the air by a bird or an aircraft.
NOUN **2** A **flight** of stairs is a set that leads from one level to another without changing direction.

flip flips, flipping, flipped VERB
If you **flip** something, you turn or move it quickly. *He **flipped** a coin.*

float floats, floating, floated
VERB **1** Something that **floats** is supported by water and does not sink.
VERB **2** Something that **floats** through the air moves along gently, supported by the air.

flock flocks NOUN
A **flock** is a group of birds, sheep or goats.
See Collective nouns on page 268

flood floods NOUN
A **flood** is a large amount of water covering an area that is usually dry.

floor floors
NOUN **1** The **floor** of a room is the flat part that you walk on.
NOUN **2** A **floor** of a building is all the rooms on that level. *Our flat is on the third floor.*

flop flops, flopping, flopped VERB
If someone or something **flops**, they fall loosely and rather heavily.

flour NOUN
Flour is a powder made by grinding grain such as wheat. It is used to make things like bread and cakes.

flow flows, flowing, flowed VERB
If liquid **flows** in a certain direction, it moves there steadily.

flower flowers NOUN
A **flower** is the part of a plant that has coloured petals. When the petals fade, fruit or seeds develop.

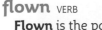

flown VERB
Flown is the past participle of **fly**.

flu NOUN
Flu is an illness that gives you a fever and makes you ache all over. Flu is an abbreviation of **influenza**.

fluffy fluffier, fluffiest ADJECTIVE
Something that is **fluffy** is very soft and light.

fluid fluids NOUN
Fluid is another word for liquid.

flute flutes NOUN
A **flute** is a musical wind instrument consisting of a long tube with holes and keys.

flutter flutters, fluttering, fluttered VERB
If something **flutters**, it flaps or waves with small quick movements.

fly flies, flying, flew, flown
NOUN **1** A **fly** is a small insect with two wings.
See Insects on page 264
VERB **2** When a bird, insect or aircraft **flies**, it moves through the air.

foam NOUN
Foam is a mass of tiny bubbles.

focus focuses, focusing, focused VERB
If you **focus** something like a camera or a telescope, you adjust it so that you can see through it clearly.

fog fogs NOUN
Fog is a thick mist of water droplets in the air.
foggy ADJECTIVE

fold folds, folding, folded
NOUN **1** **Folds** in material are the curves in it when it does not hang flat. *The curtains hung in soft folds.*
VERB **2** If you **fold** something, you bend it so that one part lies over another.

folder folders NOUN
A **folder** is a piece of folded cardboard for keeping papers in.

folk folks NOUN
Folk or folks are people.

follow follows, following, followed
VERB **1** If you **follow** someone who is moving, you move along behind them.
VERB **2** If one thing **follows** another, it happens after it.

a
b
c
d
e
f
g
h
i
j
k
l
m
n
o
p
q
r
s
t
u
v
w
x
y
z

VERB 3 If you **follow** instructions or advice, you do what you are told.

fond fonder, fondest ADJECTIVE
If you are **fond** of someone, you like them very much.

font fonts NOUN
In printing, a **font** is a complete set of numbers and letters of one style and size.

food NOUN
Food is what people and animals eat to stay alive.

foolish ADJECTIVE
Something or somebody **foolish** is silly or unwise.

foot feet
NOUN 1 Your **feet** are the parts of your body that touch the ground when you stand or walk.

NOUN 2 A **foot** is a measure of length, equal to about 30 centimetres.

football footballs
NOUN 1 Football is a game between two teams who try to kick a ball into each other's goal.

NOUN 2 A **football** is a large ball used in games of football.

footballer footballers NOUN
A **footballer** is a person who plays football.

footprint footprints NOUN
A **footprint** is a mark in the shape of a foot that a person or animal leaves on a surface.

footstep footsteps NOUN
A **footstep** is the sound made by someone walking.

for
PREPOSITION 1 You use **for** to show that something is to be used by or given to a particular person. *I bought a present for my brother.*

PREPOSITION 2 You use **for** to explain the reason, cause or purpose of something. *I'm going shopping for a pair of shoes.*

PREPOSITION 3 You use **for** to show a distance, time or quantity. *I have been waiting here for ages.*

PREPOSITION 4 If you are **for** something, you support it. *My parents are all for the new school.*

forbid forbids, forbidding, forbade, forbidden VERB
If someone **forbids** you to do something, they order you not to do it.

force forces, forcing, forced
VERB 1 If you **force** someone or something, you use your power or strength to make them do what you want. *Dad forced me to save half my pocket money.*
NOUN 2 A **force** is a push or a pull.
NOUN 3 The **force** of something is also the powerful effect it has. *The force of the storm damaged many trees.*

forecast forecasts, forecasting, forecast
VERB 1 If someone **forecasts** something, they say what they think is going to happen in the future.
NOUN 2 A weather **forecast** tells you what sort of weather to expect.

forehead foreheads NOUN
Your **forehead** is the front of your head, between your hair and eyebrows.

foreign ADJECTIVE
Something that is **foreign** is to do with a country that is not your own.

forest forests NOUN
A **forest** is a large area where trees grow close together.

forgave VERB
Forgave is the past tense of **forgive**.

forget forgets, forgetting, forgot, forgotten VERB
If you **forget** something, you do not remember or think about it.

forgive forgives, forgiving, forgave, forgiven VERB
If you **forgive** someone who has done something bad, you stop being cross with them.

fork forks
NOUN **1** A **fork** is a tool with three or four prongs on the end of a handle. You use a small fork for eating and a large fork for digging in the garden.
NOUN **2** A **fork** in a road or tree is the point where it divides into two.

form forms, forming, formed
NOUN **1** A **form** is a piece of paper with questions on it and spaces where you should write the answers.
NOUN **2** A **form** is also a class in school.
VERB **3** When something **forms**, it takes shape.

formal ADJECTIVE
Something **formal** is correct and serious.

fortnight fortnights NOUN
A **fortnight** is two weeks.

fortunate
ADJECTIVE **1** Someone who is **fortunate** has good luck.
ADJECTIVE **2** Something that is **fortunate** brings you success or gives you an advantage.

fortune fortunes
NOUN **1 Fortune** is good or bad luck.
NOUN **2** A **fortune** is a lot of money.

forty NOUN
Forty is the number 40.

forward ADVERB
If you move **forward** or **forwards**, you move the way you are facing.
look forward PHRASE If you **look forward** to something, you want it to happen.

fossil fossils NOUN
A **fossil** is the hardened remains of a prehistoric animal or plant that are found inside a rock.

fought VERB
Fought is the past tense of **fight**.

foul fouler, foulest ADJECTIVE
If something is **foul**, it is extremely unpleasant.

found VERB
Found is the past tense of **find**.

foundation foundations NOUN
The **foundations** of a building are the solid layers of material put below the ground to support it.

fountain fountains NOUN
A **fountain** is a jet or spray of water forced up into the air by a pump.

four NOUN
Four is the number 4.

fourteen NOUN
Fourteen is the number 14.

fox foxes NOUN
A **fox** is a wild animal like a dog, with reddish-brown fur and a thick tail.

a
b
c
d
e
f
g
h
i
j
k
l
m
n
o
p
q
r
s
t
u
v
w
x
y
z

A B C D E F G H I J K L M N O P Q R S T U V W X Y Z

fraction fractions

NOUN **1** In maths, a **fraction** is a part of a whole number, for example ¼.
See Fractions on page 278

NOUN **2** A **fraction** is also a tiny part of something.

fracture fractures NOUN

A **fracture** is a crack or break in something, especially a bone.

fragile ADJECTIVE

Something that is **fragile** is easily broken or damaged.

fragment fragments NOUN

A **fragment** of something is a small piece or part of it.

frame frames NOUN

A **frame** is the part surrounding something like a window or picture, or the lenses of a pair of glasses.

freckle freckles NOUN

Freckles are small, light brown spots on someone's skin.

free

ADJECTIVE **1** If a person or animal is **free**, they can go where they want. *Matthew opened the cage and set the bird **free**.*

ADJECTIVE **2** If something is **free**, it does not cost anything.

freedom NOUN

freeze freezes, freezing, froze, frozen

VERB **1** If a liquid **freezes**, it becomes solid because the temperature is low.

VERB **2** If you **freeze** something, you store it at a very low temperature.

freezer freezers NOUN

A **freezer** is a refrigerator for freezing and storing food.

frequent ADJECTIVE

If something is **frequent**, it happens often.

frequency NOUN **frequently** ADVERB

fresh fresher, freshest

ADJECTIVE **1** If food is **fresh**, it has been picked or made recently.

ADJECTIVE **2** **Fresh** water is water that is not salty.

ADJECTIVE **3** If you feel **fresh**, you feel rested and full of energy.

ADJECTIVE **4** **Fresh** air is the air outside.

friction NOUN

Friction is the force which is produced when two surfaces rub against each other.

Friday Fridays NOUN

Friday is the day between Thursday and Saturday.

fridge fridges NOUN

A **fridge** is a large metal container. It is kept cool so that the food in it stays fresh longer. Fridge is an abbreviation of **refrigerator**.

friend friends NOUN

A **friend** is someone you know well and like very much.

friendly friendlier, friendliest ADJECTIVE

If you are **friendly** to someone, you behave in a kind and pleasant way to them.

fright NOUN

Fright is a sudden feeling of fear.

frighten frightens, frightening, frightened VERB

If something **frightens** you, it makes you afraid.

frightening ADJECTIVE

Something that is **frightening** makes you feel afraid.

frog frogs NOUN

A **frog** is a small amphibious animal with smooth skin, big eyes, and long back legs which it uses for jumping.
See Amphibians on page 264

from

PREPOSITION **1 From** tells you where someone or something started. *The river flows **from** the north.*

PREPOSITION **2** If you take something **from** an amount, you reduce the amount by that much. *If you take five **from** 20 you are left with 15.*

PREPOSITION **3** You use **from** to state the range of something. *Lunchtime is **from** 12 o'clock to 1 o'clock.*

front fronts

NOUN **1** The **front** of something is the part that faces forward.

ADJECTIVE **2** A **front** room or garden is on the side of a building that faces the street.

in front PHRASE **In front** means ahead or further forward.

in front of PHRASE If you do something **in front of** someone, you do it while they are there. *They agreed to meet **in front of** the cinema.*

frost frosts NOUN

When there is a **frost**, the weather is very cold and the ground becomes covered with tiny ice crystals.

frown frowns, frowning, frowned VERB

If you **frown**, your eyebrows are drawn together. People frown when they are angry, worried, or thinking hard.

froze VERB

Froze is the past tense of **freeze**.

frozen

VERB **1 Frozen** is the past participle of **freeze**.

ADJECTIVE **2** If something like a lake or river is **frozen**, its surface has turned to ice.

ADJECTIVE **3** If you say you are **frozen**, you mean you are very cold.

fruit fruits NOUN

A **fruit** is the part of a plant that develops from the flower and contains the seeds. Many fruits are good to eat.
See Fruit on page 260

fry fries, frying, fried VERB

When you **fry** food, you cook it in a pan that contains hot fat or oil.

fuel fuels NOUN

Fuel is something like petrol or coal, that is burned to provide heat or power.

full fuller, fullest ADJECTIVE

If something is **full**, there is no room for anything more.

full stop full stops NOUN

A **full stop** is the punctuation mark (.) which you use at the end of a sentence.
See Punctuation on page 270

fun NOUN

Fun is something enjoyable that makes you feel happy.

funeral funerals NOUN

A **funeral** is a ceremony held when a person has died. The body is buried or burned.

funnel funnels

NOUN **1** A **funnel** is an open cone which narrows to a tube. You use a funnel to pour liquid into containers.

NOUN **2** A **funnel** is also a metal chimney on a ship or steam engine.

a b c d e f g h i j k l m n o p q r s t u v w x y z

81

A
B
C
D
E
F
G
H
I
J
K
L
M
N
O
P
Q
R
S
T
U
V
W
X
Y
Z

funny **funnier, funniest**

ADJECTIVE **1 Funny** people or things make you laugh.

ADJECTIVE **2** Something that is **funny** is rather strange or surprising.

funnily ADVERB

fur NOUN

Fur is the soft thick body hair of many animals.

furry ADJECTIVE

furious ADJECTIVE

Someone who is **furious** is extremely angry.

furniture NOUN

Furniture is large objects such as tables, beds and chairs, that people have in rooms.

further **furthest**

ADJECTIVE **1 Further** is a comparative form of **far**.

ADJECTIVE **2 Further** can mean more. *Write for further details.*

ADVERB **3** If someone goes **further** than someone else, they travel a longer way.

fury NOUN

Fury is violent or extreme anger.

fuss **fusses, fussing, fussed**

NOUN **1** A **fuss** is worried or anxious behaviour that is unnecessary and often not welcome. *I don't know why you're making such a fuss about it.*

VERB **2** If someone **fusses**, they worry about unimportant things.

future **futures**

NOUN **1** The **future** is the time that is to come.

ADJECTIVE **2 Future** is to do with time that is to come. *We need to look after the environment for future generations.*

NOUN **3** The **future tense** of a verb is the form used to talk about something that will happen in the future. For example, the sentence "Ben will be at school tomorrow" is in the future tense.

Gg

gain gains, gaining, gained
NOUN **1** A **gain** is an increase in the amount of something.
VERB **2** If you **gain** from something, you get something good out of it.
VERB **3** If a clock or watch **gains**, it moves too fast.

galaxy galaxies
NOUN **1** A **galaxy** is a large group of stars and planets in space.
NOUN **2** The **galaxy** is the group of stars and planets that the earth belongs to.
galactic ADJECTIVE

gale gales NOUN
A **gale** is a strong wind.

gallery galleries
NOUN **1** A **gallery** is a place that shows paintings or sculptures.
NOUN **2** In a hall or theatre, a **gallery** is a raised area at the back where people can sit and get a good view of what is happening.

gallon gallons NOUN
A **gallon** is a measure of volume equal to about four and a half litres.

gallop gallops, galloping, galloped VERB
When a horse **gallops**, it runs fast.

game games NOUN
A **game** is something you play for sport or fun. Most games have rules.

gang gangs NOUN
A **gang** is a group of people who do things together.

gap gaps NOUN
A **gap** is a space between two things, or a hole in something solid.

garage garages
NOUN **1** A **garage** is a building in which someone can keep a car.
NOUN **2** A **garage** is also a place that sells petrol or repairs cars.

garden gardens NOUN
A **garden** is land next to a house where people can grow things like trees, flowers or grass.

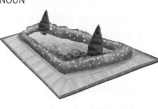

garlic NOUN
Garlic is the small white bulb of an onion-like plant which has a strong taste and smell. It is used in cooking.

garment garments NOUN
A **garment** is a piece of clothing.

gas gases NOUN
Gas is a substance that is not liquid or solid. Air is a mixture of gases. Another type of gas is used as a fuel for cookers and central heating.

gasp gasps, gasping, gasped VERB
When you **gasp**, you take a short quick breath through your mouth, especially when you are surprised or in pain.

gate gates NOUN
A **gate** is a type of door that is used at the entrance to a garden or field.

gather gathers, gathering, gathered
VERB **1** If people or animals **gather**, they come together in a group.
VERB **2** If you **gather** things, you collect them from different places. *Early people used to* ***gather*** *berries for food.*

gave VERB
Gave is the past tense of **give**.

a
b
c
d
e
f
g
h
i
j
k
l
m
n
o
p
q
r
s
t
u
v
w
x
y
z

gaze gazes, gazing, gazed VERB
If you **gaze** at something, you look steadily at it for a long time.

general generals
ADJECTIVE **1** You use **general** when you are talking about most of the people in a group. *There was a general rush for the door when the bell rang.*
NOUN **2** A **general** is an army officer of very high rank.
generally ADVERB

generous ADJECTIVE
Someone who is **generous** is kind and willing to help others by giving them money or time.

gentle gentler, gentlest ADJECTIVE
Someone who is **gentle** is kind, calm and sensitive.
gently ADVERB

gentleman gentlemen NOUN
A **gentleman** is a polite name for a man.

genuine ADJECTIVE
Something **genuine** is real and not false or pretend.

geography NOUN
Geography is the study of the countries of the world, and of things like their rivers, mountains and people.
geographical ADJECTIVE

germ germs NOUN
A **germ** is a tiny living thing that can make people ill. You cannot see germs without using a microscope.

get gets, getting, got
VERB **1** **Get** often means the same as become. *It gets dark earlier in winter.*
VERB **2** If you **get** into a particular situation, you put yourself in that situation. *We got into a muddle.*
VERB **3** If you **get** something done, you do it or you persuade someone to do it.
VERB **4** If you **get** something, you fetch it or are given it. *I'll get us all a cup of tea.*
VERB **5** If you **get** a train, bus or plane, you travel on it.

ghost ghosts NOUN
A **ghost** is a shadowy figure of someone no longer living that some people believe they see.

giant giants
NOUN **1** In fairy stories, a **giant** is someone who is huge and strong.
ADJECTIVE **2** Anything that is much larger than usual can be called **giant**. *A giant wave was coming towards us.*

gift gifts NOUN
A **gift** is a present.

gigantic ADJECTIVE
Something **gigantic** is extremely large.

giggle giggles, giggling, giggled VERB
If you **giggle**, you make quiet little laughing noises.

gill gills NOUN
The **gills** of a fish are the organs on its sides which it uses for breathing.

ginger NOUN
Ginger is a plant root with a hot spicy flavour, used in cooking.

giraffe giraffes NOUN
A **giraffe** is a large African mammal with a very long neck.

girl girls NOUN
A **girl** is a female child.

give gives, giving, gave, given VERB
If you **give** someone something, you hand it to them or provide it for them. *Dad gave me a job cleaning the car.*

give way PHRASE
If something **gives way**, it collapses.

glacier glaciers NOUN
A **glacier** is a huge frozen river of slow-moving ice.

glad gladder, gladdest ADJECTIVE
If you are **glad**, you are happy and pleased.

glance glances, glancing, glanced
VERB **1** If you **glance** at something, you look at it quickly.
NOUN **2** A **glance** is a quick look.

glare glares, glaring, glared
VERB **1** If you **glare** at someone, you look at them angrily.
VERB **2** If the sun or a light **glares**, it shines with a very bright light.

glass glasses
NOUN **1 Glass** is a hard transparent material that is easily broken.
It is used to make windows and bottles.
NOUN **2** A **glass** is a container that you can drink from, made of glass.

glasses PLURAL NOUN
Glasses are two lenses in a frame, which some people wear over their eyes to help them see better.

gleam gleams, gleaming, gleamed VERB
If something **gleams**, it shines and reflects light.

glide glides, gliding, glided VERB
When something **glides**, it moves silently and smoothly.

glider gliders NOUN
A **glider** is an aircraft that does not have an engine, but flies by floating on air currents.

glimpse glimpses, glimpsing, glimpsed VERB
If you **glimpse** something, you see it very briefly.

glisten glistens, glistening, glistened VERB
If something **glistens**, it shines or sparkles. *Her eyes **glistened** with tears.*

glitter glitters, glittering, glittered VERB
If something **glitters**, it shines in a sparkling way. *Her diamond necklace **glittered** under the lights.*

globe globes NOUN
A **globe** is a round model of the Earth with a map of the world drawn on it.

gloomy gloomier, gloomiest
ADJECTIVE **1** If a place is **gloomy**, it is dark and dull.
ADJECTIVE **2** If people are **gloomy**, they are unhappy and not at all hopeful.
gloomily ADVERB

glossy glossier, glossiest ADJECTIVE
Something that is **glossy** is smooth and shiny.

glove gloves NOUN
A **glove** is a piece of clothing which covers your hand, with separate places for each finger.

glow glows, glowing, glowed VERB
If something **glows**, it shines with a steady dull light.

glue NOUN
Glue is a thick sticky liquid used for joining things together.

a
b
c
d
e
f
g
h
i
j
k
l
m
n
o
p
q
r
s
t
u
v
w
x
y
z

A
B
C
D
E
F
G
H
I
J
K
L
M
N
O
P
Q
R
S
T
U
V
W
X
Y
Z

gnat gnats NOUN

A **gnat** is a very small flying insect that bites people.

gnaw gnaws, gnawing, gnawed VERB

If people or animals **gnaw** something hard, they keep biting on it.

go goes, going, went, gone

VERB **1** If you **go** somewhere, you move or travel there.

VERB **2** If something **goes** well, it is successful.

VERB **3** If you are **going** to do something, you will do it.

VERB **4** If a clock or watch **goes**, it works.

goal goals

NOUN **1** A **goal** in games such as football or hockey is the space into which players try to get the ball so that they can score.

NOUN **2** It is also called a **goal** when a player gets the ball into the goal.

NOUN **3** If something is your **goal**, you hope to succeed in doing it one day.

goat goats NOUN

A **goat** is an animal with short coarse hair, horns, and a short tail.

god gods

NOUN **1** A **god** is a person or thing that people worship.

NOUN **2** The name **God** is given to the god who is worshipped by some people, such as Christians or Jews.

goddess goddesses NOUN

A **goddess** is a female god.

gold

NOUN **1 Gold** is a valuable, yellow-coloured metal that is used for making things like jewellery.

ADJECTIVE **2** Something that is **gold** in colour is warm yellow.

golden ADJECTIVE

Something that is **golden** is made of gold or is a gold colour.

goldfish NOUN

A **goldfish** is a gold or orange-coloured fish which is often kept as a pet.

golf NOUN

Golf is a game in which players use long sticks called clubs to hit a small ball into special holes.

gone VERB

Gone is the past participle of **go**.

good better, best

ADJECTIVE **1** Someone who is **good** is kind and caring, and can be trusted.

ADJECTIVE **2** A child or animal that is **good** is well-behaved and obedient.

ADJECTIVE **3** If something like a film or book is **good**, people like it.

ADJECTIVE **4** Someone who is **good** at something is skilful and successful at it.

goodbye INTERJECTION

You say **goodbye** to someone when you or they are leaving.

good night INTERJECTION

You say **good night** to someone when you or they are going to bed.

goods PLURAL NOUN

Goods are things that can be bought or sold.

goose geese NOUN

A **goose** is a large bird with a long neck and webbed feet. Its cry is a loud honking noise.

gorilla gorillas

NOUN

The **gorilla** is the largest of the apes. It lives in African forests.

got

VERB **1 Got** is the past tense of **get**.

VERB **2** You can use **have got** instead of **have**. We **have got** a map.

VERB **3** You can use **have got to** instead of **have to**, when talking about something you must do. *We **have got to** win.*

government **governments** NOUN
A **government** is the group of people who run a country and decide about important things such as medical care and old age pensions.

grab **grabs, grabbing, grabbed** VERB
If you **grab** something, you take hold of it suddenly and roughly.

graceful ADJECTIVE
Someone or something that is **graceful** moves in a smooth way which is pleasant to watch.

gradual ADJECTIVE
Something that is **gradual** happens slowly.
gradually ADVERB

graffiti NOUN
Graffiti is words or pictures that are scribbled on walls in public places.

grain **grains**
NOUN **1 Grain** is the seeds of plants like wheat or corn, that we use for food.
NOUN **2** A **grain** of something such as sand or salt is a tiny hard piece of it.

gram **grams** NOUN
A **gram** (g) is a small unit of mass and weight. One sheet of paper weighs about four grams. There are 1000 grams in a kilogram.

grammar NOUN
Grammar is the rules of a language.

grand **grander, grandest** ADJECTIVE
Buildings that are **grand** are large and look important.

grandad **grandads** NOUN
Your **grandad** is your grandfather.

grandchild **grandchildren** NOUN
Someone's **grandchild** is the child of their son or daughter.

grandfather **grandfathers** NOUN
Your **grandfather** is the father of one of your parents.

grandmother **grandmothers** NOUN
Your **grandmother** is the mother of one of your parents.

grandparent **grandparents** NOUN
Your **grandparents** are your parents' parents.

granny **grannies** NOUN
INFORMAL Your **granny** is your grandmother.

grape **grapes** NOUN
A **grape** is a small green or purple fruit. Grapes grow in bunches on vines. They can be eaten raw, used for making wine, or dried to make raisins, sultanas or currants.
See Fruit on page 260

grapefruit **grapefruits** NOUN
A **grapefruit** is a large round fruit. It is like an orange but it is larger and has a pale yellow skin.
See Fruit on page 260

graph **graphs** NOUN
A **graph** is a diagram which shows how two sets of information are related.

grasp **grasps, grasping, grasped**
VERB **1** If you **grasp** something, you hold it firmly.
VERB **2** If you **grasp** an idea, you understand it.

a
b
c
d
e
f
g
h
i
j
k
l
m
n
o
p
q
r
s
t
u
v
w
x
y
z

A
B
C
D
E
F
G
H
I
J
K
L
M
N
O
P
Q
R
S
T
U
V
W
X
Y
Z

grass **grasses** NOUN
Grass is a common green plant with long thin leaves. It grows on lawns and in parks.

grasshopper **grasshoppers** NOUN
A **grasshopper** is an insect. It has long back legs and can jump well. The male makes a chirping sound by rubbing its back legs against its wings.
See *Insects* on page 264

grate **grates, grating, grated**
NOUN **1** A **grate** is a framework of metal bars in a fireplace.
VERB **2** If you **grate** food, you shred it into small pieces.

grateful ADJECTIVE
If you are **grateful** for something nice that someone has done, you have warm feelings towards them and want to thank them.

grave **graver, gravest; graves**
ADJECTIVE **1** Something that is **grave** is important, serious and worrying.
NOUN **2** A **grave** is a place where a dead person is buried.

gravel NOUN
Gravel is small stones used for making roads and paths.

gravity NOUN
Gravity is the force that makes things fall when you drop them.

gravy NOUN
Gravy is a brown sauce made from meat juices.

graze **grazes, grazing, grazed**
VERB **1** When animals **graze**, they eat grass.
VERB **2** If you **graze** your skin, you scrape it against something and hurt yourself.

grease
NOUN **1** **Grease** is a thick oil which is put on the moving parts of cars and other machines to make them work smoothly.
NOUN **2** **Grease** is also an oily substance produced by your skin and found in your hair.
greasy ADJECTIVE

great **greater, greatest**
ADJECTIVE **1** You say something is **great** when it is large in size, number or amount. *The waves threw a **great** shower of pebbles onto the seafront.*
ADJECTIVE **2 Great** also means important. *I like to hear about **great** scientists.*
ADJECTIVE **3** INFORMAL **Great** can mean wonderful. *Paul had a **great** time.*

greedy **greedier, greediest** ADJECTIVE
Someone who is **greedy** wants more than they need of something.
greedily ADVERB

green **greener, greenest**
ADJECTIVE **1** Something that is **green** is the colour of grass.
See *Colours and shapes* on page 266
ADJECTIVE **2 Green** is used to describe people who are interested in protecting the environment.

greenhouse **greenhouses** NOUN
A **greenhouse** is a building which has glass walls and a glass roof. It is used to grow plants in.

greet **greets, greeting, greeted** VERB
When you **greet** someone, you look pleased to see them, and say something friendly.

greeting **greetings** NOUN
A **greeting** is something friendly that you say or do when you meet someone.

grew VERB
Grew is the past tense of **grow**.

grey **greyer, greyest**
ADJECTIVE
Something that is **grey** is the colour of clouds on a rainy day.
See *Colours and shapes* on page 266

grid **grids** NOUN
A **grid** is a pattern of lines crossing each other to form squares.

grief NOUN
Someone who feels **grief** is very sad, often because a person or animal they love has died.

grill grills, grilling, grilled VERB
If you **grill** food, you cook it on metal bars under or over heat.

grim grimmer, grimmest
ADJECTIVE **1** If a situation or piece of news is **grim**, it is unpleasant and worrying.
ADJECTIVE **2** If someone looks **grim**, they are serious because they are worried or angry about something.

grin grins, grinning, grinned VERB
If you **grin**, you give a broad smile.

grind grinds, grinding, ground
VERB **1** If you **grind** something, such as pepper, you crush it into a fine powder.
VERB **2** If you **grind** your teeth, you rub your upper and lower teeth together.

grip grips, gripping, gripped
VERB **1** If you **grip** something, you take hold of it firmly.
VERB **2** If something **grips** you, you find it very interesting.

groan groans, groaning, groaned VERB
If you **groan**, you make a long low sound of pain or unhappiness.

groove grooves NOUN
A **groove** is a deep line cut into a surface.

ground grounds
NOUN **1** The **ground** is the surface of the earth or the floor of a room.
NOUN **2** A **ground** is an area of land where people play sports such as football or cricket.

PLURAL NOUN **3** The **grounds** of a large house are the land around it which belongs to it.
VERB **4** **Ground** is the past tense of **grind**.

group groups NOUN
A **group** of things or people is a number of them that are linked together in some way.

grow grows, growing, grew, grown
VERB **1** When a person **grows**, they get bigger. All living things can grow.
VERB **2** If you **grow** plants, you put seeds or young plants in the ground and look after them.
VERB **3** When someone **grows up**, they gradually change from being a child into being an adult.

growl growls, growling, growled VERB
When an animal **growls**, it makes a low rumbling sound, usually because it is angry.

grown VERB
Grown is the past participle of **grow**.

grown-up grown-ups NOUN
INFORMAL A **grown-up** is an adult.

growth NOUN
Growth means getting bigger.

grub grubs NOUN
A **grub** is a wormlike insect that has just hatched from its egg.

grumble grumbles, grumbling, grumbled VERB
If you **grumble**, you complain in a bad-tempered way.

grunt grunts, grunting, grunted VERB
When a pig **grunts**, it makes a low rough noise.

a
b
c
d
e
f
g
h
i
j
k
l
m
n
o
p
q
r
s
t
u
v
w
x
y
z

A
B
C
D
E
F
G
H
I
J
K
L
M
N
O
P
Q
R
S
T
U
V
W
X
Y
Z

guarantee guarantees, guaranteeing, guaranteed
VERB **1** If someone or something **guarantees** something, they make certain that it will happen.
NOUN **2** A **guarantee** is a written promise that if something you have bought goes wrong it will be replaced or mended free.

guard guards, guarding, guarded
VERB **1** If you **guard** a person or object, you stay near to them to keep them safe or to make sure they do not escape.
NOUN **2** A **guard** is a person who guards something or somewhere.

guess guesses, guessing, guessed VERB
If you **guess** something, you give an answer without knowing if it is right.

guest guests NOUN
A **guest** is someone who stays at your home or who goes to an event because they have been invited.

guide guides, guiding, guided
VERB **1** If you **guide** someone, you show them where to go or what to do.
NOUN **2** A **guide** is someone who shows you round places.

guidebook guidebooks NOUN
A **guidebook** is a book that gives information about a place.

guilty guiltier, guiltiest
ADJECTIVE **1** If you are **guilty** of doing something wrong, you did it.
ADJECTIVE **2** If you feel **guilty**, you are unhappy because you have done something wrong.

guinea pig guinea pigs NOUN
A **guinea pig** is a small furry animal without a tail, often kept as a pet.

guitar guitars NOUN
A **guitar** is a musical instrument with strings that you play with your fingers.

gulf gulfs NOUN
A **gulf** is a large area of sea which stretches a long way into the land.

gulp gulps, gulping, gulped
VERB **1** If you **gulp** food or drink, you swallow large amounts of it.
VERB **2** If you **gulp**, you swallow air because you are nervous.

gum gums
NOUN **1** Your **gums** are the firm flesh your teeth are set in.
NOUN **2** Gum is a soft sweet that people chew but do not swallow.
NOUN **3** Gum is also glue for sticking paper.

gumboot gumboots NOUN
Gumboots are long rubber boots that you wear to keep your feet dry.

gun guns NOUN
A **gun** is a weapon which fires bullets or shells.

gunpowder NOUN
Gunpowder is a powder that explodes when it is lit. It is used for making things such as fireworks.

gurdwara gurdwaras
NOUN A **gurdwara** is a place where Sikhs worship.

gust gusts NOUN
A **gust** is a sudden rush of wind.

gutter gutters
NOUN **1** A **gutter** is the edge of a road next to the pavement, where rain collects and flows away.
NOUN **2** A **gutter** is also an open pipe at the edge of a roof, where rain collects and flows away.

gym gyms
NOUN **1** Gym is physical exercises, especially ones using equipment such as bars and ropes. Gym is an abbreviation of **gymnastics**.
NOUN **2** A **gym** is a room with special equipment for physical exercises. Gym here is an abbreviation of **gymnasium**.

Hh

habit **habits** NOUN
A **habit** is something that you do often or regularly, sometimes without thinking about it.

habitat **habitats** NOUN
The **habitat** of an animal or plant is its natural home.

had VERB
Had is the past tense of **have**.

haddock NOUN
A **haddock** is an edible sea fish.

hail **hails, hailing, hailed**
NOUN **1 Hail** is frozen rain. It falls in small balls of ice called hailstones.
VERB **2** When it is **hailing**, frozen rain is falling.

hair **hairs** NOUN
Your **hair** is made up of a large number of fine threads that grow on your head. Hair also grows on other parts of the body and on the bodies of some other animals.

hairdresser **hairdressers** NOUN
A **hairdresser** is trained to cut and style people's hair.

hairy **hairier, hairiest** ADJECTIVE
Someone or something that is **hairy** is covered with hair.

hajj NOUN
The **hajj** is the journey to Mecca that every Muslim must make at least once in their life if they are healthy and wealthy enough to do so.

half **halves**
NOUN **1** A **half** is one of two equal parts of something.
See Fractions on page 278

ADVERB **2** When you are talking about time, you can use **half** to mean 30 minutes after a particular hour. *She was home by **half** past three.*

halfway ADVERB
Halfway is the middle of the distance between two points. *He stopped **halfway** down the stairs.*

hall **halls**
NOUN **1** A **hall** is the room just inside the front door of a home which leads into other rooms.
NOUN **2** A **hall** is also a large room or building used for public events.

Halloween NOUN
Halloween is October 31. Children celebrate it by dressing up, often as ghosts and witches.

halve **halves, halving, halved** VERB
If you **halve** something, you divide it into two equal parts.

ham NOUN
Ham is meat from the back leg of a pig. It is specially treated so that it can be kept for a long time.

hamburger **hamburgers** NOUN
A **hamburger** is a piece of minced meat shaped into a flat disc. Hamburgers are often eaten in a bread roll.

hammer **hammers** NOUN
A **hammer** is a tool that is used for hitting things, such as nails into wood.

hammock **hammocks** NOUN
A **hammock** is a piece of strong cloth or netting which is hung between two supports and used as a bed.

hamster **hamsters** NOUN
A **hamster** is a small furry rodent which is often kept as a pet. Hamsters have very short tails, and large cheek pouches for carrying food.

hand **hands, handing, handed**
NOUN **1** Your **hand** is the part of your body which is at the end of your arm. It has four fingers and a thumb.

NOUN **2** The **hands** of a clock point to the numbers to tell you the time.

VERB **3** When you **hand** something to someone, you pass it to them.

handbag **handbags** NOUN

A **handbag** is a small bag that women use to carry things such as money and keys.

handkerchief **handkerchiefs** NOUN

A **handkerchief** is a small square of fabric that you use for wiping your nose.

handle **handles, handling, handled**

NOUN **1** The **handle** of an object is the part you hold to pick it up and carry it.

NOUN **2** The **handle** of a door or window is the knob or lever that is used for opening or closing it.

VERB **3** If you **handle** something, you touch or feel it with your hands.

handlebar **handlebars** NOUN

Handlebars are the bar and handles at the front of a bicycle, used for steering.

handsome ADJECTIVE

A **handsome** man has a very attractive face.

handwriting NOUN

Someone's **handwriting** is the way in which they write with a pen or pencil.

handy **handier, handiest**

ADJECTIVE **1** If something is **handy**, it is near. *I like to keep my glasses **handy**.*

ADJECTIVE **2** If an object is **handy**, it is easy to handle or use.

hang **hangs, hanging, hung** VERB

If you **hang** something up, you fix it there so that it does not touch the ground. ***Hang** your coat on the hook.*

hanger **hangers** NOUN

A **hanger** is a curved piece of metal, wood or plastic that you hang clothes on.

Hanukkah or Chanukah NOUN

Hanukkah is the eight-day Jewish festival of lights.

happen **happens, happening, happened**

VERB **1** If something **happens**, it takes place.

*What **happens** if I press this button?*

VERB **2** If you **happen** to do something, you do it by chance. *I **happened** to be near the phone when it rang.*

happiness NOUN

Happiness is a feeling of great pleasure.

happy **happier, happiest** ADJECTIVE

If you are **happy**, you feel good because something nice has happened or because most things are the way you want.

happily ADVERB

harbour **harbours** NOUN

A **harbour** is an area of deep water where boats can stay safely.

hard **harder, hardest**

ADJECTIVE **1** An object that is **hard** is very firm and stiff.

ADJECTIVE **2** If something is **hard** to do, you can only do it with a lot of effort.

harden **hardens, hardening, hardened**

VERB

If something **hardens**, it becomes hard or gets harder.

hardly ADVERB

If you can **hardly** do something, you can only just do it. *The box was so heavy I could **hardly** lift it.*

hardware

NOUN **1** **Hardware** is tools and equipment made of metal.

NOUN **2** **Hardware** is also computer machinery.

hare **hares** NOUN

A **hare** is an animal like a large rabbit, but with longer ears and legs. It does not live in a burrow but rests in grass or in a ploughed field.

harm NOUN
Harm is injury to a person or animal.
harmful ADJECTIVE **harmless** ADJECTIVE

harness **harnesses**
NOUN **1** A **harness** is a set of straps which fit round a person's body to hold the person firmly in place.
NOUN **2** A horse's **harness** is a set of straps fastened round its head or body.

harsh **harsher, harshest**
ADJECTIVE **1** A person who is **harsh** is unkind.
ADJECTIVE **2** Weather that is **harsh** is cold and unpleasant.
ADJECTIVE **3** A voice or other sound that is **harsh** sounds rough and unpleasant.

harvest **harvests** NOUN
Harvest is the time when farmers cut and gather their ripe crop.

has VERB
Has is a present tense form of **have**.

hat **hats** NOUN
A **hat** is a head covering for wearing outside.

hatch **hatches, hatching, hatched** VERB
When a baby bird, insect or other animal **hatches**, it comes out of its egg by breaking the shell.

hate **hates, hating, hated** VERB
If you **hate** something, you have a strong feeling of dislike for it.

haul **hauls, hauling, hauled** VERB
To **haul** something means to move it with a long steady pull.

haunted ADJECTIVE
A place that is **haunted** is often visited by a ghost.

have **has, having, had**
VERB **1** **Have** can be used with other verbs to form the past tense. *I **have** already seen that film.*
VERB **2** If you **have** something, you own or possess it. *We **have** two tickets for the football match.*
VERB **3** If you **have** to do something, you must do it.

haven't VERB
Haven't is a contraction of **have not**.

hawk **hawks** NOUN
A **hawk** is a large bird of prey that eats small animals.

hay NOUN
Hay is grass which has been cut and dried to feed animals.

he PRONOUN
He is used to refer to a man, boy or male animal that has already been mentioned.

head **heads, heading, headed**
NOUN **1** Your **head** is the part of your body which has your brain, eyes and mouth in it.
NOUN **2** The **head** of something is the top, start or most important end. *Our teacher sat at the **head** of the table.*
NOUN **3** The **head** of a group or organization is the person in charge.
VERB **4** If you **head** in a particular direction, you move that way.
VERB **5** To **head** a ball means to hit it with your head.

headache **headaches** NOUN
A **headache** is a pain in your head.

a
b
c
d
e
f
g
h
i
j
k
l
m
n
o
p
q
r
s
t
u
v
w
x
y
z

93

A
B
C
D
E
F
G
H
I
J
K
L
M
N
O
P
Q
R
S
T
U
V
W
X
Y
Z

heading **headings** NOUN
A **heading** is a title at the top of a piece of writing.

headlight **headlights** NOUN
The **headlights** on a motor vehicle are the large powerful lights at the front.

headline **headlines**
NOUN **1** A **headline** is the title of a newspaper article printed in large type.
NOUN **2** The **headlines** are the main points of the radio or television news.

headphones PLURAL NOUN
Headphones are a pair of small speakers that you wear over or in your ears to listen to a recording without other people hearing.

headquarters NOUN
The **headquarters** of an organization is the place where the leaders of the organization work.

head teacher **head teachers** NOUN
The **head teacher** is the teacher who is in charge of a school.

heal **heals, healing, healed** VERB
If something **heals**, it becomes healthy or normal again.

health NOUN
A person's **health** is how their body is, and whether they are well or ill.

healthy **healthier, healthiest**
ADJECTIVE **1** Someone who is **healthy** is well and not suffering from any illness.
ADJECTIVE **2** Something that is **healthy** is good for your health.

heap **heaps** NOUN
A **heap** is a lot of things piled up, usually rather untidily.

hear **hears, hearing, heard** VERB
When you **hear** sounds, you notice them by using your ears.

hearing NOUN
Hearing is the sense which makes it possible for you to be aware of sounds.

heart **hearts**
NOUN **1** Your **heart** is the organ that pumps the blood round inside your body.
NOUN **2** A **heart** is a shape like a heart, used especially as a symbol of love.

heat **heats, heating, heated**
NOUN **1** **Heat** is warmth.
VERB **2** To **heat** something means to raise its temperature.

heather NOUN
Heather is a plant with small purple or white flowers that grows wild on hills and moorland.

heaven NOUN
Heaven is a place of happiness where God is believed to live.

heavy **heavier, heaviest** ADJECTIVE
Something that is **heavy** weighs a lot or weighs more than usual.

Hebrew NOUN
Hebrew is an ancient language now spoken in Israel, where it is the official language.

hedge **hedges** NOUN
A **hedge** is a row of bushes growing close together.

hedgehog hedgehogs NOUN

A **hedgehog** is a small animal with sharp spikes all over its back. It defends itself by rolling up into a ball.

heel heels

NOUN **1** Your **heel** is the back part of your foot.
NOUN **2** The **heel** of a shoe is the raised part underneath, at the back.

height heights

NOUN **1** The **height** of a person is how tall they are.

NOUN **2** The **height** of an object is its measurement from bottom to top.

held VERB

Held is the past tense of **hold**.

helicopter helicopters NOUN

A **helicopter** is an aircraft with large blades which turn very quickly. It can take off vertically, hover and fly.

hello INTERJECTION

You say **hello** to someone when you meet them.

helmet helmets NOUN

A **helmet** is a hard hat that you wear to protect your head.

help helps, helping, helped

VERB **1** To **help** someone means to make something better or easier for them.
VERB **2** If you **help yourself** to something, you take it. *Help yourself to sandwiches.*
VERB **3** If you can't **help** something, you cannot control it or change it. *I can't help feeling sorry for him.*
helpful ADJECTIVE

helping helpings NOUN

A **helping** of food is the amount of it that you get in a single serving.

helpless ADJECTIVE

Someone who is **helpless** cannot cope on their own.

hem hems NOUN

The **hem** of a piece of material is the part that is folded over and sewn.

hemisphere hemispheres NOUN

A **hemisphere** is one half of a sphere. It can also be half of the Earth.
See Solid shapes on page 266

hen hens

NOUN **1** A **hen** is a female chicken.
NOUN **2** A **hen** can also be any female bird.

heptagon heptagons NOUN

A **heptagon** is a flat shape with seven straight sides.
See Colours and shapes on page 266

her

PRONOUN **1** You use **her** to refer to a woman, girl or any female animal that has already been mentioned. *I like Nina. I often play with her.*
ADJECTIVE **2** You also use **her** to show that something belongs to a particular female. *My little sister won't eat her food.*

herb herbs NOUN

A **herb** is a plant whose leaves are used as a medicine or to flavour food.

herd herds NOUN

A **herd** is a large group of animals of one kind that live together.
See Collective nouns on page 268

here ADVERB

You say **here** to mean the place where you are. *I'll stand here and wait.*
here and there PHRASE **Here and there** means in various places. *Bits of paper were lying here and there on the floor.*

a
b
c
d
e
f
g
h
i
j
k
l
m
n
o
p
q
r
s
t
u
v
w
x
y
z

A B C D E F G H I J K L M N O P Q R S T U V W X Y Z

hero **heroes**

NOUN **1** A **hero** is a man or boy who has done something brave and good.

NOUN **2** The **hero** of a story is the man or boy that the story is about.

See **heroine**

heroine **heroines**

NOUN **1** A **heroine** is a woman or girl who has done something brave and good.

NOUN **2** The **heroine** of a story is the woman or girl that the story is about.

See **hero**

heron **herons** NOUN

A **heron** is a bird that lives near water and eats fish.

herring **herrings** NOUN

A **herring** is an edible sea fish.

herself PRONOUN

If a girl or woman does something **herself**, no one else does it. *The baby pulled **herself** up.*

hesitate **hesitates, hesitating, hesitated**
VERB

If you **hesitate**, you pause while you are doing something, or just before you do it.

hexagon **hexagons** NOUN

A **hexagon** is a flat shape with six straight sides.

hexagonal ADJECTIVE

See Colours and shapes on page 266

hibernate **hibernates, hibernating, hibernated** VERB

When certain animals, such as bears, **hibernate**, they spend the winter in a sleep-like state.

hide **hides, hiding, hid, hidden**

VERB **1** If you **hide** somewhere, you go where you cannot be seen.

VERB **2** If you **hide** something, you put it in a place where it cannot be seen.

hidden ADJECTIVE

high **higher, highest**

ADJECTIVE **1** Something that is **high** is a long way from the bottom to the top. *The wall round the garden is quite **high**.*

ADJECTIVE OR ADVERB **2** If something is **high**, it is a long way up. *There was an aeroplane **high** above her.*

hill **hills** NOUN

A **hill** is a rounded area of land which is higher than the land surrounding it.

him PRONOUN

You use **him** to refer to a man, boy or any male animal that has already been mentioned. *James asked me to ring **him** back.*

himself PRONOUN

If a boy or man does something **himself**, no one else does it. *Rahul hurt **himself** quite badly.*

Hindu **Hindus** NOUN

A **Hindu** is a person who believes in Hinduism, an Indian religion which has many gods. Hindus believe that people have another life on earth after death.

hinge **hinges** NOUN

Hinges are pieces of metal, wood or plastic that are used to hold a door or lid so that it can swing freely.

hint **hints, hinting, hinted**

NOUN **1** A **hint** is a suggestion, clue or helpful piece of advice.

VERB **2** If you **hint**, or **hint at** something, you suggest it in a way that is not obvious. *I **hinted** that I would like a bicycle for my birthday.*

hip **hips** NOUN

Your **hips** are the two parts at the sides of your body between your waist and your upper legs.

hippopotamus **hippopotamuses** or **hippopotami** NOUN
A **hippopotamus** is a large African animal with thick skin and short legs. It lives in herds on the banks of large rivers, and spends a lot of time in the water. It is often called a **hippo** for short.

hire **hires, hiring, hired** VERB
If you **hire** something, you pay money so that you can use it for a time.

his ADJECTIVE OR PRONOUN
You use **his** to show that something belongs to a man, boy or any male animal. *Robert combed **his** hair.*

hiss **hisses, hissing, hissed** VERB
To **hiss** means to make a long "sss" sound.

historical ADJECTIVE
Historical stories are stories about things that happened in the past.

history **histories** NOUN
History is a study or record of the past.

hit **hits, hitting, hit** VERB
If you **hit** something, you touch it quickly and hard.

hive **hives** NOUN
A **hive** is a house for bees, made so that the beekeeper can collect their honey. See **beehive**

hoard **hoards, hoarding, hoarded**
VERB **1** If you **hoard** things, you save or store them even though they may no longer be useful.
NOUN **2** A **hoard** is a store of things that has been saved or hidden.

hoarse **hoarser, hoarsest** ADJECTIVE
A **hoarse** voice sounds rough.

hobby **hobbies** NOUN
A **hobby** is something you enjoy doing in your spare time, such as collecting stamps or bird-watching.

hockey NOUN
Hockey is a game in which two teams use long sticks with curved ends to try and hit a small ball into the other team's goal.

hold **holds, holding, held**
VERB **1** When you **hold** something, you keep it in your hand or arms.
VERB **2** If something **holds** a particular amount of something, it can contain that amount. *This jug **holds** one litre.*

hole **holes** NOUN
A **hole** is an opening or space in something. *The dog buried his bone in a **hole** in the garden.*

Holi NOUN
Holi is a Hindu festival celebrated in spring.

holiday **holidays** NOUN
A **holiday** is time away from school or work.

hollow ADJECTIVE
Something that is **hollow** has a space inside it. *The owl lived in a **hollow** tree trunk.*

holly NOUN
Holly is an evergreen tree with prickly leaves. It often has bright red berries in winter.

home **homes** NOUN
Your **home** is the place where you live and feel you belong.

home page **home pages** NOUN
On the Internet, a person or organization's **home page** is the main page of information about them.

homesick ADJECTIVE
If you are **homesick**, you are sad because you are away from home.

A
B
C
D
E
F
G
H
I
J
K
L
M
N
O
P
Q
R
S
T
U
V
W
X
Y
Z

homework NOUN

Homework is school work that children do at home.

honest ADJECTIVE

Someone who is **honest** tells the truth and can be trusted.

honey NOUN

Honey is a sweet sticky food that is made by bees.

hood hoods NOUN

A **hood** is a part of a coat or jacket that you can pull over your head.

hoof hooves or hoofs NOUN

The **hoof** of an animal such as a horse is the hard bony part of its foot.

hook hooks NOUN

A **hook** is a curved piece of metal or plastic that is used for catching, holding or hanging things, for example a picture hook.

hoop hoops NOUN

A **hoop** is a large ring, often used as a toy.

hoot hoots, hooting, hooted

VERB **1** To **hoot** means to make a long "oo" sound like an owl.
VERB **2** If a car horn **hoots**, it makes a loud honking noise.

hop hops, hopping, hopped

VERB **1** If you **hop**, you jump on one foot.
VERB **2** When animals or birds **hop**, they jump with two feet together.

hope hopes, hoping, hoped VERB

If you **hope** that something will happen, you want it to happen.

hopeful ADJECTIVE

If you are **hopeful**, you are fairly sure that something you want to happen will happen.

hopeless

ADJECTIVE **1** You say a situation is **hopeless** when it is very bad and you do not think it will get better.
ADJECTIVE **2** If somebody is **hopeless** at doing something, they cannot do it well. *I'm hopeless at arithmetic.*

horizon horizons NOUN

The **horizon** is the line in the far distance where the sky seems to touch the land or the sea.

horizontal ADJECTIVE

Something that is **horizontal** is level, like the horizon.
See **vertical**

horn horns

NOUN **1 Horns** are the hard pointed growths on the heads of animals such as goats.
NOUN **2** A **horn** is a musical instrument made of brass.
NOUN **3** On vehicles, a **horn** makes a loud noise as a warning.

horrible ADJECTIVE

Someone or something that is **horrible** is awful or very unpleasant.
horribly ADVERB

horror NOUN
Horror is a strong feeling of fear or disgust.

horse **horses** NOUN
A **horse** is a large animal which people can ride. Horses are also used for pulling things like carts.

horseshoe **horseshoes** NOUN
A **horseshoe** is a piece of metal shaped like a U. It is fixed under a horse's hoof, to protect it.

hose **hoses** NOUN
A **hose** is a long tube that sprays water.

hospital **hospitals** NOUN
A **hospital** is a place where sick and injured people are cared for.

hot **hotter, hottest**
ADJECTIVE **1** Something that is **hot** has a high temperature.
ADJECTIVE **2** If you feel **hot**, you feel too warm to be comfortable.
ADJECTIVE **3** You say food is **hot** if it has a strong taste caused by spices. *This curry is too **hot** for me.*

hotel **hotels** NOUN
A **hotel** is a building where people pay to stay, usually for a few nights.

hour **hours** NOUN
An **hour** is a period of 60 minutes. There are 24 hours in a day.

house **houses** NOUN
A **house** is a building where people live.

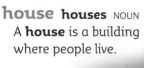

hover **hovers, hovering, hovered** VERB
When a bird or aircraft **hovers**, it stays in the same place in the air.

how
ADVERB **1** You can use **how** in questions to ask about the way something is done or known. *How did you know that?*
ADVERB **2** **How** can also be used to ask about a measurement or quantity. *How much is the fare to the town centre?*
ADVERB **3** **How** is often used in greetings. *How are you?*

however ADVERB
You use **however** when you are adding a comment that is surprising after what you have just said. *I was sure I was going to win the race. **However**, a younger girl came first.*

howl **howls, howling, howled** VERB
To **howl** means to make a long, loud cry. *The dog **howls** when I sing.*

hug **hugs, hugging, hugged** VERB
If you **hug** someone, you put your arms round them and hold them close.

huge ADJECTIVE
Something that is **huge** is extremely big.

hum **hums, humming, hummed** VERB
If you **hum**, you sing with your lips closed.

human **humans** NOUN
A **human** is a person.

humour
NOUN **1** **Humour** is the quality of being funny.
NOUN **2** **Humour** is also the ability to be amused by certain things. *She's got a peculiar sense of **humour**.*

hump **humps** NOUN
A **hump** is a large lump on the back of an animal such as a camel, which is used for storing fat and water.

hundred **hundreds** NOUN
A **hundred** is the number 100.

hung VERB
Hung is the past tense of **hang**.

a
b
c
d
e
f
g
h
i
j
k
l
m
n
o
p
q
r
s
t
u
v
w
x
y
z

A
B
C
D
E
F
G
H
I
J
K
L
M
N
O
P
Q
R
S
T
U
V
W
X
Y
Z

hungry **hungrier, hungriest** ADJECTIVE
When you are **hungry**, you want to eat.
hungrily ADVERB

hunt **hunts, hunting, hunted**
VERB **1** To **hunt** means to chase wild animals to kill them for food or sport.
VERB **2** If you **hunt** for something, you look for it.

hurricane **hurricanes** NOUN
A **hurricane** is a storm with very high winds.

hurry **hurries, hurrying, hurried** VERB
If you **hurry** somewhere, you go there as quickly as you can.

hurt **hurts, hurting, hurt**
VERB **1** If part of your body **hurts**, you feel pain.
VERB **2** If you have been **hurt**, you have been injured.
ADJECTIVE **3** If someone feels **hurt**, they feel unhappy because someone has been unkind to them.

husband **husbands** NOUN
A woman's **husband** is the man she is married to.

hut **huts** NOUN
A **hut** is a small simple building with one or two rooms.

hutch **hutches** NOUN
A **hutch** is a cage made of wood and wire netting. Pets such as rabbits are kept in hutches.

hygiene NOUN
Hygiene is keeping yourself and your surroundings clean, especially to stop the spread of disease.

hymn **hymns** NOUN
A **hymn** is a Christian song in praise of God.

hyphen **hyphens** NOUN
A **hyphen** is a punctuation mark (-) used to join together words or parts of words, for example "left-handed".
*See **Punctuation** on page 270*

Ii

I PRONOUN
You use **I** to talk about yourself. *I like ice cream.*

ice **ices, icing, iced**
NOUN **1 Ice** is water that has frozen solid.
VERB **2** If you **ice** cakes, you cover them with icing.

iceberg **icebergs** NOUN
An **iceberg** is a large mass of ice floating in the sea.

ice cream **ice creams**
NOUN
Ice cream is a very cold sweet-tasting creamy food.
See Other foods on page 261

ice skate **ice skates** NOUN
An **ice skate** is a boot with a metal blade fixed underneath. You wear it when you skate on ice.

icicle **icicles** NOUN
An **icicle** is a pointed piece of ice which hangs from roofs, or wherever water has been dripping and freezing.

icing NOUN
Icing is a mixture of powdered sugar and water or egg whites. It is used to cover cakes as a decoration.

icon **icons** NOUN
If you describe something or someone as an **icon**, you mean that they are important as a symbol of something.

ICT NOUN
ICT is an abbreviation of **Information and Communication Technology**. It is the use of computers, telephones, television and radio to store, organize and give out information.

icy **icier, iciest** ADJECTIVE
Something which is **icy** has ice on it, or is very cold. *Be careful; the road is **icy**.*

idea **ideas**
NOUN **1** If you have an **idea**, you suddenly think of a way of doing something.
NOUN **2** An **idea** is a picture in your mind.

ideal ADJECTIVE
The **ideal** person or thing is the best one possible for the situation.

identical ADJECTIVE
Things that are **identical** are exactly the same in every detail.

idle **idler, idlest** ADJECTIVE
An **idle** person is someone who does not do very much.

if CONJUNCTION
You use **if** to talk about things that might happen, or that might have happened. *You can watch TV **if** you do your homework first.*

a
b
c
d
e
f
g
h
i
j
k
l
m
n
o
p
q
r
s
t
u
v
w
x
y
z

A
B
C
D
E
F
G
H
I
J
K
L
M
N
O
P
Q
R
S
T
U
V
W
X
Y
Z

igloo **igloos** NOUN
An **igloo** is a dome-shaped house built out of blocks of snow.

ignore **ignores, ignoring, ignored** VERB
If you **ignore** someone, you deliberately take no notice of them.

ill ADJECTIVE
Someone who is **ill** has something wrong with their health.

illness **illnesses** NOUN
An **illness** is something like a cold or measles that people can suffer from.

illustrate **illustrates, illustrating, illustrated** VERB
If you **illustrate** something, you add pictures to it.

illustration **illustrations** NOUN
An **illustration** is a picture or diagram in a book or magazine.

I'm
I'm is a contraction of **I am**.

imaginary ADJECTIVE
Something that is **imaginary** is not real. It is only in your mind. *She has **imaginary** talks with famous people.*

imagination NOUN
Your **imagination** is your ability to think of ideas, or to form pictures in your mind.

imagine
imagines, imagining, imagined
VERB
When you **imagine** something, you form a picture of it in

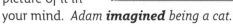

your mind. *Adam **imagined** being a cat.*

imam **imams** NOUN
An **imam** is a person who leads a group in prayer in a mosque.

imitate **imitates, imitating, imitated** VERB
If you **imitate** someone, you copy the way they speak or behave.

imitation **imitations** NOUN
An **imitation** is a copy of something else.

immediately ADVERB
If something happens **immediately**, it happens right away.

impatient ADJECTIVE
Someone who is **impatient** does not like to be kept waiting.

important
ADJECTIVE **1** If someone says something is **important**, they mean it matters a lot.
ADJECTIVE **2** Someone who is **important** has a lot of power in a particular group.

impossible ADJECTIVE
Something that is **impossible** cannot be done.

impressive ADJECTIVE
If something is **impressive**, people admire it, usually because it is large or important.

imprison **imprisons, imprisoning, imprisoned** VERB
If someone is **imprisoned**, they are locked up, usually in a prison.

improve **improves, improving, improved** VERB
If something **improves**, it gets better.

improvement **improvements** NOUN
An **improvement** is a change in something that makes it better.

in
PREPOSITION **1** You use **in** to say where something is, or where it is going. *Put it **in** the fridge.*
PREPOSITION **2** You also use **in** to say when something should happen. *I'll be home **in** 20 minutes.*
ADVERB **3** You use **in** to mean at home. *Is anybody **in**?*

inch **inches** NOUN
An **inch** is a unit of length equal to about two and a half centimetres. There are 12 inches to a foot.

include **includes, including, included** VERB
If you **include** something in a whole thing, you make it part of the whole thing. *Batteries are included.*

increase **increases, increasing, increased** VERB **1** If something **increases**, it becomes greater.
NOUN **2** An **increase** is a rise in the number, level or amount of something.

index **indexes** NOUN
An **index** is an alphabetical list at the back of a book that helps you find the things you want to read about.

individual ADJECTIVE
Individual means to do with one particular person, rather than a whole group.

indoors ADVERB
If you are **indoors**, you are inside a building.

industry NOUN
Industry is the work involved in making things in factories.

infant **infants** NOUN
An **infant** is a baby or young child.

influence **influences** NOUN
An **influence** is the effect that someone or something has on you, that can change the way you think or behave. *That boy is a bad influence on you.*

informal
ADJECTIVE **1 Informal** means relaxed. You usually speak or behave in this way when you are with people you know well.
ADJECTIVE **2** In a dictionary, a word shown as **informal** is more suitable for everyday talk than it is for writing.

information NOUN
If someone gives you **information** about something, they tell you about it.

infuriate **infuriates, infuriating, infuriated** VERB
If someone or something **infuriates** you, they make you extremely angry.

ingredient **ingredients** NOUN
Ingredients are the things that are used to make something, especially in cookery.

inhabit **inhabits, inhabiting, inhabited** VERB
If you **inhabit** a place, you live there.

inhabitant **inhabitants** NOUN
The **inhabitants** of a place are the people who live there.

initial **initials** NOUN
An **initial** is the first letter of a name. *David Hunt's initials are D.H.*

injection **injections** NOUN
If a doctor or nurse gives you an **injection**, they put medicine into your body with a special needle.

injure **injures, injuring, injured** VERB
If something **injures** a person or animal, it damages part of their body.
injury NOUN

ink **inks** NOUN
Ink is the coloured liquid that is used for writing and printing.

a
b
c
d
e
f
g
h
i
j
k
l
m
n
o
p
q
r
s
t
u
v
w
x
y
z

103

inland ADVERB

If you go **inland**, you go away from the coast towards the middle of a country.

inn **inns** NOUN

An **inn** is a small hotel.

innocent ADJECTIVE

Someone who is **innocent** has not done anything wrong.

insect **insects** NOUN

An **insect** is a small animal with six legs and usually wings. Ants, flies, butterflies and beetles are all insects.

See Insects on page 264

insert **inserts, inserting, inserted** VERB

If you **insert** an object into something, you put it into it. *She **inserted** the key in the lock.*

inside ADVERB, PREPOSITION OR ADJECTIVE

Inside means in something. *It was raining so they had to play **inside**... It was very cold **inside** the church... He hid his money in an **inside** pocket.*

insist **insists, insisting, insisted** VERB

If you **insist** on doing something, you refuse to give in.

inspect **inspects, inspecting, inspected** VERB

If you **inspect** something, you look at every part of it carefully.

inspire **inspires, inspiring, inspired** VERB

If something **inspires** you, it gives you new ideas and enthusiasm.

instant ADJECTIVE

Something **instant** happens immediately. *The new band was an **instant** success.*

instead ADVERB

Instead means in place of. *Take the stairs **instead** of the lift.*

instruction **instructions**

NOUN **1** An **instruction** is something that someone tells you to do.

PLURAL NOUN **2 Instructions** are words that tell you how to do something.

instrument **instruments**

NOUN **1** An **instrument** is a tool that is used to do a particular job.

NOUN **2** An **instrument** is also an object such as a piano or guitar, that you play to make music.

insult **insults, insulting, insulted** VERB

If you **insult** someone, you offend them by being rude to them.

intelligent ADJECTIVE

A person who is **intelligent** can understand, learn and think things out quickly and well.

intend **intends, intending, intended** VERB

If you **intend** to do something, you have decided to do it or plan to do it.

interactive ADJECTIVE

If a computer is **interactive**, information can pass in both directions between itself and the person using it.

interest **interests** NOUN

If you have an **interest** in something, you want to learn or hear more about it.

interesting ADJECTIVE

If something is **interesting**, it attracts or keeps your attention.

interfere interferes, interfering, interfered VERB
If something **interferes** with something else, it gets in the way. *Don't let TV interfere with your homework.*

interjection interjections NOUN
An **interjection** is a word you say suddenly to show surprise, pain or anger, such as "Ouch!" or "Wow!".

international ADJECTIVE
If something is **international**, it involves different countries. *This is an important international match.*

Internet NOUN
The **Internet** is a worldwide communication system that people use through computers.

interpret interprets, interpreting, interpreted VERB
If you **interpret** what someone says or does, you say what it means.

interrupt interrupts, interrupting, interrupted
VERB **1** If you **interrupt** someone, you start talking before they have finished what they were saying.
VERB **2** If you **interrupt** what someone is doing, you make them stop doing it for a while.

interval intervals NOUN
An **interval** is a short break during a play or concert.

interview interviews, interviewing, interviewed VERB
If you **interview** someone, you ask them questions about themselves.

into
PREPOSITION **1** If you go **into** something, you go inside it. *Come into the house.*
PREPOSITION **2** If you bump or crash **into** something, you bump or crash against it.

introduce introduces, introducing, introduced VERB
If you **introduce** one person to another, you tell them each other's name so that they can get to know each other.

introduction introductions NOUN
An **introduction** is a piece of writing at the beginning of a book, which usually tells you what it is about.

invent invents, inventing, invented
VERB **1** If you **invent** a story or an excuse, you make it up.
VERB **2** If someone **invents** something, such as a machine or an instrument, they are the first person to think of it.

invention inventions NOUN
An **invention** is something that is a completely new idea. *She is working on an invention that will help people.*

inventor inventors NOUN
An **inventor** is someone who thinks of new ideas and tries them out to see if they will work.

inverse NOUN
If you turn something upside down or back to front, you have its **inverse**. *Subtraction is the inverse of addition.*

inverted commas PLURAL NOUN
Inverted commas are punctuation marks (" ") or (' ') used in writing to show where speech begins and ends.

investigate investigates, investigating, investigated VERB
If you **investigate** something, you try to find out all the facts about it.

a
b
c
d
e
f
g
h
i
j
k
l
m
n
o
p
q
r
s
t
u
v
w
x
y
z

A
B
C
D
E
F
G
H
I
J
K
L
M
N
O
P
Q
R
S
T
U
V
W
X
Y
Z

invisible ADJECTIVE
If something is **invisible**, it cannot be seen. For example, germs are invisible unless you use a microscope.

invitation invitations NOUN
When you get an **invitation**, someone asks you to come to something such as a party.

invite invites, inviting, invited VERB
If you **invite** someone, you ask them to come to your home, or a party.

involve involves, involving, involved VERB
If a situation **involves** someone or something, it includes or concerns them. *This project will involve a lot of work.*

iron irons
NOUN **1 Iron** is a hard metal used to make steel, and things like gates.
NOUN **2** An **iron** is an object with a handle and a flat base. You can heat it and use it to smooth clothes.

irritable ADJECTIVE
If you are feeling **irritable**, you could easily become annoyed.

irritate irritates, irritating, irritated
VERB **1** If something **irritates** you, it annoys you.
VERB **2** If something **irritates** part of your body, it makes it sore or itchy.

is VERB
Is is a present tense form of **be**. *She is six years old.*
See **be**

Islam NOUN
Islam is the Muslim religion, which teaches that there is only one God, Allah. Mohammed is his prophet.
Islamic ADJECTIVE

island islands NOUN
An **island** is a piece of land completely surrounded by water.

ISP ISPs NOUN
An **ISP** is an abbreviation for **Internet service provider**. It is a company that provides access to the Internet.

it PRONOUN
You use **it** to talk about a thing or an animal. *This is a good book – have you read it?*

IT NOUN
IT is an abbreviation of **information technology**. It is the use of computers to store and analyse information.

italics PLURAL NOUN
Italics are letters printed in a special sloping way. *This sentence is in italics.*

itch itches, itching, itched VERB
When your skin **itches**, it makes you feel that you want to scratch it.

it's
It's is a contraction of **it is**.

its ADJECTIVE
You use **its** to show that something belongs to something that has already been mentioned. *The lion lifted its head.*

itself PRONOUN
If an animal does something **itself**, no one else does it. *The cat washed itself.*

ivory NOUN
Ivory is the hard smooth creamy material that comes from the tusks of some animals, such as elephants.

ivy NOUN
Ivy is an evergreen plant which creeps along the ground and up walls.

Jj

jab jabs NOUN
A **jab** is an injection to prevent illness.

jacket jackets NOUN
A **jacket** is a short coat.

jagged ADJECTIVE
Something **jagged** has an uneven edge with sharp points on it.

jail jails NOUN
A **jail** is a building where criminals are locked up.

jam jams, jamming, jammed
NOUN **1 Jam** is a food that is made by cooking fruit with a lot of sugar. You usually spread jam on bread.
See Other foods on page 261

NOUN **2** A **jam** is when there are so many people or vehicles in a place it is impossible for them to move.
VERB **3** If something **jams**, it becomes fixed and will not move.

January NOUN
January is the first month of the year. It has 31 days.

jar jars NOUN
A **jar** is a glass container with a wide top used for storing food.

jaw jaws NOUN
Your **jaw** is the bone in which your teeth are set. Some animals, like crocodiles, have very large jaws.

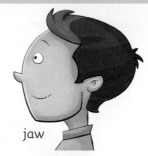
jaw

jealous ADJECTIVE
Someone who is **jealous** feels upset because someone else has what they want.

jeans PLURAL NOUN
Jeans are trousers that are usually made with a strong cotton cloth.

jelly jellies NOUN
Jelly is a clear sweet food that wobbles when you move it.

jerk jerks, jerking, jerked VERB
If something **jerks**, it moves suddenly and sharply.

jersey jerseys NOUN
A **jersey** is a knitted piece of clothing for the upper part of your body.

jet jets
NOUN **1** A **jet** is a stream of liquid, gas or flame forced out under pressure.
NOUN **2** A **jet** is also a plane that is able to fly very fast.

Jew Jews NOUN
A **Jew** is a person who follows the religion of Judaism.

jewel jewels NOUN
A **jewel** is a precious stone, such as a diamond or a ruby, used to make things like rings and necklaces.

jewellery NOUN
Jewellery is the name for ornaments that people can wear, like rings and necklaces. It is often made of valuable metal such as gold or silver and may be decorated with precious stones.

Jewish ADJECTIVE
Jewish means to do with Judaism or Jews.

a b c d e f g h i j k l m n o p q r s t u v w x y z

A B C D E F G H I J K L M N O P Q R S T U V W X Y Z

jigsaw jigsaws NOUN

A **jigsaw** is a puzzle consisting of a picture on cardboard. The picture has been cut up into small pieces that have to be put together again.

job jobs

NOUN **1** A **job** is the work that someone does to earn money.

NOUN **2** A **job** can also be anything that has to be done. *There are always plenty of jobs to do when I get home.*

jog jogs, jogging, jogged

VERB **1** To **jog** means to run slowly, often as a form of exercise.

VERB **2** If you **jog** something, you knock it slightly so that it shakes or moves.

VERB **3** If someone or something **jogs** your memory, they remind you of something.

join joins, joining, joined

VERB **1** When two things **join**, they come together.

VERB **2** If you **join** a club or organization, you become a member of it.

NOUN **3** A **join** is a place where two things are fastened together. *Look! You can't see the join.*

joint joints

NOUN **1** A **joint** is a part of your body, such as your elbow or knee, where two bones meet and are able to move.

NOUN **2** A **joint** can also be any place where two things are fastened together.

NOUN **3** A **joint** is also a large piece of meat for roasting.

joke jokes NOUN

A **joke** is something that you say or do to make people laugh.

jolt jolts, jolting, jolted

VERB **1** To **jolt** something means to move or shake it roughly and violently.

NOUN **2** A **jolt** is a sudden jerky movement.

NOUN **3** A **jolt** is also an unpleasant shock or surprise.

jot jots, jotting, jotted VERB

If you **jot** something down, you write it quickly in the form of a short note.

journal journals

NOUN **1** A **journal** is a diary which someone keeps regularly.

NOUN **2** A **journal** is also a magazine that deals with a particular subject, for example a medical journal.

journalist journalists NOUN

A **journalist** is a person whose job is to gather news and write about it for a newspaper or magazine, or present it on television or radio.

journey journeys NOUN

If you go on a **journey**, you travel from one place to another.

joy NOUN

Joy is a feeling of great happiness.

joyful ADJECTIVE

Judaism NOUN

Judaism is the religion of the Jewish people. It is based on the Old Testament of the Bible, and the Talmud or book of laws and traditions.

judge judges

NOUN **1** In law, a **judge** is a person who has the power to decide how the law should be used.

NOUN **2** The **judge** of a competition is a person who has been asked to choose the winner.

jug jugs NOUN

A **jug** is a container with a lip or spout used for holding or serving liquids.

juggle juggles, juggling, juggled VERB

If you **juggle** with objects, you keep throwing them into the air and catching them one at a time, so that there are several in the air at once.

juggler NOUN

juice NOUN

Juice is the liquid that comes from fruit such as oranges when you squeeze them.

juicy juicier, juiciest ADJECTIVE

Juicy food has a lot of juice in it.

July NOUN

July is the seventh month of the year. It has 31 days.

jumble jumbles, jumbling, jumbled

NOUN **1** **Jumble** is an untidy muddle of things.

NOUN **2** **Jumble** is also things like clothes and books that people no longer want.

VERB **3** If you **jumble** things, you mix them up untidily.

jump jumps, jumping, jumped

VERB **1** When you **jump**, you spring off the ground using your leg muscles.

VERB **2** If you **jump** something, you spring off the ground and move over or across it. *He jumped a low wall.*

VERB **3** If something or somebody makes you **jump**, you make a sudden sharp movement of surprise.

jumper jumpers NOUN

A **jumper** is a knitted piece of clothing for the top part of the body.

junction junctions NOUN

A **junction** is a place where roads or railway lines meet or cross.

June NOUN

June is the sixth month of the year. It has 30 days.

jungle jungles NOUN

A **jungle** is a dense tropical forest.

junior ADJECTIVE

Junior means younger, or less important.

junk NOUN

Junk is old or second-hand articles that are sold cheaply or thrown away.

just

ADVERB **1** If you say that something has **just** happened, you mean it happened a short time ago.

ADVERB **2** If you say you are **just** going to do something, you mean you will do it very soon.

justice NOUN

Justice is fairness in the way that people are treated.

justify justifies, justifying, justified VERB

If you **justify** an action or idea, you explain why it is reasonable or necessary.

a
b
c
d
e
f
g
h
i
j
k
l
m
n
o
p
q
r
s
t
u
v
w
x
y
z

Kk

kangaroo kangaroos NOUN

A **kangaroo** is a large Australian animal which moves forward by jumping on its back legs.

keen keener, keenest ADJECTIVE

Someone who is **keen** to do something wants to do it very much.

keep keeps, keeping, kept

VERB **1** If you **keep** something for somebody, you save it for them.

VERB **2** If you **keep** doing something, you do it over and over again.

VERB **3** If something **keeps** you a certain way, you stay that way because of it. *That dog is keeping me awake.*

kennel kennels NOUN

A **kennel** is a small house for a dog.

kept VERB

Kept is the past tense of **keep**.

kerb kerbs NOUN

The **kerb** is the edge of the pavement.

ketchup NOUN

Ketchup is a cold tomato sauce.

kettle kettles NOUN

A **kettle** is a covered container used to boil water.

key keys

NOUN **1** A **key** is a specially shaped piece of metal that fits into a lock.

NOUN **2** The **keys** on something like a computer keyboard or a piano are the buttons that you press to use it.

ADJECTIVE **3 Key** words or sentences are an important part of a piece of text.

keyboard keyboards NOUN

A **keyboard** is a row of buttons called keys on a piano or computer.

kick kicks, kicking, kicked VERB

If you **kick** something, you hit it with your foot.

kid kids

NOUN **1** A **kid** is a young goat.
See Young animals on page 265
NOUN **2** INFORMAL A **kid** is a child.

kidnap kidnaps, kidnapping, kidnapped VERB

If someone **kidnaps** another person, they take them away by force.

kill kills, killing, killed VERB

To **kill** someone or something means to cause them to die.

kilogram kilograms NOUN

A **kilogram** (kg) is a unit of mass and weight. One kilogram, or kilo, is equal to 1000 grams.

kilometre kilometres NOUN

A **kilometre** is a unit of distance equal to 1000 metres.

kind kinds; kinder, kindest

NOUN **1** If you talk about a **kind** of object, you mean a sort of object.

ADJECTIVE **2** Someone who is **kind** behaves in a gentle, caring way.

kindness NOUN

king kings NOUN

A **king** is a man who rules a country. Kings are not chosen by the people, but are born into a royal family.

kingdom kingdoms

NOUN **1** A **kingdom** is a country or region that is ruled by a king or queen.

NOUN **2** The animal **kingdom** is all the animals in the world. *This creature is the largest in the animal kingdom.*

kiss **kisses, kissing, kissed** VERB
If you **kiss** someone, you touch them with your lips.

kit **kits** NOUN
A **kit** is a set of things that are used for a particular purpose. *Have you seen my first aid kit?*

kitchen **kitchens** NOUN
A **kitchen** is a room that is used for cooking and washing-up.

kite **kites**
NOUN **1** A **kite** is a frame covered with paper or cloth which you fly in the sky at the end of a piece of string.
NOUN **2** In maths, a **kite** is a flat shape with four sides, with two pairs of the same length and none of the sides parallel to each other.
See Colours and shapes on page 266

kitten **kittens** NOUN
A **kitten** is a young cat.
See Young animals on page 265

kiwi **kiwis** NOUN
A **kiwi** is a type of bird found in New Zealand. Kiwis cannot fly.

knee **knees** NOUN
Your **knee** is the joint where your leg bends.

kneel **kneels, kneeling, kneeled** or **knelt** VERB
When you **kneel**, you bend your legs until your knees are touching the ground.

knew VERB
Knew is the past tense of **know**.

knickers PLURAL NOUN
Knickers are pants worn by women and girls.

knife **knives** NOUN
A **knife** is a sharp metal tool that you use to cut things.

knit **knits, knitting, knitted** VERB
If you **knit**, you make something from wool using two long needles.

knob **knobs**
NOUN **1** A **knob** is a round handle on a door or a drawer.
NOUN **2** A **knob** is also a round button on a piece of equipment such as a radio.

knock **knocks, knocking, knocked** VERB
If you **knock** on something, you hit it hard.

knot **knots** NOUN
A **knot** is a tie in something such as string or cloth.

know **knows, knowing, knew**
VERB **1** If you **know** a fact, you have it in your mind and do not need to learn it.
VERB **2** If you **know** somebody, you have met them before.

knowledge NOUN
Knowledge is all the facts and information that you know.

knuckle **knuckles** NOUN
Your **knuckles** are the bony parts where your fingers join your hands and where your fingers bend.

koala **koalas** NOUN
A **koala** is an Australian animal that looks like a small bear with grey fur.

Koran NOUN
The **Koran** is the holy book of Islam.

a
b
c
d
e
f
g
h
i
j
k
l
m
n
o
p
q
r
s
t
u
v
w
x
y
z

111

Ll

label **labels** NOUN
A **label** is a small notice that tells you what something is or gives you information. *Read the **label** on the medicine bottle.*

laboratory **laboratories** NOUN
A **laboratory** is a place where scientists work, using special equipment.

labour NOUN
Labour is hard work.

lace **laces**
NOUN **1 Lace** is a very fine decorated cloth made with a lot of holes in it.
NOUN **2 Laces** are cords that you use to fasten your shoes.

lack **lacks, lacking, lacked** VERB
If you **lack** something, you do not have it when you need it.

ladder **ladders** NOUN
A **ladder** is a wooden or metal frame used for climbing up things like walls or trees.

ladle **ladles** NOUN
A **ladle** is a big deep spoon with a long handle, which is used to serve soup.
ladle VERB

lady **ladies** NOUN
Lady is a polite name for a woman. *I think this **lady** was in front of me.*

ladybird **ladybirds** NOUN
A **ladybird** is a small round flying beetle with spots on its wings.
See Insects on page 264

laid VERB
Laid is the past tense of **lay**.

lain VERB
Lain is the past participle of **lie**.

lake **lakes** NOUN
A **lake** is a large area of fresh water with land all round it.

lamb **lambs** NOUN
A **lamb** is a young sheep.
See Young animals on page 265

lame ADJECTIVE
An animal which is **lame** cannot walk properly.

lamp **lamps** NOUN
A **lamp** is an object that gives light.

lamppost **lampposts** NOUN
A **lamppost** is a tall column in the street, with a lamp at the top.

land **lands, landing, landed**
NOUN **1 Land** is the part of the world that is solid, dry ground.
VERB **2** When an aircraft **lands**, it comes down from the air on to land or water.

landmark **landmarks** NOUN
A **landmark** is a building or a feature of the land that can be used to find out where you are.

landscape **landscapes** NOUN
A **landscape** is everything you can see when you look across an area of land.

lane **lanes**
NOUN **1** A **lane** is a narrow road, especially in the country.

NOUN **2** A **lane** is also part of a main road or motorway. It is marked with lines to guide drivers.

language languages NOUN
A **language** is the words that are used by the people of a country when they speak or write to each other.

lantern lanterns NOUN
A **lantern** is a lamp in a container. It has sides which the light can shine through but which stop the wind from blowing out the light.

lap laps, lapping, lapped
NOUN **1** Your **lap** is the flat area formed by the tops of your legs when you are sitting down.
VERB **2** When an animal **laps** up liquid, it drinks using its tongue to get the liquid into its mouth.

laptop laptops NOUN
A **laptop** is a portable computer small enough to fit on your lap.

large larger, largest ADJECTIVE
Something **large** is big.

larva larvae NOUN
A **larva** is an insect at an early stage of its life. It looks likes a short fat worm.

laser lasers NOUN
A **laser** is a machine which produces a narrow beam of light. Lasers are used for many different things, including medical operations.

last lasts, lasting, lasted
ADJECTIVE **1** The **last** thing or event is the most recent one. *I saw him last week.*
ADVERB **2** If something happens **last**, it happens after everything else. *I came last in the race.*
VERB **3** If something **lasts**, it continues to exist or happen. *Her speech lasted an hour.*
at last PHRASE If something happens **at last**, it happens after a long time.

late later, latest
ADJECTIVE OR ADVERB **1** If you are **late** arriving somewhere, you get there after the time you were supposed to.

ADJECTIVE OR ADVERB **2** **Late** means near the end of a period of time. *We had a picnic in the late afternoon.*

lately ADVERB
If something has happened **lately**, it happened not long ago. *Have you seen your cousin lately?*

laugh laughs, laughing, laughed VERB
When you **laugh**, you make the sound people make when they are happy or think something is funny.
laughter NOUN

launch launches, launching, launched
VERB **1** When a rocket or satellite is **launched**, it is sent into the sky.
VERB **2** To **launch** a ship means to send it into the water for the first time.

launderette launderettes NOUN
A **launderette** is a shop where people pay to use washing machines.

lava NOUN
Lava is a very hot, liquid rock which comes out of volcanoes.

lavatory lavatories
NOUN **1** A **lavatory** is a toilet.
NOUN **2** A **lavatory** is also the room where the lavatory is.

law laws NOUN
A **law** is a rule that is made by the government.

113

A
B
C
D
E
F
G
H
I
J
K
L
M
N
O
P
Q
R
S
T
U
V
W
X
Y
Z

lawn **lawns** NOUN
A **lawn** is an area of short grass in a garden or park.

lawnmower **lawnmowers** NOUN
A **lawnmower** is a machine for cutting the grass on lawns.

lawyer **lawyers** NOUN
A **lawyer** is a person who understands the law and can advise people about it.

lay **lays, laying, laid**
VERB **1** If you **lay** something somewhere, you put it there carefully.
VERB **2** If you **lay** the table, you put things like knives and forks on the table ready for a meal.
VERB **3** When a bird **lays** an egg, it produces the egg out of its body.

layer **layers** NOUN
A **layer** is a single thickness of something that lies on top of or underneath something else.

layout **layouts** NOUN
The **layout** of something is the way it is arranged.

lazy **lazier, laziest** ADJECTIVE
Someone who is **lazy** does not want to work or do anything hard.
lazily ADVERB

lead **leads, leading, led**
(*rhymes with* **feed**) VERB **1** If you **lead** someone to a particular place, you go with them to show them the way.
VERB **2** Someone who **leads** a group of people is in charge of them.

VERB **3** If you are **leading** in a race or game, you are winning at that point.
NOUN **4** A dog's **lead** is a long thin piece of leather or a chain. You fix one end to the collar and hold the other end.
(*rhymes with* **fed**) NOUN **5** Lead is a grey, heavy metal.
NOUN **6** The **lead** in a pencil is the centre part of it that makes a mark on paper.

leader **leaders** NOUN
The **leader** of a group of people is the person who is in charge.

leaf **leaves** NOUN
A **leaf** is one of the flat green parts of a plant. Different sorts of plant have differently shaped leaves.

leaflet **leaflets** NOUN
A **leaflet** is a piece of paper with information or advertising printed on it.

leak **leaks, leaking, leaked**
VERB **1** If a pipe or container **leaks**, it has a hole which lets gas or liquid escape.
VERB **2** If liquid or gas **leaks**, it escapes from a pipe or container.

lean **leans, leaning, leant** or **leaned; leaner, leanest**
VERB **1** When you **lean** somewhere, you bend your body in that direction.
VERB **2** When you **lean** on something, you rest your body against it for support.
ADJECTIVE **3** Lean meat has little or no fat.

leap **leaps, leaping, leapt** or **leaped** VERB
If you **leap** somewhere, you jump over a long distance or high in the air.

leap year **leap years** NOUN
A **leap year** is a year with 366 days. There is a leap year every four years.

learn **learns, learning, learnt** or **learned**
VERB
When you **learn** something, you get to know it or find out how to do it.

least

NOUN **1** The **least** is the smallest possible amount of something. *That is the **least** of my problems.*

ADJECTIVE OR ADVERB **2 Least** is a superlative form of **little**, meaning very small in amount. *We bought the **least** expensive bike... She ate the **least** of all of them.*

leather NOUN

Leather is the specially treated skin of animals. It is used for making things like shoes and furniture.

leave leaves, leaving, left

VERB **1** When you **leave** a place, you go away from it.

VERB **2** If you **leave** someone somewhere, they stay behind after you go away.

VERB **3** In maths, when you take one number from other, it **leaves** a third number.

led VERB

Led is the past tense of **lead**.

ledge ledges NOUN

A **ledge** is a narrow shelf on the side of a cliff or rock face, or on the outside of a building.

leek leeks NOUN

A **leek** is a long white vegetable with green leaves.
See Vegetables on page 260

left

VERB **1 Left** is the past tense of **leave**.

NOUN **2** The **left** is the side that you begin reading on in English.

ADJECTIVE OR ADVERB **3 Left** means on or towards the left side of something. *Turn **left** at the end of the road.*

leg legs

NOUN **1 Legs** are the parts of your body which stretch from the hips to the feet.

NOUN **2** The **legs** of an object such as a table are the parts which rest on the floor and support the object's weight.

leg

legend legends NOUN

A **legend** is an old and popular story which may or may not be true.

leisure NOUN

Leisure is time when you do not have to work and can do things that you enjoy.

lemon lemons NOUN

A **lemon** is a yellow, oval fruit. Lemons are juicy but they taste sour.
See Fruit on page 260

lemonade NOUN

Lemonade is a drink made from lemons, sugar and water.

lend lends, lending, lent VERB

If you **lend** something to someone, you let them have it for a while.

length lengths

NOUN **1** The **length** of something is the distance that it measures from one end to the other.

NOUN **2** The **length** of something like a holiday is the period of time that it lasts.

lens lenses NOUN

A **lens** is a curved piece of glass that makes light go in a certain way. Lenses are used in things like cameras, telescopes and glasses.

lent VERB

Lent is the past tense of **lend**.

leopard leopards NOUN

A **leopard** is a large wild cat that lives in the forests of Africa and Asia. It has yellow fur with black spots.

a
b
c
d
e
f
g
h
i
j
k
l
m
n
o
p
q
r
s
t
u
v
w
x
y
z

A B C D E F G H I J K L M N O P Q R S T U V W X Y Z

less ADJECTIVE OR ADVERB

Less is a comparative form of **little**, meaning not as much. *A shower uses **less** water than a bath.*

lesson **lessons** NOUN

A **lesson** is a short period of time when you are taught something.

let **lets, letting, let**

VERB **1** If you **let** someone do something, you allow them to do it.

VERB **2** If someone **lets** a house or flat that they own, they rent it out.

letter **letters**

NOUN **1** A **letter** is a written message to someone, usually sent through the post.

NOUN **2 Letters** are written symbols which go together to make words.

letter box **letter boxes**

NOUN **1** A **letter box** is an oblong gap in the front door of a house or flat.

NOUN **2** A **letter box** is also a large metal container where you post letters.

lettuce **lettuces** NOUN

A **lettuce** is a plant with large green leaves that you eat raw in salads.

See Vegetables on page 260

level **levels**

ADJECTIVE **1** A surface that is **level** is smooth, flat and parallel to the ground.

ADVERB **2** If you are **level** with someone, you are next to them.

NOUN **3** The **level** of a liquid is the height it comes up to. *After heavy rain the river rose to a dangerous **level**.*

lever **levers**

NOUN **1** A **lever** is a long bar that you put under a heavy object and press down on to make the object move.

NOUN **2** A **lever** is also a handle on a machine that you pull down to make the machine work.

liar **liars** NOUN

A **liar** is a person who tells lies.

library **libraries** NOUN

A **library** is a building where books are kept for people to come and read or borrow.

lick **licks, licking, licked** VERB

If you **lick** something, you move your tongue across it.

lid **lids** NOUN

A **lid** is a cover for a box or other container.

lie **lies, lying, lay, lain; lied**

VERB **1** To **lie** somewhere means to rest there horizontally.

VERB **2** To **lie** means to say something that is not true.

life **lives** NOUN

The **life** of a person or animal is the time between their birth and death.

lifeboat **lifeboats** NOUN

A **lifeboat** is a boat that is used to rescue people in danger at sea.

lifetime NOUN

Your **lifetime** is the period of time during which you are alive.

lift **lifts, lifting, lifted**

VERB **1** If you **lift** something, you move it to a higher position.

NOUN **2** A **lift** is a machine like a small room that carries passengers from one floor to another in a building.

light lights, lighting, lighted or lit; lighter, lightest

NOUN **1** **Light** is the brightness from the sun, moon, fire or lamps, that lets you see things.

NOUN **2** A **light** is a lamp or other object that gives out brightness.

VERB **3** To **light** something means to cause light to shine on it or in it.

VERB **4** To **light** a fire means to make it start burning.

ADJECTIVE **5** A place that is **light** is bright because of the sun or the use of lamps.

ADJECTIVE **6** A **light** colour is pale.

ADJECTIVE **7** A **light** object does not weigh much.

lighthouse lighthouses NOUN

A **lighthouse** is a tower with a powerful flashing light at the top, which is used to guide ships or to warn them of danger.

lightning NOUN

Lightning is a bright flash of light in the sky produced by natural electricity during a thunderstorm.

like likes, liking, liked

PREPOSITION **1** If one thing is **like** another, it is similar to it.

VERB **2** If you **like** someone or something, you find them pleasant.

likely likelier, likeliest ADJECTIVE

Something that is **likely** will probably happen or is probably true.

limb limbs NOUN

A **limb** is an arm or leg.

limit limits NOUN

A **limit** is a line or a point beyond which something cannot go. *There is a speed* **limit** *on this road.*

limp limps, limping, limped; limper, limpest

VERB **1** If you **limp**, you walk unevenly because you have hurt your leg or foot.

ADJECTIVE **2** Something that is **limp** is soft and floppy. *This lettuce is a bit* **limp**.

line lines

NOUN **1** A **line** is a long thin mark. Some writing paper has lines on it to show you where to write.

NOUN **2** A **line** of people or things is a number of them in a row.

NOUN **3** In a piece of writing, a **line** is a number of words together. *A limerick has five* **lines**.

NOUN **4** A railway **line** is one of the heavy metal rails that trains run on.

linen NOUN

Linen is a kind of cloth made from a plant called flax. It is used for things like sheets and tablecloths.

liner liners NOUN

A **liner** is a large passenger ship that makes long journeys.

link links

NOUN **1** A **link** is one of the rings in a chain.

NOUN **2** A **link** is also a connection between two things. *There's a high speed rail* **link** *between the two main cities.*

lion lions NOUN

A **lion** is a large wild cat. Lions live in parts of Africa and Asia, in groups called prides.

lip lips NOUN

Your **lips** are the top and bottom outer edges of your mouth.

liquid liquids NOUN

A **liquid** is anything which is not a solid or a gas, and which can be poured.

list lists NOUN

A **list** is a set of things that are written one below the other.

A
B
C
D
E
F
G
H
I
J
K
L
M
N
O
P
Q
R
S
T
U
V
W
X
Y
Z

listen listens, listening, listened VERB
If you **listen** to a sound that you can hear, you pay attention to it.
listener NOUN

lit VERB
Lit is the past tense of **light**.

literacy NOUN
Literacy is the ability to read and write. See **numeracy**

literature NOUN
Novels, plays and poetry are referred to as **literature**.

litre litres NOUN
A **litre** is a unit used to measure volume and capacity. A litre is equal to 1000 millilitres.

litter litters
NOUN **1 Litter** is rubbish left lying untidily outside.
NOUN **2** A **litter** is a group of animals born to the same mother at the same time.
See Collective nouns on page 268

little less, lesser, least
ADJECTIVE **1** Something or someone that is **little** is small in size.
ADVERB **2 Little** can mean not much. *Our lazy cat does very little.*

live lives, living, lived
(*rhymes with* **give**) VERB **1** If you **live** in a place, that is where your home is.
VERB **2** To **live** means to be alive.
(*rhymes with* **hive**) ADJECTIVE **3** A **live** animal is living.
ADJECTIVE **4 Live** television or radio is broadcast as it happens.

lively livelier, liveliest ADJECTIVE
Someone who is **lively** is cheerful and full of energy.

liver livers NOUN
Your **liver** is a large organ in your body. Its job is to clean your blood.

living
ADJECTIVE **1 Living** things are plants, animals and humans that are alive. All living things need food to grow.
NOUN **2** Someone who earns a **living** earns enough money to buy all the things they need. *She earns a living as an artist.*

living room living rooms NOUN
The **living room** in a house is the room where the family spend most of their time.

lizard lizards NOUN
A **lizard** is a small reptile with four short legs and a long tail. It has a rough dry skin. The babies hatch from eggs.
See Reptiles on page 264

load loads, loading, loaded
NOUN **1** A **load** is things which are being carried somewhere.
VERB **2** When you **load** a machine, you put something into it so it will work.

loaf loaves NOUN
A **loaf** is bread that has been baked into one shape. You cut a loaf into slices.

lobster lobsters
NOUN
A **lobster** is a sea animal with a hard shell, two large claws and eight legs.

local ADJECTIVE
Local means belonging to the area where you live or work. *I read about it in the local paper.*

locate locates, locating, located VERB
To **locate** someone or something is to find out where they are.

location locations NOUN
A **location** is a place, or the position of something. *The school is being moved to a new location.*

lock locks, locking, locked
VERB **1** If you **lock** something, you close it and fasten it with a key.
NOUN **2** A **lock** is used to keep something, such as a door or case, closed. You can only open a lock with the right key.

locomotive **locomotives** NOUN
A **locomotive** is the engine which pulls trains along railway tracks.

loft **lofts** NOUN
A **loft** is the space under the roof of a house, often used for storing things.

log **logs** NOUN
A **log** is a piece of a thick branch from a tree.

lollipop **lollipops** NOUN
A **lollipop** is a hard sweet on a stick.

lolly **lollies** NOUN
Lolly is an abbreviation of **lollipop**. A **lolly** is also a piece of flavoured ice or ice cream on a stick.

lonely **lonelier, loneliest** ADJECTIVE
Someone who is **lonely** is sad because they are on their own, or do not have any friends.

long **longer, longest; longs, longing, longed**
ADJECTIVE **1** Something **long** takes up more time than usual. *It was a **long** film.*
ADJECTIVE **2** Something that is **long** is far from one end to the other. *It's a **long** way from London to New York.*
VERB **3** If you **long** for something, you want it very much.

look **looks, looking, looked**
VERB **1** If you **look** in a particular direction, you turn your eyes that w ay.
VERB **2** If you say how someone **looks**, you tell them how they seem to you.
VERB **3** If you **look after** someone, you care for them.

VERB **4** If you **look for** someone or something, you try to find them.
VERB **5** If you are **looking forward** to something, you want it to happen because you think you will enjoy it.

loop **loops** NOUN
A **loop** is a circular shape in something long and thin. For example, when you tie shoelaces, the bow has two loops in it.

loose **looser, loosest**
ADJECTIVE **1** Something that is **loose** is not firmly fixed. *I've got a **loose** tooth.*
ADJECTIVE **2** Things that are **loose** are not fixed together. *She had four **loose** sheets of paper in her bag.*

lord **lords**. NOUN
Hundreds of years ago, a **lord** was a man who had a lot of power. Now, **Lord** is a title in front of some men's names in Britain.

lorry **lorries** NOUN
A **lorry** is a large road vehicle that is used to carry loads.

lose **loses, losing, lost**
VERB **1** If you **lose** something, you cannot find it.
VERB **2** If someone **loses** weight, they become thinner.
VERB **3** If you **lose** something like a game or a race, someone does better than you.

lost
ADJECTIVE **1** If you are **lost**, you cannot find your way or do not know where you are.

VERB **2 Lost** is the past tense of **lose**.

lot **lots** NOUN
A **lot** of something, or **lots** of something, is a large amount of it.

lottery **lotteries** NOUN
A **lottery** is a way of raising money by selling tickets. The winner is chosen by chance.

loud **louder, loudest** ADJECTIVE
A **loud** sound is one that makes a lot of noise. *The firework went off with a **loud** bang.*

loudspeaker **loudspeakers** NOUN
A **loudspeaker** is a piece of equipment that is used so that sounds can be heard. Microphones, radios and CD players all need loudspeakers.

lounge **lounges** NOUN
A **lounge** in a house or hotel is a room where people sit and relax.

love **loves, loving, loved**
VERB **1** If you **love** someone, you have strong feelings of affection for them.
VERB **2** If you **love** something, you like it very much. *I **love** pizza.*

lovely **lovelier, loveliest** ADJECTIVE
Something that is **lovely** is very pleasing to look at or listen to.

low **lower, lowest** ADJECTIVE
Something that is **low** measures only a short distance from the ground to the top. *He jumped over the **low** wall.*

lower **lowers, lowering, lowered**
VERB **1** If you **lower** something, you move it slowly downwards. *As it was getting dark, she **lowered** the blind.*
VERB **2** If you **lower** your voice, you speak more quietly.

lower-case ADJECTIVE
Lower-case letters are the small letters of the alphabet, such as a, b, c and d. *The letters down the side of this page are **lower-case**.*
See **upper-case**

loyal ADJECTIVE
If you are **loyal** to someone, you always support them.

luck NOUN
Luck is something that seems to happen without any reason. Luck can be good or bad.

lucky **luckier, luckiest** ADJECTIVE
Someone who is **lucky** seems to have good luck.
luckily ADVERB

luggage NOUN
Luggage is all the suitcases, bags and things that you take with you when you are travelling.

lump **lumps**
NOUN **1** A lump is a piece of something solid. *She takes one **lump** of sugar in her tea.*

NOUN **2** A **lump** on someone's body is a small swelling.

lunar ADJECTIVE
Lunar is used to describe something that is to do with the moon.

lunch **lunches**
NOUN
Lunch is a meal that you have in the middle of the day.

lung **lungs** NOUN
Your **lungs** are the two parts of your body inside your chest that fill with air when you breathe.

luxury **luxuries** NOUN
A **luxury** is something quite expensive to buy, which you like very much but do not need.
luxurious ADJECTIVE

lying VERB
Lying is the present participle of **lie**.

A
B
C
D
E
F
G
H
I
J
K
L
M
N
O
P
Q
R
S
T
U
V
W
X
Y
Z

Mm

machine **machines** NOUN

A **machine** is a piece of equipment which does a particular kind of work. It is usually powered by an engine or by electricity.

machinery NOUN

Machinery is machines in general.

mad **madder, maddest**

ADJECTIVE **1** Someone who is **mad** has an illness in their mind.

ADJECTIVE **2** If you describe someone as **mad**, you mean they are foolish or silly.

ADJECTIVE **3** INFORMAL Someone who is **mad** is angry.

ADJECTIVE **4** INFORMAL If you are **mad** about someone or something, you like them very much.

made VERB

Made is the past tense of **make**.

magazine **magazines** NOUN

A **magazine** is a thin book which comes out regularly, usually once a week or once a month. It has articles, stories and pictures.

maggot **maggots** NOUN

A **maggot** looks like a tiny worm. Maggots change into flies.

magic

NOUN **1** In stories, **magic** is the thing that makes impossible things happen.

ADJECTIVE **2 Magic** tricks entertain and puzzle people.

magical ADJECTIVE

magician **magicians**

NOUN **1** In stories, a **magician** is a man who has magic powers.

NOUN **2** A **magician** is also a real person who can do magic tricks.

magnet **magnets** NOUN

A **magnet** is a special piece of metal. It pulls or attracts iron or steel towards it. Magnets can also push other magnets away.

magnetic ADJECTIVE

magnificent ADJECTIVE

Something that is **magnificent** is very grand.

magnifying glass **magnifying glasses** NOUN

A **magnifying glass** is a piece of glass that makes objects appear to be bigger than they really are.

magpie **magpies** NOUN

A **magpie** is a bird of the crow family. It has black and white markings and a long tail.

mail

NOUN **1 Mail** is things like letters and parcels that are sent through the post.

NOUN **2 Mail** is also another name for **e-mail**.

main ADJECTIVE

The **main** part of something is the most important part.

maize NOUN

Maize is a tall plant that produces sweet corn.

major ADJECTIVE
You use **major** to describe something important. *This is a **major** discovery.*

make makes, making, made
VERB **1** If you **make** something new, you use your skill to shape it or put it together.
VERB **2** To **make** something happen is to cause it. *My new boots **made** a loud squeak.*
VERB **3** If you **make** a mistake, you do something wrong.
VERB **4** If you **make** someone do something, you force them to do it. *My mum **makes** me eat vegetables.*

male males NOUN
A **male** is a person or animal that belongs to the sex that cannot have babies.
male ADJECTIVE

mammal mammals NOUN
A **mammal** is a warm-blooded animal. Female mammals give birth to live babies. They feed their babies with milk from their own bodies.

man men NOUN
A **man** is an adult male human being. See **woman**

manage manages, managing, managed
VERB **1** If you **manage** to do something, you succeed in doing it. *He **managed** to get a seat on the bus.*
VERB **2** Someone who **manages** an organization is in charge of it.

mane manes NOUN
The **mane** of an animal such as a horse or a male lion is the long thick hair that grows from its neck.

mango mangoes or mangos NOUN
A **mango** is a sweet yellowish fruit which grows in tropical countries.
*See **Fruit** on page 260*

manner manners
NOUN **1** The **manner** in which you do something is how you do it.

NOUN **2** Your **manner** is the way in which you behave and talk. *It is good **manners** to be polite.*

mantelpiece mantelpieces NOUN
A **mantelpiece** is a shelf over a fireplace.

manufacture manufactures, manufacturing, manufactured VERB
To **manufacture** goods is to make them in a factory.

many
ADJECTIVE **1** If there are **many** people or things, there are a large number of them.
ADJECTIVE **2** You also use **many** to ask how great a quantity is or to give information about it. *How **many** tickets do you want?*

map maps NOUN
A **map** is a drawing of a particular area as it would look from above.

marathon marathons NOUN
A **marathon** is a race in which people have to run 26 miles (about 42 kilometres) along roads.

marble marbles
NOUN **1** Marble is a very hard stone which shines when it is polished. Statues and parts of buildings are sometimes made of marble.
NOUN **2** Marbles is a children's game played with small coloured glass balls. These balls are also called marbles.

march **marches, marching, marched**
VERB
When you **march**, you walk with quick regular steps like a soldier.

March NOUN
March is the third month of the year. It has 31 days.

mare **mares** NOUN
A **mare** is an adult female horse.

margarine NOUN
Margarine is a food that looks like butter but is made from vegetable oil and animal fats. You can spread it on bread and use it for cooking.

margin **margins** NOUN
The **margin** is the blank space at each side on a written or printed page.

mark **marks**
NOUN **1** A **mark** is a small stain. *I can't get that mark off your shirt.*
NOUN **2** A **mark** is also something that has been written or drawn. *He made little marks on the paper with his pencil.*
NOUN **3** At school, a **mark** is a letter or number showing how well you have done in homework or in a test.

market **markets** NOUN
A **market** is a place with many small stalls selling different goods.

marmalade NOUN
Marmalade is a jam made from fruit like oranges or lemons. People often eat it spread on toast for breakfast.

marriage **marriages** NOUN
Marriage is the state or relationship of living together in a legal partnership.

married ADJECTIVE
Someone who is **married** has a partner in marriage.

marry **marries, marrying, married** VERB
If you **marry** someone, you take them as your partner in marriage.

marsh **marshes** NOUN
A **marsh** is an area of land which is always very wet and muddy.

marvellous ADJECTIVE
Something that is **marvellous** is wonderful.

masculine ADJECTIVE
Masculine refers to qualities and things that are typical of men.

mask **masks** NOUN
A **mask** is something you wear over your face to protect or disguise you.

mass **masses**
NOUN **1** A **mass** of things is a large number of them grouped together.
See **weight**
NOUN **2** The **mass** of something is the amount of matter it contains. Mass is measured in grams and kilograms. People often say "weight" when they mean "mass". Mass and weight are different. If you were on the moon, you would weigh less than on Earth but your mass would not change.
See **weight**
NOUN **3** In the Roman Catholic church, a **Mass** is a religious service.

massive ADJECTIVE
Something **massive** is extremely large.

mast **masts** NOUN
A **mast** is the tall upright pole that supports the sail of a boat.

a
b
c
d
e
f
g
h
i
j
k
l
m
n
o
p
q
r
s
t
u
v
w
x
y
z

A
B
C
D
E
F
G
H
I
J
K
L
M
N
O
P
Q
R
S
T
U
V
W
X
Y
Z

mat mats

NOUN **1** A **mat** is a small piece of carpet.

NOUN **2** A **mat** is also something used to protect a table from plates or glasses.

match matches, matching, matched

NOUN **1** A **match** is an organized game of something like tennis or football.

NOUN **2** A **match** is also a thin stick of wood that can make a flame.

VERB **3** If you **match** things, you find a connection between them. *Match the animals with the countries they come from.*

mate mates

NOUN **1** INFORMAL A **mate** is a friend.

NOUN **2** An animal's **mate** is its partner.

material materials

NOUN **1** **Material** is cloth.

NOUN **2** A **material** is anything that can be used to make something else. Wood, stone, plastic and water are all materials.

mathematics NOUN

Mathematics is the study of numbers, quantities and shapes.

maths NOUN

Maths is an abbreviation of **mathematics**.

matter matters, mattering, mattered

VERB **1** If something **matters** to you, you care about it and feel it is important.

NOUN **2** A **matter** is something that you have to deal with or think about. *This is a matter for the police.*

mattress mattresses NOUN

A **mattress** is a large flat cushion which is put on a bed to make it comfortable to lie on.

maximum

ADJECTIVE **1** The **maximum** amount is the most that is possible or allowed. *The maximum score for this question is five marks.*

NOUN **2** The **maximum** is the most that is possible or allowed. *Pupils are allowed a maximum of five pounds to spend.*

may VERB

If someone says you **may** do something, you are allowed to do it.

May NOUN

May is the fifth month of the year. It has 31 days.

maybe ADVERB

You say **maybe** when something is possible but you are not sure about it. *Maybe we could go tomorrow.*

mayor mayors NOUN

The **mayor** of a town or city is the man or woman who has been chosen to be its head.

maze mazes NOUN

A **maze** is a system of paths which is made like a puzzle so that it is difficult to find your way through it.

me PRONOUN

You use **me** when you are talking about yourself. *Can you hear me?*

meadow meadows NOUN

A **meadow** is a field of grass and wild flowers.

meal **meals** NOUN
A **meal** is food that people eat, usually at set times during the day.

mean **means, meaning, meant; meaner, meanest**
VERB **1** If you ask what something **means**, you want it explained to you.
VERB **2** If you **mean** what you say, you are serious about it.
VERB **3** If something **means** a lot to you, it is important to you.
VERB **4** If you **mean** to do something, you intend to do it. *I **meant** to phone you, but I didn't have time.*
ADJECTIVE **5** Someone who is **mean** does not like spending money or sharing.

meaning **meanings** NOUN
The **meaning** of a word or sentence is the thing or idea that it is explaining. *Do you know the **meaning** of the proverb "Look before you leap"?*

meanwhile ADVERB
Meanwhile means while something else is happening.

measles NOUN
Measles is an illness caught especially by children. It gives you a fever and red spots on your skin.

measure **measures, measuring, measured**
VERB **1** If you **measure** something, you find out how large or heavy it is.
NOUN **2** A **measure** is a unit in which something such as size or speed is expressed. *Kilometres are a **measure** of distance.*
See *Measures* on page 278

measurement **measurements** NOUN
A **measurement** is a result that you get by measuring something.

meat **meats** NOUN
Meat is the flesh of animals that is cooked and eaten.

mechanical ADJECTIVE
A **mechanical** object has moving parts and is used to do a physical task.

medal **medals** NOUN
A **medal** is a small metal disc or cross given as an award for bravery or as a prize for sport.

medical ADJECTIVE
Medical means to do with medicine or the care of people's health.

medicine **medicines** NOUN
Medicine is a tablet or liquid given to people who are ill to make them better.

medium ADJECTIVE
Medium means somewhere in the middle of two extremes. *He's of **medium** height − neither tall nor short.*

meet **meets, meeting, met** VERB
If you **meet** someone, you go to the same place at the same time as they do.

meeting **meetings** NOUN
A **meeting** is when a group of people meet to talk about particular things.

megabyte **megabytes** NOUN
A **megabyte** is a measurement of how much data can be stored on a computer.

melon **melons** NOUN
A **melon** is a large fruit that is sweet and juicy inside. It has a thick, hard green or yellow skin.
See Fruit on page 260

melt **melts, melting, melted** VERB
When something like ice **melts**, it changes from a solid into a liquid because it has become warmer.

member **members** NOUN
A **member** of a group is one of the people, animals or things belonging to that group.
membership NOUN

a
b
c
d
e
f
g
h
i
j
k
l
m
n
o
p
q
r
s
t
u
v
w
x
y
z

A
B
C
D
E
F
G
H
I
J
K
L
M
N
O
P
Q
R
S
T
U
V
W
X
Y
Z

memorize **memorizes, memorizing, memorized**; also spelt **memorise** VERB
If you **memorize** something, you learn it so that you can repeat it exactly using only your memory.

memory **memories**
NOUN **1** Your **memory** is what allows you to remember things.
NOUN **2** A **memory** is something you remember from the past.
NOUN **3** The **memory** of a computer is the part where information is stored.

men NOUN
Men is the plural of **man**.

mend **mends, mending, mended** VERB
If you **mend** something that is broken or does not work, you put it right so that it can be used again.

mental ADJECTIVE
Mental means to do with your mind or brain. For example, mental maths is working out the answers to calculations in your head.

mention **mentions, mentioning, mentioned** VERB
If you **mention** something, you talk about it briefly.

menu **menus**
NOUN **1** A **menu** is a list of food that you can order in a restaurant.
NOUN **2** A **menu** on a computer is a list of choices.

mercury NOUN
Mercury is a silver-coloured metal. Liquid mercury is used in thermometers.

mercy NOUN
If you show **mercy** to someone, you do not hurt or punish them.

merry **merrier, merriest** ADJECTIVE
Merry means happy and cheerful.

mess **messes** NOUN
If you say something is a **mess**, you mean it is very untidy.
messy ADJECTIVE

message **messages** NOUN
A **message** is words that you send or leave when you cannot speak directly to someone.

messenger **messengers** NOUN
A **messenger** is a person who takes a message to someone.

met VERB
Met is the past tense of **meet**.

metal **metals** NOUN
A **metal** is a hard, strong material that melts when it is heated, such as iron, gold or steel. Metals are used to make things like jewellery, tools, cars and machines.

meteor **meteors** NOUN
A **meteor** is a piece of rock or metal moving through space. Meteors burn very brightly when they enter the earth's atmosphere.

meter **meters** NOUN
A **meter** is an instrument for measuring something, such as the amount of gas that you have used.

method **methods** NOUN
A **method** is a particular way of doing something.

metre metres

NOUN **1** A **metre** (m) is a measure of length. It is equal to 100 centimetres.

NOUN **2** In poetry, **metre** is the rhythmic arrangement of words and syllables.

miaow NOUN

A **miaow** is the short high-pitched sound that a cat makes.

mice NOUN

Mice is the plural of **mouse**.

microchip microchips NOUN

A **microchip** is a small piece of silicon on which electronic circuits for a computer are printed.

microphone microphones NOUN

A **microphone** is a piece of equipment that is used to make sounds louder, or to record them.

microscope microscopes NOUN

A **microscope** is a piece of equipment which makes small objects appear much larger.

microscopic ADJECTIVE

microwave microwaves NOUN

A **microwave** is a type of oven which cooks food very quickly.

midday NOUN

Midday is 12 o'clock (noon) in the middle of the day.

middle middles

NOUN **1** The **middle** of something is the part furthest from the edges.

ADJECTIVE **2** The **middle** one in a series or a row is the one that has an equal number of people or things on each side of it.

midnight NOUN

Midnight is 12 o'clock at night.

might

VERB **1** If you say something **might** happen, you are not sure if it will.

VERB **2** If you say something **might** be true, you are not sure about it.

migrate migrates, migrating, migrated

VERB

When birds, fish or animals **migrate**, they move to another place at a particular time of year so that they can find food.

mild milder, mildest

ADJECTIVE **1** Something that is **mild** is gentle and does no harm. *You need to use a **mild** shampoo.*

ADJECTIVE **2** **Mild** weather in the winter is warmer than usual.

mile miles NOUN

A **mile** is a unit of distance equal to about one and a half kilometres.

military ADJECTIVE

Military means to do with the armed forces of a country.

milk NOUN

Milk is the white liquid that female mammals make in their bodies to feed their young. People drink milk from cows and use it to make butter, cheese and yogurt.

See Drinks on page 261

mill mills

NOUN **1** A **mill** is a building in which grain is crushed to make flour.

NOUN **2** A **mill** is also a factory used for making things such as cotton or paper.

millennium millennia or millenniums

NOUN

A **millennium** is a period of 1000 years.

millilitre millilitres NOUN

A **millilitre** is a measure of volume and capacity. There are 1000 millilitres in a litre.

millimetre millimetres NOUN

A **millimetre** (mm) is a measure of length. There are 1000 millimetres in a metre. There are 10 millimetres in a centimetre.

million

millions NOUN

A **million** is the number 1,000,000.

a
b
c
d
e
f
g
h
i
j
k
l
m
n
o
p
q
r
s
t
u
v
w
x
y
z

A B C D E F G H I J K L M N O P Q R S T U V W X Y Z

millionaire **millionaires** NOUN
A **millionaire** is a person who has more than a million pounds or dollars.

mince NOUN
Mince is meat which has been cut into very small pieces.

mincemeat NOUN
Mincemeat is a sticky mixture of dried fruit and other sweet things.

mind **minds, minding, minded**
NOUN **1** Your **mind** is your ability to think, together with your memory and all the thoughts you have.
NOUN **2** If you **change your mind**, you change a decision you have made.
VERB **3** If you **mind** about something, it worries you or makes you angry.

mine **mines**
PRONOUN **1** **Mine** refers to something belonging to the person who is speaking or writing. *That bag is **mine**.*

NOUN **2** A **mine** is a place under the ground where people dig out things like diamonds, coal or other minerals.
NOUN **3** A **mine** can be a bomb hidden in the ground or underwater, which explodes when people or things touch it.

mineral **minerals** NOUN
Minerals are substances such as tin, salt or coal that are formed naturally in rocks and in the earth.

minibus **minibuses** NOUN
A **minibus** is a van with seats in the back that is used as a small bus.

minimum **minimums**
ADJECTIVE **1** A **minimum** amount of something is the smallest amount that is possible, allowed or needed.
NOUN **2** The **minimum** is the smallest amount of something that is possible, allowed or needed.

minister **ministers**
NOUN **1** A **minister** is an important member of the government of a country.
NOUN **2** A **minister** is also a person in charge of a church.

minor ADJECTIVE
Something that is **minor** is not very important or serious. *She had a **minor** accident.*

mint **mints**
NOUN **1** **Mint** is a small plant. Its leaves have a strong taste and smell, and are used in cooking.
NOUN **2** A **mint** is a kind of sweet.
NOUN **3** A **mint** is also a place where coins are made.

minus
PREPOSITION **1** You use **minus** to show that one number is being subtracted from another. For example, ten minus six equals four (written $10 - 6 = 4$).
ADJECTIVE **2** **Minus** is used when talking about temperatures below 0° Celsius. *The temperature is **minus** two degrees.*

minute **minutes**
(*said* **min**-nit) NOUN **1** A **minute** is a unit of time equal to 60 seconds.
(*said* my-**nyoot**) ADJECTIVE **2** Something **minute** is extremely small.

miracle **miracles**
NOUN **1** A **miracle** is a wonderful event, believed to have been caused by God.
NOUN **2** A **miracle** can also be any very surprising event. *By some **miracle** he got to school early.*

mirror **mirrors** NOUN
A **mirror** is a piece of glass that reflects light. When you look in a mirror you can see yourself.

misbehave **misbehaves, misbehaving, misbehaved** VERB
If a child **misbehaves**, they are naughty or behave badly.

mischief NOUN
Mischief is silly things that some children do to annoy other people.

mischievous
ADJECTIVE **1** A **mischievous** person likes to have fun by embarrassing people or playing tricks.
ADJECTIVE **2** A **mischievous** child is often naughty but does not do any real harm.

miserable ADJECTIVE
Someone who is **miserable** is very unhappy.
miserably ADVERB

misery NOUN
Misery is great unhappiness.

misfortune **misfortunes** NOUN
Misfortune is bad luck.

mislay **mislays, mislaying, mislaid** VERB
If you **mislay** something, you forget where you have put it.

mislead **misleads, misleading, misled** VERB
To **mislead** someone is to give them an idea that is not true.

misprint **misprints** NOUN
A **misprint** is a mistake in something that has been printed, for example "cow" instead of "cot".

miss **misses, missing, missed**
VERB **1** If you are aiming at something and **miss**, you fail to hit it.
VERB **2** If you **miss** a bus or train, you are too late to get on it.
VERB **3** If you **miss** somebody, you are lonely without them.

Miss NOUN
Miss is used before the name of a girl or an unmarried woman.

missile **missiles** NOUN
A **missile** is a weapon that goes through the air and explodes when it reaches its target.

missing ADJECTIVE
If something is **missing**, it is not in its usual place and you cannot find it.

misspell **misspells, misspelling, misspelt** or **misspelled** VERB
If you **misspell** a word, you spell it wrongly.

mist **mists** NOUN
A **mist** is a large number of tiny drops of water in the air. When there is a mist, you cannot see very far.
misty ADJECTIVE

mistake **mistakes** NOUN
A **mistake** is something that is done wrong.

misunderstand **misunderstands, misunderstanding, misunderstood** VERB
If you **misunderstand** someone, you do not understand them properly.

mix **mixes, mixing, mixed** VERB
If you **mix** things, you stir them or put them together. *The children made paste by **mixing** flour and water.*

mixture **mixtures** NOUN
A **mixture** is several different things mixed up.

moan **moans, moaning, moaned** VERB
If you **moan**, you make a low sad sound because you are in pain or trouble.

moat **moats** NOUN
A **moat** is a wide water-filled ditch around a building such as a castle.

a
b
c
d
e
f
g
h
i
j
k
l
m
n
o
p
q
r
s
t
u
v
w
x
y
z

129

A
B
C
D
E
F
G
H
I
J
K
L
M
N
O
P
Q
R
S
T
U
V
W
X
Y
Z

mobile mobiles

ADJECTIVE **1** If you are **mobile**, you are able to travel or move to another place.

NOUN **2 Mobile** is an abbreviation of **mobile phone**.

NOUN **3** A **mobile** is a decoration that you hang up so that it moves around when a breeze blows.

mobile phone mobile phones NOUN

A **mobile phone** is a telephone you can carry about.

model models

NOUN **1** A **model** is a small copy of something. It shows what it looks like or how it works.

NOUN **2** A **model** is also someone who shows clothes to people by wearing them.

modern ADJECTIVE

Modern is to do with new ideas and equipment. *We live in a **modern** house.*

modest ADJECTIVE

People who are **modest** do not boast about themselves.

moist moister, moistest ADJECTIVE

Something that is **moist** is slightly wet.
moisten VERB

moisture NOUN

Moisture is tiny drops of water in the air or on a surface.

mole moles

NOUN **1** A **mole** is a small burrowing animal with tiny eyes and dark silky fur.

NOUN **2** A **mole** is also a small dark lump on someone's skin.

moment moments

NOUN **1** A **moment** is a very short time.

NOUN **2** A **moment** is also a point in time when something happens. *At that **moment**, the teacher came into the room.*

Monday Mondays NOUN

Monday is the day between Sunday and Tuesday.

money NOUN

Money is the coins or banknotes you use to buy something.

monitor monitors NOUN

A **monitor** is the part of a computer that contains the screen.

monkey monkeys NOUN

A **monkey** is an animal that lives in hot countries. It has a long tail and climbs trees.

monster monsters NOUN

A **monster** is an imaginary creature that is large and terrifying.

month months NOUN

A **month** is a measure of time. There are 12 months in a year.

mood moods NOUN

Your **mood** is the way you are feeling about things at a particular time, such as how cheerful or angry you are.

moon moons NOUN

The **moon** is a satellite that moves round the Earth. It shines in the sky at night. You can only see it because the moon's surface reflects sunlight.

moonlight NOUN

Moonlight is the light that comes from the moon at night.

moor moors NOUN

A **moor** is an open area of land covered mainly with grass and heather.

moose NOUN

A **moose** is a large North American deer. Moose have very flat, branch-shaped horns called antlers.

mop **mops** NOUN
A **mop** is a tool for washing floors. It has a long handle with sponge or pieces of string fixed to the end.

more ADJECTIVE OR ADVERB
More means a greater number or amount of something. It is the comparative of "many" or "much". *Tanya thinks football is* **more** *fun than maths... He's got* **more** *chips than me.*

morning **mornings** NOUN
Morning is the part of the day before noon.

mosque **mosques** NOUN
A **mosque** is a building where Muslims worship.

mosquito **mosquitoes** or **mosquitos**
NOUN
A **mosquito** is a small flying insect that lives in damp places. The female bites people and other animals to suck their blood.
*See **Insects** on page 264*

moss **mosses** NOUN
Moss is a small green plant without roots. It grows in flat clumps on trees, rocks and damp ground.

most ADJECTIVE, ADVERB OR NOUN
Most means the greatest number or amount of something. It is the superlative of "many" or "much". *I saw the* **most** *fantastic film... **Most** children like sweets... The* **most** *I can give you is three pieces.*

moth **moths** NOUN
A **moth** is an insect like a butterfly that usually flies at night.

mother **mothers** NOUN
A **mother** is a woman who has a child or children of her own.

motion **motions** NOUN
A **motion** is a movement.

motive **motives** NOUN
A **motive** is a reason for doing something. *There was no* **motive** *for the attack.*

motor **motors** NOUN
A **motor** is part of a vehicle or machine. The motor uses fuel to make the vehicle or machine work.

motorbike
motorbikes NOUN
A **motorbike** is a two-wheeled vehicle that is driven by an engine.

motorway **motorways** NOUN
A **motorway** is a wide road built for fast travel over long distances.

mould **moulds**
NOUN **1 Mould** is a soft grey or green substance that can form on old food.
NOUN **2** A **mould** is a container used to make something into a particular shape, for example a jelly mould.

moult **moults, moulting, moulted** VERB
When an animal **moults**, it loses its hair or feathers so that new ones can grow.

mount **mounts, mounting, mounted**
VERB
If you **mount** a horse, you climb on its back.

mountain **mountains** NOUN
A **mountain** is a very high piece of land with steep sides.

mouse **mice**
NOUN **1** A **mouse** is a small rodent with a long tail.
NOUN **2** A **mouse** is also a small object that you use to move the cursor on a computer screen.

a
b
c
d
e
f
g
h
i
j
k
l
m
n
o
p
q
r
s
t
u
v
w
x
y
z

131

A B C D E F G H I J K L M N O P Q R S T U V W X Y Z

moustache **moustaches** NOUN
A man's **moustache** is hair growing on his upper lip.

mouth **mouths**
NOUN **1** Your **mouth** is your lips, or the space behind them where your tongue and teeth are.
NOUN **2** The **mouth** of a cave or hole is the entrance to it.
NOUN **3** The **mouth** of a river is the place where it flows into the sea.

move **moves, moving, moved**
VERB **1** To **move** means to go to a different place or position.
VERB **2** To **move** something means to change its place or position.
movement NOUN

movie **movies** NOUN
A **movie** is a film made for the cinema or TV.

mow **mows, mowing, mowed** VERB
If a person **mows** an area of grass, they cut it with a lawnmower.

MP3 player **MP3 players** NOUN
An **MP3 player** is a machine on which you can play music downloaded from the Internet.

Mr (said **miss**-ter)
Mr is used before a man's name.

Mrs (said **miss**-iz)
Mrs is used before the name of a married woman.

Ms (said **miz**)
Ms can be used before a woman's name. Some women choose to be called Ms because it says nothing about whether they are married or not.

much
ADVERB **1** You use **much** to show that something is true to a great extent. *I feel **much** better now.*
ADVERB **2** If something does not happen **much**, it does not happen very often.
ADJECTIVE **3** You use **much** to ask questions or give information about the size or amount of something. *How **much** money do you need?*

mud NOUN
Mud is wet sticky earth.
muddy ADJECTIVE

muddle **muddles** NOUN
If things such as papers are in a **muddle**, they are all mixed up.

mug **mugs** NOUN
A **mug** is a large deep cup, usually with straight sides and a handle.

multiple **multiples** NOUN
The **multiples** of a number are other numbers that it will divide into exactly. For example, 6, 9 and 12 are multiples of 3.

multiplication NOUN
Multiplication is when you multiply one number by another. The sign you use for multiplication is ×.

multiply **multiplies, multiplying, multiplied**
VERB **1** When something **multiplies**, it increases greatly in number. *Fleas **multiply** very fast.*
VERB **2** When you **multiply** a number, you make it bigger by a number of times. For example, two multiplied by three (two plus two plus two) equals six. $2 \times 3 = 6$ or $2 + 2 + 2 = 6$

mum **mums** NOUN
Your **mum** is your mother.

mumble **mumbles, mumbling, mumbled** VERB
If you **mumble**, you speak very quietly and not clearly.

mummy **mummies** NOUN
INFORMAL Your **mummy** is your mother.

mumps NOUN
Mumps is an illness caught especially by children. Your neck swells and your throat hurts.

munch **munches, munching, munched**
VERB
If you **munch** something, you chew it steadily and thoroughly.

murder **murders** NOUN
Murder is the deliberate killing of a person.

murmur **murmurs, murmuring, murmured** VERB
If you **murmur**, you say something very softly.

muscle **muscles** NOUN
Muscles are the parts inside your body that you use when you move.

museum **museums** NOUN
A **museum** is a building where many interesting or valuable objects are kept and displayed.

mushroom **mushrooms** NOUN
A **mushroom** is a small fungus with a short thick stem and a round top. You can eat some kinds of mushroom, but others are poisonous.

music
NOUN **1 Music** is a pattern of sounds made by people singing or playing instruments.
NOUN **2 Music** is also the written symbols that stand for musical sounds.

musical ADJECTIVE
Musical means relating to playing or studying music. *He wants to learn to play a* ***musical*** *instrument.*

musician **musicians** NOUN
A **musician** is a person who plays a musical instrument well.

Muslim **Muslims**; also spelt **Moslem**
NOUN
A **Muslim** is a person who follows the religion of Islam.

must VERB
If something **must** happen, it is important or necessary that it happens. *You* ***must*** *be home by 5 p.m.*

mustard NOUN
Mustard is a hot spicy yellow paste made from mustard seeds.

my ADJECTIVE
My refers to something belonging or relating to the person speaking or writing. *I held* ***my*** *breath.*

myself PRONOUN
Myself is used when the person speaking does something and no one else does it. *I hung the picture* ***myself***.

mysterious ADJECTIVE
Something that is **mysterious** is strange and puzzling.

mystery **mysteries**
NOUN **1** A **mystery** is something strange that cannot be explained.
NOUN **2** A **mystery** is also a story in which strange things happen.

myth **myths** NOUN
A **myth** is a story which was made up long ago to explain natural events and religious beliefs.

a
b
c
d
e
f
g
h
i
j
k
l
m
n
o
p
q
r
s
t
u
v
w
x
y
z

133

Nn

nail nails

NOUN **1** A **nail** is a small piece of metal with a sharp point at one end, which you hammer into objects to hold them together.

NOUN **2** Your **nails** are the thin hard areas at the ends of your fingers and toes.

naked ADJECTIVE

Someone who is **naked** is not wearing any clothes.

name names NOUN

A **name** is what someone or something is called.

nappy nappies NOUN

A **nappy** is a thick piece of soft material wrapped round a baby's bottom to help keep it dry and clean.

narrative narratives NOUN

A **narrative** is a story or an account of events.

narrow narrower, narrowest ADJECTIVE

Something **narrow** is a short distance from one side to the other. *The stream was **narrow** enough to jump across.*

nasty nastier, nastiest

ADJECTIVE **1** Something that is **nasty** is very unpleasant.

ADJECTIVE **2** Someone who is **nasty** is very unkind.

nastily ADVERB

nation nations NOUN

A **nation** is a country with its own laws.

national ADJECTIVE

Something that is **national** is to do with the whole of a country. *The Observer is a **national** newspaper.*

native

ADJECTIVE **1** Your **native** country is the country where you were born.

ADJECTIVE **2** Your **native** language is the language that you first learned to speak.

ADJECTIVE **3** Animals or plants that are **native** to a place live there naturally. They have not been brought there by people.

natural

ADJECTIVE **1** **Natural** means existing or happening in nature. For example, an earthquake is a natural disaster.

ADJECTIVE **2** Something that is **natural** is normal and to be expected.

nature natures

NOUN **1** **Nature** is animals, plants and all the other things in the world not made by people.

NOUN **2** The **nature** of a person or thing is their basic character.

naughty naughtier, naughtiest ADJECTIVE

A child who is **naughty** behaves badly.

navigate navigates, navigating, navigated VERB

When someone **navigates**, they work out the direction in which a ship, plane or car should go, using maps and sometimes instruments.

navy navies

NOUN **1** A **navy** is the part of a country's armed forces that fights at sea.

ADJECTIVE **2** Something that is **navy** is a very dark blue.

See Colours and shapes on page 266

See Colours and shapes on page 266

near nearer, nearest

ADJECTIVE **1** Something that is **near** is not far away. *Where is the **nearest** garage?*

ADVERB **2** If you are **near** something or somewhere, you are not far away from it. *We must be getting **nearer**.*

nearly ADVERB
Nearly means almost but not quite. *I nearly caught him but he ran off.*

neat neater, neatest ADJECTIVE
Something that is **neat** is very tidy and clean.

necessary ADJECTIVE
Something that is **necessary** is needed or must be done.
necessarily ADVERB

neck necks NOUN
Your **neck** is the part of your body that joins your head to the rest of your body.

necklace necklaces NOUN
A **necklace** is a piece of jewellery that you wear around your neck.

need needs, needing, needed
VERB **1** If you **need** something, you must have it in order to live and be healthy.
VERB **2** Sometimes you **need** something to help you do a particular job. *Now I need a paintbrush.*
VERB **3** If you **need** to do something, you have to do it.

needle needles
NOUN **1** A **needle** is a small thin piece of metal used for sewing. It has a hole in one end and a sharp point at the other. You put thread through the hole.
NOUN **2** A **needle** is also a thin metal tube with a sharp point, that people like doctors use to give injections.
NOUN **3 Needles** are long thin pieces of metal or plastic used for knitting.
NOUN **4** The thin leaves on pine trees are called **needles**.

negative
ADJECTIVE **1** A **negative** sentence is one that has the word "no" or "not" in it.
ADJECTIVE **2** A **negative** number is less than zero.

neglect neglects, neglecting, neglected
NOUN
If you **neglect** something, you do not look after it.

neighbour neighbours NOUN
Your **neighbour** is someone who lives near you.

neighbourhood neighbourhoods NOUN
A **neighbourhood** is a district where people live. *This is a friendly neighbourhood.*

nephew nephews NOUN
Someone's **nephew** is a son of their sister or brother.
See **niece**

nerve nerves
NOUN **1** Your **nerves** are the long thin threads in your body that carry messages between your brain and the other parts of your body.
NOUN **2 Nerve** is courage. *I wanted to go on the ride but I hadn't got the nerve.*

nervous
ADJECTIVE **1** If you are **nervous**, you are worried about doing something.
ADJECTIVE **2** A **nervous** person is easily frightened.

nest nests NOUN
A **nest** is a place that a bird or other animal makes for its babies.

net nets
NOUN **1 Net** is material made from threads woven together with small spaces in between.
NOUN **2** The **net** is the same as the Internet.
NOUN **3** In maths, the **net** of a three-dimensional shape is the flat shape that you could fold to make the three-dimensional shape.
ADJECTIVE **4** The **net** weight of something is its weight without its wrapping.

netball NOUN
Netball is a game played by two teams of seven players. Each team tries to score goals by throwing a ball through a net at the top of a pole.

a
b
c
d
e
f
g
h
i
j
k
l
m
n
o
p
q
r
s
t
u
v
w
x
y
z

A
B
C
D
E
F
G
H
I
J
K
L
M
N
O
P
Q
R
S
T
U
V
W
X
Y
Z

nettle nettles NOUN
A **nettle** is a wild plant covered with little hairs that sting.

network networks
NOUN **1** A **network** is a large number of lines or roads that cross each other at many points.
NOUN **2** A **network** is also a group of computers that are connected to each other.

never ADVERB
Never means at no time in the past or future. *You must **never** cross the road without looking carefully.*

new newer, newest
ADJECTIVE **1** Something that is **new** has just been made or bought. *They have built some **new** houses close to us.*
ADJECTIVE **2 New** can mean different. *We've got a **new** car – it's only a year old.*

news NOUN
News is information about something that has just happened.

newspaper
newspapers NOUN
A **newspaper** is sheets of paper that are printed and sold regularly. Newspapers contain news and articles.

newt newts NOUN
A **newt** is a small animal that looks like a lizard. It lives near water.
See Amphibians on page 264

next
ADJECTIVE **1** The **next** period or thing is the one that comes immediately after this one. *The **next** programme will follow after the break.*
ADJECTIVE **2** The **next** place is the one nearest to you. *She's in the **next** room.*

nib nibs NOUN
A **nib** is a small pointed piece of metal at the end of a pen. Ink comes out of the nib as you write.

nibble nibbles, nibbling, nibbled VERB
If you **nibble** something, you eat it slowly by taking small bites out of it.

nice nicer, nicest
ADJECTIVE **1** You say something is **nice** when you like it. *This cake is **nice**.*
ADJECTIVE **2** If you say the weather is **nice**, it is warm and pleasant.
ADJECTIVE **3** If you are **nice** to people, you are friendly and kind.

nickname nicknames NOUN
A **nickname** is a name that is given to a person by friends or family. *The baby's name is Sam but his **nickname** is Dribbler.*

niece nieces NOUN
Someone's **niece** is a daughter of their sister or brother.
See **nephew**

night nights NOUN
The **night** is the time between evening and morning when it is dark.

nightmare nightmares NOUN
A **nightmare** is a frightening dream.

nil NOUN
Nil is zero or nothing, especially in sports scores. *At half-time the score was still **nil**-**nil**.*

nine NOUN
Nine is the number 9.

nineteen NOUN
Nineteen is the number 19.

ninety NOUN
Ninety is the number 90.

no

INTERJECTION **1** You say **no** when you do not want something or do not agree. *"More tea?"* *"**No**, thank you."*

ADJECTIVE **2** You can use **no** to mean not any. *I had **no** help at all.*

ADVERB **3** You can use **no** to mean not. *Competition entries must be in **no** later than Friday.*

nobody PRONOUN
Nobody means not a single person.

nod **nods, nodding, nodded** VERB
If you **nod**, you move your head quickly down and up to answer yes to a question, or to show that you agree.

noise **noises**
NOUN **1** A **noise** is a sound that someone or something makes.
NOUN **2** **Noise** is loud or unpleasant sounds.

noisy **noisier, noisiest** ADJECTIVE
A **noisy** person or thing makes a lot of loud noise. *It was a very **noisy** party.*

none PRONOUN
None means not any, or not one. ***None** of us wanted to go.*

non-fiction NOUN
Non-fiction is writing that is based on fact. For example, dictionaries are non-fiction.
See **fiction**

nonsense NOUN
Nonsense is words that do not make sense.

noon NOUN
Noon is 12 o'clock in the middle of the day.

no one or **no-one** PRONOUN
No one means not a single person.

normal ADJECTIVE
Something that is **normal** is what you would expect.

north NOUN
North is one of the four main points of the compass. If you face the point where the sun rises, north is on your left.
See **compass point**
northern ADJECTIVE

north-east NOUN
North-east is halfway between north and east.

north-west NOUN
North-west is halfway between north and west.

nose **noses** NOUN
Your **nose** is the part of your face that sticks out above your mouth. It is used for smelling and breathing.

nostril **nostrils** NOUN
Your **nostrils** are the two openings at the end of your nose. You breathe through your nostrils.

not ADVERB
Not is used to make a sentence mean the opposite. *I am **not** very happy.*

note **notes**
NOUN **1** A **note** is a short written message.
NOUN **2** You take **notes** to help you remember what has been said.
NOUN **3** A **note** is also a single sound in music.
NOUN **4** A bank **note** is a printed piece of paper that is used as money.

nothing PRONOUN
Nothing means not anything.

notice **notices, noticing, noticed**
VERB **1** If you **notice** something, you pay attention to it. *She **noticed** that it was raining.*
NOUN **2** A **notice** is a sign that tells people something. *The **notice** said, "Cameras are not allowed in the museum".*

a
b
c
d
e
f
g
h
i
j
k
l
m
n
o
p
q
r
s
t
u
v
w
x
y
z

nought NOUN
Nought is the number 0, or zero.

noun nouns NOUN
In grammar, a **noun** is a word which names a person, a thing or an idea. "James", "newt", and "success" are all nouns.
See Noun on page 268

nourishment NOUN
Nourishment is the food that you need in order to grow and stay healthy.
nourishing ADJECTIVE

novel novels NOUN
A **novel** is a long written story that has been made up by the author. Novels are fiction.

November NOUN
November is the 11th month of the year. It has 30 days.

now ADVERB
Now means at the present time.

nowhere ADVERB
Nowhere means not anywhere.

nude ADJECTIVE
Someone who is **nude** is not wearing any clothes.

nudge nudges, nudging, nudged VERB
If you **nudge** somebody, you push them gently, usually with your elbow.

nuisance nuisances NOUN
If you say that someone or something is a **nuisance**, you mean they annoy you.

numb ADJECTIVE
If something is **numb**, it does not feel anything. *My foot is so cold it is **numb**.*

number numbers NOUN
A **number** is a word or sign that tells you how many of something there are.
See Numbers on page 278

numeracy NOUN
Numeracy is the ability to understand and work with numbers.

numerous ADJECTIVE
If there are **numerous** things or people, there are a lot of them.

nurse nurses NOUN
A **nurse** is a person whose job is to care for people who are ill or injured.

nursery nurseries
NOUN **1** A **nursery** is a place where young children can be looked after during the day.
NOUN **2** A **nursery** can also be a place where plants are grown and sold.

nut nuts
NOUN **1** A **nut** is the hard fruit of certain trees such as walnuts and chestnuts.
NOUN **2** A **nut** is also a small piece of metal with a hole in it. It screws onto a bolt to fasten things together.

nylon NOUN
Nylon is a strong artificial material.

123

Oo

oak oaks NOUN
An **oak** is a large tree with nuts called acorns. The wood of oak trees is often used to make furniture.

oar oars NOUN
An **oar** is a wooden pole with a wide flat end, used for rowing a boat.

oasis oases NOUN
An **oasis** is a place in a desert where water and plants are found.

oats PLURAL NOUN
Oats are the grains of a cereal. They are used especially for making porridge or for feeding animals.

obedient ADJECTIVE
If you are **obedient**, you do what you are told to do.

obey obeys, obeying, obeyed VERB
If you **obey** someone, you do as they say.

object objects
NOUN **1** An **object** is anything that you can touch or see, and that is not alive.
NOUN **2** In grammar, the **object** of a verb or preposition is the word or phrase which describes the person or thing affected. In the sentence "She fed the cat", "cat" is the object.

oblong oblongs NOUN
An **oblong** is a four-sided shape with two parallel short sides and two parallel long sides.
See **rectangle**
See also Colours and shapes on page 266

observe observes, observing, observed
VERB
If you **observe** something or somebody, you watch them carefully.

obstinate ADJECTIVE
Someone who is **obstinate** is determined to do what they want and will not change their mind.

obvious ADJECTIVE
Something that is **obvious** is easy to see or understand.

occasion occasions NOUN
An **occasion** is an important event or celebration.

occasional ADJECTIVE
Occasional means happening sometimes, but not regularly or often.
occasionally ADVERB

occupant occupants NOUN
The **occupant** of a place is the person who lives or works there.

occupy occupies, occupying, occupied
VERB **1** To **occupy** a place means to live, stay or work in it.
VERB **2** If something **occupies** you, you are busy doing it or thinking about it.
ADJECTIVE **3** If something like a chair is **occupied**, someone is using it.

occur occurs, occurring, occurred
VERB **1** When something **occurs**, it happens.
VERB **2** If something **occurs** to you, you suddenly think of it or realize it.

ocean oceans
NOUN
An **ocean** is one of the five large seas on the earth's surface.

a
b
c
d
e
f
g
h
i
j
k
l
m
n
o
p
q
r
s
t
u
v
w
x
y
z

A
B
C
D
E
F
G
H
I
J
K
L
M
N
O
P
Q
R
S
T
U
V
W
X
Y
Z

o'clock ADVERB
You say **o'clock** after numbers when you say a time that is exactly on the hour.

octagon octagons NOUN
An **octagon** is a flat shape with eight straight sides.
octagonal ADJECTIVE
See Colours and shapes on page 266

October NOUN
October is the 10th month of the year. It has 31 days.

octopus octopuses NOUN
An **octopus** is a sea animal with eight long arms called tentacles.

odd odder, oddest
ADJECTIVE **1** If you say something is **odd**, you mean it is strange or unusual.
ADJECTIVE **2 Odd** numbers are those which cannot be divided exactly by two. 13, 25 and 79 are odd numbers.
ADJECTIVE **3 Odd** things are those which do not belong in a pair or a set. *You can't go out wearing **odd** socks.*
odds and ends PHRASE **Odds and ends** are small unimportant things. *His pockets were full of **odds and ends**.*

odour odours NOUN
An **odour** is a particular smell.

of PREPOSITION
You use **of** to show that one thing belongs to another. *Police searched the homes **of** the criminals.*

off
PREPOSITION **1 Off** can show movement away from or out of a place. *They stepped **off** the plane.*
ADVERB **2 Off** can mean not switched on. *He turned the radio **off**.*
ADVERB **3 Off** can also mean time spent away from work. *He took the afternoon **off**.*
ADVERB **4** People use **off** to show a reduction. *All right, I'll take ten per cent **off**.*
ADJECTIVE **5** If food is **off**, it is going bad.

offend offends, offending, offended VERB
If you **offend** someone, you upset them by doing or saying something rude.
offensive ADJECTIVE

offer offers, offering, offered
VERB **1** If you **offer** something to someone, you ask them if they would like to have it.
VERB **2** If you **offer** to do something, you say you will do it without being asked.

office offices NOUN
An **office** is a room where people work at desks.

officer officers
NOUN **1** An **officer** is a member of the police, or of a government organization.
NOUN **2** An **officer** is also a person in the army, navy or air force who gives orders to other people.

official ADJECTIVE
Something that is **official** is written or done by the government or by someone else in charge.

often ADVERB
If something happens **often**, it happens many times.

oil oils
NOUN **1 Oil** is a smooth thick liquid that is found under the ground. It is used to keep machines running smoothly, and also for fuel.
NOUN **2 Oil** can also be made from plants or animals. This oil can sometimes be used for cooking.

OK or okay

INTERJECTION **1** You can say **OK** to show that you agree to something.

ADJECTIVE **2** If someone is **OK**, they are safe and well.

old older, oldest

ADJECTIVE **1** Someone or something **old** has been in the world for many years.

ADJECTIVE **2** You say something is **old** if it has been used a lot, or you have had it for a long time. *These are my old shoes.*

ADJECTIVE **3** If you ask how **old** someone is, you want to know how long they have lived. *How old is your baby?*

old-fashioned ADJECTIVE

Something **old-fashioned** belongs to the past and has been replaced by something more modern.

olive olives NOUN

An **olive** is a small green or black fruit. Olives are eaten as a snack, or used to make oil for cooking.

omelette omelettes

NOUN

An **omelette** is a food made by beating eggs and cooking them.

on

PREPOSITION **1** If someone or something is **on** a surface, it is resting there. *There was a large box on the table.*

ADJECTIVE **2** When something that uses electricity is **on**, it is using electricity. *The television is on.*

once

ADVERB **1** If something happens **once**, it happens one time only.

ADVERB **2** **Once** means at some time in the past. *Once, the Romans ruled in Britain.*

at once PHRASE If you do something **at once**, you do it straight away.

one

NOUN **1** **One** is the number 1.

PRONOUN **2** **One** refers to a particular thing or person. *I think Tim's idea is the best one.*

onion onions NOUN

An **onion** is a small round vegetable with a brown papery skin and a very strong taste.

online ADJECTIVE

If you are **online**, your computer is connected to the Internet.

only

ADJECTIVE **1** **Only** means one and no more. *She was the only girl in the group.*

ADJECTIVE **2** An **only** child is someone who has no brothers or sisters.

ADVERB **3** You say **only** when you mean one person or thing and not others. *He's only interested in football.*

ADVERB **4** You can say **only** when something is not very important. *It was only a sparrow.*

ADVERB **5** **Only** can be used when something was less than you expected. *It only took me ten minutes.*

onto PREPOSITION

If something moves **onto** a surface, it moves to a place on that surface. *The cat climbed onto her lap.*

open opens, opening, opened

VERB **1** If you **open** a door, you move it so that people can go through it.

VERB **2** If you **open** a box or a bottle, you take the lid off or unfasten it.

VERB **3** When flowers **open**, you can see their petals.

ADJECTIVE **4** When a place such as a shop or library is **open**, you can use it.

opening openings NOUN

An **opening** is a hole or space that things or people can go through.

opera operas NOUN

An **opera** is a musical play in which most of the words are sung.

A
B
C
D
E
F
G
H
I
J
K
L
M
N
O
P
Q
R
S
T
U
V
W
X
Y
Z

operate operates, operating, operated

VERB **1** When someone **operates** a machine, they make it work.

VERB **2** When doctors **operate**, they cut open a patient's body to remove or repair a damaged part.

operation operations NOUN

An **operation** is when doctors cut open a patient's body to remove or repair a damaged part.

opinion opinions NOUN

An **opinion** is what someone thinks about something.

opponent opponents NOUN

An **opponent** is someone who is against you in an argument or a contest.

opposite opposites

NOUN **1** The **opposite** of something is the thing that is most different from it. *Hot is the* **opposite** *of cold.*

PREPOSITION **2** If one person or thing is **opposite** another, they are on the other side of something. *In the train I sat* **opposite** *a small boy.*

optician opticians NOUN

An **optician** is someone who tests people's eyes, and sells glasses and contact lenses.

or CONJUNCTION

Or is used to link two alternatives or choices. *You need to decide whether to stay* **or** *leave.*

orange oranges

NOUN **1** An **orange** is a round fruit with a thick skin. Oranges are juicy and sometimes sweet. *See Fruit on page 260*

ADJECTIVE **2** Something that is **orange** has a colour between red and yellow.
See Colours and shapes on page 266

orbit orbits, orbiting, orbited VERB

If something **orbits** a planet or the Sun, it goes round and round it.

orchard orchards NOUN

An **orchard** is an area of land where fruit trees are grown.

orchestra orchestras NOUN

An **orchestra** is a large group of musicians who play different instruments together.

order orders, ordering, ordered

NOUN **1** An **order** is something you are told to do.

VERB **2** If you **order** something, for example in a restaurant, you ask for it to be brought to you.

NOUN **3 Order** is the way a set of things is organized. A dictionary is written in alphabetical order.

ordinary ADJECTIVE

Something that is **ordinary** is not special in any way.

organ organs

NOUN **1** An **organ** is a part of your body that does a special job, for example your heart, lungs or stomach.

NOUN **2** An **organ** is also a large musical instrument like a piano. It has pipes that air is forced through to make the sounds.

organic ADJECTIVE

Food that is **organic** has been produced without the use of chemicals.

organization organizations; also spelt **organisation** NOUN

An **organization** is a large group of people

who work together. For example, the police force is an organization.

organize organizes, organizing, organized; also spelt **organise**

VERB **1** If you **organize** an event, you plan and arrange it.

VERB **2** If you **organize** things, you arrange them in a sensible order.

origin origins

NOUN **1** The **origin** of something is how and why it started.

NOUN **2** You can refer to where someone comes from as their **origin**. *She was of Swedish origin.*

original

ADJECTIVE **1** Something that is **original** is new and not a copy.

ADJECTIVE **2** If you say someone's ideas are **original**, you mean they are clever at thinking of new ways of doing things.

ornament ornaments NOUN

An **ornament** is an object that you put somewhere because you think it is nice to look at.

orphan orphans NOUN

An **orphan** is a child whose parents are dead.

ostrich ostriches NOUN

An **ostrich** is the largest living bird. It cannot fly, but it can run very fast. Ostriches live in sandy places in Africa. Their eggs are large, weighing more than a kilo each.

other

ADJECTIVE **1** When you say **other** things or other people, you can mean more of the same kind. *He found it hard to make friends with other children.*

ADJECTIVE **2** You can also use **other** to mean different. *We got lost last time. I think we'll try some other way.*

every other PHRASE **Every other** means one in every two. *We meet every other week.*

otherwise ADVERB

You say **otherwise** to explain what will happen if you do not do something.

I'd better take an umbrella, otherwise I'll get soaked.

otter otters NOUN

An **otter** is an animal with brown fur, short legs and a long tail. Otters swim well and eat fish.

ought VERB

If you **ought** to do something, you should do it. *I ought to leave early.*

our ADJECTIVE

Our refers to something belonging or relating to the speaker or writer and one or more other people. *We recently sold our house.*

ours PRONOUN

You use **ours** when you are talking about something that belongs to you and one or more other people. *That car is ours.*

ourselves PRONOUN

Ourselves is used when the people speaking do something and no one else does it. *We made the beds ourselves.*

out

ADVERB **1** **Out** means towards the outside of a place. *Two dogs rushed out of the house.*

ADVERB **2** **Out** can also mean not at home. *She was out when I rang last night.*

ADVERB **3** **Out** can mean no longer shining or burning. *The lights went out.*

outdoors ADVERB

If you are **outdoors**, you are not inside a building.

a
b
c
d
e
f
g
h
i
j
k
l
m
n
o
p
q
r
s
t
u
v
w
x
y
z

143

A B C D E F G H I J K L M N O P Q R S T U V W X Y Z

outer ADJECTIVE

The **outer** parts of something are the parts furthest from the centre. *The **outer** layer of an onion is brown and papery.*

outing outings NOUN

An **outing** is a short trip somewhere to enjoy yourself.

outline outlines NOUN

An **outline** is the shape of something, especially when you cannot see any details.

outside

NOUN **1** The **outside** of something is the part which surrounds the rest of it. *They painted the **outside** of the building.*

ADVERB **2** You can use **outside** with a verb to mean out of a building. *Let's go **outside**.*

PREPOSITION **3** If something is **outside** a place or a container, it is next to it but not in it. *The bicycle was chained up **outside** the church.*

oval ovals

NOUN **1** An **oval** is a shape like an egg.

ADJECTIVE **2 Oval** describes something shaped like an egg, such as an oval mirror or oval frame.

See Colours and shapes on page 266

oven ovens NOUN

The **oven** is the part of a cooker that you use for baking or roasting food.

over

PREPOSITION **1 Over** something means directly above it or covering it. *He put his hands **over** his eyes.*

PREPOSITION **2** A view **over** an area is a view across that area. *The front windows look out **over** the sea.*

PREPOSITION **3** Something that is **over** a particular amount is more than that amount.

PREPOSITION **4** If something happens **over** a period of time, it happens during that period. *I went skiing **over** Christmas.*

ADVERB **5** If you lean **over**, you bend your body in a particular direction.

ADVERB **6** You can use **over** to show movement from one place to another. *She went **over** to the door.*

overalls PLURAL NOUN

Overalls are a piece of clothing with trousers and jacket in one. You wear overalls to protect your other clothes when you are working.

overboard ADVERB

If someone falls **overboard**, they fall over the side of a ship into the water.

overcoat overcoats NOUN

An **overcoat** is a thick warm coat that people wear in winter.

overdue ADJECTIVE

If someone or something is **overdue**, they are late. *My library book is **overdue**.*

overflow overflows, overflowing, overflowed

VERB **1** If a liquid **overflows**, it spills over the edges of its container.

VERB **2** If a river **overflows**, it flows over its banks.

overgrown ADJECTIVE

If a place is **overgrown**, it is thickly covered with plants and weeds, usually because it has not been looked after for a long time.

overhead ADVERB

Overhead means above you. *Seagulls were flying **overhead**.*

overhear **overhears, overhearing, overheard** VERB
If you **overhear** someone's conversation, you hear what they are saying to someone else.

overlap **overlaps, overlapping, overlapped** VERB
If one thing **overlaps** another, one part of it covers part of the other thing.

overseas ADVERB
If you go **overseas**, you go to a country which is on the other side of a sea or ocean.

oversleep **oversleeps, oversleeping, overslept** VERB
If you **oversleep**, you sleep longer than you meant to, and wake up late.

overtake **overtakes, overtaking, overtook, overtaken** VERB
If you **overtake** someone, you pass them because you are moving faster than they are.

owe **owes, owing, owed**
VERB **1** If you **owe** someone money, they have lent it to you and you have not yet paid it back.
VERB **2** If you **owe** someone something, such as thanks, you need to give it to them.

owl **owls** NOUN
An **owl** is a bird with a flat face and large eyes. Usually owls hunt at night for small animals.

own **owns, owning, owned**
VERB **1** If you **own** something, it belongs to you.
VERB **2** If you **own up** to something wrong, you say that you did it.
on your own PHRASE If you are **on your own**, you are alone. If you do something **on your own**, you do it without any help.

owner **owners** NOUN
The **owner** of something is the person it belongs to.

ox **oxen** NOUN
Oxen are cattle which are used for carrying or pulling things.

oxygen NOUN
Oxygen is a gas that forms part of the air we breathe. Other animals and plants also need oxygen to live, and things will not burn without it.

oyster **oysters** NOUN
An **oyster** is a large flat shellfish. Some oysters produce pearls.
See **pearl**

ozone NOUN
Ozone is a form of oxygen.
ozone layer PHRASE The **ozone layer** is the part of the Earth's atmosphere that protects living things from the dangerous rays of the Sun.

a b c d e f g h i j k l m n o p q r s t u v w x y z

145

Pp

pace paces
NOUN **1** The **pace** of something is the speed at which it happens.
NOUN **2** A **pace** is a step that you take when you walk.

pack packs, packing, packed
VERB **1** When you **pack**, you put your clothes in a case or bag.
NOUN **2** A **pack** is a set of playing cards.
NOUN **3** A **pack** of wolves or other animals is a group that hunts together.
See Collective nouns on page 268

package packages NOUN
A **package** is a small parcel.

packaging NOUN
Packaging is the container that something is sold or sent in.

packet packets NOUN
A **packet** is a thin cardboard box or paper container.

pad pads
NOUN **1** A **pad** is a number of pieces of paper fixed together on one side.
NOUN **2** An animal's **pads** are the soft parts under its paws.

paddle paddles, paddling, paddled
VERB **1** If you **paddle** in the sea, you stand or walk in the shallow water.
VERB **2** If you **paddle** a small boat such as a canoe, you use a special type of oar called a paddle to move the boat along.

padlock padlocks NOUN
A **padlock** is a special kind of lock. You can use it to lock gates and bicycles.

page pages NOUN
A **page** is one side of a piece of paper in a book or newspaper.

paid VERB
Paid is the past tense of **pay**.

pail pails NOUN
A **pail** is a bucket.

pain pains NOUN
A **pain** is an unpleasant feeling that you have in part of your body if you have been hurt or are ill.

painful ADJECTIVE
If you say that something is **painful**, you mean it is hurting you.
painfully ADVERB

paint paints, painting, painted
NOUN **1** **Paint** is a coloured liquid that you put onto a surface to make it look fresh.
VERB **2** When you **paint** a picture, you use paint to make a picture on paper or canvas.

painting paintings NOUN
A **painting** is a picture that has been painted.

pair pairs
NOUN **1** A **pair** is a set of two things that go together. *I need a new **pair** of shoes.*
NOUN **2** Some objects, such as trousers and scissors, have two main parts which are the same size and shape. This sort of object is also called a **pair**.

palace palaces

NOUN

A **palace** is a large important house, especially one which is the home of a king, queen or president.

pale paler, palest

ADJECTIVE

Something that is **pale** is light in colour, and not strong or bright.

palm palms

NOUN **1** The **palm** of your hand is the inside surface of it. Your fingers and thumb are not part of your palm.

NOUN **2** A **palm** is a tree which grows in hot countries. It has long pointed leaves that grow out of the top of a tall trunk.

pan pans NOUN

A **pan** is a container with a long handle that is used for cooking.

pancake pancakes NOUN

A **pancake** is a thin flat cake made of flour, eggs and milk, which is fried.

panda pandas NOUN

A **panda** is an animal like a black and white bear that lives in the bamboo forests of China.

pane panes NOUN

A **pane** is a sheet of glass in a window or door.

panic panics, panicking, panicked VERB

If you **panic**, you suddenly get so worried you cannot act sensibly.

pant pants, panting, panted VERB

If you **pant**, you breathe quickly with your mouth open. You usually pant when you have been running fast.

panther panthers NOUN

Panther is another name for a black leopard.

pantomime pantomimes NOUN

A **pantomime** is a funny musical play for children.

pants PLURAL NOUN

Pants are a piece of clothing that you wear under your other clothes. They have two holes for your legs and elastic round the waist.

paper papers

NOUN **1 Paper** is the material that you write on or wrap things in.

NOUN **2** A newspaper is also called a **paper**.

parachute parachutes NOUN

A **parachute** is a large piece of thin cloth. It has strings fixed to it so that a person attached to it can float down to the ground from an aircraft.

parade parades NOUN

A **parade** is a lot of people marching in the road on a special day.

paragraph paragraphs NOUN

A **paragraph** is a section of a piece of writing. Paragraphs begin on a new line.

parallel ADJECTIVE

Two lines or other things that are **parallel** are the same distance apart all the way along. *The road along the sea front is **parallel** with the sea.*

paralysed ADJECTIVE

Someone who is **paralysed** cannot move or feel some or all of their body.

parcel parcels NOUN

A **parcel** is one or more objects wrapped in paper. This is usually done so that it can be sent by post.

parent parents NOUN

Your **parents** are your mother and father.

a
b
c
d
e
f
g
h
i
j
k
l
m
n
o
p
q
r
s
t
u
v
w
x
y
z

A
B
C
D
E
F
G
H
I
J
K
L
M
N
O
P
Q
R
S
T
U
V
W
X
Y
Z

park parks, parking, parked
NOUN **1** A **park** is an area of land with grass and trees, usually in a town. People go there to walk or play.

VERB **2** When someone **parks** a vehicle, they put it somewhere until they need it again.

parliament parliaments NOUN
The **parliament** of a country is the people who make the country's laws.

parrot parrots
NOUN

A **parrot** is brightly-coloured bird with a curved beak.

parsnip parsnips NOUN
A **parsnip** is a long, pointed, cream-coloured root vegetable.
See Vegetables on page 260

part parts
NOUN **1** A **part** of something is one of the pieces that it is made from. *We need a new part for the washing machine.*

NOUN **2** A **part** is also a particular bit of something such as an area or a body. *This part of the park is for young children only.*

NOUN **3** If you have a **part** in a play, you are one of the people in it.

particular ADJECTIVE
When you talk about a **particular** person or thing, you mean just that person or thing and not others of the same kind.

partly ADVERB
Partly means not completely. *The table was partly covered with a cloth.*

partner partners NOUN
Your **partner** is the person you are doing something with, for example when dancing or playing games.

part of speech parts of speech NOUN
A **part of speech** is one of the groups that words are divided into in grammar, such as a noun or an adjective.
See Parts of speech on page 268

party parties NOUN
A **party** is a group of people having fun together.

pass passes, passing, passed
VERB **1** If you **pass** someone, you go past them without stopping.

VERB **2** If you **pass** something to someone, you hand it to them.

VERB **3** If you **pass** a test or an exam, you are successful in it.

passage passages
NOUN **1** A **passage** is a long narrow space with walls on both sides.

NOUN **2** A **passage** is also a section in a piece of writing. *There's a wonderful passage in the book that describes their arrival at the castle.*

passenger passengers NOUN
A **passenger** is a person who travels in a vehicle but is not the driver.

passive NOUN
In grammar, the **passive** or **passive voice** is the form of the verb in which the person or thing to which an action is being done is the subject of the sentence. For example, the sentence "The ball was hit by the boy" is in the passive.
See **voice**

Passover NOUN
Passover is a Jewish festival held in spring.

passport passports NOUN
A **passport** is a book with your name and photograph in it, that you need when you leave your own country.

password passwords NOUN
A **password** is a secret word or phrase that you must say to be allowed into a particular place.

past

NOUN **1** The **past** is the period of time before the present.

ADVERB **2** If you go **past** something, you move towards it and continue until you are on the other side.

PREPOSITION **3** You use **past** when you are telling the time. *It's ten **past** three.*

NOUN **4** In grammar, the **past tense** of a verb is the form used to show that something happened in the past.

pasta NOUN

Pasta is a type of food made from flour, eggs and water, which is formed into different shapes. Spaghetti, macaroni and noodles are types of pasta.
*See **Other foods** on page 261*

paste pastes NOUN

Paste is a thick wet mixture that is easy to spread.

pastime pastimes NOUN

A **pastime** is something you like to do in your free time.

pastry NOUN

Pastry is a food made of flour, fat and water, rolled flat and used for making pies.

pasture pastures NOUN

Pasture is land that is used for farm animals to graze on.

pat pats, patting, patted VERB

If you **pat** something, you hit it gently, usually with your open hand.

patch patches NOUN

A **patch** is a piece of material you put over a hole in something to mend it.

path paths NOUN

A **path** is a strip of ground that people walk on.

patience NOUN

Patience is being able to wait calmly for something, or to do something difficult without giving up.

patient patients

ADJECTIVE **1** If you are **patient**, you are able to wait calmly for something, or to do something difficult without giving up.

NOUN **2** A **patient** is someone who is being treated by a doctor.

patrol patrols, patrolling, patrolled VERB

When people like the police **patrol** a particular area, they go round it to make sure there is no trouble or danger.

pattern patterns NOUN

A **pattern** is a regular way something is organized. For example, lines and shapes can make patterns.

pause pauses, pausing, paused VERB

If you **pause** while you are doing something, you stop for a moment.

pavement pavements NOUN

A **pavement** is a path with a hard surface beside a road, so that people can walk in safety.

paw paws NOUN

A **paw** is the foot of some animals. Paws have claws at the front and soft pads underneath.

pay pays, paying, paid VERB

When a person **pays** someone, they give them money in exchange for work or for things that they have bought.
payment NOUN

a
b
c
d
e
f
g
h
i
j
k
l
m
n
o
p
q
r
s
t
u
v
w
x
y
z

A
B
C
D
E
F
G
H
I
J
K
L
M
N
O
P
Q
R
S
T
U
V
W
X
Y
Z

PC PCs
NOUN **1** A **PC** is a personal computer.
NOUN **2** In Britain, a **PC** is also a police constable.

PE NOUN
PE is an abbreviation of **physical education**.

pea peas NOUN
Peas are round green seeds which are eaten as a vegetable. They grow inside a covering called a pod.
See Vegetables on page 260

peace
NOUN **1** **Peace** is a feeling of quiet and calm.
NOUN **2** When a country has **peace** or is **at peace**, it is not fighting a war.

peaceful ADJECTIVE
A **peaceful** place is quiet and calm.

peach peaches NOUN
A **peach** is a round juicy fruit with a large stone in the middle. It has sweet yellow flesh and a yellow and red skin.
See Fruit on page 260

peacock peacocks NOUN
A **peacock** is a large male bird with bright blue and green feathers, and long tail feathers which it spreads in a fan. The female is called a peahen.

peak peaks
NOUN **1** The **peak** of a mountain is the pointed top of it.
NOUN **2** The **peak** of a cap is the part that sticks out at the front.

peanut peanuts NOUN
Peanuts are small hard seeds which grow under the ground. You can buy roasted and salted peanuts to eat.

pear pears NOUN
A **pear** is a sweet juicy fruit which grows on trees. It is narrow near its stalk, and wider and rounded at the bottom.
See Fruit on page 260

pearl pearls NOUN
A **pearl** is a hard round object which grows inside the shell of an oyster. It is creamy-white in colour. Pearls are used to make valuable jewellery.

pebble pebbles NOUN
A **pebble** is a small smooth stone found on seashores and river beds.

peck pecks, pecking, pecked VERB
When a bird **pecks**, it bites at something with its beak.

peculiar ADJECTIVE
Something that is **peculiar** is strange or unusual.

pedal pedals NOUN
The **pedals** on a cycle are the two parts that you push with your feet to make it move.

pedestrian pedestrians NOUN
A **pedestrian** is a person who is walking.

peek peeks, peeking, peeked VERB
If you **peek** at something, you have a quick look at it.

peel peels, peeling, peeled VERB
If you **peel** fruit or vegetables, you remove the skin.

peep peeps, peeping, peeped VERB
If you **peep** at something, you look at it very quickly, and usually secretly.

peg pegs
NOUN **1** A **peg** is a thin piece of metal or plastic that is used to hang things on.
NOUN **2** A **peg** is also a small clip that is used to hold washing on a line.

pelican pelicans NOUN
A **pelican** is a water bird. Its large beak has a soft lower part like a pouch.

pen pens NOUN
A **pen** is a long thin tool that you use to write in ink.

pence NOUN
Pence is a plural form of **penny**.

pencil **pencils** NOUN
A **pencil** is a long thin piece of wood with a dark material called graphite in the middle. It is used for writing or drawing.

pendulum
pendulums NOUN
A **pendulum** is a large weight which hangs from a clock. It swings from side to side to keep the clock going at the right speed.

penguin
penguins NOUN
A **penguin** is a large black and white bird found in the Antarctic. Penguins cannot fly. They use their wings for swimming in the water.

penny **pennies** or **pence** NOUN
A **penny** is a small British coin. A hundred pence are worth one pound. The abbreviation for pence is p.

pentagon **pentagons** NOUN
A **pentagon** is a flat shape that has five straight sides.
pentagonal ADJECTIVE
See Colours and shapes on page 266

people PLURAL NOUN
People are men, women and children.

pepper **peppers**
NOUN **1** **Pepper** is a hot-tasting powder which is used to flavour food.
NOUN **2** A **pepper** is a red, green or yellow vegetable. It can be cooked or eaten raw in salads.
See Food and drink on pages 260 and 261

per cent PHRASE
You use **per cent** to talk about amounts as a proportion of 100. For example, ten per cent (10%) means 10 out of every 100.

perch **perches** NOUN
A **perch** is a short piece of wood for a bird to stand on.

percussion ADJECTIVE
Percussion instruments are instruments that you play by hitting them. Drums and cymbals are percussion instruments.

perfect
ADJECTIVE **1** Something that is **perfect** is done so well it could not be done better.
ADJECTIVE **2** If you say something is **perfect**, you mean it is wonderful.
perfectly ADVERB

perform **performs, performing, performed** VERB
If someone **performs**, they do something to entertain an audience.

performance **performances** NOUN
A **performance** is something done in front of people, like acting or dancing.

perfume **perfumes**
NOUN **1** A **perfume** is a pleasant smell.
NOUN **2** **Perfume** is a liquid that you put on your body so that you smell nice.

perhaps
ADVERB **1** If you say **perhaps** something will happen, you mean it might happen but you are not sure.
ADVERB **2** You can also say **perhaps** when you are suggesting something. *He's late – perhaps he missed the train.*

perimeter **perimeters** NOUN
The **perimeter** of a shape is the distance all round it.

period **periods** NOUN
A **period** is a particular length of time. *Mrs Smith will be away for a period of six months.*

periscope **periscopes** NOUN
A **periscope** is a tube with mirrors. When you look in one end, you can see what would otherwise be out of sight.

permanent ADJECTIVE
Something that is **permanent** lasts for ever, or for a very long time.

a
b
c
d
e
f
g
h
i
j
k
l
m
n
o
p
q
r
s
t
u
v
w
x
y
z

A B C D E F G H I J K L M N O P Q R S T U V W X Y Z

permission NOUN
If you have **permission** to do something, you are allowed to do it.

permit **permits, permitting, permitted** VERB
If someone **permits** you to do something, they allow you to do it.

persist **persists, persisting, persisted** VERB
If you **persist**, you go on doing something even when it is difficult or other people have told you to stop.

person **people** NOUN
A **person** is a man, woman or child.

personal ADJECTIVE
Personal matters relate to your feelings, relationships and health, which you may not want to talk about with other people.

personality **personalities** NOUN
Your **personality** is your character and nature. *She's got a very lively* **personality**.

persuade **persuades, persuading, persuaded** VERB
If someone **persuades** you to do something you did not want to do, you agree because they gave you a good reason.
persuasion NOUN

persuasive
ADJECTIVE **1** Someone who is **persuasive** is good at persuading others to believe or do a particular thing.
ADJECTIVE **2** **Persuasive** text aims to persuade the reader of something.

pest **pests** NOUN
A **pest** is an insect, rat or other small animal that causes damage.

pester **pesters, pestering, pestered** VERB
If you **pester** someone, you keep bothering them.

pet **pets** NOUN
A **pet** is a tame animal that you keep and look after in your home.

petal **petals** NOUN
A **petal** is part of a flower. Petals may have bright colours or scents to attract insects.

petrol NOUN
Petrol is a liquid used as fuel in motor vehicles.

phantom **phantoms** NOUN
A **phantom** is a ghost.

phone **phones** NOUN
Phone is an abbreviation of **telephone**.

photo **photos** NOUN
Photo is an abbreviation of **photograph**.

photocopy **photocopies** NOUN
A **photocopy** is a copy of a document produced by a photocopier.

photograph **photographs** NOUN
A **photograph** is a picture that is made using a camera.

phrase **phrases** NOUN
A **phrase** is a short group of words used together.

physical
ADJECTIVE **1** **Physical** means to do with things that can be touched or seen.
ADJECTIVE **2** **Physical** also means to do with a person's body, rather than their mind.
physically ADVERB

piano **pianos** NOUN
A **piano** is a large musical instrument with black and white keys that you press with your fingers.

pick **picks, picking, picked**
VERB **1** To **pick** means to choose. *We need to* **pick** *three more people for our team.*
VERB **2** When you **pick** flowers or fruit, you take them off the plant.
VERB **3** If you **pick** something **up**, you lift it up from where it is.

pickle **pickles** NOUN
Pickles are vegetables or fruit that have been kept in vinegar or salt water.

picnic **picnics** NOUN
A **picnic** is a meal that you take with you and eat out of doors.

picture **pictures** NOUN
A **picture** is a drawing, painting or photograph.

pie **pies** NOUN
A **pie** is fruit, vegetables, meat or fish baked in pastry.

piece **pieces** NOUN
A **piece** is a part of something.

pier **piers** NOUN
A **pier** is a long platform which sticks out over the sea. Piers often have some kind of entertainment on them.

pierce **pierces, piercing, pierced** VERB
If a sharp object **pierces** something, it goes through it and makes a hole in it.

pig **pigs** NOUN
A **pig** is a farm animal kept for its meat. It has pinkish skin and short legs.

pigeon **pigeons** NOUN
A **pigeon** is a large bird with grey feathers, often seen in towns.

piglet **piglets** NOUN
A **piglet** is a young pig.
See *Young animals* on page 265

pile **piles** NOUN
A **pile** is a lot of things, such as books, which have been put one on top of the other.

pill **pills** NOUN
A **pill** is medicine made into a small round object that you swallow.

pillar **pillars** NOUN
A **pillar** is a tall post made of something such as stone or brick. It usually helps to hold up a building.

pillow **pillows** NOUN
A **pillow** is a bag filled with soft material to rest your head on in bed.

pilot **pilots** NOUN
A **pilot** is a person who is trained to fly an aircraft.

pimple **pimples** NOUN
A **pimple** is a small red spot, especially on your face.

pin **pins** NOUN
A **pin** is a small thin piece of metal with a point at one end. Pins can be pushed through things such as pieces of paper or cloth, to hold them together.

pincers
PLURAL NOUN **1** The **pincers** of a crab or lobster are its front claws.
PLURAL NOUN **2 Pincers** are also a tool used for gripping and pulling things.

pinch **pinches, pinching, pinched** VERB
If someone **pinches** you, they squeeze part of you quickly between their thumb and first finger.

pine **pines** NOUN
A **pine** is a tall evergreen tree with sharp thin leaves called needles.

pineapple **pineapples** NOUN
A **pineapple** is a large oval fruit with yellow flesh and a thick, lumpy skin. Pineapples grow in hot countries.

pink **pinker, pinkest** ADJECTIVE
Something that is **pink** has a colour between white and red.
See *Colours and shapes* on page 266

pint **pints** NOUN
A **pint** is a measure for liquids. A pint is equal to just over half a litre.

a b c d e f g h i j k l m n o p q r s t u v w x y z

pipe **pipes** NOUN

A **pipe** is a long hollow tube, usually made of metal or plastic. Pipes are used to carry liquid or gas.

pirate **pirates** NOUN

In the past, a **pirate** was a robber who stole from ships.

pistol **pistols** NOUN

A **pistol** is a small gun.

pit **pits**

NOUN **1** A **pit** is a large hole that has been dug in the ground.

NOUN **2** A **pit** is also a coal mine.

pitch **pitches, pitching, pitched**

NOUN **1** A **pitch** is an area of ground where a game such as hockey or football is played.

NOUN **2** The **pitch** of a sound is how high or low it is.

VERB **3** When you **pitch** a tent, you put it up so that you can use it.

pity

NOUN **1** If you feel **pity** for someone, you feel sorry for them.

NOUN **2** If you say something is a **pity**, you mean it is disappointing. *What a **pity** Mark isn't coming.*

pizza **pizzas** NOUN

A **pizza** is a flat round piece of dough covered with cheese, tomato and other savoury food.

place **places**

NOUN **1** A **place** is any building or area.

NOUN **2** A **place** is also the position where something belongs. *Please put the tools back in their right **place**.*

plague **plagues** NOUN

A **plague** is a disease that spreads quickly and kills many people.

plaice NOUN

A **plaice** is a flat sea fish.

plain **plainer, plainest; plains**

ADJECTIVE **1** A **plain** object has no pattern on it. *She wore a **plain** skirt.*

ADJECTIVE **2** If something is **plain**, it is clear and easy to see.

NOUN **3** A **plain** is a large, flat area of land with very few trees on it.

plait **plaits, plaiting, plaited**

VERB **1** If you **plait** three lengths of hair or rope together, you twist them over each other in turn.

NOUN **2** A **plait** is a length of hair that has been plaited.

plan **plans, planning, planned**

NOUN **1** If you have a **plan**, you have thought of a way of doing something.

NOUN **2** A **plan** is a drawing that shows what something looks like from above.

VERB **3** If you **plan** what you are going to do, you decide exactly how to do it.

plane **planes**

NOUN **1** A **plane** is a flying vehicle. It has wings and one or more engines. Plane is an abbreviation of **aeroplane**.

NOUN **2** A **plane** is also a tool used for smoothing wood.

planet **planets** NOUN

A **planet** is a large round object in space that moves around a star. Earth is one of the nine planets that go round the sun.

plank **planks** NOUN

A **plank** is a long flat piece of wood.

plant **plants, planting, planted**

NOUN **1** A **plant** is any living thing that is not an animal. Plants can make their own food.

VERB **2** When you **plant** things, such as seeds, flowers or trees, you put them in the ground so that they will grow.

A B C D E F G H I J K L M N O P Q R S T U V W X Y Z

plaster plasters
NOUN **1** A **plaster** is a strip of sticky material used for covering small cuts.
NOUN **2 Plaster** is a smooth paste that dries and forms a hard layer. It is used to cover walls and ceilings inside buildings.

plastic
NOUN **1 Plastic** is a light artificial material that does not break easily. It is used to make all sorts of things, such as buckets, bowls and plates.
ADJECTIVE **2** Something that is **plastic** is made of plastic.

plate plates NOUN
A **plate** is a flat dish for food.

platform platforms
NOUN **1** A **platform** is the area in a station where you wait for the train.
NOUN **2** A **platform** is also a raised area for people to stand on so that they can be seen more easily.

play plays, playing, played
VERB **1** When you **play**, you spend time doing things you enjoy.
VERB **2** When one person or team **plays** another, they take part in a game and each side tries to win.
VERB **3** If you **play** a musical instrument, you make musical sounds with it.
NOUN **4** A **play** is a story which is acted on the stage, or on radio or television.

player players NOUN
A **player** is a person who takes part in a sport or game.

playground playgrounds NOUN
A **playground** is a piece of land for children to play on.

playtime NOUN
Playtime is a break in the school day when you can play.

pleasant ADJECTIVE
If something is **pleasant**, you enjoy it or like it.

please pleases, pleasing, pleased VERB
If you **please** someone, you make them feel happy.

pleasure NOUN
Pleasure is a feeling of happiness or enjoyment.

pleat pleats NOUN
A **pleat** is a permanent fold in fabric.
pleated ADJECTIVE

plenty NOUN
If there is **plenty** of something, there is more than enough of it.

pliers PLURAL NOUN
Pliers are a tool used for pulling out small things like nails, or for bending or cutting wire.

plot plots, plotting, plotted
NOUN **1** A **plot** is a secret plan.
NOUN **2** The **plot** of a film, novel or play is the story and the way it develops.
NOUN **3** A **plot** of land is a small piece that has been marked out for a special purpose such as building houses or growing vegetables.
VERB **4** If people **plot** something, they plan secretly to do it.

plough ploughs NOUN
A **plough** is a farming tool that is pulled across a field to turn the soil over.

a
b
c
d
e
f
g
h
i
j
k
l
m
n
o
p
q
r
s
t
u
v
w
x
y
z

155

pluck plucks, plucking, plucked
VERB **1** When someone **plucks** a musical instrument, such as a guitar, they pull the strings and let them go quickly.
VERB **2** When you **pluck** a feather, flower or fruit, you pull it from where it is growing.

plug plugs, plugging, plugged
NOUN **1** A **plug** is a thick piece of rubber or plastic that fits in the drain hole of a bath or washbasin.
NOUN **2** A **plug** is also a small object that joins pieces of equipment to the electricity supply.
VERB **3** If someone **plugs** a hole, they block it with something.

plum plums NOUN
A **plum** is a small fruit with a thin, dark red or yellow skin and juicy flesh. It has a large stone in the middle.
See Fruit on page 260

plumber plumbers NOUN
A **plumber** is a person who fits and mends water pipes.

plump plumper, plumpest ADJECTIVE
Someone or something that is **plump** is rather fat.

plunge plunges, plunging, plunged VERB
If someone **plunges** into the water, they dive or throw themselves into it.

plural plurals NOUN
Plural means more than one. *The **plural** of "boy" is "boys"... The **plural** of "box" is "boxes".*
See **singular**
See also Plurals on page 277

plus
PREPOSITION **1** You use **plus** (+) to show that one number is being added to another. *Two **plus** two equals four.*
PREPOSITION **2** You can use **plus** when you mention an additional item. *You get a television **plus** a free radio.*

p.m. ADVERB
p.m. is the time between 12 noon and 12 midnight.
See **a.m.**

poach poaches, poaching, poached VERB
If you **poach** an egg, you remove its shell and cook the egg gently in boiling water.

pocket pockets NOUN
A **pocket** is a small bag that is sewn into clothing.

pod pods NOUN
A **pod** is a seed cover. Peas and beans grow inside pods.
See **pea**

podcast podcasts NOUN
A **podcast** is a computer file containing sound that can be downloaded and listened to on a computer or MP3 player.

poem poems NOUN
A **poem** is a piece of writing in short lines, which sometimes rhyme. The lines usually have a particular rhythm.

poet poets NOUN
A **poet** is a person who writes poems.

poetry NOUN
Poetry is writing in which the lines have a rhythm and sometimes rhyme.

point points, pointing, pointed
NOUN **1** The **point** of something such as a pin is the sharp end of it.
NOUN **2** A **point** is a position or time. *I'll call you at some **point** during the day.*
NOUN **3** The **point** of doing something is the reason for doing it. *The **point** of playing is to have fun.*
NOUN **4** In a game or sport, a **point** is part of the score.
NOUN **5** The decimal **point** in a number is the dot separating the whole number from the fraction.
VERB **6** If you **point** at something, you show where it is by using your finger.
VERB **7** If something **points** in a particular direction, it faces that way.

pointed ADJECTIVE
Something that is **pointed** has a point at one end.

poison poisons NOUN
Poison is something that harms or kills

people or animals if it gets into their body.
poisonous ADJECTIVE

poke **pokes, poking, poked** VERB
If you **poke** something, you push it hard with your finger.

polar bear **polar bears** NOUN
A **polar bear** is a large white bear that lives near the North Pole.

pole **poles**
NOUN **1** A **pole** is a long round post, used especially for holding things up.
NOUN **2** A **pole** is also one of the two points on the Earth that are the furthest from the equator. They are known as the North Pole and the South Pole.

police PLURAL NOUN
The **police** are an organization whose job is to protect people and their belongings, and to make sure that people obey the law.
policeman NOUN **policewoman** NOUN

police officer **police officers** NOUN
A **police officer** is a policeman or policewoman.

polish **polishes, polishing, polished**
NOUN **1 Polish** is a substance that you put on an object to clean and shine it.
VERB **2** If you **polish** something, you put polish on it or rub it with a cloth to make it shine.

polite ADJECTIVE
Someone who is **polite** is well-behaved and thinks about other people's feelings.

politician **politicians** NOUN
A **politician** is a person involved in the government of a country.

politics NOUN
Politics is the study of the way in which a country is governed.

pollen NOUN
Pollen is a fine, yellow powder in flowers that the wind or insects carry to other flowers to make seeds.

pollution NOUN
Pollution is making things like the air and water dirty and dangerous to live in or use.

polyester NOUN
Polyester is an artificial fibre used especially to make clothes.

polygon **polygons** NOUN
A **polygon** is a flat shape with three or more straight sides.

polythene NOUN
Polythene is a thin plastic material that is often made into bags.

pond **ponds** NOUN
A **pond** is a small lake.

pony **ponies** NOUN
A **pony** is a kind of horse which is smaller than an ordinary horse.

ponytail **ponytails** NOUN
A **ponytail** is long hair which is tied behind the head and hangs down like a tail.

pool **pools** NOUN
A **pool** is a small area of still or slow-moving water.

poor **poorer, poorest**
ADJECTIVE **1** Someone who is **poor** has very little money and few belongings.
ADJECTIVE **2** Something that is **poor** is not good. *If my work is **poor**, I have to do it again.*

pop **pops**
NOUN **1 Pop** is modern music played and enjoyed especially by young people.
NOUN **2** A **pop** is a short sharp sound.

popcorn NOUN

Popcorn is a snack made from a type of corn that pops open when heated.

poppy **poppies** NOUN

A **poppy** is a plant with a large red flower on a hairy stem.

popular ADJECTIVE

If someone or something is **popular**, they are liked by a lot of people.

population

NOUN **1** The **population** of a country or area is all the people who live in it.

NOUN **2** The **population** of a place is also the number of people who live there.

porch **porches** NOUN

A **porch** is a sheltered place at the entrance to a building.

porcupine **porcupines** NOUN

A **porcupine** is an animal with lots of stiff hairs called quills on its back.

pork NOUN

Pork is meat from a pig.

porridge NOUN

Porridge is a thick sticky food made from oats cooked in water or milk.

port **ports** NOUN

A **port** is a place where boats come to load and unload.

portable ADJECTIVE

Something that is **portable** is made to be easily carried, for example a portable television.

porter **porters** NOUN

A **porter** is a person whose job is to look after

the entrance of a building, greeting and directing visitors.

portion **portions** NOUN

A **portion** of food is the amount that is given to one person at a meal.

portrait **portraits** NOUN

A **portrait** is a picture of a person.

position **positions**

NOUN **1** The **position** of someone or something is the place where they are.

NOUN **2** Someone's **position** can also be the way they are sitting or standing. *Try to stay in that position while I draw you.*

positive

ADJECTIVE **1** If you are **positive** about something, you are very sure about it.

ADJECTIVE **2** **Positive** numbers are those which are greater than zero.

possess **possesses, possessing, possessed** VERB

If you **possess** something, you have it or own it.

possession NOUN

possible

ADJECTIVE **1** Something that is **possible** can be done.

ADJECTIVE **2** You can also use **possible** to talk about something that may happen but is not certain. *It's possible we might go abroad next year.*

possibly ADVERB

post **posts, posting, posted**

NOUN **1** **Post** is letters or parcels that are collected and delivered.

NOUN **2** A **post** is a strong piece of wood or metal fixed upright in the ground.

VERB **3** If you **post** a letter, you send it to someone by putting it in a postbox.

postcard **postcards** NOUN

A **postcard** is a piece of thin card, often with a picture on one side, that you can use to send a message to someone.

postcode **postcodes** NOUN

A **postcode** is the letters and numbers at the end of an address to help the sorting of mail.

A B C D E F G H I J K L M N O P Q R S T U V W X Y Z

poster posters NOUN

A **poster** is a large notice or picture that is put on a wall or notice board.

postman postmen NOUN

A **postman** is a man whose job is to deliver letters and parcels sent by post.

post office post offices NOUN

A **post office** is a building where you can take things to be posted.

postpone postpones, postponing, postponed VERB

If you **postpone** something, you put it off until later. *We had to postpone the picnic because the weather was so bad.*

pot pots NOUN

A **pot** is a round container for things like paint or jam, or for growing plants in.

potato potatoes NOUN

A **potato** is a round vegetable that grows under the ground. Potatoes can be boiled, baked or fried. *See Vegetables on page 260*

pottery NOUN

Pottery is objects such as dishes and ornaments that are made from clay.

pouch pouches

NOUN **1** A **pouch** is a small bag for keeping things in.
NOUN **2** A **pouch** can also be a pocket of skin on an animal. Female kangaroos and other marsupials have a pouch on their stomach. Their babies grow in this pouch. Hamsters have pouches in their cheeks for storing food.

pounce pounces, pouncing, pounced VERB

When an animal **pounces** on something, it leaps on it and grabs it.

pound pounds

NOUN **1** The **pound** (£) is a unit of money in Britain and in some other countries.
NOUN **2** A **pound** is also a unit of weight equal to just under half a kilogram.

pour pours, pouring, poured

VERB **1** If you **pour** a liquid out of a container, you make it flow out by tipping the container.
VERB **2** When it is raining heavily, you can say that it is **pouring**.

powder NOUN

Powder is something that has been ground into tiny pieces.

power powers

NOUN **1** If someone or something has **power**, they have control over other people.
NOUN **2** The **power** of something, such as the wind or the sea, is its strength.

powerful ADJECTIVE

If someone or something is **powerful**, they are very strong.

practical

ADJECTIVE **1** **Practical** people are good at working with their hands.
ADJECTIVE **2** **Practical** ideas are ones that are likely to work.

practice NOUN

Practice is doing something many times so that you get better at it.

practise practises, practising, practised VERB

If you **practise**, you do something again and again, in order to get better at it. *She has been practising this piece of music for months.*

praise praises, praising, praised VERB

If someone **praises** you for something you have done, they say how well you have done it.

a
b
c
d
e
f
g
h
i
j
k
l
m
n
o
p
q
r
s
t
u
v
w
x
y
z

159

A
B
C
D
E
F
G
H
I
J
K
L
M
N
O
P
Q
R
S
T
U
V
W
X
Y
Z

pram **prams** NOUN
A **pram** is a small carriage that a baby can be pushed around in.

prawn **prawns** NOUN
A **prawn** is a small edible shellfish with a long tail.

pray **prays, praying, prayed** VERB
When someone **prays**, they speak to the god they believe in, to give thanks or to ask for help.

prayer **prayers** NOUN
A **prayer** is the words someone says when they are praying.

precious ADJECTIVE
Something that is **precious** is worth a lot of money.

precise ADJECTIVE
Something that is **precise** is exact and accurate in every detail. *Take precise measurements of the room.*
precisely ADVERB

predator **predators** NOUN
A **predator** is an animal that kills and eats other animals.

predict **predicts, predicting, predicted** VERB
If someone **predicts** an event, they say that it will happen in the future.

prefer **prefers, preferring, preferred** VERB
If you **prefer** someone or something, you like that person or thing better than another.

prefix **prefixes** NOUN
A **prefix** is a letter or group of letters added to the beginning of a word to make a new word, for example "dis-", "pre-" and "un-".
See Prefixes on page 270

pregnant ADJECTIVE
A woman who is **pregnant** is expecting a baby.

prehistoric ADJECTIVE
Something that is **prehistoric** belongs to the time before history was written down.

preparations PLURAL NOUN
Preparations are all the things that have to be done before an event. *The children were busy with preparations for the school play.*

prepare **prepares, preparing, prepared**
VERB **1** If you **prepare** for something that is going to happen, you get ready for it.
VERB **2** If you **prepare** someone or something, you get them ready.

preposition **prepositions** NOUN
In grammar, a **preposition** is a word such as "by", "for" or "with", that goes in front of a noun group. In the sentence "She fell into the pond", "into" is a preposition and "the pond" is a noun group.

present **presents, presenting, presented**
NOUN **1** A **present** is something that you give to someone for them to keep.

ADJECTIVE **2** If someone is **present** somewhere, they are there.
NOUN **3** The **present** is the time now.
VERB **4** If someone **presents** you with something, they give it to you. *The mayor presented her with a certificate.*
VERB **5** The person who **presents** a show introduces each part or each guest.
NOUN **6** The **present tense** of a verb is the form used to show something is happening now.

preserve preserves, preserving, preserved
VERB **1** If you **preserve** something, you do something to keep it the way it is.
VERB **2** To **preserve** food means to stop it from going bad.

president presidents NOUN
The **president** of a country or an organization is the head of it.

press presses, pressing, pressed
VERB **1** If you **press** something against something else, you hold it there firmly. *He pressed the phone against his ear.*
NOUN **2** Newspapers and the journalists who work for them are called the **press**.

pressure NOUN
Pressure is the force of one thing pressing or pushing on another.

pretend pretends, pretending, pretended VERB
If you **pretend**, you act as though something is true although it is not. *Let's pretend to be working.*

pretty prettier, prettiest ADJECTIVE
Someone who is **pretty** is nice to look at.

prevent prevents, preventing, prevented VERB
If you **prevent** someone from doing something, you stop them doing it.

prey NOUN
The **prey** of an animal is the creatures that it hunts for food.
bird of prey PHRASE A **bird of prey** is a bird such as an eagle or a hawk, that kills and eats smaller birds and animals.

price prices NOUN
The **price** of something is the amount of money that you must pay to buy it.

prick pricks, pricking, pricked VERB
To **prick** something means to make a tiny hole with something sharp.

prickle prickles NOUN
Prickles are small sharp points or thorns on plants.

pride
NOUN **1** **Pride** is the good feeling you have when you have done something well.
NOUN **2** A **pride** of lions is a group of lions that live together.
See Collective nouns on page 268

prime minister prime ministers NOUN
The **prime minister** of a country is the leader of that country's government.

prince princes NOUN
A **prince** is the son of a king or queen.

princess princesses NOUN
A **princess** is the daughter of a king or queen, or the wife of a prince.

print prints, printing, printed
VERB **1** When someone **prints** something such as a poster or a newspaper, they use a machine to make lots of copies of it.
VERB **2** If you **print** words, you write in letters that are not joined together.

printer printers
NOUN **1** A **printer** is a machine that is linked to a computer to print information on paper.
NOUN **2** A **printer** is also a person who prints things like books and magazines.

print-out print-outs NOUN
A **print-out** is a printed copy of information from a computer.

a
b
c
d
e
f
g
h
i
j
k
l
m
n
o
p
q
r
s
t
u
v
w
x
y
z

prism prisms

NOUN **1** A **prism** is an object made of clear glass with many flat sides. It separates light passing through it into the colours of the rainbow.

NOUN **2** A **prism** is also any three-dimensional shape that has the same size and shape of face at each end.

prison prisons NOUN

A **prison** is a building where people are kept when they have broken the law.

prisoner prisoners

NOUN **1** A **prisoner** is someone who is kept in prison as a punishment.

NOUN **2** A **prisoner** is also someone who has been captured by an enemy.

private ADJECTIVE

If something is **private**, it is for one person or group only. *All the rooms have a **private** bath.*

in private PHRASE If you do something **in private**, you do it without other people being there.

prize prizes NOUN

A **prize** is something that is given to someone as a reward.

probable ADJECTIVE

Something that is **probable** is likely to be true, or likely to happen.

probably ADVERB

problem problems

NOUN **1** A **problem** is something that is difficult.

NOUN **2** A **problem** is also something, like a puzzle, that you have to work out.

process processes NOUN

A **process** is a series of actions for doing or making something.

procession processions NOUN

A **procession** is a line of people walking or riding through the streets on a special occasion.

prod prods, prodding, prodded VERB

If you **prod** something, you push it with your finger.

produce produces, producing, produced

VERB **1** To **produce** something means to make it.

VERB **2** If you **produce** an object from somewhere such as a pocket, you bring it out so that it can be seen.

VERB **3** Someone who **produces** a play, film or television programme gets it ready to show to the public.

product products

NOUN **1** A **product** is something that is made to be sold.

NOUN **2** In maths, the **product** of two numbers is the answer you get when you multiply them together. For example, the product of four and two is eight.

profit profits NOUN

A **profit** is the money you gain when you sell something for more than it cost you to make or buy.

program programs NOUN

A **program** is a set of instructions that a computer uses in order to do particular things.

programme programmes

NOUN **1** A radio or television **programme** is the thing that is being broadcast.

NOUN **2** A **programme** is a plan of things that will take place.

progress progresses, progressing, progressed

NOUN **1** **Progress** is moving forward or getting better at something. *I'm making **progress** with my spelling.*

VERB **2** If you **progress**, you get better at something.

project **projects** NOUN
A **project** is work that you do to learn about something and then write about it.

promise **promises, promising, promised** VERB
If you **promise** to do something, you mean you really will do it.

pronoun **pronouns**
NOUN **1** In grammar, a **pronoun** is a word that is used to replace a noun.
NOUN **2** **Personal pronouns** replace the subject or object of a sentence. In the sentence "She caught a fish", "she" is a personal pronoun.
NOUN **3** **Possessive pronouns** replace the subject or object when you want to show who owns it. In the sentence "This book is mine", "mine" is a possessive pronoun.
See *Pronoun* on page 269

pronounce **pronounces, pronouncing, pronounced** VERB
To **pronounce** a word means to say it in a particular way.

pronunciation NOUN
Pronunciation is the way a word is usually said.

proof NOUN
Proof of something is the facts that show that it is true or that it exists.

prop **props, propping, propped** VERB
If you **prop** an object somewhere, you support it against something.

propeller **propellers** NOUN
A **propeller** is the blades that turn to drive an aircraft or ship.

proper
ADJECTIVE **1** **Proper** means right. *Put those things back in the proper place.*
ADJECTIVE **2** You can also use **proper** to mean real. *You need a proper screwdriver for that job.*

properly ADVERB
If something is done **properly**, it is done correctly.

proper noun **proper nouns** NOUN
A **proper noun** is the name of a particular person or place. It starts with a capital letter. "Ben" and "London" are both proper nouns. See *Noun* on page 268

property **properties**
NOUN **1** Someone's **property** is the things that belong to them.
NOUN **2** A **property** is a building and the land belonging to it.

prophet **prophets** NOUN
A **prophet** is a person who predicts what will happen in the future.

proportion **proportions** NOUN
The **proportion** of one amount to another is its size in comparison with the other amount. *There was a large proportion of boys in the class.*

prose NOUN
Prose is written language that is not poetry or a play.

protect **protects, protecting, protected** VERB
To **protect** someone or something is to prevent them from being harmed.
protection NOUN

protein **proteins** NOUN
Protein is a substance found in meat, eggs and milk that is needed by bodies for growth.

protest **protests** NOUN
A **protest** is something you say or do to show that you disagree with something.

proud **prouder, proudest** ADJECTIVE
If you feel **proud**, you feel glad about something you have done, or about something that belongs to you. *She was proud of her new bike.*

prove **proves, proving, proved** VERB
When you **prove** something, you show that it is definitely true.

a b c d e f g h i j k l m n o p q r s t u v w x y z

163

A
B
C
D
E
F
G
H
I
J
K
L
M
N
O
P
Q
R
S
T
U
V
W
X
Y
Z

proverb **proverbs** NOUN

A **proverb** is a short sentence that people say which gives advice about life. For example, the proverb "Look before you leap" means that you should think carefully before you do something.

provide **provides, providing, provided**
VERB

If you **provide** something for someone, you give it to them so that they have it when they need it.

prune **prunes, pruning, pruned**

VERB **1** When someone **prunes** a tree, they cut off some of the branches so that it will grow better.

NOUN **2** A **prune** is a dried plum.

pub **pubs** NOUN

A **pub** is a building where people go to drink and talk with their friends.

public ADJECTIVE

Something that is **public** can be used by anyone. For example, anyone can pay to travel on public transport, such as trains and buses.

publish **publishes, publishing, published** VERB

When a company **publishes** a book, newspaper or magazine, they print copies of it and sell them.
publisher NOUN

pudding **puddings** NOUN

A **pudding** is a sweet food which is usually eaten after the main part of a meal.

puddle **puddles** NOUN

A **puddle** is a small shallow pool of liquid.

pull **pulls, pulling, pulled**

VERB **1** When you **pull** something, you hold it firmly and move it towards you.

VERB **2** When you **pull** a curtain, you move it across a window.

VERB **3** When a vehicle **pulls away, pulls out** or **pulls in**, it moves in that direction.

pulley **pulleys** NOUN

A **pulley** is for lifting heavy weights. The weight is attached to a rope or a chain which passes over a wheel.

pullover **pullovers** NOUN

A **pullover** is a jumper.

pulse NOUN

Your **pulse** is the regular beating of blood through your body. You can feel your pulse in your neck or wrist.

pump **pumps, pumping, pumped**

NOUN **1** A **pump** is a machine that is used to force gas or liquid to move the way it is wanted.

VERB **2** To **pump** is to force gas or liquid somewhere using a pump. *I must **pump** up these balloons.*

pumpkin **pumpkins** NOUN

A **pumpkin** is a very large, orange-coloured vegetable with a thick skin. It is soft inside, with a lot of seeds.

pun **puns** NOUN

A **pun** is a joke using a word which has two different meanings. For example, the sentence "My dog's a champion boxer" has a pun on the word "boxer".

punch **punches, punching, punched** VERB

If you **punch** someone, you hit them hard with your fist.

punctual ADJECTIVE

Someone who is **punctual** arrives somewhere or does something at exactly the right time.

punctuation NOUN

Punctuation is the marks such as full stops and commas that you use in writing.
punctuate VERB
*See **Punctuation** on page 270*

*See **Punctuation** on page 270*

puncture **punctures** NOUN

A **puncture** is a small hole in a tyre. When a tyre has a puncture, the air inside escapes and the tyre goes flat.

punish **punishes, punishing, punished**
VERB

To **punish** someone means to make them

suffer because they have done something wrong.
punishment NOUN

pupil **pupils**

NOUN **1** The **pupils** at a school are the children who go there.

NOUN **2** Your **pupils** are the small round black holes in the centre of your eyes.

puppet **puppets** NOUN

A **puppet** is a kind of doll that you can move. Some puppets have strings which you can pull. Others are made so that you can put your hand inside.

puppy **puppies** NOUN

A **puppy** is a young dog.
See *Young animals* on page 265

purchase **purchases, purchasing, purchased** VERB

When you **purchase** something, you buy it.

pure **purer, purest** ADJECTIVE

Something that is **pure** is not mixed with anything else.

purple ADJECTIVE

Something that is **purple** is of a reddish-blue colour.
See *Colours and shapes* on page 266

purpose **purposes** NOUN

A **purpose** is the reason for doing something.
on purpose PHRASE If you do something **on purpose**, you mean to do it. It does not happen by accident.

purr **purrs, purring, purred** VERB

When a cat **purrs**, it keeps making a low sound that shows it is happy.

purse **purses** NOUN

A **purse** is a small bag that people keep their money in.

push **pushes, pushing, pushed** VERB

When you **push** something, you press it hard.

pushchair **pushchairs** NOUN

A **pushchair** is a small folding chair on wheels in which a baby or toddler can be wheeled around.

put **puts, putting, put**

VERB **1** When you **put** something somewhere, you move it there.
VERB **2** If you **put** something **off**, you delay doing it.
VERB **3** If you **put** a light **out**, you make it stop shining.

puzzle **puzzles, puzzling, puzzled**

VERB **1** If something **puzzles** you, you do not understand it.
NOUN **2** A **puzzle** is a game or question that needs a lot of thought to solve it.

pyjamas PLURAL NOUN

Pyjamas are loose trousers and a top that people wear in bed.

pyramid **pyramids**

NOUN **1** A **pyramid** is a solid shape with a flat base and flat triangular faces that meet at the top in a point.
See *Solid shapes* on page 266
PLURAL NOUN **2** The **Pyramids** are ancient stone structures built over the bodies of Egyptian kings and queens.

a
b
c
d
e
f
g
h
i
j
k
l
m
n
o
p
q
r
s
t
u
v
w
x
y
z

Qq

quack quacks, quacking, quacked VERB
When a duck **quacks**, it makes a loud harsh sound.

quadrilateral quadrilaterals NOUN
A **quadrilateral** is a flat shape with four straight sides.
See Colours and shapes on page 266

quaint quainter, quaintest ADJECTIVE
Something that is **quaint** is unusual and rather pretty.

qualify qualifies, qualifying, qualified
VERB **1** When someone **qualifies**, they pass the examination they need to do a particular job.
VERB **2** You **qualify** if you get enough points in a competition to go on to the next stage.

quality qualities NOUN
The **quality** of something is how good or bad it is, compared with other things of the same kind.

quantity quantities NOUN
A **quantity** is an amount you can measure or count. *We shall need a huge **quantity** of food for the weekend.*

quarrel quarrels NOUN
A **quarrel** is an angry argument.

quarry quarries NOUN
A **quarry** is a deep hole that has been dug in a piece of land. Quarries are dug to provide materials such as stone for building and other work.

quarter quarters NOUN
A **quarter** is one of four equal parts of something.
See Fractions on page 278

quay quays (said kee) NOUN
A **quay** is a place where boats are tied up to be loaded or unloaded.

queen queens
NOUN **1** A **queen** is a woman who rules a country. Queens are not chosen by the people. They are born into a royal family.

NOUN **2** The wife of a king is also called a **queen**.
NOUN **3** In the insect world, a **queen** is a large female bee, ant or wasp which can lay eggs.

query queries, querying, queried
NOUN **1** A **query** is a question.
VERB **2** If you **query** something, you ask about it because you think it might not be right.

question questions NOUN
A **question** is words you say or write when you want to ask something.

question mark question marks NOUN
A **question mark** is the punctuation mark (**?**) which you use in writing at the end of a question. *See Punctuation on page 270*

A B C D E F G H I J K L M N O P Q R S T U V W X Y Z

questionnaire questionnaires NOUN

A **questionnaire** is a list of questions which asks for information for a survey.

queue queues NOUN

A **queue** is a line of people or vehicles waiting for something.

quick quicker, quickest

ADJECTIVE **1** Someone or something that is **quick** moves very fast.

ADJECTIVE **2** Something that is **quick** lasts only a short time. *I'll have a **quick** look at it.*

quickly ADVERB

Things that happen **quickly** happen very fast.

quiet quieter, quietest

ADJECTIVE **1** Someone or something that is **quiet** makes only a little noise or no noise at all.

ADJECTIVE **2 Quiet** also means peaceful. *Let's have a **quiet** evening at home.*

quilt quilts NOUN

A **quilt** is a soft cover for a bed.

quit quits, quitting, quit

VERB **1** If you **quit** something, you stop doing it. ***Quit** teasing me!*

VERB **2** If you **quit**, you leave. *My dad has just **quit** his job.*

quite

ADVERB **1 Quite** means rather. *I think he's **quite** nice.*

ADVERB **2 Quite** can also mean completely. *The work is now **quite** finished.*

quiver quivers, quivering, quivered

VERB **1** If something **quivers**, it trembles.

NOUN **2** A **quiver** is a container for carrying arrows.

quiz quizzes NOUN

A **quiz** is a game or test. Someone tries to find out how much you know by asking you questions.

quotation quotations NOUN

A **quotation** is an extract from a book or speech that you use in your own work.

quotation marks PLURAL NOUN

Quotation marks are punctuation marks (" ") or (' ') used in writing to show where speech begins and ends.

quote quotes, quoting, quoted

VERB **1** If you **quote** something that someone has written or said, you repeat their exact words.

NOUN **2** A **quote** is a piece out of a book or speech.

quotient quotients NOUN

In maths, a **quotient** is a whole number you get when you divide one number into another. For example, if you divide eight by two, the quotient is four.

a
b
c
d
e
f
g
h
i
j
k
l
m
n
o
p
q
r
s
t
u
v
w
x
y
z

Rr

A
B
C
D
E
F
G
H
I
J
K
L
M
N
O
P
Q
R
S
T
U
V
W
X
Y
Z

rabbi **rabbis** NOUN
A **rabbi** is a Jewish religious leader.

rabbit **rabbits** NOUN
A **rabbit** is a small furry animal with long ears.

race **races, racing, raced**
NOUN **1** A **race** is a competition to see who is the fastest.
NOUN **2** A **race** is also a large group of people who look alike in some way. For example, different races have different skin colour, or differently shaped eyes.
VERB **3** If you **race** someone, you try to beat them in a race.

racist **racists** NOUN
If someone is a **racist**, they believe that some people are better than others because they belong to a particular race.

rack **racks** NOUN
A **rack** is a frame that is used for holding things or for hanging things on.

racket **rackets**
NOUN **1** A **racket** is a bat with an oval frame and strings across and down it. It is used in tennis and similar games.
NOUN **2** If someone makes a **racket**, they make a loud unpleasant noise.

radar NOUN
Radar is a way of showing the position and speed of ships and aircraft when they cannot be seen. Radio signals give the information on a screen.

radiator **radiators**
NOUN **1** A **radiator** is a hollow metal object that can be filled with liquid in order to heat a room.

NOUN **2** In a car, the **radiator** holds the water that is used to cool the engine.

radio **radios** NOUN
A **radio** is a piece of equipment which receives sounds through the air. You can use a radio to listen to programmes that are broadcast.

radish **radishes** NOUN
A **radish** is a small salad vegetable with a red skin and white flesh.
See Vegetables on page 260

radius **radii** NOUN
The **radius** of a circle is the length of a straight line drawn from its centre to any point on its edge.

raffle **raffles** NOUN
A **raffle** is a competition. You buy a numbered ticket and win a prize if your number is chosen.

raft **rafts** NOUN
A **raft** is a floating platform. Rafts are often made of large pieces of wood fixed together.

rag **rags**
NOUN **1** A **rag** is a piece of old cloth that you can use to clean or wipe things.
NOUN **2** **Rags** are old torn clothes.

rage NOUN
Rage is great anger. *Dad's face showed his rage.*

ragged ADJECTIVE
Clothes that are **ragged** are old and torn.

raid **raids** NOUN
A **raid** is a sudden attack against an enemy.

rail **rails**
NOUN **1** A **rail** is a horizontal bar that is firmly fixed to posts. Rails are used as fences, or for people to lean on.
NOUN **2** **Rails** are the heavy metal bars that trains run on.

railing **railings** NOUN
A **railing** is a kind of fence made from metal bars.

railway **railways** NOUN
A **railway** is a route along which trains travel on metal rails.

rain **rains, raining, rained**
NOUN **1** **Rain** is water that falls from the clouds in small drops.
VERB **2** When it is **raining**, rain is falling.

rainbow **rainbows** NOUN
A **rainbow** is an arch of different colours that sometimes appears in the sky when the sun shines through rain.

rainforest **rainforests** NOUN
A **rainforest** is a dense forest in a tropical area where there is a lot of rain.

raise **raises, raising, raised**
VERB **1** If you **raise** something, you move it so that it is higher.
VERB **2** If you **raise** your voice, you speak more loudly.
VERB **3** To **raise** money for a cause means to get people to give money towards it.

raisin **raisins** NOUN
A **raisin** is a dried grape.

rake **rakes** NOUN
A **rake** is a garden tool with a row of metal teeth fixed to a long handle.

ram **rams, ramming, rammed**
VERB **1** If one vehicle **rams** another, it crashes into it.
NOUN **2** A **ram** is an adult male sheep.

Ramadan NOUN
Ramadan is the ninth month of the Muslim year, when Muslims eat and drink nothing from sunrise to sunset.

ramp **ramps** NOUN
A **ramp** is a sloping surface between two places at different levels.

ran VERB
Ran is the past tense of **run**.

ranch **ranches** NOUN
In the United States, a **ranch** is a large farm for raising cattle, sheep or horses.

rang VERB
Rang is the past tense of **ring**.

range **ranges**
NOUN **1** The **range** of something is the area or distance over which it can be used.
NOUN **2** A **range** is a row of hills or mountains.

rank **ranks** NOUN
A **rank** is a position that a person holds in an organization. The higher the rank, the more important they are.

rap **raps, rapping, rapped**
VERB **1** If you **rap** something, you hit it with a series of quick blows.
NOUN **2** **Rap** is a style of poetry spoken to music with a strong beat.

rapid ADJECTIVE
Something that is **rapid** is very quick.

rare **rarer, rarest** ADJECTIVE
Something that is **rare** is not often seen, or does not happen very often.

rash **rashes** NOUN
A **rash** is a lot of spots that appear on your skin in certain illnesses.

raspberry **raspberries** NOUN
A **raspberry** is a small red fruit which is soft and juicy, with a lot of small seeds called pips.
See *Fruit* on page 260

rat **rats** NOUN
A **rat** is a rodent with a long tail.

a
b
c
d
e
f
g
h
i
j
k
l
m
n
o
p
q
r
s
t
u
v
w
x
y
z

A B C D E F G H I J K L M N O P Q R S T U V W X Y Z

rate rates NOUN
The **rate** that something happens is how quickly or slowly, or how often it happens.

rather
ADVERB **1 Rather** means quite. *I'm rather angry about that.*
ADVERB **2** You can say **rather** if there is something else you want to do. *I don't want to go out. I'd rather watch television.*

rattle rattles, rattling, rattled
VERB **1** When something **rattles**, it makes short rapid knocking sounds. *Can you stop that window rattling?*
NOUN **2** A baby's **rattle** is a toy that makes a noise when it is shaken.

raw ADJECTIVE
Food that is **raw** is not cooked.

ray rays NOUN
A **ray** is a line of light.

razor razors NOUN
A **razor** is a tool that people use for shaving.

reach reaches, reaching, reached
VERB **1** When you **reach** a place, you arrive there.
VERB **2** If you **reach** somewhere, you stretch out your hand. *He reached across the table for the salt.*

react reacts, reacting, reacted VERB
When you **react** to something, you behave in a particular way because of it. *He reacted badly to the news.*
reaction NOUN

read reads, reading, read
VERB **1** When you **read**, you look at words and understand what they mean.
VERB **2** When you **read aloud**, you say the words that are written.

reading readings NOUN
Reading is the activity of reading books or other written material.

ready ADJECTIVE
If someone or something is **ready**, they are properly prepared for doing something.

real
ADJECTIVE **1** Something that is **real** is true. It is not imaginary. *I've seen a real princess.*
ADJECTIVE **2** You also say **real** when you mean the thing itself and not a copy. *I've got a lovely toy pony. But Jenny's got a real one.*

realize realizes, realizing, realized; also spelt **realise** VERB
If you **realize** something, you work it out or notice it. *I've just realized you must be Tara's sister.*

really ADVERB
You can use **really** to make something you are saying stronger. *I really don't like that boy.*

rear NOUN
The **rear** of something is the part that is at the back of it.

rearrange rearranges, rearranging, rearranged VERB
To **rearrange** something means to organize or arrange it in a different way.

reason reasons NOUN
The **reason** for something is why it happens. *I'm sorry I'm late, but there is a good reason.*

reasonable
ADJECTIVE **1** People who are **reasonable** behave in a fair and sensible way.
ADJECTIVE **2** A price that is **reasonable** seems fair and not too high.
reasonably ADVERB

rebel rebels, rebelling, rebelled VERB
To **rebel** means to fight against authority.
rebellious ADJECTIVE

receive receives, receiving, received VERB
When you **receive** something, you get it after it has been given or sent to you.

recent ADJECTIVE
Something that is **recent** happened only a short time ago.
recently ADVERB

recipe **recipes** NOUN
A **recipe** is a list of ingredients and instructions for cooking something.

recite **recites, reciting, recited** VERB
When you **recite** something like a poem, you say it aloud from memory.

reckon **reckons, reckoning, reckoned** VERB
If you **reckon** that something is true, you think it is true.

recognize **recognizes, recognizing, recognized**; also spelt **recognise** VERB
If you **recognize** someone, you realize that you know who they are.

recommend **recommends, recommending, recommended** VERB
If you **recommend** something to someone, you tell them it is good.

record **records, recording, recorded**
(*said* **rek**-ord) NOUN **1** If you keep a **record** of something, you keep a written account or store information in a computer.
NOUN **2** A **record** is also the best that has been done so far.
NOUN **3** A **record** is also a piece of music that has been put on a tape or compact disc.
(*said* ri-**kord**) VERB **4** If someone **records** information, they write it down, put it onto tape or film, or into a computer.
VERB **5** To **record** sound means to put it on tape or compact disc.

recorder **recorders** NOUN
A **recorder** is a small musical instrument which you play by blowing into one end and putting your fingers over the holes.

recover **recovers, recovering, recovered** VERB
When you **recover** from something such as an illness, you become well again.

recreation NOUN
Recreation is all the things that you like doing in your spare time.
recreational ADJECTIVE

rectangle **rectangles** NOUN
A **rectangle** is a flat shape with four straight sides and four right angles.
rectangular ADJECTIVE
See Colours and shapes on page 266

recycle **recycles, recycling, recycled** VERB
To **recycle** used products means to process them so they can be used again.

red **redder, reddest** ADJECTIVE
Something that is **red** is the colour of a ripe tomato.
See Colours and shapes on page 266

redraft **redrafts, redrafting, redrafted** VERB
If you **redraft** a piece of text, you make another draft.

reduce **reduces, reducing, reduced** VERB
To **reduce** something means to make it smaller in size or amount.

reed **reeds** NOUN
A **reed** is a plant with a tall hollow stem. Reeds grow in or near water.

reef **reefs** NOUN
A **reef** is a long line of rocks that is just below the surface of the sea.

a
b
c
d
e
f
g
h
i
j
k
l
m
n
o
p
q
r
s
t
u
v
w
x
y
z

171

reel **reels** NOUN
A **reel** is a round object that you wrap thread, wire or film around.

refer **refers, referring, referred** VERB
If you **refer** to someone or something, you mention them.

referee **referees** NOUN
A **referee** is a person whose job is to make sure that the players in a game follow the rules properly.

refill **refills, refilling, refilled**
NOUN **1** A **refill** is a full container that replaces an empty one. *Have you got a **refill** for this pen?*
VERB **2** If you **refill** something, you fill it again after it has been emptied.

reflect **reflects, reflecting, reflected**
VERB **1** When a surface **reflects** rays of something like light or heat, the rays bounce back from the surface.
VERB **2** When a mirror **reflects** a person or thing, it shows what they look like.

reflection **reflections** NOUN
A **reflection** is what you see when you look in a mirror or shiny surface.

refreshing ADJECTIVE
Something that is **refreshing** makes you feel energetic or cool again after you have been tired or hot.

refreshments PLURAL NOUN
Refreshments are drinks and snacks.

refrigerator **refrigerators** NOUN
A **refrigerator** is a large cooled container in which you store food to keep it fresh. A refrigerator is often called a **fridge** for short.

refugee **refugees** NOUN
A **refugee** is a person who has been forced to leave their country and live elsewhere, for example because of a war.

refuse **refuses, refusing, refused**
(*said* rif-**yooz**) VERB **1** If you **refuse** to do something, you say you will not do it.
(*said* **ref**-yoos) NOUN **2** **Refuse** is rubbish or waste.

region **regions** NOUN
A **region** is a large area of land.

register **registers, registering, registered**
NOUN **1** A **register** is an official list or record of things.
VERB **2** When something is **registered**, it is recorded on an official list. *The car was **registered** in my mother's name.*

regret **regrets, regretting, regretted** VERB
If you **regret** something, you wish it had not happened.

regular
ADJECTIVE **1** Something that is **regular** does not change its pattern, for example a regular heartbeat.
ADJECTIVE **2** A **regular** polygon has all its angles and sides equal.

rehearsal **rehearsals** NOUN
A **rehearsal** is a practice of a play, dance or piece of music, to prepare for a public performance.

reign **reigns, reigning, reigned**
VERB **1** When a king or queen **reigns**, they rule a country.
NOUN **2** The **reign** of a king or queen is the period during which they reign.

rein reins NOUN
A **rein** is one of the leather straps that are used to control a horse.

reindeer NOUN
A **reindeer** is a large deer that lives in cold northern countries.

relate relates, relating, related VERB
If something **relates** to something else, it is connected or concerned with it.

related
ADJECTIVE **1** People who are **related** belong to the same family.
ADJECTIVE **2** If one thing is **related** to another, there is a connection between them. *A graph shows how two sets of numbers are **related**.*

relation relations NOUN
If someone is your **relation**, they belong to the same family as you.

relative relatives NOUN
If someone is your **relative**, they belong to the same family as you.

relax relaxes, relaxing, relaxed VERB
When you **relax**, you stop worrying and feel more calm.

release releases, releasing, released VERB
If someone **releases** a person or animal that has been trapped or held in some way, they set them free.

reliable ADJECTIVE
If something or someone is **reliable**, you can depend on them.

relief NOUN
Relief is the feeling you have if you do not need to worry about something any more.

relieved ADJECTIVE
If you are **relieved**, you are glad because you can stop worrying about something.

religion religions NOUN
A **religion** is a set of beliefs about a god, or about several gods.
religious ADJECTIVE

reluctant ADJECTIVE
If you are **reluctant** to do something, you do not want to do it.
reluctantly ADVERB

rely relies, relying, relied
VERB **1** If you **rely** on someone, you need them and depend on them.
VERB **2** If you can **rely** on someone to do something, you can trust them to do it.

remain remains, remaining, remained
VERB **1** If you **remain** in a place, you stay there and do not go away.
PLURAL NOUN **2** The **remains** of something are the parts that are left after most of it has been destroyed. *They found the **remains** of an ancient pyramid.*

remainder
NOUN **1** The **remainder** of something is the part that is left. *He gulped down the **remainder** of his coffee.*
NOUN **2** In maths, the **remainder** is the amount left over when one number cannot be exactly divided by another. For example, if nine is divided by four, the answer is two remainder one.

remark remarks, remarking, remarked
VERB
If you **remark** on something, you mention it. *The teacher **remarked** on his strange haircut.*

remarkable ADJECTIVE
Someone or something that is **remarkable** is unusual in some way so that people notice them and feel surprised.

remember remembers, remembering, remembered VERB
If you can **remember** something, you can bring it back into your mind. *Can you **remember** that actor's name?*

a b c d e f g h i j k l m n o p q r s t u v w x y z

A
B
C
D
E
F
G
H
I
J
K
L
M
N
O
P
Q
R
S
T
U
V
W
X
Y
Z

remind **reminds, reminding, reminded**
VERB **1** If someone or something **reminds** you to do something, they make you remember it. *That* ***reminds*** *me – I must get a card for Leah.*
VERB **2** If someone **reminds** you of someone else, something about them makes you think of the other person.

remote **remoter, remotest** ADJECTIVE
Remote areas are far away from places where most people live.

remote control NOUN
Remote control is a system of controlling a machine from a distance, using radio or electronic signals.

removal **removals**
NOUN **1** The **removal** of something is the act of taking it away or getting rid of it.
NOUN **2** A **removal company** takes furniture from one building to another when people move house.

remove **removes, removing, removed**
VERB
If you **remove** something from somewhere, you take it off or away.

renewable ADJECTIVE
Renewable resources are ones such as wind, water, and sunlight, which are constantly replacing themselves and therefore do not become used up.

rent **rents** NOUN
Rent is the amount of money you pay regularly for a house or flat.

repair **repairs, repairing, repaired** VERB
If you **repair** something that is broken or not working, you mend it.

repeat **repeats, repeating, repeated** VERB
If you **repeat** something, you say it or do it again.
repetition NOUN

replace **replaces, replacing, replaced**
VERB **1** If you **replace** something, you put it back where it was before.
VERB **2** If you **replace** something that is old, lost or broken, you get a new one.

reply **replies, replying, replied** VERB
When you **reply**, you answer someone.

report **reports, reporting, reported**
VERB **1** If you **report** that something has happened, you tell someone about it. *He* ***reported*** *the theft to the police.*
NOUN **2** A **report** is an account of an event or situation.

reporter **reporters** NOUN
A **reporter** is someone who works for a newspaper, radio or television. Their job is to find out what is happening in the world so that their report can be printed or broadcast.

represent **represents, representing, represented**
VERB **1** If you **represent** someone, you act for them. *The class chose Meena to* ***represent*** *them.*
VERB **2** If a sign or symbol **represents** something, it stands for it.

reptile **reptiles** NOUN
A **reptile** is a cold-blooded animal with a scaly skin. Female reptiles lay eggs. Snakes and crocodiles are reptiles.
See Reptiles on page 264

request **requests, requesting, requested**
VERB **1** If you **request** something, you ask for it politely.
NOUN **2** A **request** is a polite demand for something.

require **requires, requiring, required**
VERB
If you **require** something, you need it.

rescue **rescues, rescuing, rescued** VERB
If you **rescue** someone, you save them from danger.

research **researches, researching, researched**
NOUN **1 Research** is studying something and trying to find out facts about it.
VERB **2** If you **research** something, you try to discover facts about it.

resent **resents, resenting, resented** VERB
If you **resent** something, you feel angry about it.

reserve **reserves, reserving, reserved**
VERB
If you **reserve** something, like a book at the library, you arrange for it to be kept for you.

resign **resigns, resigning, resigned** VERB
If someone **resigns** from a job, they say they want to leave it.

resist **resists, resisting, resisted** VERB
If you **resist** something, you fight against it and do not give up.

resource **resources** NOUN
The **resources** of a country, organization or person are the materials, money or skills they have.

respect **respects, respecting, respected**
VERB
If you **respect** someone, you look up to them and think their opinions are important.

respectable ADJECTIVE
Someone who is **respectable** behaves in a way that other people think is right.

respond **responds, responding, responded** VERB
When you **respond** to someone, you react to them by doing or saying something.
response NOUN

responsible
ADJECTIVE **1** If you are **responsible** for something, it is your job to deal with it, and you are to blame if it goes wrong.
ADJECTIVE **2** A **responsible** person behaves properly and sensibly.

rest **rests, resting, rested**
VERB **1** When you **rest**, you sit or lie down and keep still for a while.
NOUN **2** A **rest** is a period of time when you do not work.
NOUN **3** The **rest** is all the things in a group that are left. *I've done some of the washing-up. I'll do the **rest** tomorrow.*

restaurant **restaurants** NOUN
A **restaurant** is a place where meals are served.

restless ADJECTIVE
If you feel **restless**, you find it hard to relax.

result **results**
NOUN **1** A **result** is something that happens because of something else. *The milk boiled over and the **result** was a real mess.*
NOUN **2** A **result** is also the score at the end of a game.

retire **retires, retiring, retired** VERB
When someone **retires**, they stop doing their job, usually because they are getting old.

retreat **retreats, retreating, retreated**
VERB
If you **retreat** from something difficult or dangerous, you move backwards away from it. *The army **retreated** from the enemy.*

a
b
c
d
e
f
g
h
i
j
k
l
m
n
o
p
q
r
s
t
u
v
w
x
y
z

A
B
C
D
E
F
G
H
I
J
K
L
M
N
O
P
Q
R
S
T
U
V
W
X
Y
Z

return **returns, returning, returned**
VERB **1** When you **return** to a place, you go back there after you have been away.
VERB **2** If you **return** something to someone, you give it back to them.
NOUN **3** A **return** is a ticket for the journey to a place and back again.

reveal **reveals, revealing, revealed** VERB
If you **reveal** something that has been secret or hidden, you tell people about it or show it to them.

revenge NOUN
Revenge is something a person does to hurt someone who has hurt them.

reverse **reverses, reversing, reversed**
VERB **1** If a car **reverses**, it goes backwards.
VERB **2** If you **reverse** the order of things, you put them in the opposite order.

revise **revises, revising, revised**
VERB **1** If you **revise** something, you alter it or correct it.
VERB **2** When you **revise**, you read something again so that you can learn it for a test.
revision NOUN

revolting ADJECTIVE
Something that is **revolting** is horrible and disgusting.

reward **rewards** NOUN
A **reward** is something you are given for doing well.

rhinoceros **rhinoceroses** NOUN
A **rhinoceros** is a large African or Asian animal with a thick skin and one or two horns on its nose. Rhinoceroses are often called **rhinos** for short.

rhyme **rhymes, rhyming, rhymed** VERB
If two words **rhyme**, they have a similar sound. For example, "dog" rhymes with "log".

rhythm **rhythms** NOUN
Rhythm is a regular pattern of sound or movement. Music and dancing have rhythm.

rib **ribs** NOUN
Your **ribs** are the curved bones that go from your backbone to your chest.

ribbon **ribbons** NOUN
A **ribbon** is a long narrow piece of fine cloth. It is used for tying things together, or as a decoration.

rice NOUN
Rice is white or pale brown grains which are boiled and eaten.
See Other foods on page 261

rich **richer, richest** ADJECTIVE
Someone who is **rich** has a lot of money or valuable things.

rid PHRASE
When you **get rid of** something that you do not want, you remove it or throw it away.

riddle **riddles** NOUN
A **riddle** is a kind of puzzle. You ask a question which has a funny answer.

ride **rides, riding, rode, ridden**
NOUN **1** A **ride** is a journey using a bus, car, train, horse or bicycle.
VERB **2** When a person **rides** a horse or a bicycle, they sit on it and control it.
VERB **3** When you **ride** in a vehicle such as a car, you travel in it.

ridiculous ADJECTIVE
If you say something is **ridiculous**, you mean it is foolish.

right
ADJECTIVE **1** If something is **right**, it is correct.
ADJECTIVE OR ADVERB **2** **Right** means on or towards the right side of something. Most people write with their right hand.

right angle **right angles** NOUN
A **right angle** is an angle or turn of 90 degrees.

rigid ADJECTIVE
Something that is **rigid** is very stiff and does not bend or stretch.

rim **rims**
NOUN **1** The **rim** of a container, such as a cup, is the edge round the top.
NOUN **2** The **rim** of a round object, such as a wheel, is the outside edge of it.

rind **rinds** NOUN
The **rind** of a fruit such as an orange or a lemon is its thick outer skin.

ring **rings, ringing, rang, rung**
NOUN **1** A **ring** is an ornament that people wear on a finger.
NOUN **2** Anything in the shape of a circle can be called a **ring**.
VERB **3** If you **ring** someone, you phone them.
VERB **4** When a bell **rings**, it makes a loud clear sound.

rinse **rinses, rinsing, rinsed** VERB
When you **rinse** something, you wash it in clean water with no soap.

rip **rips, ripping, ripped** VERB
If someone **rips** something, they tear it violently.

ripe **riper, ripest** ADJECTIVE
When fruit or grain is **ripe**, it is ready to be eaten or harvested.

ripple **ripples** NOUN
A **ripple** is a little wave on the surface of water.

rise **rises, rising, rose, risen**
VERB **1** If something **rises**, it moves upwards.
VERB **2** When the sun or the moon **rises**, it appears above the horizon.

risk **risks** NOUN
A **risk** is a danger that something bad might happen.

take a risk PHRASE If someone **takes a risk**, they do something knowing that it could be dangerous.
risky ADJECTIVE

rival **rivals** NOUN
Your **rival** is someone who is trying to win the same things as you are.

river **rivers** NOUN
A **river** is a large amount of fresh water flowing towards the sea.

road **roads** NOUN
A **road** is a long piece of hard ground, specially treated so that people and vehicles can travel along it easily.

roam **roams, roaming, roamed** VERB
If you **roam**, you wander around without any particular purpose.

roar **roars, roaring, roared** VERB
If something **roars**, it makes a very loud noise like a lion. *The car **roared** off down the road.*

roast **roasts, roasting, roasted** VERB
When someone **roasts** meat or other food, they cook it in an oven or over a fire.

rob **robs, robbing, robbed** VERB
If someone **robs** you, they steal something from you.
robber NOUN **robbery** NOUN

robin **robins** NOUN
A **robin** is a small brown bird with a red neck and chest.

robot **robots** NOUN
A **robot** is a machine which is programmed to move and perform tasks automatically.

a b c d e f g h i j k l m n o p q r s t u v w x y z

177

rock rocks, rocking, rocked

NOUN **1 Rock** is the very hard material that is in the earth. Cliffs and mountains are made of rock.

NOUN **2** A **rock** is a large piece of rock.

VERB **3** When something **rocks**, it moves slowly backwards and forwards, or from side to side.

NOUN **4 Rock** or **rock music** is music with a very strong beat.

NOUN **5 Rock** is also a sweet shaped into long hard sticks.

rocky ADJECTIVE

rocket rockets

NOUN **1** A **rocket** is a space vehicle, usually shaped like a long pointed tube.

NOUN **2 Rockets** are fireworks that explode when they are high in the air.

rod rods NOUN

A **rod** is a long thin pole or bar, usually made of wood or metal. *His uncle gave him a new fishing rod.*

rode VERB

Rode is the past tense of **ride**.

rodent rodents NOUN

A **rodent** is a small mammal with sharp front teeth for gnawing. Rats, mice, squirrels and hamsters are rodents.

roll rolls, rolling, rolled

VERB **1** When something **rolls**, or when you roll it, it moves along a surface, turning over and over.

NOUN **2** A **roll** of something like paper is a long piece of it that has been rolled into a tube.

NOUN **3** A **roll** is a small loaf of bread for one person.

Rollerblade Rollerblades NOUN

TRADEMARK **Rollerblades** are roller skates which have the wheels set in one straight line on the bottom of the boot.

roller skate roller skates NOUN

Roller skates are shoes with four small wheels underneath.

ROM NOUN

ROM is an abbreviation for **read-only memory**. It is the permanent part of a computer's memory. The information stored there can be read but not changed.

roof roofs

NOUN **1** The **roof** of a building or car is the covering on top of it.

NOUN **2** The **roof** of your mouth or of a cave is the highest part.

room rooms

NOUN **1** A **room** is a section in a building, divided from other rooms by walls.

NOUN **2** If there is plenty of **room**, there is a lot of space.

root roots

NOUN **1** A **root** is the part of a plant that grows underground.

NOUN **2** The **root** of a hair, tooth or nail is the part that you cannot see because it is covered with skin.

rope ropes NOUN

Rope is thick strong string.

rose roses

NOUN **1** A **rose** is a flower. Most roses grow on thorny stems.

VERB **2 Rose** is also the past tense of **rise**.

A B C D E F G H I J K L M N O P Q R S T U V W X Y Z

rot rots, rotting, rotted
VERB **1** When vegetables and other foods **rot**, they go bad.
VERB **2** When wood **rots**, it goes soft and can easily be pulled to pieces.

rotate rotates, rotating, rotated VERB
When something **rotates**, it turns with a circular movement.

rotten ADJECTIVE
Something that is **rotten** has gone bad or soft so that it cannot be used.

rough rougher, roughest
ADJECTIVE **1** If something is **rough**, the surface is uneven and not smooth.
ADJECTIVE **2** If someone is being **rough**, they are not being gentle.
ADJECTIVE **3** A **rough** estimate is not meant to be exact.
ADJECTIVE **4** A **rough** draft is an early version of something you are writing.

roughly
ADVERB **1** If you say **roughly**, you mean approximately. *There are roughly twice as many boys as girls in this club.*
ADVERB **2** If someone speaks **roughly** to you, they sound angry and aggressive.

round rounder, roundest
ADJECTIVE **1** Something **round** is shaped like a ball or a circle.
PREPOSITION **2** If something is **round** something else, it surrounds it. *There was a wall round the garden.*
PREPOSITION **3** If something moves **round** you, it keeps moving in a circle with you in the centre.
ADVERB **4** If you turn or look **round**, you turn so you are facing a different way.
round up PHRASE or **round down** PHRASE If you **round a number**, you raise it up or lower it down to the nearest 10, 100 or 1000. *If you round 34 to the nearest ten, it would be 30... 675 rounded up to the nearest hundred is 700.*

roundabout roundabouts
NOUN **1** A **roundabout** is a place where several roads meet, with a circle in the centre which vehicles have to go round.

NOUN **2** A **roundabout** is also a large machine at a fair that children can sit on and go round and round.

rounders NOUN
Rounders is a game in which players run between posts after hitting the ball.

route routes NOUN
A **route** is a way from one place to another. *Aryan took his usual route to school.*

routine routines
ADJECTIVE **1** **Routine** things happen regularly.
NOUN **2** Your **routine** is the usual way that you do things.

row rows, rowing, rowed
(*rhymes with* **snow**) NOUN **1** A **row** of people or things is several of them arranged in a line.
VERB **2** When you **row** a boat, you use oars to make it move through the water.
(*rhymes with* **now**) NOUN **3** A **row** is a noisy argument.

royal
ADJECTIVE **1** Someone who is **royal** belongs to the family of a king or queen.
ADJECTIVE **2** Something that is **royal** is connected with a royal family.

rub rubs, rubbing, rubbed VERB
When you **rub** something, you wipe it hard.

rubber rubbers
NOUN **1** **Rubber** is a strong stretchy material that is made from the sap of a tree. It is used to make things like tyres.
NOUN **2** A **rubber** is a small piece of rubber used to get rid of pencil marks.

rubbish
NOUN **1** **Rubbish** is waste material, such as used paper or empty tins.
NOUN **2** If you say something is **rubbish**, you think it is of very poor quality. *This new television programme is rubbish.*

a
b
c
d
e
f
g
h
i
j
k
l
m
n
o
p
q
r
s
t
u
v
w
x
y
z

179

A
B
C
D
E
F
G
H
I
J
K
L
M
N
O
P
Q
R
S
T
U
V
W
X
Y
Z

ruby **rubies** NOUN
A **ruby** is a dark red jewel.

rude **ruder, rudest** ADJECTIVE
If someone is **rude**, they behave badly and are not polite. *It's **rude** to stare at people.*

rug **rugs** NOUN
A **rug** is a piece of thick material like a small carpet.

rugby NOUN
Rugby is a game played with an oval ball. Two teams try to score points by carrying the ball across a line, or by kicking the ball over a bar.

ruin **ruins, ruining, ruined**
VERB **1** To **ruin** something means to spoil it completely. *Mark and Joe **ruined** my party by fighting.*
NOUN **2** The **ruins** of a building are the parts of it that are left after it has fallen down or been badly damaged.

rule **rules, ruling, ruled**
VERB **1** To **rule** a country means to be in charge of the way the country works.
NOUN **2** **Rules** tell you what you are allowed to do and what you are not allowed to do. They are used in games, and in places such as schools.

ruler **rulers**
NOUN **1** A **ruler** is a person who rules a country.
NOUN **2** A **ruler** is also a long flat piece of wood or plastic with straight edges, used for measuring or drawing straight lines.

rumour **rumours** NOUN
A **rumour** is a story or piece of information which a lot of people are talking about, but which may not be true.

run **runs, running, ran, run**
VERB **1** When you **run**, you move quickly, leaving the ground during each stride.
VERB **2** When liquid **runs**, it flows. *Don't leave the hot water **running**.*
VERB **3** Someone who **runs** something, like a school or country, is in charge of it.

VERB **4** When a vehicle such as a train or bus **runs** somewhere, it travels at set times. *The bus **runs** every 20 minutes.*
VERB **5** If you **run** out of something, you have no more of it left.

rung **rungs**
NOUN **1** A **rung** is a wooden or metal step on a ladder.
VERB **2** **Rung** is the past participle of **ring**.

running
NOUN **1** **Running** is the activity of running, especially as a sport.
ADJECTIVE **2** **Running** water is flowing rather than standing still.

runway **runways** NOUN
A **runway** is a long narrow strip of ground at an airport which planes use when they take off or land.

rush **rushes, rushing, rushed** VERB
If you **rush** somewhere, you go there quickly.

rust **rusts, rusting, rusted**
NOUN **1** **Rust** is a reddish-brown substance that forms on iron or steel which has been in contact with water.
VERB **2** When something **rusts**, rust forms on it.
rusty ADJECTIVE

rustle **rustles, rustling, rustled** VERB
When something **rustles**, it makes soft sounds as it moves. *Dry leaves **rustled** underfoot.*

rut **ruts** NOUN
A **rut** is a deep groove in the ground made by the wheels of a vehicle.

Ss

sack **sacks** NOUN
A **sack** is a large strong bag made of cloth or plastic.

sad **sadder, saddest** ADJECTIVE
If you are **sad**, you are unhappy because something has happened that you do not like.

saddle **saddles** NOUN
A **saddle** is a seat for a rider on a horse or bicycle.

safari **safaris** NOUN
A **safari** is a journey to see wild animals.

safe **safer, safest; safes**
ADJECTIVE **1** If you are **safe**, you are not in any danger.
ADJECTIVE **2** If something is in a **safe** place, it cannot be lost or stolen.
NOUN **3** A **safe** is a strong metal cupboard with special locks. People keep money or valuable things in a safe.
safety NOUN

said VERB
Said is the past tense of **say**.

sail **sails, sailing, sailed**
NOUN **1** A **sail** is a large piece of material fixed to a boat. The wind blows against the sail and pushes the boat along.
NOUN **2** A **sail** is also one of the flat pieces of wood on the top of a windmill.
VERB **3** To **sail** a boat means to make it move across water using its sails.

sailor **sailors** NOUN
A **sailor** is a person who works on a ship as a member of the crew.

salad **salads** NOUN
A **salad** is a mixture of raw vegetables, for example lettuce, cucumber and tomatoes.
*See **Other foods** on page 261*

sale **sales**
NOUN **1** The **sale** of anything is the selling of it for money.
NOUN **2** A **sale** is a time when a shop sells things at less than their usual price.

saliva NOUN
Saliva is the liquid in your mouth that helps you eat food.

salmon NOUN
A **salmon** is a large silvery fish. Salmon live in the sea, but they swim up rivers to lay their eggs.

salt NOUN
Salt is a white powder or crystal with a bitter taste. Salt is found in the earth and in sea water. It is used to flavour or preserve food.
*See **Other foods** on page 261*

salute **salutes, saluting, saluted**
NOUN **1** A **salute** is a sign of respect used especially in the armed forces.
VERB **2** If you **salute** someone, you give them a salute.

same
ADJECTIVE **1** If two things are the **same**, they are exactly like each other in some way. *Look! Your dress is the **same** as mine.*
ADJECTIVE **2** **Same** means one shared thing and not two different ones. *Amy and I are in the **same** class.*

a
b
c
d
e
f
g
h
i
j
k
l
m
n
o
p
q
r
s
t
u
v
w
x
y
z

181

A
B
C
D
E
F
G
H
I
J
K
L
M
N
O
P
Q
R
S
T
U
V
W
X
Y
Z

182

sample samples NOUN
A **sample** of something is a small quantity of it that you can try.

sand NOUN
Sand is tiny grains of rock, shells and other material. Most deserts and beaches are made of sand.

sandal sandals NOUN
Sandals are light shoes for warm weather. The soles are held on by straps which go over your foot.

sandwich sandwiches NOUN
A **sandwich** is two slices of bread with a layer of food in between.
See Other foods on page 261

sang VERB
Sang is the past tense of **sing**.

sank VERB
Sank is the past tense of **sink**.

sap NOUN
Sap is the liquid that carries food through plants and trees.

sardine sardines NOUN
A **sardine** is a small sea fish.

sari saris NOUN
A **sari** is a piece of clothing worn especially by Asian women.

sat VERB
Sat is the past tense of **sit**.

satchel satchels NOUN
A **satchel** is a leather or cloth bag with a long strap.

satellite satellites
NOUN **1** A **satellite** is a natural object in space that moves around a larger object. The moon is a satellite of the Earth.
NOUN **2** A **satellite** is also an object sent into space to send signals back to Earth.

satellite dish satellite dishes NOUN
A **satellite dish** is an aerial which receives signals from an artificial satellite.

satisfactory ADJECTIVE
Something that is **satisfactory** is good enough for its purpose.

satisfy satisfies, satisfying, satisfied VERB
To **satisfy** someone means to give them enough of something to make them pleased or contented.

Saturday Saturdays NOUN
Saturday is the day between Friday and Sunday.

sauce sauces NOUN
A **sauce** is a thick liquid served with other food to add to the taste.

saucepan saucepans NOUN
A **saucepan** is a deep metal cooking pot, usually with a long handle. Most saucepans have lids.

saucer saucers NOUN
A **saucer** is a small plate on which you stand a cup.

sausage sausages NOUN
A **sausage** is a finely minced meat mixture put into a skin.

savage ADJECTIVE
A **savage** animal is wild and fierce.

save saves, saving, saved
VERB **1** If you **save** someone or something, you help them to escape from harm or danger. *He fell in the river and his father dived in to save him.*
VERB **2** If you **save** money, you gradually collect it by not spending it all.

savings PLURAL NOUN
Your **savings** are the money you have saved.

saw saws, sawing, sawed, sawn
VERB **1** **Saw** is the past tense of **see**.
NOUN **2** A **saw** is a tool for cutting wood and other materials. It has a blade with sharp teeth along one edge.
VERB **3** If you **saw** something, you cut it with a saw.

sawdust NOUN
Sawdust is the dust and small bits of wood made when wood is sawn.

say **says, saying, said** VERB
When you **say** something, you speak words.

scald **scalds, scalding, scalded** VERB
If you **scald** yourself, you burn yourself with very hot liquid or steam.

scale **scales**
NOUN **1** The **scale** of a map is how its size relates to the place in the real world.
NOUN **2** The **scales** of a fish or reptile are the small pieces of hard skin covering its body.

scales PLURAL NOUN
Scales are a piece of equipment you use for weighing things.

scamper **scampers, scampering, scampered** VERB
When people or small animals **scamper**, they move quickly and lightly.

scan **scans, scanning, scanned**
VERB **1** If you **scan** a piece of writing, you look through it quickly.
VERB **2** If a machine **scans** something, it examines it using a beam of light, X-rays or sound waves.

scar **scars** NOUN
A **scar** is a mark that is left on the skin after a wound has healed.

scarce **scarcer, scarcest** ADJECTIVE
Something that is **scarce** is not often found.

scare **scares, scaring, scared** VERB
Someone or something that **scares** you makes you feel frightened.

scarecrow **scarecrows** NOUN
A **scarecrow** is an object in the shape of a person, put in a field of crops to frighten birds away.

scared ADJECTIVE
If you are **scared**, you are frightened.

scarf **scarves** NOUN
A **scarf** is a piece of cloth that you wear round your neck to keep you warm.

scarlet ADJECTIVE
Something **scarlet** is a bright red colour.

scatter **scatters, scattering, scattered**
VERB **1** If you **scatter** things, you throw or drop a lot of them all over an area.
VERB **2** If people **scatter**, they suddenly move away in different directions.

scene **scenes**
NOUN **1** The **scene** of an event is the place where it happened. *The police went to the scene of the crime.*
NOUN **2** A **scene** is part of a play or film in which things happen in one place.

scenery
NOUN **1** **Scenery** is what you can see when you are out in the country.
NOUN **2** **Scenery** is also all the cloths and boards that are used as a background for the stage in a theatre.

scent **scents** NOUN
A **scent** is a pleasant smell.

scheme **schemes, scheming, schemed**
NOUN **1** A **scheme** is a plan for doing something.
VERB **2** When people **scheme**, they make secret plans.

school **schools**
NOUN **1** A **school** is a place for teaching and learning.
See School and study on page 262
NOUN **2** You can refer to a large group of dolphins or fish as a **school**.
See Collective nouns on page 268

science NOUN
Science is the study of plants and animals, materials, and things like electricity, forces, light and sound.

science fiction NOUN
Science fiction is stories about events happening in the future or in other parts of the universe.

a
b
c
d
e
f
g
h
i
j
k
l
m
n
o
p
q
r
s
t
u
v
w
x
y
z

scientist scientists NOUN
A **scientist** is a person who finds out why things happen by doing tests and by careful study.

scissors PLURAL NOUN
Scissors are a cutting tool with two sharp blades.

scoop scoops, scooping, scooped
VERB **1** If you **scoop** something up, you pick it up using a spoon or the palm of your hand.
NOUN **2** A **scoop** is an object like a large spoon which is used for picking up food such as ice cream.

score scores, scoring, scored
VERB **1** If someone **scores**, they get a goal or other point in a game.
NOUN **2** The **score** in a game is the total number of points made by the two teams or players.

scowl scowls, scowling, scowled VERB
If you **scowl**, you look very cross.

scramble scrambles, scrambling, scrambled VERB
If you **scramble** over rough or difficult ground, you move over it quickly, using your hands to help you.

scrap scraps NOUN
A **scrap** of something is a small piece of it. *I need a scrap of paper.*

scrapbook scrapbooks NOUN
A **scrapbook** is a book in which you stick things such as pictures or newspaper articles.

scrape scrapes, scraping, scraped VERB
If you **scrape** something, you take off its surface by pulling a rough or sharp object over it.

scratch scratches, scratching, scratched
VERB **1** If you **scratch** your skin, you rub your fingernails against it.

VERB **2** If you **scratch** something, you damage it by making small cuts on it. *I fell into the hedge and scratched my bike.*
NOUN **3** A **scratch** is a small cut.

scream screams, screaming, screamed VERB
If you **scream**, you shout or cry in a loud high-pitched voice.

screech screeches, screeching, screeched VERB
To **screech** means to make an unpleasant high-pitched noise. *The car wheels screeched.*

screen screens NOUN
A **screen** is a flat surface on which pictures or words are shown, for example a television or computer screen.

screw screws, screwing, screwed
NOUN **1** A **screw** is a small sharp piece of metal used for fixing things together.
VERB **2** If you **screw** things together, you fix them together using screws.
VERB **3** If you **screw** something onto something else, you fix it there by twisting it round and round. *He screwed the top back onto the bottle of water.*

screwdriver screwdrivers NOUN
A **screwdriver** is a tool used for turning screws.

scribble scribbles, scribbling, scribbled VERB
If you **scribble**, you write quickly and roughly.

script scripts NOUN
The **script** of a play or film is the written version of it.

scroll scrolls, scrolling, scrolled VERB
If you **scroll** through text on a computer screen, you move the text up or down to find the information that you need. *I scrolled down to find the name.*

scrub scrubs, scrubbing, scrubbed VERB
If you **scrub** something, you rub it hard with a stiff brush and water.

sculptor **sculptors** NOUN
A **sculptor** is someone who makes sculptures.

sculpture **sculptures**
NOUN **1** A **sculpture** is a statue or model made by shaping stone, clay or other materials.

NOUN **2 Sculpture** is the art of making sculptures.

sea **seas** NOUN
The **sea** is the salty water that covers about three-quarters of the earth.

seagull **seagulls** NOUN
Seagulls are common white, grey and black birds that live near the sea.

seahorse **seahorses** NOUN
A **seahorse** is a small fish which swims upright, with a head that looks like a horse's head.

seal **seals, sealing, sealed**
NOUN **1** A **seal** is a large mammal with flippers that lives partly on land and partly in the sea.
VERB **2** If you **seal** an envelope, you stick down the flap.

seam **seams** NOUN
A **seam** is the line where two pieces of material are sewn together.

search **searches, searching, searched**
VERB
If you **search** for something, you try to find it by looking carefully.

search engine **search engines** NOUN
A **search engine** is a computer program that searches for documents on the Internet.

seaside NOUN
The **seaside** is a place by the sea, especially one where people go for their holidays.

season **seasons** NOUN
A **season** is one of the four parts of a year: spring, summer, autumn and winter.
*See **Weather and seasons** on page 263*

seat **seats** NOUN
A **seat** is a place where you can sit, for example a chair or a stool.

seat belt **seat belts** NOUN
A **seat belt** is a strap that you fasten across your body for safety when travelling in a car, coach or aircraft.

seaweed NOUN
Seaweed is a plant that grows in the sea.

second **seconds**
ADJECTIVE **1** The **second** item in a series is the one counted as number two.
NOUN **2** A **second** is a short period of time. There are 60 seconds in a minute.

second person NOUN
In grammar, the **second person** is the person who is addressed in speech or writing. It is expressed as "you".

secret **secrets** NOUN
A **secret** is something that only a few people know and that they are not to tell other people.

secretary **secretaries** NOUN
A **secretary** is a person who is employed by an organization to keep records, write letters and do office work.

a
b
c
d
e
f
g
h
i
j
k
l
m
n
o
p
q
r
s
t
u
v
w
x
y
z

185

A
B
C
D
E
F
G
H
I
J
K
L
M
N
O
P
Q
R
S
T
U
V
W
X
Y
Z

section **sections** NOUN
A **section** of something is one of the separate parts it is divided into.

secure
ADJECTIVE **1** If you feel **secure**, you feel safe and confident.
ADJECTIVE **2** If something is **secure**, it is fixed firmly in position.
security NOUN

see **sees, seeing, saw, seen**
VERB **1** If you **see** something, you are looking at it or you notice it.
VERB **2** To **see** something also means to understand it. *I **see** what you mean.*
VERB **3** If you **see** someone, you visit them or meet them. *I went to **see** the doctor.*

seed **seeds** NOUN
The **seeds** of a plant are the small hard parts from which new plants grow.

seek **seeks, seeking, sought** VERB
If you **seek** someone or something, you try to find them.

seem **seems, seeming, seemed**
VERB **1** If you say that someone **seems**, for example, to be happy or sad, you mean that is the way they look. *Tim **seems** to be a bit upset today.*
VERB **2** If something **seems** a certain way, that is the way it feels to you. *I only waited for ten minutes but it **seemed** like hours.*

seen VERB
Seen is the past participle of **see**.

seesaw **seesaws** NOUN
A **seesaw** is a long plank. A child sits on each end and they move up and down in turn.

segment **segments** NOUN
A **segment** of something is a small part of it.

seize **seizes, seizing, seized** VERB
If you **seize** something, you grab it firmly.

select **selects, selecting, selected** VERB
When you **select** someone or something, you choose them.

selfish ADJECTIVE
People who are **selfish** only think about themselves. They do not care about other people.

sell **sells, selling, sold** VERB
When someone **sells** something, they give it in exchange for money.

Sellotape NOUN
TRADEMARK **Sellotape** is a transparent sticky tape.

semicircle
semicircles NOUN
A **semicircle** is half of a circle.
*The children stood in a **semicircle**.*
See Colours and shapes on page 266

semicolon
semicolons NOUN
A **semicolon** is the punctuation mark (;) which is used in writing to separate different parts of a sentence or list, or to show a pause.
See Punctuation on page 270

semifinal **semifinals** NOUN
The **semifinals** are the two matches in a competition played to decide who plays in the final.

send **sends, sending, sent**
VERB **1** When you **send** something to someone, you arrange for it to be delivered to them.
VERB **2** If someone **sends** someone somewhere, they tell them to go there. *She was **sent** home because she was ill.*
VERB **3** If someone **sends** for you, you get a message to go and see them.

senior ADJECTIVE
People who are **senior** are older or more important.

sensation sensations NOUN
A **sensation** is a physical feeling.

sense senses
NOUN **1** Your **senses** are your power to see, hear, smell, touch and taste.
NOUN **2** **Sense** is knowing the right thing to do. *You should have had more sense.*
NOUN **3** If something makes **sense**, you can understand it.

sensible ADJECTIVE
People who are **sensible** know what is the right thing to do.
sensibly ADVERB

sensitive
ADJECTIVE **1** If someone or something is **sensitive**, they are easily hurt. *He is very sensitive about his big ears.*
ADJECTIVE **2** If you are **sensitive** to other people's feelings, you understand them.

sent VERB
Sent is the past tense of **send**.

sentence sentences NOUN
A **sentence** is a group of words that mean something.

separate separates, separating, separated
ADJECTIVE **1** If two things are **separate**, they are not connected.
VERB **2** To **separate** people or things means to part them. *Separate the yolk from the white.*

September NOUN
September is the ninth month of the year. It has 30 days.

sequel sequels NOUN
A **sequel** to a book or film is another book or film which continues the story.

sequence sequences NOUN
A **sequence** of events is a number of them coming one after the other.

series
NOUN **1** A **series** is a number of things of the same kind that follow each other.
NOUN **2** A radio or television **series** is a set of programmes about the same thing.

serious
ADJECTIVE **1** People who are **serious** are often quiet and do not laugh very much.
ADJECTIVE **2** Things that are **serious** are important and need careful thought.
ADJECTIVE **3** A **serious** problem or situation is very bad and worrying.

servant servants NOUN
A **servant** is someone paid to work in another person's house.

serve serves, serving, served
VERB **1** If you **serve** food or drink to people, you give it to them.

VERB **2** To **serve** customers in a shop means to help them to buy what they want.

service services NOUN
A **service** is something useful that a person or company does for people.

serviette serviettes NOUN
A **serviette** is a small piece of cloth or paper that you use to wipe your hands and mouth when you are eating.

set sets, setting, set
NOUN **1** A **set** is a number of things of the same kind that belong together, for example a set of golf clubs or a set of tools.
VERB **2** When something such as jelly or concrete **sets**, it becomes firm or hard.
VERB **3** When the sun **sets**, it goes down behind the horizon.
VERB **4** When you **set** a clock or control, you adjust it to a particular position.

settee settees NOUN
A **settee** is a long, comfortable seat for two or more people.

a
b
c
d
e
f
g
h
i
j
k
l
m
n
o
p
q
r
s
t
u
v
w
x
y
z

A
B
C
D
E
F
G
H
I
J
K
L
M
N
O
P
Q
R
S
T
U
V
W
X
Y
Z

setting settings NOUN
The **setting** of a story or play is where it takes place. *That old castle would make a great setting for a creepy story.*

settle settles, settling, settled
VERB **1** If you **settle**, you sit or make yourself comfortable.
VERB **2** If something such as dust or snow **settles**, it sinks slowly and becomes still.
VERB **3** If you **settle** something, you decide it.

seven NOUN
Seven is the number 7.

seventeen NOUN
Seventeen is the number 17.

seventy NOUN
Seventy is the number 70.

several ADJECTIVE
Several people or things means a number of them. *He was gone for several hours.*

severe ADJECTIVE
Severe is used to describe something extremely bad or unpleasant. *She woke with severe toothache.*

sew sews, sewing, sewed VERB
When someone **sews**, they join pieces of cloth together by using a needle and thread.

sewer sewers NOUN
A **sewer** is a large underground pipe that carries rainwater and waste away from houses and other buildings.

sex sexes NOUN
The two **sexes** are the two groups that people and other living things are divided into. One sex is male and the other is female. Only female animals can have babies.

shabby shabbier, shabbiest ADJECTIVE
Something that is **shabby** looks old and nearly worn out.

shade shades, shading, shaded
NOUN **1 Shade** is the darkness in a place where the sun cannot reach. *She sat in the shade of an apple tree.*
NOUN **2** A **shade** is something that covers a light to stop it shining in your eyes.
VERB **3** If you **shade** something, you stop the sun from shining on it.
NOUN **4 Shade** is how dark or light a colour is. *I love this shade of blue.*

shadow shadows NOUN
A **shadow** is a dark shape. It is formed when something opaque blocks the light coming from a lamp, a torch or the sun.

shake shakes, shaking, shook, shaken
VERB **1** If you **shake** something, or it shakes, it moves quickly from side to side or up and down.
VERB **2** If your voice **shakes**, it trembles because you are nervous or angry.

shaky shakier, shakiest ADJECTIVE
If someone or something is **shaky**, they are weak and unsteady.
shakily ADVERB

shall should VERB
Shall is used with "I" and "we" to refer to the future. *I shall go shopping tomorrow... I should wait till next week to open my present.*

shallow shallower, shallowest ADJECTIVE
Something that is **shallow**, such as a hole, a container or water, measures only a short distance from top to bottom.

shame
NOUN **1 Shame** is an unhappy feeling that people have when they have done something wrong or foolish.
NOUN **2** If you say something is a **shame**, you mean you are sorry about it. *It's a shame you can't come round.*

shampoo shampoos NOUN
Shampoo is a soapy liquid that you use for washing your hair.

shape shapes

NOUN **1** The **shape** of something is the form of its outline, for example whether it is round or square.

NOUN **2** A **shape** is something that has its outside edges joining in a particular way. Shapes can be flat (two-dimensional), like a circle or a triangle, or solid (three-dimensional), like a cube or sphere.

See Colours and shapes on page 266

share shares, sharing, shared

VERB **1** If you **share** something with another person, you both use it. *She **shared** a bedroom with her sister.*

VERB **2** If you **share** something among a group of people, you divide it so that everyone gets some.

NOUN **3** A **share** of something is a portion of it.

shark sharks NOUN

Sharks are large powerful fish with sharp teeth.

sharp sharper, sharpest

ADJECTIVE **1** A **sharp** object has a fine edge or point that is good for cutting or piercing things.

ADJECTIVE **2** A **sharp** person is quick to notice or understand things.

ADJECTIVE **3** A **sharp** pain is sudden and hurts a lot.

sharpen sharpens, sharpening, sharpened VERB

If you **sharpen** something, you make its edge or point sharper.

shatter shatters, shattering, shattered VERB

If something **shatters**, it breaks into a lot of small pieces.

shave shaves, shaving, shaved VERB

When a man **shaves**, he removes hair from his face with a razor.

shawl shawls NOUN

A **shawl** is a large piece of woollen cloth. Shawls are worn by women over their shoulders or head. They are also used to wrap babies in.

she PRONOUN

She is used to refer to a woman or girl who has already been mentioned.

shear shears, shearing, sheared VERB

To **shear** a sheep means to cut the wool off it.

shed sheds, shedding, shed

NOUN **1** A **shed** is a small building used for storing things.

VERB **2** When a tree **sheds** its leaves, they fall off.

sheep NOUN

A **sheep** is a farm animal with a thick woolly coat. Sheep are kept for meat or wool.

sheet sheets

NOUN **1** A **sheet** is a large piece of thin cloth which is put on a bed.

NOUN **2** A **sheet** of something, such as paper or glass, is a thin flat piece.

shelf shelves NOUN

A **shelf** is something flat which is fixed to a wall or inside a cupboard. It is for putting things on.

shell shells

NOUN **1** The **shell** of an egg or nut is the hard covering round it.

NOUN **2** The **shell** of an animal such as a tortoise is the hard covering on its back.

shelter shelters, sheltering, sheltered

NOUN **1** A **shelter** is a small building or covered place where people or animals can be safe from bad weather or danger.

VERB **2** If you **shelter** in a place, you stay there and are safe.

a
b
c
d
e
f
g
h
i
j
k
l
m
n
o
p
q
r
s
t
u
v
w
x
y
z

189

A
B
C
D
E
F
G
H
I
J
K
L
M
N
O
P
Q
R
S
T
U
V
W
X
Y
Z

shepherd shepherds NOUN
A **shepherd** is a person who looks after sheep.

sheriff sheriffs NOUN
In America, a **sheriff** is a person who keeps the law in a county.

shield shields, shielding, shielded
NOUN **1** A **shield** is a large piece of strong material like metal or plastic which soldiers or policemen carry to protect themselves.
VERB **2** To **shield** someone means to protect them from something.

shift shifts, shifting, shifted
VERB **1** If you **shift** something, you move it.
VERB **2** If something **shifts**, it moves.
NOUN **3** A **shift** is a set period during which people work in a factory or hospital. *My dad works the night shift.*

shin shins NOUN
Your **shin** is the front part of your leg, between your knee and your ankle.

shine shines, shining, shone
VERB **1** When something **shines**, it gives out a bright light.
VERB **2** If you make an object **shine**, you make it bright by polishing it.
shiny ADJECTIVE

ship ships NOUN
A **ship** is a large boat which carries passengers or cargo.

shirt shirts NOUN
A **shirt** is a light piece of clothing for the top part of your body, with a collar, sleeves, and buttons down the front.

shiver shivers, shivering, shivered VERB
When you **shiver**, your body shakes slightly, usually because you are cold or frightened.

shock shocks, shocking, shocked
NOUN **1** If you have a **shock**, something happens suddenly which upsets you.
VERB **2** If you **shock** someone, you give them an unpleasant surprise.
shocking ADJECTIVE

shoe shoes, shoeing, shod
NOUN **1 Shoes** are strong coverings for your feet.
VERB **2** To **shoe** a horse means to fix horseshoes onto its hooves.

shone VERB
Shone is the past tense of **shine**.

shook VERB
Shook is the past tense of **shake**.

shoot shoots, shooting, shot
NOUN **1** A **shoot** is a new part growing from a plant or tree.
VERB **2** To **shoot** means to fire a bullet from a gun, or an arrow from a bow.
VERB **3** If someone **shoots** in a game such as football, they try to score a goal.
VERB **4** When a film is **shot**, it is filmed.

shop shops, shopping, shopped
NOUN **1** A **shop** is a place where things are sold.
VERB **2** When you **shop**, you go to the shops to buy things.
shopping NOUN

shopkeeper
shopkeepers NOUN
A **shopkeeper** is a person who owns or looks after a small shop.

shopping NOUN
Your **shopping** is the goods you have bought in a shop.

shore shores NOUN

The **shore** of a sea or lake is the land along the edge of it.

short shorter, shortest

ADJECTIVE **1** Someone who is **short** is not as tall as most other people.

ADJECTIVE **2** Something that is **short** is not very long.

PHRASE **3** If one word is **short for** another, it is a quick way of saying it. *Phone is **short for** telephone.*

shorts PLURAL NOUN

Shorts are trousers with short legs.

shot shots

VERB **1 Shot** is the past tense of **shoot**.

NOUN **2** A **shot** is when a gun is fired.

NOUN **3** In football and tennis, a **shot** is the act of kicking or hitting the ball.

should

VERB **1** You use **should** to say that something ought to happen. *You **should** write a thank-you letter.*

VERB **2** You also use **should** to say that you expect something to happen. *We **should** have heard by now.*

shoulder shoulders NOUN

Your **shoulders** are the parts of your body between your neck and the tops of your arms.

shout shouts, shouting, shouted VERB

If you **shout** something, you say it very loudly.

shove shoves, shoving, shoved VERB

If you **shove** someone or something, you push them roughly.

shovel shovels, shovelling, shovelled

NOUN **1** A **shovel** is a tool like a spade with a rounded blade.

VERB **2** If you **shovel** earth or snow, you move it with a shovel.

show shows, showing, showed, shown

VERB **1** If you **show** someone something, you let them see it. ***Show** me your passport.*

VERB **2** If you **show** someone how to do something, you do it yourself so that they can watch you.

VERB **3** If something **shows**, people can see it. *Do you think that mark will **show**?*

VERB **4** If you **show** your feelings, you let people see them.

NOUN **5** A **show** is something that you watch at the theatre or on television.

shower showers

NOUN **1** A **shower** is a piece of equipment which sprays you with water so that you can wash yourself.

NOUN **2** A **shower** is also a short period of rain or snow.

shrank VERB

Shrank is the past tense of **shrink**.

shred shreds, shredding, shredded

NOUN **1** A **shred** of paper or material is a small narrow piece of it. *He tore the paper into **shreds**.*

VERB **2** If you **shred** something, you cut or tear it into small pieces.

shriek shrieks, shrieking, shrieked VERB

If you **shriek**, you give a sudden sharp scream.

shrill shriller, shrillest ADJECTIVE

A **shrill** sound is loud and high-pitched, like a whistle.

shrimp shrimps NOUN

A **shrimp** is a small edible shellfish with a long tail and many legs.

a
b
c
d
e
f
g
h
i
j
k
l
m
n
o
p
q
r
s
t
u
v
w
x
y
z

191

shrink shrinks, shrinking, shrank, shrunk VERB
If something **shrinks**, it becomes smaller.

shrivel shrivels, shrivelling, shrivelled VERB
When something **shrivels**, it becomes dry and curled up.

shrug shrugs, shrugging, shrugged VERB
If you **shrug** your shoulders, you raise them slightly to show that you are not interested in something.

shrunk VERB
Shrunk is the past participle of **shrink**.

shudder shudders, shuddering, shuddered VERB
If you **shudder**, you tremble with fear or horror.

shuffle shuffles, shuffling, shuffled
VERB **1** If you **shuffle**, you walk without lifting your feet properly off the ground.
VERB **2** If you **shuffle** a pack of cards, you mix them up before you begin a game.

shut shuts, shutting, shut
VERB **1** If you **shut** something, such as a door, you move it so that it fills a gap.

VERB **2** When a shop **shuts** you can no longer go into it.
ADJECTIVE **3** If something is **shut**, it is closed.

shy shier, shiest ADJECTIVE
A **shy** person is nervous with people they do not know well.

sick sicker, sickest ADJECTIVE
If you are **sick**, you are ill.

side sides
NOUN **1** The **side** of something is to the left or right of it. *He parted his hair on the left side.*
NOUN **2** The **side** of something can be the edge of it. *A triangle has three sides.*
NOUN **3** The **sides** of a river are its banks.
NOUN **4** The **sides** of a piece of paper are its front and back.
NOUN **5** The two **sides** in a game are the teams playing against each other.
ADJECTIVE **6** A **side** road is a small road leading off a larger one.

sideways ADVERB
Sideways means moving or facing towards one side. *She had to squeeze sideways through the gap.*

sigh sighs, sighing, sighed VERB
When you **sigh**, you breathe out heavily. People usually sigh when they are tired, sad or bored.

sight NOUN
Sight is being able to see.

sign signs, signing, signed
VERB **1** If you **sign** something, you write your name on it.
NOUN **2** A **sign** is a mark that means something, for example a plus sign (+).
NOUN **3** **Signs** can be words, pictures or symbols that tell you something.
NOUN **4** You can make a **sign** with your body that means something to other people. For example, if you shake your head it is a sign that you mean "No".

signal signals, signalling, signalled
NOUN **1** A **signal** is a message that is given by signs. For example, a flashing light is a signal that a driver is turning left or right.
VERB **2** If you **signal** to someone, you do something to give them a message.

signature signatures NOUN
Your **signature** is the way you write your own name.

sign language NOUN
Sign language is a way of communicating using your hands. It is often used by deaf people.

Sikh **Sikhs** NOUN
A **Sikh** is a person who believes in Sikhism, an Indian religion which teaches that there is only one God.

silence NOUN
Silence is when there is no noise.

silent
ADJECTIVE **1** If someone or something is **silent**, they are not saying anything or making any noise.
ADJECTIVE **2** A **silent** letter is one that is written but not pronounced, for example, the "g" in the word "gnat".
See Silent letters on page 267

silhouette **silhouettes** NOUN
A **silhouette** is the outline of a dark shape against a light background.

silk **silks** NOUN
Silk is a fine soft cloth. It is made from threads produced by a kind of caterpillar called a silkworm.
silky ADJECTIVE

silly **sillier, silliest** ADJECTIVE
If someone says you are **silly**, they mean you are behaving in a foolish or childish way.

silver NOUN
Silver is a greyish-white metal used for making jewellery.

similar ADJECTIVE
If things are **similar**, they are rather alike.

simile **similes** NOUN
A **simile** is an expression in which a person or thing is described as being similar to someone or something else. "She went as red as a beetroot" is a simile.

simple **simpler, simplest** ADJECTIVE
Something that is **simple** is easy to do or understand.
simply ADVERB

simplify **simplifies, simplifying, simplified** VERB
To **simplify** something means to make it easier to do or understand.

since
PREPOSITION **1 Since** means from a particular time until now. *I've been waiting **since** half past three.*
CONJUNCTION **2 Since** also means because. *I had a drink, **since** I was feeling thirsty.*

sincere ADJECTIVE
If you are **sincere**, you say things that you really mean.
sincerely ADVERB

sing **sings, singing, sang, sung**
VERB **1** If you **sing** a song, you make music with your voice.

VERB **2** When birds **sing**, they make pleasant sounds.

single
ADJECTIVE **1 Single** means one of something. *We can't park here. It's a **single** yellow line.*
ADJECTIVE **2** People who are **single** are not married.
ADJECTIVE **3** A **single** bed or bedroom is for one person.
ADJECTIVE **4** A **single** ticket only allows you to travel one way.

singular NOUN
Singular means one. *The **singular** of "girls" is "girl"... The **singular** of "children" is "child".*
See **plural**

sink **sinks, sinking, sank, sunk**
NOUN **1** A **sink** is a large basin with water taps and a drain.

A
B
C
D
E
F
G
H
I
J
K
L
M
N
O
P
Q
R
S
T
U
V
W
X
Y
Z

VERB 2 If something **sinks**, it moves slowly down until it disappears, especially below the surface of water.

VERB 3 To **sink** something sharp into an object means to make it go deeply into it. *The tiger sank its teeth into his leg.*

sip **sips, sipping, sipped** VERB
If you **sip** a drink, you drink it a little at a time.

sir NOUN
Sir is a polite way of addressing a man. *Please sir, can I leave early?*

siren **sirens** NOUN
A **siren** is something that makes a loud wailing noise as a warning. Fire engines, police cars and ambulances have sirens.

sister **sisters** NOUN
Your **sister** is a girl or woman who has the same parents as you.

sit **sits, sitting, sat**
VERB 1 When you **sit**, you put your bottom on something such as a chair or the floor.
VERB 2 When a bird **sits** on its eggs, it covers them with its body to hatch them.

site **sites** NOUN
A **site** is a piece of ground that is used for a particular purpose. *Let's stop at the next camp site.*

situation **situations**
NOUN 1 A **situation** is the place where something is. *Our hotel was in a lovely situation.*
NOUN 2 A **situation** is the things that are happening to you. *You have put me in a difficult situation.*

six NOUN
Six is the number 6.

sixteen NOUN
Sixteen is the number 16.

sixty NOUN
Sixty is the number 60.

size **sizes** NOUN
The **size** of something is how big or small it is.

sizzle **sizzles, sizzling, sizzled** VERB
If something **sizzles**, it makes a hissing sound. *The meat sizzled in the frying pan.*

skate **skates**
NOUN 1 Skates are ice skates or roller skates.
NOUN 2 A **skate** is an edible flat sea fish.

skateboard **skateboards** NOUN
A **skateboard** is a narrow board on wheels which you stand on and ride for fun.

skeleton **skeletons** NOUN
Your **skeleton** is all the bones in your body joined together. It supports your body and protects your organs.

sketch **sketches** NOUN
A **sketch** is a quick drawing.

ski **skis** NOUN
Skis are long pieces of wood, metal or plastic that you fasten to special boots so that you can move easily on snow.

skid **skids, skidding, skidded** VERB
If a vehicle **skids**, it slides out of control, for example because the road is wet or icy.

skill **skills** NOUN
Skill is the ability to do something well.
skilful ADJECTIVE

skim **skims, skimming, skimmed**
VERB 1 If you **skim** something from the surface of a liquid, you remove it.
VERB 2 If you **skim** a piece of writing, you read it to get a general idea of what it is about.

skin **skins**
NOUN 1 Your **skin** is the natural covering of your body.
NOUN 2 The **skin** of a fruit or vegetable is its outer covering.

skinny **skinnier, skinniest** ADJECTIVE
Someone **skinny** is very thin.

skip skips, skipping, skipped

VERB **1** When you **skip**, you move along almost as though you were dancing, with little jumps.

VERB **2** If you **skip** with a rope, you swing the rope over your head and under your feet while jumping.

VERB **3** If you **skip** something, you miss it out. *I'm going to **skip** lunch.*

NOUN **4** A **skip** is a large metal container for holding rubbish and rubble.

skirt skirts NOUN

A **skirt** is a piece of clothing worn by women and girls. It hangs from the waist.

skull skulls NOUN

Your **skull** is the bony part of your head. It protects your brain, which is inside it.

sky skies NOUN

The **sky** is the space around the earth which you can see when you stand outside and look upwards.

skyscraper skyscrapers NOUN

A **skyscraper** is a very tall building.

slab slabs NOUN

A **slab** is a thick flat piece of something such as stone or concrete.

slack slacker, slackest ADJECTIVE

Something that is **slack** is loose, and not firmly stretched.

slam slams, slamming, slammed VERB

If you **slam** a door, you shut it hard so that it makes a loud noise.

slang NOUN

Slang is words that you use in everyday talk but not when you are writing or being polite.

slant slants, slanting, slanted VERB

If something **slants**, it is not straight but lies at an angle.

slap slaps, slapping, slapped VERB

If you **slap** someone, you hit them with the palm of your hand.

slate slates NOUN

Slate is a dark grey rock that can be split into thin layers. It is often used for roofs.

sledge sledges NOUN

A **sledge** is a vehicle on runners used for travelling over snow.

sleek sleeker, sleekest ADJECTIVE

Hair or fur that is **sleek** is smooth and shiny.

sleep sleeps, sleeping, slept VERB

When you **sleep**, you close your eyes and your whole body rests.

sleepy ADJECTIVE

sleet NOUN

Sleet is a mixture of snow and rain.

sleeve sleeves NOUN

The **sleeves** of a coat or jumper are the parts that cover your arms.

sleigh sleighs NOUN

A **sleigh** is a sledge pulled by animals.

slept VERB

Slept is the past tense of **sleep**.

slice slices, slicing, sliced

NOUN **1** A **slice** is a thin piece of food that has been cut from a larger piece.

VERB **2** If you **slice** food, you cut it into thin pieces.

slide slides, sliding, slid

VERB **1** When something **slides**, it moves smoothly over a surface.

NOUN **2** A **slide** is a piece of playground equipment for sliding down.

slight slighter, slightest ADJECTIVE

Something that is **slight** is small. *She has a **slight** cut.*

slightly ADVERB

slim slimmer, slimmest ADJECTIVE

Someone who is **slim** has a body that is thin but not too thin.

a
b
c
d
e
f
g
h
i
j
k
l
m
n
o
p
q
r
s
t
u
v
w
x
y
z

A
B
C
D
E
F
G
H
I
J
K
L
M
N
O
P
Q
R
S
T
U
V
W
X
Y
Z

slime NOUN
Slime is a thick slippery substance which covers a surface and which looks unpleasant. *The pond was covered in green **slime**.*
slimy ADJECTIVE

sling slings, slinging, slung
NOUN **1** A **sling** is a piece of cloth which you hang from your neck to support a broken or injured arm.
VERB **2** If you **sling** something somewhere, you throw it carelessly.

slip slips, slipping, slipped
VERB **1** If you **slip**, you accidentally slide and lose your balance.
VERB **2** If you **slip** somewhere, you go there quickly and quietly. *She **slipped** out of the house.*
NOUN **3** A **slip** of paper is a small piece of paper.

slipper slippers
NOUN
Slippers are soft loose shoes that people wear in the house.

slippery ADJECTIVE
Something that is **slippery** is smooth, wet or greasy. It is difficult to keep hold of or to walk on.

slit slits, slitting, slit
VERB **1** If you **slit** something, you make a long narrow cut in it. *He **slit** open the envelope.*
NOUN **2** A **slit** is a long narrow opening in something.

slope slopes NOUN
A **slope** is a flat surface which has one end higher than the other.

slot slots NOUN
A **slot** is a narrow opening in something, usually for putting coins in.

slow slower, slowest
ADJECTIVE **1** Something that is **slow** moves along without much speed.

ADJECTIVE **2** If a watch or clock is **slow**, it shows a time that is earlier than the correct time.
slowly ADVERB

slug slugs NOUN
A **slug** is a small slow-moving animal with a long slimy body, like a snail but without a shell.

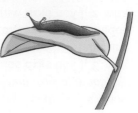

sly slyer, slyest ADJECTIVE
Someone who is **sly** is good at tricking people in a not very nice way.

smack smacks, smacking, smacked VERB
If a person **smacks** someone, they hit them with an open hand.

small smaller, smallest ADJECTIVE
Something that is **small** is not as large as other things of the same kind.

smart smarter, smartest ADJECTIVE
Someone who is **smart** looks neat and clean.

smash smashes, smashing, smashed
VERB **1** If something **smashes**, it falls and hits the ground. It makes a loud noise and breaks into lots of pieces. *The cup **smashed** when she dropped it.*
VERB **2** If someone or something **smashes** an object, they drop it or hit it so that it breaks into lots of pieces.

smell smells, smelling, smelled or smelt
VERB **1** When you **smell** something, you notice it with your nose.
VERB **2** If something **smells** nice or nasty, people's noses tell them about it.
NOUN **3** Your sense of **smell** is your ability to smell things.

smile smiles, smiling, smiled VERB
When you **smile**, the corners of your mouth move upwards and you look happy.

smoke smokes, smoking, smoked
NOUN **1 Smoke** is a mixture of gas and small particles sent into the air when something burns.
VERB **2** If something is **smoking**, smoke is coming from it.

smooth smoother, smoothest

ADJECTIVE **1** Something which is **smooth** has no roughness, lumps or holes in it.

ADJECTIVE **2** A **smooth** ride is one that is comfortable because there are no bumps.

smother smothers, smothering, smothered

VERB **1** If someone **smothers** a fire, they cover it with something in order to put it out.

VERB **2** If a lot of things **smother** something, they cover it all over. *The grass was **smothered** in daisies.*

smudge smudges, smudging, smudged

NOUN **1** A **smudge** is a dirty mark left on something.

VERB **2** If you **smudge** something, you make it dirty by touching it.

smug smugger, smuggest ADJECTIVE

Someone who is **smug** is too pleased with how good or clever they are.

smuggle smuggles, smuggling, smuggled VERB

To **smuggle** things or people into or out of a place means to take them there secretly, or against the law.

snack snacks NOUN

A **snack** is a small amount of food that you eat quickly. *I had some yoghurt and crackers for a **snack**.*

snag snags NOUN

A **snag** is a small problem.

snail snails NOUN

A **snail** is a small slow-moving animal with a shell on its back.

snake snakes NOUN

A **snake** is a long thin reptile with scales on its skin and no legs.

See Reptiles on page 264

snap snaps, snapping, snapped

VERB **1** If something **snaps**, it breaks suddenly with a sharp cracking noise.

VERB **2** If a dog **snaps** at you, it tries to bite you.

VERB **3** If someone **snaps** at you, they speak crossly.

NOUN **4 Snap** is a children's card game.

snarl snarls, snarling, snarled VERB

When an animal **snarls**, it makes a fierce sound in its throat while showing its teeth.

snatch snatches, snatching, snatched VERB

If you **snatch** something, you take it quickly and suddenly.

sneak sneaks, sneaking, sneaked VERB

If you **sneak** somewhere, you go there very quietly, being careful that other people do not see or hear you.

sneer sneers, sneering, sneered VERB

If a person **sneers** at something, they show that they don't like it much.

sneeze sneezes, sneezing, sneezed VERB

When you **sneeze**, you blow out suddenly through your nose, making a loud noise.

sniff sniffs, sniffing, sniffed VERB

If you **sniff**, you breathe in through your nose hard enough to make a sound.

snooze snoozes, snoozing, snoozed VERB

If you **snooze**, you sleep lightly for a short time, especially during the day.

snore snores, snoring, snored VERB

When people **snore**, they breathe very noisily while they are sleeping.

a
b
c
d
e
f
g
h
i
j
k
l
m
n
o
p
q
r
s
t
u
v
w
x
y
z

A
B
C
D
E
F
G
H
I
J
K
L
M
N
O
P
Q
R
S
T
U
V
W
X
Y
Z

snow snows, snowing, snowed
NOUN **1 Snow** is flakes of ice crystals which fall from the sky in cold weather.
VERB **2** When it **snows**, snow falls from the sky.

snowball snowballs NOUN
A **snowball** is a ball of snow for throwing.

snowboard snowboards NOUN
A **snowboard** is a narrow board that you stand on in order to slide quickly through snow.

snowflake snowflakes NOUN
A **snowflake** is a soft piece of falling snow.

snowman snowmen NOUN
A **snowman** is a pile of snow that is made to look like a person.

snug snugger, snuggest ADJECTIVE
If you feel **snug**, you are warm and comfortable.

snuggle snuggles, snuggling, snuggled
VERB
If you **snuggle** somewhere, you cuddle up to something or someone.

so
ADVERB **1** You use **so** to talk about something without repeating the same words. *She laughed, and* **so** *did the teacher.*
ADVERB **2** You can use **so** in front of adjectives and adverbs to make them stronger. *You are* **so** *funny.*
CONJUNCTION **3** You use **so** to talk about the reason for doing something. *I was cold,* **so** *I put on a coat.*

soak soaks, soaking, soaked
VERB **1** When liquid **soaks** something, it makes it very wet.
VERB **2** When something **soaks** up a liquid, the liquid is drawn up into it.

soap soaps NOUN
Soap is a substance made of natural oils and fats, used for washing yourself.

soar soars, soaring, soared VERB
If something **soars** into the air, it goes quickly up into it.

sob sobs, sobbing, sobbed VERB
When someone **sobs**, they cry in a noisy way, breathing in short breaths.

soccer NOUN
Soccer is another word for the game of football.

society societies
NOUN **1 Society** is people in general.
NOUN **2** A **society** is an organization for people who have the same interests.

sock socks NOUN
A **sock** is a soft piece of clothing which covers your foot and ankle.

socket sockets NOUN
A **socket** is a place on a wall or on a piece of electrical equipment into which you can put a plug or bulb.

sofa sofas NOUN
A **sofa** is a long comfortable seat for more than one person. Sofas have a back, and usually arms.

soft softer, softest
ADJECTIVE **1** Something that is **soft** changes shape easily when you touch it.
ADJECTIVE **2** A **soft** sound or voice is quiet and gentle.
ADJECTIVE **3** A **soft** light or colour is not too bright.

software NOUN
Software is computer programs.

soggy soggier, soggiest ADJECTIVE
Something that is **soggy** is wet and often heavy.

soil NOUN
Soil is the top layer of earth, which plants can grow in.

solar

ADJECTIVE **1 Solar** is used to describe something that is to do with the sun.

ADJECTIVE **2 Solar** power uses the sun's energy to provide light and heat.

sold VERB

Sold is the past tense of **sell**.

soldier soldiers NOUN

A **soldier** is a person in an army.

sole soles

NOUN **1** The **sole** of your foot, shoe or sock is the underneath surface of it.

NOUN **2** A **sole** is also a flat sea fish.

solemn ADJECTIVE

Someone or something that is **solemn** is serious, rather than cheerful.

solid

ADJECTIVE **1** Something that is **solid** is firm and always keeps its shape. Metal, wood and rock are all solid.

ADJECTIVE **2** Something **solid** is not hollow.

ADJECTIVE **3** A **solid** shape is a three-dimensional shape such as a cylinder or a cone.

See *Solid shapes* on page 266

solo solos

NOUN **1** A **solo** is a piece of music played or sung by one person alone.

ADJECTIVE **2** A **solo** performance or activity is done by one person alone.

solution solutions

NOUN **1** A **solution** is the answer to a problem.

NOUN **2** A **solution** can also be a liquid in which something, like a powder, has been dissolved.

solve solves, solving, solved VERB

If you **solve** a problem, you find an answer to it.

some ADJECTIVE

You use **some** to talk about an amount when you are not saying how much there is. *There's **some** money on the table.*

somebody PRONOUN

You use **somebody** to talk about a person without saying exactly who you mean.

somehow ADVERB

You use **somehow** to talk about a way of doing something when you do not know exactly how.

someone PRONOUN

You use **someone** to talk about a person without saying exactly who you mean.

somersault somersaults NOUN

A **somersault** is a forwards or backwards roll in which you place your head on the ground and bring your body over it. You can also do a somersault in the air using a trampoline.

something PRONOUN

You use **something** to talk about a thing without saying exactly what you mean. *We need **something** to hold the door open.*

sometimes ADVERB

Sometimes means occasionally, rather than always or never.

somewhere

ADVERB **1 Somewhere** is used to talk about a place without saying exactly where it is. *It must be around **somewhere**.*

ADVERB **2 Somewhere** can be used to give an approximate amount, number or time. *It was **somewhere** between 11 o'clock and midnight.*

a b c d e f g h i j k l m n o p q r s t u v w x y z

A
B
C
D
E
F
G
H
I
J
K
L
M
N
O
P
Q
R
S
T
U
V
W
X
Y
Z

son **sons** NOUN
A boy is the **son** of his parents.

song **songs** NOUN
A **song** is a piece of music with words.

soon **sooner, soonest** ADVERB
Soon means in the near future.

soot NOUN
Soot is a black powder that comes from burning coal or wood.

sore **sorer, sorest** ADJECTIVE
If part of your body is **sore**, it hurts. *Her throat was so **sore** she couldn't talk.*

sorrow **sorrows** NOUN
Sorrow is feeling very sad.

sorry **sorrier, sorriest**
ADJECTIVE **1** If you feel **sorry** about something, you feel disappointed or sad. *I was **sorry** to leave all my friends.*
ADJECTIVE **2** If you feel **sorry** for someone, you feel sad for them.

sort **sorts, sorting, sorted**
NOUN **1** The different **sorts** of something are the different types of it.
VERB **2** If you **sort** things, you put them into groups. ***Sort** your socks into pairs.*
all sorts PHRASE **All sorts** of things means lots of different things.

sought VERB
Sought is the past tense of **seek**.

sound **sounds** NOUN
A **sound** is something that you hear.

soup **soups** NOUN
Soup is liquid food made by boiling meat, fish or vegetables in water.
See Other foods on page 261

sour **sourer, sourest**
ADJECTIVE **1** Something that is **sour** tastes sharp.
ADJECTIVE **2** **Sour** milk is no longer fresh.

source **sources**
NOUN **1** The **source** of something is the place that it has come from.
NOUN **2** The **source** of a river or stream is the place where it begins.

south NOUN
South is one of the four main points of the compass. If you face the point where the sun rises, south is on your right.
See **compass point**
southern ADJECTIVE

south-east NOUN
South-east is halfway between south and east.

south-west NOUN
South-west is halfway between south and west.

souvenir **souvenirs** NOUN
A **souvenir** is something you keep to remind you of a person or place.

sow **sows, sowing, sowed**
(*rhymes with* **no**) VERB **1** To **sow** seeds means to plant them in the ground.
(*rhymes with* **now**) NOUN **2** A **sow** is an adult female pig.

space **spaces**
NOUN **1** **Space** is the area that is empty in a place, building or container. *There's enough **space** for a bigger chair in my room.*
NOUN **2** **Space** is also the place far above the Earth where there is no air.

spaceship **spaceships** NOUN
A **spaceship** is a vehicle that carries people through space.

spacesuit **spacesuits** NOUN
A **spacesuit** is a special suit that is worn by an astronaut, which covers the whole body.

spade **spades** NOUN
A **spade** is a tool for digging, with a flat metal blade and a long handle.

spaghetti NOUN
Spaghetti is long thin pieces of pasta.

span **spans** NOUN
The **span** of something is the total length of it from end to end. For example, when a bird stretches its wings, the distance from wing tip to wing tip is called its "wing span".

spanner **spanners** NOUN
A **spanner** is a tool with a specially shaped end that fits round a nut to turn it.

spare **spares, sparing, spared**
ADJECTIVE **1** Something that is **spare** is extra to what is needed. *Do you have a **spare** pencil you can lend me?*
VERB **2** If you **spare** something, you make it available. *Can you **spare** me some time?*

spark **sparks** NOUN
A **spark** is a tiny piece of fire. It can fly up from something burning, or it can be caused by electricity.

sparkle **sparkles, sparkling, sparkled**
VERB
If something **sparkles**, it shines with a lot of small bright points of light.

sparrow **sparrows** NOUN
A **sparrow** is a small bird with brown and grey feathers.

speak **speaks, speaking, spoke, spoken**
VERB **1** When you **speak**, you use your voice to say words.
VERB **2** If you **speak** a foreign language, you know it and can use it.

speaker **speakers** NOUN
A **speaker** is a person who is speaking or making a speech.

spear **spears, spearing, speared**
NOUN **1** A **spear** is a weapon consisting of a long pole with a sharp point.
VERB **2** To **spear** something means to push or throw a pointed object into it. *He **speared** a potato with his fork.*

special
ADJECTIVE **1** Something that is **special** is more important or better than other things of its kind.
ADJECTIVE **2** **Special** can also mean that something is for a particular use. *You need a **special** tool for this job.*

speck **specks** NOUN
A **speck** is a tiny piece of something. *There wasn't a **speck** of dust anywhere.*

spectator **spectators** NOUN
A **spectator** is a person who is watching something.

speech **speeches**
NOUN **1** **Speech** is the ability to speak or the act of speaking.
NOUN **2** A **speech** is a formal talk given to an audience.
NOUN **3** In a play, a **speech** is a group of lines spoken by one of the characters.

speechless ADJECTIVE
If you are **speechless**, you cannot speak for a short time, usually because something has amazed you.

speech marks PLURAL NOUN
Speech marks are punctuation marks (" ") or (' ') used in writing to show where speech begins and ends.
See Punctuation on page 270

speed **speeds, speeding, sped or speeded**
NOUN **1** The **speed** of something is how fast it moves.
VERB **2** Someone who is **speeding** is moving very fast, or too fast.

spell **spells, spelling, spelt or spelled**
VERB **1** When you **spell** a word, you name or write its letters in order.
NOUN **2** A **spell** is a short time. *We're in for a **spell** of bad weather.*

a
b
c
d
e
f
g
h
i
j
k
l
m
n
o
p
q
r
s
t
u
v
w
x
y
z

201

NOUN **3** A **spell** is also the words used to perform magic.

spellcheck spellchecks, spellchecking, spellchecked VERB

If you **spellcheck** something you have written on a computer, you use a program to check whether you have made any spelling mistakes.

spelling NOUN

The **spelling** of a word is the correct order of letters in it.

spend spends, spending, spent

VERB **1** When you **spend** money, you buy things with it.

VERB **2** To **spend** time or energy means to use it.

sphere NOUN

A **sphere** is an object or shape that is like a ball.

spherical ADJECTIVE

See Solid shapes on page 266

spice spices NOUN

A **spice** is the powder or seeds from a particular plant which people put in food to give it flavour.

spicy ADJECTIVE

spider spiders NOUN

A **spider** is a small animal with eight legs. Some spiders make webs that they use to catch insects for food.

spike spikes NOUN

A **spike** is a long piece of metal with a sharp point at one end.

spill spills, spilling, spilled or spilt VERB

If you **spill** a liquid, you let it flow out of a container by mistake.

spin spins, spinning, spun

VERB **1** If something **spins**, it turns round and round quickly.

VERB **2** When someone **spins**, they make thread by twisting together pieces of fibre using a machine.

VERB **3** When spiders **spin**, they give out a sticky thread and make it into a web.

spinach NOUN

Spinach is a vegetable with large green leaves.

See Vegetables on page 260

spine spines

NOUN **1** Your **spine** is your backbone.

NOUN **2** **Spines** are long sharp points on an animal's body or on a plant.

spiral spirals NOUN

A **spiral** is a continuous curve which winds round and round, with each curve above or outside the previous one.

spire spires NOUN

The **spire** of a church is the tall cone-shaped structure on top.

spite spites, spiting, spited VERB

If you do something to **spite** someone, you do it deliberately to hurt or annoy them.

in spite of PHRASE When you say that you are doing something **in spite of** something else, you mean that you are not going to let it stop you. *In spite of the rain, I'm still going out.*

spiteful ADJECTIVE

A **spiteful** person does or says nasty things to people to hurt them.

spitefully ADVERB

splash splashes, splashing, splashed

VERB **1** If you **splash** around in water, you disturb the water in a noisy way.

VERB **2** If liquid **splashes** something, it scatters over it in a lot of small drops.

NOUN **3** A **splash** is the sound made when something hits or falls into water.

splendid ADJECTIVE
Splendid means extremely good.

splinter splinters, splintering, splintered
NOUN **1** A **splinter** is a thin sharp piece of wood or glass which has broken off a larger piece.
VERB **2** If something **splinters**, it breaks into thin sharp pieces.

split splits, splitting, split
VERB **1** If something is **split**, it divides into two or more. *The village was **split** in two by the new road.*
VERB **2** If people **split** something between them, they share it.

spoil spoils, spoiling, spoiled or spoilt
VERB **1** If you **spoil** something, you damage it, or make it less good than it was.
VERB **2** To **spoil** children means to give them everything they want, so that they become selfish.

spoke spokes
VERB **1** **Spoke** is the past tense of **speak**.
NOUN **2** The **spokes** of a wheel are the bars which connect the hub to the rim.

spoken VERB
Spoken is the past participle of **speak**.

sponge sponges
NOUN **1** A **sponge** is a soft thing with holes in it. It soaks up water and you use it for washing things.
NOUN **2** A **sponge** or **sponge cake** is a very light cake.

sponsor sponsors, sponsoring, sponsored
VERB **1** If an organization **sponsors** something, such as an event or someone's training, it gives money to pay for it.
VERB **2** If you **sponsor** someone who is doing something for charity, you agree to give them a sum of money for the charity if they manage to do it.

spoon spoons NOUN
A **spoon** is a tool like a small shallow bowl with a long handle. It is used for eating, mixing or serving food.

sport sports NOUN
Sports are games that you play which exercise your body.

spot spots, spotting, spotted
NOUN **1** **Spots** are small round marks on a surface. Some fabrics have a pattern of spots.
NOUN **2** A **spot** can be a particular place. *This would be a nice **spot** for a picnic.*
NOUN **3** A **spot** can also be a small raised mark on a person's skin.
VERB **4** If you **spot** something, you notice it.

spotless ADJECTIVE
Something that is **spotless** is perfectly clean.

spout spouts NOUN
A **spout** is a tube with an end like a lip, for pouring liquid. *Teapots have a **spout**.*

sprang VERB
Sprang is the past tense of **spring**.

sprawl sprawls, sprawling, sprawled VERB
If you **sprawl**, you sit or lie with your legs and arms spread out.

spray sprays, spraying, sprayed
NOUN **1** **Spray** is lots of small drops of liquid splashed or forced into the air.
VERB **2** To **spray** a liquid over something means to cover it with small drops of the liquid.

a
b
c
d
e
f
g
h
i
j
k
l
m
n
o
p
q
r
s
t
u
v
w
x
y
z

spread **spreads, spreading, spread**

VERB **1** If you **spread** something, you arrange it over a surface. *They **spread** their wet clothes out to dry.*

VERB **2** If you **spread** something, such as butter, you put a thin layer of it onto something.

VERB **3** If you **spread** parts of your body, such as your arms, you stretch them out until they are far apart.

spring **springs, springing, sprang, sprung**

NOUN **1** **Spring** is the season between winter and summer.

NOUN **2** A **spring** is a coil of wire which returns to its shape after being pressed or pulled.

NOUN **3** A **spring** is also a place where water comes up through the ground.

VERB **4** To **spring** means to jump. *The leopard **sprang** on its prey.*

sprinkle **sprinkles, sprinkling, sprinkled**

VERB

If you **sprinkle** a liquid or powder over something, you scatter it over it.

sprint **sprints, sprinting, sprinted** VERB

To **sprint** means to run fast over a short distance.

sprout **sprouts, sprouting, sprouted**

VERB **1** When something **sprouts**, it starts to grow.

NOUN **2** **Sprouts** are small round green vegetables.

See Vegetables on page 260

sprung VERB

Sprung is the past participle of **spring**.

spun VERB

Spun is the past tense of **spin**.

spurt **spurts, spurting, spurted** VERB

When a liquid or flame **spurts** out, it comes out quickly in a powerful stream. *Blood **spurted** from his arm.*

spy **spies, spying, spied**

NOUN **1** A **spy** is a person sent to find out secret information about a country or organization.

VERB **2** If you **spy** on someone, you watch them secretly.

square **squares**

NOUN **1** A **square** is a shape with four equal sides and four right angles.

See Colours and shapes on page 266

NOUN **2** The **square** of a number is the number multiplied by itself. For example, the square of 3, written 3^2, is 3×3.

ADJECTIVE **3** **Square** is used before units of length when talking about the area of something. *The room measures 25 **square** metres.*

squash **squashes, squashing, squashed**

VERB **1** If you **squash** something, you press it so that it loses its shape.

NOUN **2** If there is a **squash** in a place, there are a lot of people pressed against each other.

NOUN **3** **Squash** is a drink made from fruit juice, sugar and water.

squat **squats, squatting, squatted** VERB

If you **squat**, you crouch down, balancing on your feet with your legs bent.

squawk **squawks, squawking, squawked** VERB

When a bird **squawks**, it makes a loud harsh noise.

squeak **squeaks, squeaking, squeaked**

VERB

If something **squeaks**, it makes a short high-pitched sound.

squeal **squeals, squealing, squealed** VERB

When things or people **squeal**, they make a long high-pitched sound.

squeeze squeezes, squeezing, squeezed
VERB **1** When you **squeeze** something, you press it firmly from two sides.
VERB **2** When you **squeeze** something into a small amount of time or space, you manage to fit it in.

squirrel squirrels NOUN
A **squirrel** is a small furry animal with a long bushy tail.

squirt squirts, squirting, squirted VERB
If a liquid **squirts**, it comes out of a narrow opening in a thin fast stream.

stable stables NOUN
A **stable** is a building in which horses are kept.

stack stacks, stacking, stacked
NOUN **1** A **stack** of things is a pile of them, one on top of the other.
VERB **2** If you **stack** things, you arrange them one on top of the other in a pile.

stadium stadiums NOUN
A **stadium** is a large place where you go to watch games.

staff NOUN
The **staff** of an organization are the people who work for it.

stag stags NOUN
A **stag** is an adult male deer.

stage stages
NOUN **1** A **stage** is a part of a process that lasts for a period of time. *The final **stage** is really difficult.*
NOUN **2** In a theatre, the **stage** is a raised platform where the actors perform.

stagger staggers, staggering, staggered
VERB **1** If someone **staggers**, they walk unsteadily.
VERB **2** If something **staggers** you, it amazes you.

stain stains NOUN
A **stain** is a mark on something that is difficult to remove.

stair stairs NOUN
A **stair** is one of a set of steps in a building going from one floor to another.

staircase staircases NOUN
A **staircase** is a set of stairs.

stake stakes NOUN
A **stake** is a pointed wooden post that can be hammered into the ground and used as a support.

stale staler, stalest ADJECTIVE
Stale food or air is not fresh.

stalk stalks, stalking, stalked
NOUN **1** A **stalk** is the main stem of a plant.
VERB **2** To **stalk** a person or animal means to follow them slowly and quietly.

stall stalls
NOUN **1** A **stall** is a large table on which there are goods for sale.
PLURAL NOUN **2** In a theatre, the **stalls** are the seats at the lowest level, in front of the stage.

stallion stallions NOUN
A **stallion** is an adult male horse.

stammer stammers, stammering, stammered VERB
When someone **stammers**, they hesitate and repeat some sounds when they speak.

stamp stamps, stamping, stamped
NOUN **1** A **stamp** is a small piece of gummed paper which you stick on a letter or parcel before posting it.
VERB **2** If you **stamp**, you lift your foot and put it down hard on the ground.

a
b
c
d
e
f
g
h
i
j
k
l
m
n
o
p
q
r
s
t
u
v
w
x
y
z

205

A
B
C
D
E
F
G
H
I
J
K
L
M
N
O
P
Q
R
S
T
U
V
W
X
Y
Z

stand stands, standing, stood

VERB **1** When you **stand**, your body is upright and you are on your feet.

VERB **2** If a letter **stands for** a particular word, it is an abbreviation of that word. *So you're J Smith. What does J **stand for**?*

VERB **3** If you cannot **stand** something, you cannot bear it. *I can't **stand** that boy.*

standard standards

NOUN **1** A **standard** is how good something is. *This is not up to your usual **standard**.*

ADJECTIVE **2** Something which is **standard** is usual, and not special or extra. *Power steering is now a **standard** feature on this car.*

stank VERB

Stank is the past tense of **stink**.

star stars, starring, starred

NOUN **1** A **star** is a large ball of burning gas in space that appears as a point of light in the sky at night.

NOUN **2** A **star** is also a shape with four, five or more points sticking out in a regular pattern. *See Colours and shapes on page 266*

NOUN **3** A **star** is also a famous person in entertainment or sport.

VERB **4** If an actor or actress **stars** in a film, they have one of the most important parts i n it.

starch NOUN

Starch is a substance that gives you energy. It is found in foods such as bread and potatoes.

stare stares, staring, stared VERB

If you **stare** at something, you look at it for a long time.

starfish starfishes or starfish NOUN

A **starfish** is a flat, star-shaped sea animal with five limbs.

starling starlings NOUN

A **starling** is a common European bird with shiny dark feathers.

start starts, starting, started

VERB **1** To **start** means to begin.

VERB **2** If someone **starts** a machine or car, they use the controls to make it work.

startle startles, startling, startled VERB

If something **startles** you, it frightens you by making a sudden movement or noise.

starve starves, starving, starved VERB

When people or animals **starve**, they suffer a great deal from lack of food and sometimes die.

state states, stating, stated

NOUN **1** The **state** of someone or something is how they are. *Have you seen the **state** of the garden?*

NOUN **2** A **state** is a country, or a part of a country making some of its own laws.

VERB **3** If you **state** something, you say it clearly and formally.

in a state PHRASE If you are **in a state**, you are nervous or upset.

statement statements NOUN

A **statement** is something you say or write when you give facts or information in a formal way.

station stations

NOUN **1** A **station** is a building where trains or buses stop for passengers.

NOUN **2** A **station** is also a building for people such as the police or fire brigade.

stationary ADJECTIVE

If something like a vehicle is **stationary**, it is not moving.

stationery NOUN

Stationery is paper, pens, envelopes and other equipment used for writing.

statue statues NOUN
A **statue** is a large sculpture of a person or animal.

stay stays, staying, stayed
VERB **1** If you **stay** in a place, you do not move away from it.
VERB **2** If you **stay** with someone, you live in their house for a while.

steady steadier, steadiest
ADJECTIVE **1** If something such as a ladder is **steady**, it is firm and does not shake or move about.
ADJECTIVE **2** A **steady** look or voice is calm and controlled.
steadily ADVERB

steak steaks NOUN
A **steak** is a thick slice of meat or fish.

steal steals, stealing, stole, stolen VERB
To **steal** means to take something which does not belong to you, and keep it.

steam NOUN
Steam is the hot vapour formed when water boils.

steel NOUN
Steel is a strong metal made mostly from iron.

steep steeper, steepest ADJECTIVE
Something such as a road or hill that is **steep** slopes sharply.

steeple steeples NOUN
A **steeple** is a church tower with a high pointed top.

steer steers, steering, steered VERB
When someone **steers** something like a car or cycle, they make it go in the direction they want.

stem stems NOUN
The **stem** of a plant is the long thin centre part.

stencil stencils NOUN
A **stencil** is a thin sheet with a cut-out pattern. Ink or paint passes through the stencil to form a pattern on the surface below.

step steps
NOUN **1** A **step** is the movement you make when you lift your foot and put it down in a different place.
NOUN **2** A **step** is also a raised flat surface which you use to move from one level to another.

stepbrother stepbrothers NOUN
Your **stepbrother** is the son of your stepmother or stepfather.

stepfather stepfathers NOUN
Your **stepfather** is a man who is married to your mother but who is not your natural father.

stepmother stepmothers NOUN
Your **stepmother** is a woman who is married to your father but who is not your natural mother.

stepsister stepsisters NOUN
Your **stepsister** is the daughter of your stepmother or stepfather.

stern sterner, sternest ADJECTIVE
Someone who is **stern** is serious and expects to be obeyed.

stew stews NOUN
A **stew** is a meal which you make by cooking meat, fish or vegetables slowly for a long time.

stick sticks, sticking, stuck
NOUN **1** A **stick** is a long thin piece of wood.
VERB **2** If you **stick** a pointed object, such as a drawing pin, into something, you push it in.
VERB **3** If you **stick** two things together, you fix them with something like glue.
VERB **4** If something like a drawer **sticks**, it cannot be moved.

stick

a
b
c
d
e
f
g
h
i
j
k
l
m
n
o
p
q
r
s
t
u
v
w
x
y
z

207

A
B
C
D
E
F
G
H
I
J
K
L
M
N
O
P
Q
R
S
T
U
V
W
X
Y
Z

sticker **stickers** NOUN
A **sticker** is a small piece of paper that you can stick on to a surface. It has writing or a picture on one side.

sticky **stickier, stickiest** ADJECTIVE
Something that is **sticky**, like jam or glue, can stick to other things.

stiff **stiffer, stiffest**
ADJECTIVE **1** Something that is **stiff** is quite hard or firm. *Use a **stiff** broom to sweep up the leaves.*
ADJECTIVE **2** If a person is **stiff**, their muscles or joints hurt when they move.

stile **stiles** NOUN
A **stile** is a kind of fixed gate with a step on each side. It is made so that people can get into a field without letting animals out.

still **stiller, stillest**
ADVERB **1** You say **still** when something is the same as it was before. *I've **still** got a headache.*
ADVERB OR ADJECTIVE **2 Still** means staying in the same position without moving. *He wouldn't sit **still**.*

stilt **stilts** NOUN
Stilts are two long pieces of wood or metal on which people walk.

sting **stings, stinging, stung** VERB
If a creature or plant **stings** you, it pricks your skin and hurts you.

stink **stinks, stinking, stank, stunk** VERB
Something that **stinks** smells bad.

stir **stirs, stirring, stirred** VERB
If you **stir** a liquid, you move it around with a spoon or a stick.

stitch **stitches, stitching, stitched** VERB
If you **stitch** fabric, you push a needle and thread in and out through it.

stocking **stockings** NOUN
Stockings are long pieces of thin clothing that cover a woman's legs and feet.

stole VERB
Stole is the past tense of **steal**.

stolen
VERB **1 Stolen** is the past participle of **steal**.
ADJECTIVE **2** If something is **stolen**, it has been taken away from its owner. *The police found the **stolen** bike.*

stomach **stomachs** NOUN
Your **stomach** is the part of your body that holds food when you have eaten it.

stone **stones**
NOUN **1 Stone** is a hard dry material that is dug out of the ground. It is often used for building houses and walls.
NOUN **2** A **stone** is a small piece of rock.
NOUN **3** The **stone** in a fruit such as a plum is the large seed in the centre.
NOUN **4** A **stone** is a unit of weight equal to just over six kilograms.

stony **stonier, stoniest** ADJECTIVE
Stony ground is rough and contains a lot of stones.

stood VERB
Stood is the past tense of **stand**.

stool **stools** NOUN
A **stool** is a seat with legs but no back.

stoop **stoops, stooping, stooped** VERB
If you **stoop**, you bend your body down from the waist, usually so that you can pick something up.

stop **stops, stopping, stopped**
VERB **1** If you **stop** what you are doing, you no longer do it.
VERB **2** If you **stop** somewhere, you stay there for a short while.

store **stores, storing, stored**
VERB **1** When you **store** things, you put them away and keep them until they are wanted.
NOUN **2** A **store** is a large shop.

storey **storeys** NOUN
A **storey** is all the rooms on one floor of a building.

stork **storks** NOUN
A **stork** is a large bird with a long beak and long legs.

storm **storms** NOUN
A **storm** is bad weather with heavy rain and strong winds. Often there is thunder and lightning.
stormy ADJECTIVE

story **stories** NOUN
A **story** tells you about things that have happened. It can be about something real or something made up.

stout **stouter, stoutest**
ADJECTIVE **1** Someone **stout** is rather fat.
ADJECTIVE **2** Things such as branches that are **stout** are thick and strong.

stove **stoves** NOUN
A **stove** is a piece of equipment for heating a room or for cooking.

straight **straighter, straightest**
ADJECTIVE **1** Something which is **straight** does not bend or curve. You use a ruler to draw a straight line.
ADVERB **2** **Straight** can mean immediately and directly. *We promised to go **straight** to school.*

straighten **straightens, straightening, straightened** VERB
If you **straighten** something, you make it straight, or neat and tidy.

strain **strains, straining, strained**
VERB **1** If you **strain** to do something, you try too hard.
VERB **2** To **strain** food means to pour away the liquid from it.
VERB **3** If you **strain** a muscle, you injure it by moving awkwardly.

strange **stranger, strangest**
ADJECTIVE **1** Something that is **strange** is odd or unexpected.
ADJECTIVE **2** A **strange** place is one you have never been to before.

stranger **strangers** NOUN
A **stranger** is a person you do not know.

strap **straps** NOUN
A **strap** is a strip of something like leather which is used to carry something around, or to fasten things together.

straw **straws**
NOUN **1** **Straw** is dried stalks of cereal such as wheat.
NOUN **2** A **straw** is a thin tube of paper or plastic, which you drink through.

strawberry **strawberries** NOUN
A **strawberry** is a small red fruit. It is soft and juicy and has tiny yellow seeds on its skin.
See Fruit on page 260

stray **strays, straying, strayed**
VERB **1** If people or animals **stray**, they wander away from where they are supposed to be.
ADJECTIVE **2** A **stray** dog or cat is one that has wandered away from home.

stream **streams**
NOUN **1** A **stream** is a small river.
NOUN **2** A **stream** is also a steady flow of something like liquid or traffic.

street **streets** NOUN
A **street** is a road in a town or village, usually with buildings along it.

strength NOUN
Strength is how strong something is.

a
b
c
d
e
f
g
h
i
j
k
l
m
n
o
p
q
r
s
t
u
v
w
x
y
z

A
B
C
D
E
F
G
H
I
J
K
L
M
N
O
P
Q
R
S
T
U
V
W
X
Y
Z

stretch stretches, stretching, stretched

VERB **1** If you **stretch**, you hold out part of your body as far as you can.

VERB **2** If you **stretch** something, you pull it so that it becomes longer or wider.

NOUN **3** A **stretch** of land or water is an area of it.

strict stricter, strictest

ADJECTIVE **1** Someone who is **strict** makes you behave well.

ADJECTIVE **2** A **strict** rule or law is one that must be obeyed.

stride strides, striding, strode

VERB **1** To **stride** along means to walk quickly with long steps.

NOUN **2** A **stride** is a long step.

strike strikes, striking, struck

VERB **1** To **strike** someone or something means to hit them.

VERB **2** When a clock **strikes**, it rings a bell to show what the time is.

VERB **3** If someone **strikes** a match, they make a flame or sparks with it.

NOUN **4** A **strike** is when workers refuse to go on working.

string strings

NOUN **1** **String** is thin rope.

NOUN **2** On a musical instrument like a guitar, the **strings** are the parts that you touch to make the sounds.

strip strips, stripping, stripped

NOUN **1** A **strip** of paper, cloth or other material is a long narrow piece of it.

VERB **2** If you **strip**, you take off all your clothes.

stripe stripes NOUN

A **stripe** is a coloured line on something.

strode VERB

Strode is the past tense of **stride**.

stroke strokes, stroking, stroked VERB

If you **stroke** something, you move your hand gently over it.

stroll strolls, strolling, strolled VERB

To **stroll** means to walk along slowly in a relaxed way.

strong stronger, strongest

ADJECTIVE **1** If you are **strong**, you can work hard and carry heavy things.

ADJECTIVE **2** Objects or materials that are **strong** will not break easily.

ADJECTIVE **3** Wind or water currents that are **strong** move very fast.

ADJECTIVE **4** Smells and flavours that are **strong** are easily noticed.

struck VERB

Struck is the past tense of **strike**.

structure structures NOUN

A **structure** is something that has been built.

struggle struggles, struggling, struggled

VERB **1** If you **struggle** to do something, you try hard to do it but find it difficult.

VERB **2** If you **struggle** when you are being held by something or someone, you twist and kick to try and get free.

stubborn ADJECTIVE

Someone who is **stubborn** is determined to do what they want.

stuck

VERB **1** **Stuck** is the past tense of **stick**.

ADJECTIVE **2** If you are **stuck**, you cannot carry on because it is too difficult.

student **students** NOUN
A **student** is a person who is studying at a university or college.

studio **studios**
NOUN **1** A **studio** is a room where a photographer or artist works.

NOUN **2** A **studio** is also a place where films, television programmes or other recordings are made.

study **studies, studying, studied**
VERB **1** If you **study** a subject, you spend time learning about it.
VERB **2** If you **study** something, you look at it carefully.
NOUN **3** A **study** is a room for writing and studying.

stuff **stuffs, stuffing, stuffed**
NOUN **1** You can talk about a substance or group of things as **stuff**.
VERB **2** If you **stuff** something with objects, you fill it with them.

stumble **stumbles, stumbling, stumbled** VERB
If you **stumble** when you are walking, you trip and almost fall.

stump **stumps** NOUN
A **stump** is the small part of something, such as a tree, that remains when most of it has been removed.

stun **stuns, stunning, stunned**
VERB **1** If you are **stunned** by something, you are very surprised by it.
VERB **2** To **stun** a person or animal means to knock them unconscious by hitting them on the head.

stung VERB
Stung is the past tense of **sting**.

stunk VERB
Stunk is the past participle of **stink**.

stupid **stupider, stupidest** ADJECTIVE
Someone who is **stupid** does things that are not at all sensible.
stupidly ADVERB

sturdy **sturdier, sturdiest** ADJECTIVE
Someone or something that is **sturdy** is strong and firm.

stutter **stutters** NOUN
Someone who has a **stutter** finds it difficult to speak smoothly and often repeats sounds.

sty **sties** NOUN
A **sty** is a hut with a yard where pigs are kept.

style **styles** NOUN
The **style** of something is its design. *I'd like shoes in a different **style**.*

subheading **subheadings** NOUN
A **subheading** is a heading which is less important than the main heading. *We'll have "animals" as a main heading, and "mammals" as a **subheading**.*

subject **subjects**
NOUN **1** A **subject** is a particular thing that people study at school or college, for example science or drawing.
NOUN **2** The **subject** of a piece of writing or a conversation is the thing or person being talked about.
NOUN **3** In grammar, the **subject** is the word or words representing a person or thing doing the action. For example, in the sentence "My cat caught a bird", "my cat" is the subject.

submarine **submarines** NOUN
A **submarine** is a ship that can travel under water.

a
b
c
d
e
f
g
h
i
j
k
l
m
n
o
p
q
r
s
t
u
v
w
x
y
z

211

A
B
C
D
E
F
G
H
I
J
K
L
M
N
O
P
Q
R
S
T
U
V
W
X
Y
Z

substance substances NOUN
Any solid, powder, liquid or paste can be called a **substance**.

subtract subtracts, subtracting, subtracted VERB
If you **subtract** one number from another, you take away the first number from the second. The symbol you use for subtract is –.

subtraction NOUN
Subtraction is taking one number away from another.

suburb suburbs NOUN
A **suburb** is an area of a town or city that is away from its centre.

subway subways NOUN
A **subway** is a footpath that goes underneath a road.

succeed succeeds, succeeding, succeeded VERB
If you **succeed**, you manage to do what you set out to do.

success NOUN
Success is managing to do something that you set out to do.

successful ADJECTIVE
If you are **successful**, you achieve what you wanted to achieve.

such ADVERB
You can use **such** to emphasize something. *She's **such** a nice girl.*
such as PHRASE You can use **such as** to introduce examples of something. *I like team games **such as** football and rounders.*

suck sucks, sucking, sucked VERB
If you **suck** something, you hold it in your mouth and pull at it with your cheeks and tongue, usually to get liquid out of it.

sudden ADJECTIVE
Something that is **sudden** happens quickly and unexpectedly.
suddenly ADVERB

suffer suffers, suffering, suffered VERB
If someone is **suffering**, they feel pain or sadness.

suffix suffixes NOUN
A **suffix** is a group of letters which is added to the end of a word to form a new word, for example "-able" or "-ful".
*See **Suffixes** on page 271*

sugar NOUN
Sugar is a sweet substance used to sweeten food and drinks.

suggest suggests, suggesting, suggested VERB
If you **suggest** something to someone, you give a plan or an idea for them to think about.
suggestion NOUN

suit suits, suiting, suited
NOUN **1** A **suit** is a matching jacket and trousers or skirt.
VERB **2** If something **suits** you, it is right for you.

suitable ADJECTIVE
Something that is **suitable** for a particular purpose is right for it. *Are these shoes **suitable** for running?*

suitcase suitcases NOUN
A **suitcase** is a case that you carry clothes in when you are travelling.

sulk sulks, sulking, sulked VERB
If you **sulk**, you are silent and bad-tempered for a while because you are annoyed about something.

sultana sultanas NOUN
A **sultana** is a dried white grape.

sum sums
NOUN **1** A **sum** is an amount of money.
NOUN **2** In maths, the **sum** is the answer or total that you get when you add numbers. *The **sum** of 2 and 3 is 5.*

summarize summarizes, summarizing, summarized; also spelt **summarise** VERB
To **summarize** something means to give a short account of its main points.

summary **summaries** NOUN
If you give a **summary** of something, you give the main points.

summer **summers** NOUN
Summer is the season between spring and autumn.

summit **summits** NOUN
The **summit** of a mountain is its top.

sun **suns** NOUN
The **sun** is the star that gives us heat and light.

sunburn NOUN
Sunburn is sore skin on someone's body when they have been in the sun for too long.

Sunday **Sundays** NOUN
Sunday is the day between Saturday and Monday.

sunflower **sunflowers** NOUN
A **sunflower** is a tall plant with large yellow flowers.

sung VERB
Sung is the past participle of **sing**.

sunglasses PLURAL NOUN
Sunglasses are glasses with dark lenses that you wear to protect your eyes from the sun.

sunk VERB
Sunk is the past participle of **sink**.

sunlight NOUN
Sunlight is the bright light produced when the sun is shining.
sunlit ADJECTIVE

sunny **sunnier, sunniest** ADJECTIVE
When the weather is **sunny**, the sun is shining brightly.

sunrise **sunrises** NOUN
Sunrise is the time in the morning when the sun comes up.

sunset **sunsets** NOUN
Sunset is the time in the evening when the sun goes down.

sunshine NOUN
Sunshine is the bright light produced when the sun is shining.

super ADJECTIVE
Super means very nice or very good. *We've just seen a **super** film.*

superlative **superlatives** NOUN
In grammar, the **superlative** is the form of an adjective which has "the most" of that adjective. For example, "fattest" is the superlative of "fat".
See Adjective on page 269

*See **Adjective** on page 269*

supermarket **supermarkets** NOUN
A **supermarket** is a large shop which sells all kinds of food and things for the house.

supersonic ADJECTIVE
A **supersonic** aircraft can travel faster than the speed of sound.

superstitious ADJECTIVE
People who are **superstitious** believe in things like magic and powers that bring good or bad luck.

a
b
c
d
e
f
g
h
i
j
k
l
m
n
o
p
q
r
s
t
u
v
w
x
y
z

supper **suppers** NOUN
Supper is a meal or snack eaten in the evening.

supply **supplies, supplying, supplied**
VERB **1** If someone **supplies** you with something, they provide you with it.
NOUN **2** A **supply** of something is the amount of it which someone has. *The water* **supply** *is getting very low.*

support **supports, supporting, supported**
VERB **1** If you **support** someone, you want them to do well.
VERB **2** If something **supports** an object, it holds it up firmly.

suppose **supposes, supposing, supposed**
VERB **1** If you **suppose** that something is true, you think that it is likely to be true.
CONJUNCTION **2** You can use **suppose** or **supposing** when you are thinking about doing something. ***Supposing** we just left without saying anything, what do you think would happen?*
I suppose PHRASE You can say **I suppose** when you are not certain about something. *Yes, **I suppose** he could come.*

sure
ADJECTIVE **1** If you are **sure** something is true, you believe it is true.
ADJECTIVE **2** If something is **sure** to happen, it will definitely happen.
ADJECTIVE **3** If you are **sure** of yourself, you are very confident.
make sure PHRASE If you **make sure** of something, you check it. *Can you **make sure** we locked up properly?*

surf **surfs, surfing, surfed**
NOUN **1 Surf** is the white foam that forms on the top of waves when they break.
VERB **2** When you **surf**, you ride towards the shore on top of a large wave while standing on a special board.
VERB **3** When you **surf** the Internet, you go from website to website.

surface **surfaces** NOUN
The **surface** of something is the top or outside area of it.

surgeon **surgeons** NOUN
A **surgeon** is a doctor who performs operations.

surgery **surgeries**
NOUN **1 Surgery** is medical treatment in which part of the patient's body is cut open.
NOUN **2** A **surgery** is a room or building where a doctor or dentist works.

surname **surnames** NOUN
Your **surname** is the name you share with other members of your family.

surprise **surprises** NOUN
A **surprise** is something unexpected.

surrender **surrenders, surrendering, surrendered** VERB
If someone **surrenders**, they stop fighting and agree that they have lost.

surround **surrounds, surrounding, surrounded** VERB
If something **surrounds** something else, it is all round it.

surroundings PLURAL NOUN
Your **surroundings** are the area around you.

survey **surveys**
NOUN **1** A **survey** of something is a detailed examination of it, often in the form of a report.
VERB **2** A **survey** is also a set of questions to find out what people think about things.

survive **survives, surviving, survived** VERB
If someone **survives**, they continue to live after being close to death.

suspect **suspects, suspecting, suspected** VERB
If you **suspect** someone of doing something wrong, you think they have done it.

suspense NOUN
Suspense is excitement or worry caused by having to wait for something.

suspicious
ADJECTIVE **1** If you are **suspicious** of someone, you do not trust them.
ADJECTIVE **2** If something is **suspicious**, it makes you feel something is wrong.

swallow swallows, swallowing, swallowed
VERB **1** When you **swallow** food or drink, it goes down your throat.
NOUN **2** A **swallow** is a small bird with pointed wings and a long forked tail.

swam VERB
Swam is the past tense of **swim**.

swamp swamps NOUN
A **swamp** is an area of extremely wet land.

swan swans NOUN
A **swan** is a large white bird with a long neck that lives on rivers and lakes.

swap swaps, swapping, swapped VERB
If you **swap** something, you give it to someone and receive something else from them in exchange.

swarm swarms NOUN
A **swarm** is a large group of bees or other insects flying together.
See Collective nouns on page 268

sway sways, swaying, swayed VERB
When people or things **sway**, they lean or swing slowly from side to side.

sweat NOUN
Sweat is the salty liquid which comes from your skin when you are hot.

sweater sweaters NOUN
A **sweater** is a knitted piece of clothing covering your upper body and arms.

sweatshirt sweatshirts NOUN
A **sweatshirt** is a piece of clothing made of thick cotton. It covers your upper body and arms.

sweep sweeps, sweeping, swept VERB
If you **sweep** a floor or a path, you clean it by pushing a broom over it.

sweet sweeter, sweetest; sweets
ADJECTIVE **1** Food or drink that is **sweet** has a taste of sugar.
PLURAL NOUN **2** **Sweets** are things such as chocolates and toffees.
NOUN **3** A **sweet** can be something that is eaten after the main part of a meal.

sweet corn NOUN
Sweet corn is a long stalk covered with juicy yellow seeds that can be eaten as a vegetable.
See Vegetables on page 260

swell swells, swelling, swelled or swollen VERB
If something **swells**, it becomes larger and rounder than usual.

swept VERB
Swept is the past tense of **sweep**.

swerve swerves, swerving, swerved VERB
If something that is moving **swerves**, it suddenly changes direction.

swift swifter, swiftest ADJECTIVE
Something that is **swift** can move very quickly.

swim swims, swimming, swam, swum VERB
When you **swim**, you use your arms and legs to move through water.

swimming NOUN
Swimming is the activity of moving yourself through water.

a
b
c
d
e
f
g
h
i
j
k
l
m
n
o
p
q
r
s
t
u
v
w
x
y
z

swimming costume swimming costumes NOUN

A **swimming costume** is the clothing worn by a woman or girl when she goes swimming.

swimming pool swimming pools NOUN

A **swimming pool** is a place made for people to swim in.

swimming trunks PLURAL NOUN

Swimming trunks are shorts worn by a man or boy when they go swimming.

swing swings, swinging, swung

VERB **1** If something **swings**, it keeps moving backwards and forwards, or from side to side, while it is hanging.

NOUN **2** A **swing** is a seat that hangs from a frame and moves backwards and forwards when you sit on it.

switch switches, switching, switched

NOUN **1** A **switch** is a small control for a piece of equipment such as a light or radio.

VERB **2** To **switch** is to change one thing for another. *I switched to another school when I moved house.*

swollen ADJECTIVE

Something that is **swollen** has swelled up.

swoop swoops, swooping, swooped VERB

When a bird **swoops**, it suddenly flies downwards in a smooth curve.

swop VERB

Swop is another spelling of **swap**.

sword swords NOUN

A **sword** is a weapon with a long blade and a short handle.

swum VERB

Swum is the past participle of **swim**.

swung VERB

Swung is the past tense of **swing**.

sycamore

sycamores NOUN

A **sycamore** is a tree that has large five-pointed leaves.

syllable syllables NOUN

Each beat in a word is a **syllable**. For example, "cat" has one syllable, and "cattle" has two.

symbol symbols NOUN

A **symbol** is a sign or mark that stands for something else. For example, the symbol + stands for "plus".

symmetrical ADJECTIVE

If something is **symmetrical**, it has two halves that are exactly the same, except that one half is like a reflection of the other half.

symmetry

NOUN **1 Symmetry** is when one half of something is exactly like a mirror image of the other half.

NOUN **2** The **line of symmetry** is the dividing line between two symmetrical halves.

sympathy NOUN

If you feel **sympathy** for someone who is unhappy, you are sorry for them.

synagogue

synagogues NOUN

A **synagogue** is a building where Jewish people pray.

synonym

synonyms NOUN

Synonyms are words that have the same or similar meaning. The words "nice" and "pleasant" are synonyms.

See Synonyms on page 272

See Synonyms on page 272

syrup NOUN

Syrup is a thick sweet liquid made by boiling sugar with water.

system systems

NOUN **1** A **system** is a way of doing something. *I've got a new system for organizing my toys.*

NOUN **2** You can refer to a set of equipment as a **system**, for example a central heating system.

Tt

table tables

NOUN **1** A **table** is a piece of furniture with a flat top for putting things on.

NOUN **2** A **table** is also a set of facts or figures arranged in rows or columns.

tablet tablets

NOUN **1** A **tablet** is a small round pill made of powdered medicine.

NOUN **2** A **tablet** is also a small portable computer.

table tennis NOUN

Table tennis is a game for two or four people. You use bats to hit a small hollow ball over a low net across a table.

tackle tackles, tackling, tackled

VERB **1** If you **tackle** a difficult task, you deal with it in a determined way.

VERB **2** If you **tackle** someone in a game such as football, you try to get the ball away from them.

tactful ADJECTIVE

A **tactful** person is careful not to hurt someone else's feelings. **tactfully** ADVERB

tadpole tadpoles NOUN

Tadpoles are small water animals that grow into frogs or toads. They have long tails and round black heads.

tail tails

NOUN **1** A **tail** is the part of an animal, bird or fish that grows out of the end of its body.

NOUN **2** The back part of a plane is called the **tail**.

take takes, taking, took, taken

VERB **1** If you **take** something, you put your hand round it and carry it. *Let me take your coat.*

VERB **2** If someone **takes** you somewhere, you go there with them.

VERB **3** If a person **takes** something that does not belong to them, they steal it.

VERB **4** If you **take away** one number or amount from another, you find out how much is left.

takeaway takeaways NOUN

A **takeaway** is a hot cooked meal bought from a shop or restaurant and eaten elsewhere. The shop or restaurant is also called a **takeaway**.

talcum powder NOUN

Talcum powder, or **talc**, is a soft powder which you put on your skin to help dry it and make it smell nice.

tale tales NOUN

A **tale** is a story.

talent talents NOUN

Talent is the natural ability a person has to do something well.

talk talks, talking, talked VERB

When you **talk**, you say things to someone.

talkative ADJECTIVE

Someone who is **talkative** talks a lot.

tall taller, tallest

ADJECTIVE **1** Someone who is **tall** is higher than a lot of other people.

ADJECTIVE **2** You use **tall** to say how high somebody or something is. *My little brother is only one metre tall.*

tally tallies NOUN

A **tally** is a record of amounts which you add to as you go along.

Talmud NOUN

The **Talmud** is a collection of books explaining the ancient Jewish ceremonies and laws.

tame tamer, tamest ADJECTIVE

A **tame** animal is not afraid of humans and will not hurt them.

a
b
c
d
e
f
g
h
i
j
k
l
m
n
o
p
q
r
s
t
u
v
w
x
y
z

A
B
C
D
E
F
G
H
I
J
K
L
M
N
O
P
Q
R
S
T
U
V
W
X
Y
Z

tan **tans** NOUN
If someone has a **tan**, their skin has become darker than it usually is because they have been in the sun.

tangle **tangles, tangling, tangled**
NOUN **1** A **tangle** is a mass of things such as hairs or fibres that are knotted or coiled together and are hard to separate.
VERB **2** If something is **tangled**, it is twisted in knots.

tank **tanks**
NOUN **1** A **tank** is a large container for liquid or gas.
NOUN **2** A **tank** is also a vehicle for soldiers which moves on tracks. Tanks are covered with strong metal armour, and have guns or rockets.

tanker **tankers** NOUN
A **tanker** is a ship, truck or railway vehicle for carrying gas or liquid.

tap **taps, tapping, tapped**
NOUN **1** A **tap** is a handle which controls the flow of gas or liquid from a pipe.
VERB **2** If you **tap** something, you hit it lightly.

tape **tapes**
NOUN **1** **Tape** is a strip of sticky material which you use to stick things together.
NOUN **2** A **tape** is a long thin magnetic strip that you can record sounds or pictures on.

tar NOUN
Tar is a thick black substance that is used for making roads.

target **targets** NOUN
A **target** is something that people aim at and try to hit.

tart **tarts** NOUN
A **tart** is a piece of pastry filled with jam or fruit.

task **tasks** NOUN
A **task** is a piece of work which has to be done.

tassel **tassels** NOUN
A **tassel** is a tuft of loose threads tied by a knot and used for decoration.

taste **tastes, tasting, tasted**
NOUN **1** Your sense of **taste** is your ability to recognize the flavour of things in your mouth.
VERB **2** When you **taste** food, you take a little bit to see what it is like.

tasty **tastier, tastiest** ADJECTIVE
Something that is **tasty** has a pleasant flavour.

taught VERB
Taught is the past tense of **teach**.

tax **taxes** NOUN
Tax is money that people have to pay to the government.

taxi **taxis** NOUN
A **taxi** is a car that people pay to be driven somewhere in.

tea **teas**
NOUN **1** **Tea** is a drink made by pouring boiling water onto the dried leaves of the tea plant.
See Drinks on page 261
NOUN **2** **Tea** is also an afternoon meal.

tea bag **tea bags** NOUN
A **tea bag** is a small paper bag with tea leaves in it which is put in boiling water to make tea.

teach **teaches, teaching, taught** VERB
If someone **teaches** you something, they tell or show you how to do it.

teacher **teachers** NOUN
A **teacher** is a person whose job is to help people learn.

team **teams** NOUN
A **team** is a number of people working or playing together.

teapot **teapots** NOUN
A **teapot** is a container for making tea. It has a lid, a handle and a spout.

tear **tears, tearing, tore, torn**
(*rhymes with* **fear**) NOUN **1 Tears** are the drops of liquid that come out of your eyes when you cry.
(*rhymes with* **fair**) VERB **2** If you **tear** something, such as paper or fabric, you pull it apart.

tease **teases, teasing, teased** VERB
If someone **teases** you, they make fun of you.

teaspoon **teaspoons** NOUN
A **teaspoon** is a small spoon used for stirring drinks.

technology NOUN
Technology is the practical use of science in areas such as industry, farming or medicine.

teddy bear **teddy bears** NOUN
A **teddy bear** is a child's soft toy which looks like a friendly bear.

teenager **teenagers** NOUN
A **teenager** is someone from 13 to 19 years of age.

teeth NOUN
Teeth is the plural of **tooth**.

telephone **telephones** NOUN
A **telephone**, or **phone**, is an instrument for talking to someone else who is in another place.

telescope **telescopes** NOUN
A **telescope** is an instrument for making objects that are far away look nearer and larger.

television **televisions** NOUN
A **television** is a machine that receives signals through the air or on cable and changes them into pictures and sounds.

tell **tells, telling, told**
VERB **1** If you **tell** someone something, you let them know about it.
VERB **2** If someone **tells** you to do something, they say you must do it.
VERB **3** If you **tell** the time, you find out what the time is by looking at a clock.

temper
NOUN **1** Someone's **temper** is how cheerful or how angry they are feeling.
NOUN **2** If you lose your **temper**, you become angry.

temperature **temperatures** NOUN
The **temperature** of something is how hot or cold it is.

temple **temples** NOUN
A **temple** is a building used for the worship of a god in various religions.

temporary ADJECTIVE
Something that is **temporary** only lasts for a short time.

tempt **tempts, tempting, tempted** VERB
If something **tempts** you, you want to do it but you think it might be wrong.
tempting ADJECTIVE

tender
ADJECTIVE **1** Someone who is **tender** shows gentle and caring feelings.
ADJECTIVE **2** Meat or other food which is **tender** is very easy to cut or chew.

tennis NOUN
Tennis is a game for two or four players in which a ball is hit over a net.

tense **tenser, tensest; tenses**
ADJECTIVE **1** If you are **tense**, you are nervous and cannot relax.
NOUN **2** The **tense** of a verb is the form which shows whether you are talking about the past, present or future.

a b c d e f g h i j k l m n o p q r s t u v w x y z

A
B
C
D
E
F
G
H
I
J
K
L
M
N
O
P
Q
R
S
T
U
V
W
X
Y
Z

tent **tents** NOUN

A **tent** is a shelter made of canvas or nylon, held up by poles and ropes.

tentacle **tentacles** NOUN

The **tentacles** of an animal, such as an octopus, are its long thin arms.

term **terms** NOUN

A **term** is one of the periods that each year is divided into at school.

terrace **terraces** NOUN

A **terrace** is a row of houses joined together.

terrible ADJECTIVE

Something **terrible** is serious and unpleasant.
terribly ADVERB

terrify **terrifies, terrifying, terrified** VERB

If something **terrifies** you, it makes you feel extremely frightened.

territory **territories**

NOUN **1** The **territory** of a country is the land that it controls.

NOUN **2** An animal's **territory** is an area that it considers its own and defends when other animals try to enter it.

terror NOUN

Terror is great fear or panic.

test **tests, testing, tested**

VERB **1** If someone **tests** something, they try to find out whether it works properly.

NOUN **2** A **test** is something you have to do to show how much you know.

text **texts** NOUN

Text is any written material.

textbook **textbooks** NOUN

A **textbook** is a book about a particular subject for students to use.

texting NOUN

Texting is sending written messages using a mobile phone.

text message **text messages** NOUN

A **text message** is a written message that you send using a mobile phone.

than PREPOSITION OR CONJUNCTION

You use **than** to link two things that you are comparing. *She's older **than** me.*

thank **thanks, thanking, thanked** VERB

You **thank** people when you are grateful for something they have done.

thank you INTERJECTION

You say **thank you** to someone to show you are pleased or grateful for something that they have done for you.

that **those**

ADJECTIVE **1** You use **that** or **those** to describe something which is not the nearest one. *Give me **that** book, please.*

PRONOUN **2** You can use **that** or **those** to refer to people or things which have already been mentioned. *What about going by bus? Is **that** a good idea?*

thatched ADJECTIVE

A **thatched** roof is one made of straw or reeds.

thaw **thaws, thawing, thawed** VERB

When something that is frozen **thaws**, it melts.

the ADJECTIVE

You use **the** in front of a noun when you are referring to something in particular. *That's **the** chair I bought yesterday.*

theatre theatres NOUN
A **theatre** is a building where you go to see a play or show.

their ADJECTIVE
Their refers to something belonging or relating to people or things that have already been mentioned. *Leave it to Sam and Joe. It's **their** problem.*

them PRONOUN
Them refers to people or things which have already been mentioned. *I don't want any sprouts. I don't like **them**.*

theme themes NOUN
A **theme** is the main idea in a piece of writing, painting, film or music.

themselves PRONOUN
If people do something **themselves**, no one else does it. *My parents had to educate **themselves**.*

then ADVERB
Then refers to a particular time in the past or future. *I left the room **then**.*

there
ADVERB **1 There** means in, at, or to that place. *He's sitting over **there**.*
PRONOUN **2 There** is used to say that something exists or does not exist. *Are **there** any more crisps?*

therefore ADVERB
Therefore means as a result. *It was raining, **therefore** we stayed indoors.*

thermometer thermometers NOUN
A **thermometer** is an instrument that measures temperature.

thesaurus thesauruses NOUN
A **thesaurus** is a book in which words with similar meanings are grouped together.

these ADJECTIVE OR PRONOUN
These is the plural of **this**.

they PRONOUN
You use **they** when you are talking about more than one person, animal or thing. ***They** are all in the same class.*

thick thicker, thickest
ADJECTIVE **1** An object that is **thick** is deeper through than other things of the same kind. *I'll have a **thick** slice, please.*
ADJECTIVE **2** Something that is **thick** is made up of a lot of things growing closely together. *She has long **thick** hair.*
ADJECTIVE **3 Thick** liquids do not flow easily.

thief thieves NOUN
A **thief** is a person who steals something.

thigh thighs NOUN
Your **thighs** are the top parts of your legs above your knees.

thin thinner, thinnest
ADJECTIVE **1** Something that is **thin** is much narrower than it is long. *The witch's nose was long and **thin**.*
ADJECTIVE **2** A **thin** person weighs less than most people of the same height.
ADJECTIVE **3** Something such as paper or cloth that is **thin** has only a small distance between front and back.
ADJECTIVE **4 Thin** liquids are watery.

thing things
NOUN **1** A **thing** is an object, rather than an animal or human being.
PLURAL NOUN **2** Your **things** are your clothes or possessions.

think thinks, thinking, thought
VERB **1** When you **think**, you use your mind to consider ideas or problems.
VERB **2** If you say you **think** something is true, you mean you believe it is true but you are not sure.

a
b
c
d
e
f
g
h
i
j
k
l
m
n
o
p
q
r
s
t
u
v
w
x
y
z

A
B
C
D
E
F
G
H
I
J
K
L
M
N
O
P
Q
R
S
T
U
V
W
X
Y
Z

third thirds

ADJECTIVE **1** The **third** thing in a series is the one after the second, counted as number three.

NOUN **2** A **third** is one of three equal parts into which something can be divided.

third person NOUN

In grammar, the **third person** refers to a person, thing or group. It is expressed as "he", "she", "it", or "they".

thirsty ADJECTIVE

If you are **thirsty**, you feel that you need to drink something.

thirstily ADVERB

thirteen NOUN

Thirteen is the number 13.

thirty NOUN

Thirty is the number 30.

this these

ADJECTIVE **1** **This** is used to refer to someone or something that is nearby. *Would you like to borrow **this** book?*

PRONOUN **2** You can use **this** to introduce someone. *This is Ranjit.*

thistle thistles NOUN

A **thistle** is a wild plant with prickly leaves and purple flowers.

thorn thorns NOUN

A **thorn** is one of the sharp points on the stem of a plant such as a rose.

thorough

ADJECTIVE **1** Someone who is **thorough** is always careful in their work.

ADJECTIVE **2** A **thorough** action is one that is done carefully and completely. *The doctor gave him a **thorough** examination.*

thoroughly ADVERB

those ADJECTIVE OR PRONOUN

Those is the plural of **that**.

though

CONJUNCTION **1** You say **though** before something that makes another part of the sentence rather surprising. *She didn't take a coat, **though** it was raining.*

CONJUNCTION **2** You can use **though** to mean if. *It looks as **though** you were right.*

thought thoughts

VERB **1** **Thought** is the past tense of **think**.

NOUN **2** A **thought** is an idea that you have in your mind.

NOUN **3** **Thought** is the action of thinking carefully about something.

thoughtful

ADJECTIVE **1** If someone is **thoughtful**, they are thinking a lot.

ADJECTIVE **2** A **thoughtful** person remembers what other people want or need, and tries to be kind to them.

thoughtfully ADVERB

thoughtless ADJECTIVE

If you are **thoughtless**, you do not think about what other people feel.

thousand NOUN

A **thousand** is the number 1000.

thread threads, threading, threaded

NOUN **1** A **thread** is a long fine piece of cotton, silk, nylon or wool.

VERB **2** When you **thread** a needle, you put thread through the hole in the top.

threat threats NOUN

A **threat** is a warning that something unpleasant may happen.

threaten threatens, threatening, threatened VERB

If someone **threatens** you, they say that something unpleasant may happen if you do not do what they want.

three NOUN

Three is the number 3.

three-dimensional ADJECTIVE
A **three-dimensional** or **3D** object or shape is not flat. It has height or depth as well as length and width.
See Solid shapes on page 266

threw VERB
Threw is the past tense of **throw**.

thrill thrills NOUN
A **thrill** is a sudden feeling of great excitement or pleasure.
thrilling ADJECTIVE

throat throats
NOUN **1** Your **throat** is the back of your mouth and the top part of the passages inside your neck.
NOUN **2** The front part of your neck is also called your **throat**.

throb throbs, throbbing, throbbed
VERB **1** If a part of your body **throbs**, you feel a series of strong beats or dull pains.
VERB **2** If something **throbs**, it vibrates and makes a loud rhythmic noise.

throne thrones NOUN
A **throne** is a special chair used by kings and queens on important occasions.

through PREPOSITION
Through means moving from one side of something to the other. *We found a path **through** the woods.*

throw throws, throwing, threw, thrown
VERB
If you **throw** an object that you are holding, you send it through the air.

thrush thrushes NOUN
A **thrush** is a songbird with a brown back and a pale spotted chest.

thrust thrusts, thrusting, thrust VERB
If you **thrust** something somewhere, you push or move it there quickly with a lot of force.

thud thuds NOUN
A **thud** is a dull sound, such as a heavy object makes when it falls onto a carpet.

thumb thumbs NOUN
Your **thumb** is the short thick finger on the side of your hand.

thump thumps, thumping, thumped
VERB
If you **thump** something, you hit it hard, usually with your fist. *He shouted and **thumped** the table.*

thunder NOUN
Thunder is the loud noise that you hear after a flash of lightning in a storm.

thunderstorm thunderstorms NOUN
A **thunderstorm** is a storm with thunder, lightning and heavy rain.

Thursday Thursdays NOUN
Thursday is the day between Wednesday and Friday.

tick ticks NOUN
A **tick** is a sign to show that something is correct.

ticket tickets NOUN
A **ticket** is a small piece of card or paper that shows that you have paid for something such as a train ride.

tickle tickles, tickling, tickled VERB
When you **tickle** someone, you move your fingers lightly over their body to make them laugh.

tide tides NOUN
The **tide** is the regular change in the level of the sea on the shore.

tidy tidier, tidiest; tidies, tidying, tidied
ADJECTIVE **1** Something that is **tidy** is neat and well arranged.
VERB **2** When you **tidy** a room, you put things away in their proper place.
tidily ADVERB

a
b
c
d
e
f
g
h
i
j
k
l
m
n
o
p
q
r
s
t
u
v
w
x
y
z

223

tie ties, tying, tied

NOUN **1** A **tie** is a long narrow piece of cloth that is worn round the neck.

NOUN **2** A **tie** in a race or competition is when two people have the same result.

VERB **3** If you **tie** an object to something, you fasten it with something such as string.

tiger tigers NOUN

A **tiger** is a large wild cat that lives in Asia. Its fur is usually orange with black stripes.

tight tighter, tightest

ADJECTIVE **1** Clothes that are **tight** fit too closely to your body.

ADJECTIVE **2** Something that is **tight** is firmly fastened and difficult to move.

tights PLURAL NOUN

Tights are a piece of clothing made of thin material that fit closely over your hips, legs and feet.

tile tiles NOUN

A **tile** is a small thin piece of something such as slate or carpet, that is used to cover surfaces.

till tills

PREPOSITION OR CONJUNCTION **1 Till** means the same as until. *Wait **till** morning... Wait **till** I get back.*

NOUN **2** A **till** is a drawer or box in a shop or bank where money is kept.

tilt tilts, tilting, tilted VERB

If you **tilt** something, you make it slope.

timber NOUN

Timber is wood used for building, and making furniture.

time

NOUN **1 Time** is what is measured in seconds, minutes, hours, days and years.

See Time on page 279

NOUN **2** If it is **time** to do something, that thing ought to be done now.

times

NOUN **1 Times** is used after numbers to say how often something happens.

NOUN **2** In maths, **times** is used to link numbers that are multiplied together. *Four **times** three is twelve.*

timetable timetables NOUN

A **timetable** is a list of the times when things happen, or when trains and buses go.

timid ADJECTIVE

A **timid** person is not brave.

tin tins

NOUN **1 Tin** is a soft silvery-white metal.

NOUN **2** A **tin** is a metal container with a lid, for storing food.

tingle tingles, tingling, tingled VERB

When part of your body **tingles**, you feel a slight prickling or stinging.

tinkle tinkles, tinkling, tinkled VERB

If something **tinkles**, it makes a sound like a small bell ringing.

tinned ADJECTIVE

Tinned food has been preserved by being sealed in a tin.

tin opener tin openers NOUN

A **tin opener** is something you use for opening tins of food.

tiny tinier, tiniest ADJECTIVE

Something that is **tiny** is very small.

tip tips, tipping, tipped

VERB **1** If you **tip** an object, you move it so that it is no longer straight. *She **tipped** her chair back and almost fell over.*

NOUN **2** The **tip** of something long and narrow is the end of it.

tiptoe tiptoes, tiptoeing, tiptoed VERB

If you **tiptoe** somewhere, you walk there very quietly on your toes.

tired ADJECTIVE

If you are **tired**, you feel that you want to rest or sleep.

tissue **tissues** NOUN
A **tissue** is a piece of soft paper that you can use as a handkerchief.

title **titles**
NOUN **1** A **title** is the name of something such as a book or film.
NOUN **2** Someone's **title** is a name such as Mr, Mrs or Sir, that goes in front of their own name.

to
PREPOSITION **1** You use **to** indicate a direction in which something is going. *She went **to** the window and looked out.*
PREPOSITION **2** You use **to** when you are comparing two things. *I prefer fruit **to** chocolate.*

toad **toads** NOUN
A **toad** is an amphibian. It looks like a frog but it has a drier skin and lives mostly on land.
See *Amphibians* on page 264

toadstool **toadstools** NOUN
A **toadstool** is a type of poisonous fungus.

toast NOUN
Toast is a slice of bread made brown and crisp by heating.

today ADVERB
Today is the day that is happening now.

toddler **toddlers** NOUN
A **toddler** is a small child who has only just learned to walk.

toe **toes** NOUN
Your **toes** are the five parts at the end of your foot which you can move.

toffee **toffees** NOUN
A **toffee** is a sticky, chewy sweet made from butter and sugar.

together
ADVERB **1** If two people do something **together**, they both do it.
ADVERB **2** If two things happen **together**, they happen at the same time.

toilet **toilets**
NOUN **1** A **toilet** is a bowl connected to a drain and fitted with a seat. You use it to get rid of waste matter from your body.
NOUN **2** A **toilet** is also a small room containing a toilet.

told VERB
Told is the past tense of **tell**.

tomato **tomatoes** NOUN
A **tomato** is a soft, small red fruit. It can be cooked or eaten raw in salads.
See *Fruit* on page 260

tomorrow ADVERB
Tomorrow is the day after today.

ton **tons** NOUN
A **ton** is a unit of weight equal to about 1000 kilograms.

tongue **tongues** NOUN
Your **tongue** is the soft, moving part inside your mouth. You use your tongue for tasting, eating and speaking.

tongue twister **tongue twisters** NOUN
A **tongue twister** is a sentence or expression which is difficult to say properly. For example, "She sells seashells on the seashore" is a tongue twister.

a
b
c
d
e
f
g
h
i
j
k
l
m
n
o
p
q
r
s
t
u
v
w
x
y
z

tonight ADVERB

Tonight is the evening of today or the night that follows today.

tonne **tonnes** NOUN

A **tonne** is a metric measure of weight. It is equal to 1000 kilograms.

too

ADVERB **1 Too** means also, or as well. *I was there* ***too***.

ADVERB **2 Too** also means more than is needed. *I've had* ***too*** *much to eat.*

took VERB

Took is the past tense of **take**.

tool **tools** NOUN

A **tool** is anything that you use to help you do something, such as a hammer.

tooth **teeth**

NOUN **1** A **tooth** is one of the hard white objects in your mouth. You use your teeth for biting and chewing food.

NOUN **2** The **teeth** of a comb, saw or zip are the parts that stick out in a row.

toothbrush **toothbrushes** NOUN

A **toothbrush** is a small brush that you use for cleaning your teeth.

toothpaste NOUN

Toothpaste is a substance which you use to clean your teeth.

top **tops**

NOUN **1** The **top** of something is its highest point, part or surface.

NOUN **2** The **top** of a bottle, jar or tube is its cap or lid.

topic **topics** NOUN

A **topic** is a particular subject that you write or talk about.

torch **torches** NOUN

A **torch** is a small electric lamp which you can carry in your hand.

tore VERB

Tore is the past tense of **tear**.

torn VERB

Torn is the past participle of **tear**.

tornado **tornadoes** or **tornados** NOUN

A **tornado** is a very strong wind that moves round in a circle and can cause a lot of damage.

tortoise **tortoises** NOUN

A **tortoise** is a slow-moving reptile with a hard thick shell.

See **Reptiles** *on page 264*

toss **tosses, tossing, tossed**

VERB **1** If you **toss** something, you throw it lightly and carelessly.

VERB **2** If something **tosses**, it keeps moving from side to side.

total **totals**

NOUN **1** A **total** is the number you get when you add several numbers together.

ADJECTIVE **2 Total** means complete. *The party was a* ***total*** *success.*

touch **touches, touching, touched**

VERB **1** If you **touch** something, you feel it with your hand.

VERB **2** If two things are **touching**, there is no space between them.

tough **tougher, toughest** ADJECTIVE

Something that is **tough** is strong and difficult to cut, tear or break.

tour **tours** NOUN

A **tour** is a journey to visit interesting places.

tourist tourists NOUN
A **tourist** is a person who visits places for pleasure and interest.

tournament tournaments NOUN
A **tournament** is a competition in which lots of matches are played, until just one person or team is left.

tow tows, towing, towed VERB
If a vehicle **tows** another vehicle, it pulls it along behind.

towards
PREPOSITION **1** If you move **towards** something, you go in that direction.
PREPOSITION **2** If you give money **towards** something, you help pay for it.

towel towels NOUN
A **towel** is a piece of soft thick cloth that you use to dry yourself with.

tower towers NOUN
A **tower** is a tall narrow building or a tall part of a building.

town towns NOUN
A **town** is a place with a lot of streets and buildings where people live and work.

toy toys NOUN
A **toy** is something you play with, such as a doll or a model car.

trace traces, tracing, traced
VERB **1** If you **trace** something such as a map, you copy it by covering it with a piece of thin paper and drawing over the lines underneath.
VERB **2** If you **trace** something, you find it after looking for it.

track tracks
NOUN **1** A **track** is a rough narrow road or path.
NOUN **2** A **track** is also a special road or path that is used for racing.
NOUN **3** A railway **track** is a strip of ground with rails that trains travel on.

tracksuit tracksuits NOUN
A **tracksuit** is a loose warm suit of trousers and a top, worn for outdoor sports.

tractor tractors NOUN
A **tractor** is a vehicle with large rear wheels. Tractors are used on farms for pulling or lifting things.

trade trades NOUN
Trade is the buying and selling of goods or services. Trade can be between people, companies or countries.

trademark trademarks NOUN
A **trademark** is a name or symbol that a manufacturer always uses on its products. It is usually protected by law so that nobody else can use it.

tradition traditions NOUN
A **tradition** is something that people have done or believed in for a long time.
traditional ADJECTIVE **traditionally** ADVERB

traffic NOUN
Traffic is the movement of vehicles on the road, in the air or on water.

traffic light traffic lights NOUN
Traffic lights are special signals to control the flow of traffic. Red lights mean stop and green lights mean go.

tragedy tragedies
NOUN **1** A **tragedy** is an event or situation that is very sad.
NOUN **2** A **tragedy** is also a serious play, that usually ends with the death of the main character.
tragic ADJECTIVE

trail trails, trailing, trailed
NOUN **1** A **trail** is a rough path across open country or through forests.
NOUN **2** A **trail** is also the scent, footprints and other signs that people and animals leave behind them.
VERB **3** If you **trail** something or it **trails**, it drags along behind you.

trailer trailers
NOUN **1** A **trailer** is a vehicle pulled by a car, used for carrying things.
NOUN **2** A **trailer** can also be a series of short pieces from a film or television programme in order to advertise it.

a b c d e f g h i j k l m n o p q r s t u v w x y z

227

train **trains, training, trained**

NOUN **1** A **train** is a number of carriages or trucks which are joined together and pulled by an engine along a railway.

VERB **2** If someone **trains** you to do a job, they teach you the skills you need.

VERB **3** If you **train** a dog, you teach it to behave properly.

trainer **trainers**

NOUN **1** A **trainer** is a person who coaches people in sports such as boxing.

NOUN **2 Trainers** are special shoes people wear for running or jogging.

tram **trams** NOUN

A **tram** is a vehicle which runs on rails along the street.

trampoline **trampolines** NOUN

A **trampoline** is something that is used for jumping on. It is made of strong cloth held into a frame by springs.

transfer **transfers, transferring, transferred** VERB

If you **transfer** something, you move it to a different place or position.

translate **translates, translating, translated** VERB

If you **translate** something, you put the words into a different language.

translation NOUN

translucent ADJECTIVE

If something is **translucent**, light passes through it so that it glows.

transparent ADJECTIVE

If something is **transparent**, it lets light through and you can see through it.

transplant **transplants** NOUN

A **transplant** is an operation to put part of one person's body into another person.

transport NOUN

Transport is using vehicles to move people and things from one place to another.

trap **traps, trapping, trapped**

NOUN **1** A **trap** is something that is specially made to catch animals.

VERB **2** If a person is **trapped**, they cannot escape.

trap door **trap doors** NOUN

A **trap door** is a small door in a floor or ceiling.

trapeze **trapezes** NOUN

A **trapeze** is a bar hung from a high place by ropes. People swing from trapezes in circuses.

travel **travels, travelling, travelled** VERB

If you **travel**, you go from one place to another.

traveller NOUN

tray **trays** NOUN

A **tray** is a flat object with raised edges, used for carrying food or drinks.

treacherous ADJECTIVE

ADJECTIVE **1** A person who is **treacherous** cannot be trusted.

ADJECTIVE **2** If something like the sea is **treacherous**, it is dangerous.

treacle NOUN

Treacle is a thick sweet sticky liquid made from sugar.

tread **treads, treading, trod, trodden** VERB

If you **tread** on something, you walk on it or step on it.

treasure **treasures** NOUN

Treasure is valuable things such as jewels or paintings.

treat **treats, treating, treated**

VERB **1** If you **treat** someone in a certain way, you behave that way towards them. *My uncle treats me as if I'm five.*

VERB **2** If someone **treats** a person who is ill, they help them get well again.

NOUN **3** A **treat** is something enjoyable.

tree **trees** NOUN

A **tree** is a large plant with a hard woody trunk, branches and leaves.

tremble **trembles, trembling, trembled** VERB

If you **tremble**, you shake slightly, because you are frightened or cold.

trespass **trespasses, trespassing, trespassed** VERB

To **trespass** means to go on someone else's land without asking.

trial **trials**

NOUN **1** A **trial** is when you try something out to see if it works.

NOUN **2** In law, a **trial** is a time in court. People decide whether a person is guilty of a crime.

triangle **triangles**

NOUN

A **triangle** is a flat shape with three straight sides and three angles.

triangular ADJECTIVE
See Colours and shapes on page 266

tribe **tribes** NOUN

A **tribe** is a group of people of the same race, customs and language, who are ruled by one chief.

trick **tricks, tricking, tricked**

NOUN **1** A **trick** is a clever or skilful act that someone does to entertain people.

VERB **2** If a person **tricks** someone, they deceive them.

trickle **trickles, trickling, trickled** VERB

When a liquid **trickles**, it flows slowly in small amounts.

tricycle **tricycles** NOUN

A **tricycle** is a vehicle similar to a bicycle, but with three wheels.

tried VERB

Tried is the past tense of **try**.

tries VERB

Tries is a present tense form of **try**.

trifle **trifles** NOUN

Trifle is a cold pudding made of layers of sponge, fruit, jelly and custard.

trigger **triggers** NOUN

A **trigger** is a small lever on a gun, which is pulled to fire the gun.

trim **trims, trimming, trimmed** VERB

If a person **trims** something, such as a hedge or your hair, they cut off small amounts of it to make it neat.

trip **trips, tripping, tripped**

NOUN **1** A **trip** is a journey to a place and back again.

VERB **2** If you **trip**, you catch your foot on something and fall over.

a
b
c
d
e
f
g
h
i
j
k
l
m
n
o
p
q
r
s
t
u
v
w
x
y
z

triumph **triumphs** NOUN
A **triumph** is a great success.

triumphant ADJECTIVE
Someone who is **triumphant** feels extremely happy because they have been very successful.

trod VERB
Trod is the past tense of **tread**.

trolley **trolleys** NOUN
A **trolley** is a small cart on wheels used for carrying heavy objects.

troops PLURAL NOUN
Troops are soldiers.

trophy **trophies** NOUN
A **trophy** is a cup or shield given to the winner of a competition.

tropical ADJECTIVE
Tropical means to do with the tropics, which are the hottest part of the world, near the equator.

trot **trots, trotting, trotted** VERB
When a horse **trots**, it moves at a speed a little faster than a walk.

trouble **troubles** NOUN
Trouble is something that worries or bothers you.

trough **troughs** NOUN
A **trough** is a long narrow container which holds food or drink for farm animals.

trousers PLURAL NOUN
Trousers are a piece of clothing for the body from the waist down, with a separate part for each leg.

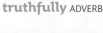

trout NOUN
A **trout** is a fish that lives in lakes and rivers.

trowel **trowels** NOUN
A **trowel** is a small garden tool with a curved and pointed blade used for planting or weeding.

truant **truants** NOUN
A **truant** is a child who stays away from school without permission.

truce **truces** NOUN
A **truce** is an agreement between two people or groups to stop fighting or quarrelling for a time.

truck **trucks**
NOUN **1** A **truck** is a large motor vehicle which is open at the back. Trucks are used for carrying heavy loads.
NOUN **2** A **truck** is also an open vehicle used for carrying things on a railway.

true **truer, truest**
ADJECTIVE **1** A **true** story or statement is based on facts and is not made up.
ADJECTIVE **2** **True** feelings are sincere.
truly ADVERB

trumpet **trumpets** NOUN
A **trumpet** is a brass musical instrument that you blow into.

trunk **trunks**
NOUN **1** The **trunk** of a tree is its main stem, from which the branches grow.
NOUN **2** An elephant's **trunk** is its long flexible nose.
NOUN **3** A **trunk** is also a large box with a lid used for storing things.

trust **trusts, trusting, trusted** VERB
If you **trust** someone, you believe that they are honest and will not do anything to hurt you.

truth NOUN
The **truth** is the facts about something or someone, rather than things that are imagined or made up.

truthful ADJECTIVE
A **truthful** person is honest and tells the truth.
truthfully ADVERB

try tries, trying, tried

VERB **1** If you **try** to do something, you do your best to do it.

VERB **2** If you **try** something, you test it to see what it is like.

T-shirt T-shirts NOUN

A **T-shirt** is a simple short-sleeved cotton shirt with no collar.

tub tubs NOUN

A **tub** is a round container for food.

tube tubes

NOUN **1** A **tube** is a round hollow pipe.

NOUN **2** A **tube** is also a container with a cap at one end that you squeeze to get the contents out.

tuck tucks, tucking, tucked VERB

If you **tuck** something, you put the end of it under or into something else. *He **tucked** his shirt into his trousers.*

Tuesday Tuesdays NOUN

Tuesday is the day after Monday and before Wednesday.

tuft tufts NOUN

A **tuft** of something, such as hair, is a bunch of it growing closely together.

tug tugs, tugging, tugged VERB

If you **tug** something, you give it a quick strong pull.

tug-of-war NOUN

A **tug-of-war** is a sport in which two teams pull against each other on opposite ends of a rope.

tulip tulips NOUN

A **tulip** is a spring flower shaped like an upside-down bell.

tumble tumbles, tumbling, tumbled

VERB If you **tumble**, you fall over and over.

tuna NOUN

Tuna are large edible fish that live in warm seas.

tune tunes NOUN

A **tune** is a series of musical notes that are nice to listen to.

tunnel tunnels

NOUN

A **tunnel** is a long passage under the ground or through a hill.

turkey turkeys

NOUN

A **turkey** is a large bird that is kept on a farm for its meat.

turn turns, turning, turned

VERB **1** When you **turn**, you move so that you are facing a different way.

VERB **2** When you **turn** something, you move it round.

VERB **3** When something **turns into** something else, it becomes that thing. *When water freezes, it **turns into** ice.*

NOUN **4** If people take **turns** to do something, they do it one after the other.

turnip turnips NOUN

A **turnip** is a round root vegetable with a white or yellow skin.

See Vegetables on page 260

turquoise ADJECTIVE

Something **turquoise** is a blue-green colour.

See Colours and shapes on page 266

turtle turtles NOUN

A **turtle** is a large reptile with a thick shell. It lives mostly in the sea.

See Reptiles on page 264

tusk tusks NOUN

Tusks are long pointed teeth that some animals have. For example, elephants and walruses have tusks.

TV TVs NOUN

TV is an abbreviation of **television**.

a
b
c
d
e
f
g
h
i
j
k
l
m
n
o
p
q
r
s
t
u
v
w
x
y
z

twelve NOUN
Twelve is the number 12.

twenty NOUN
Twenty is the number 20.

twice ADVERB
Twice means two times.

twig **twigs** NOUN
A **twig** is a small thin branch of a tree or bush.

twilight NOUN
Twilight is the time after sunset when it is just getting dark.

twin **twins** NOUN
If two people are **twins**, they have the same mother and were born on the same day.

twinkle **twinkles, twinkling, twinkled** VERB
If something **twinkles**, it shines with little flashes.

twirl **twirls, twirling, twirled** VERB
If something **twirls**, or if you twirl it, it spins round and round.

twist **twists, twisting, twisted**
VERB **1** When you **twist** something, you turn one end in the opposite direction to the other.
VERB **2** When something **twists**, it moves or bends into a strange shape.

two NOUN
Two is the number 2.

two-dimensional ADJECTIVE
Something that is **two-dimensional**, or **2D**, is a flat shape. For example, a circle is two-dimensional.

tying VERB
Tying is the present participle of **tie**.

type **types, typing, typed**
NOUN **1 Type** means kind or sort. *What **type** of plant is it?*
VERB **2** If you **type** words, you use a computer or typewriter.

typhoon **typhoons** NOUN
A **typhoon** is a storm with extremely strong winds.

typical ADJECTIVE
Something that is **typical** is what you would expect.

tyre **tyres** NOUN
A **tyre** is a thick ring of rubber fitted round each wheel of a vehicle.

Uu

ugly **uglier, ugliest** ADJECTIVE
Someone or something that is **ugly** is not pleasant to look at.

umbrella **umbrellas** NOUN
An **umbrella** is a shelter from the rain. It consists of a folding frame covered in thin cloth, attached to a long stick.

unable ADJECTIVE
If you are **unable** to do something, you cannot do it.

unaware ADJECTIVE
If you are **unaware** of something, you do not know about it.

unbearable ADJECTIVE
Something **unbearable** is so unpleasant, painful or upsetting you feel you cannot stand it.

unbelievable
ADJECTIVE **1** Something **unbelievable** is extremely great or surprising. *She showed* **unbelievable** *courage.*
ADJECTIVE **2 Unbelievable** can also be used to describe something that is so unlikely you cannot believe it.

uncertain ADJECTIVE
If you are **uncertain**, you are not sure what to do.

uncle **uncles** NOUN
Your **uncle** is the brother of one of your parents, or your aunt's husband.

uncomfortable ADJECTIVE
If you are **uncomfortable**, you do not feel easy.

uncommon ADJECTIVE
Something **uncommon** does not often happen, or is not often seen.

unconscious ADJECTIVE
Someone who is **unconscious** is unable to see, hear or feel anything that is going on. This is usually because they have fainted or have been badly injured.

under
PREPOSITION **1 Under** means below or beneath.
PREPOSITION **2 Under** can also mean less than. *Children* **under** *five can go in free.*

underground
ADJECTIVE **1** Something **underground** is below the surface of the ground.
NOUN **2** The **underground** is a railway that runs in tunnels under some cities.

undergrowth NOUN
Undergrowth is bushes or plants growing together under the trees in a forest or jungle.

underline **underlines, underlining, underlined** VERB
If you **underline** a word or sentence, you draw a line under it.

underneath PREPOSITION OR ADVERB
Underneath means below or beneath. *They found the missing card* **underneath** *the table... They couldn't move the car because their cat was* **underneath***.*

understand **understands, understanding, understood** VERB
If you **understand** something, you know what it means.

a b c d e f g h i j k l m n o p q r s t u v w x y z

233

A B C D E F G H I J K L M N O P Q R S T U V W X Y Z

underwear NOUN
Your **underwear** is the clothing that you wear next to your skin under your other clothes.

undo undoes, undoing, undid, undone VERB
If you **undo** something that is tied up, you untie it.

undress undresses, undressing, undressed VERB
When you **undress**, you take off your clothes.

uneasy ADJECTIVE
If you are **uneasy**, you are worried that something is wrong.

unemployed ADJECTIVE
Someone who is **unemployed** does not have a job.

uneven ADJECTIVE
Something that is **uneven** does not have a flat, smooth surface.

unexpected ADJECTIVE
Something that is **unexpected** surprises you.
unexpectedly ADVERB

unfair ADJECTIVE
If you think that something is **unfair**, it does not seem right or reasonable to you.
unfairly ADVERB

unfortunate
ADJECTIVE **1** Someone who is **unfortunate** is unlucky.
ADJECTIVE **2** If you say something is **unfortunate**, you mean you wish it had not happened.
unfortunately ADVERB

unfriendly ADJECTIVE
Someone who is **unfriendly** is not kind to you.

ungrateful ADJECTIVE
If someone is **ungrateful**, they are not thankful for something that has been given to them or done for them.

unhappy unhappier, unhappiest ADJECTIVE
Someone who is **unhappy** is sad or miserable.
unhappily ADVERB

unhealthy unhealthier, unhealthiest
ADJECTIVE **1** Someone who is **unhealthy** is often ill.
ADJECTIVE **2** Something that is **unhealthy** is likely to cause illness.

uniform uniforms NOUN
A **uniform** is a special set of clothes that is worn by people to show that they belong to the same group.

unique ADJECTIVE
If something is **unique**, it is the only one of its kind.

unit units
NOUN **1** A **unit** is an amount that is used for measuring things. For example, a second is a unit of time.
NOUN **2** In maths, the number of ones is the number of **units**. *The number 37 has 3 tens and 7 units.*

unite unites, uniting, united VERB
If people **unite**, they work as a group.
united ADJECTIVE

universe NOUN
The **universe** is the whole of space including all the stars and planets.

university universities NOUN
A **university** is a place where people can carry on their education when they have left school.

unkind ADJECTIVE

Someone who is **unkind** is rather cruel and unpleasant.

unleaded ADJECTIVE

Unleaded petrol has a smaller amount of lead in it, in order to reduce the pollution from vehicles.

unless CONJUNCTION

You use **unless** to introduce a condition which is necessary for something else to happen. *I won't come **unless** you invite me.*

unlike PREPOSITION

If one thing is **unlike** another, the two things are different.

unlikely ADJECTIVE

If something is **unlikely**, it is probably not true or probably will not happen.

unload unloads, unloading, unloaded

VERB

If people **unload** something, such as a lorry, they take the load off it.

unlock unlocks, unlocking, unlocked

VERB

If you **unlock** something, such as a door, you open it with a key.

unlucky ADJECTIVE

Someone who is **unlucky** has bad luck.

unluckily ADVERB

unnatural ADJECTIVE

Something **unnatural** is strange because it is not usual. *There was an **unnatural** stillness.*

unnaturally ADVERB

unnecessary ADJECTIVE

Something that is **unnecessary** is not needed.

unpack unpacks, unpacking, unpacked

VERB

When you **unpack**, you take everything out of a suitcase, bag or box.

unpleasant ADJECTIVE

Something that is **unpleasant** is rather nasty and not enjoyable.

unpopular ADJECTIVE

Someone or something that is **unpopular** is disliked by most people.

unsafe ADJECTIVE

If something like a building or a machine is **unsafe**, it is dangerous.

unselfish ADJECTIVE

People who are **unselfish** care more about other people than they do about themselves.

untidy untidier, untidiest

ADJECTIVE **1** Someone who is **untidy** does not care whether things are neat and well arranged.

ADJECTIVE **2** An **untidy** place is not neat or well arranged.

untie unties, untying, untied VERB

If you **untie** something, you undo the knots in the string around it.

until PREPOSITION OR CONJUNCTION

Until means up to a certain time. *The shop was open **until** midnight... He waited **until** the dog was asleep.*

untrue ADJECTIVE

Something that is **untrue** is false and not based on facts.

unusual ADJECTIVE

Someone or something that is **unusual** is different from the ordinary.

up

PREPOSITION OR ADVERB **1 Up** means towards or in a higher place. *She ran **up** the stairs... It was high **up** in the mountains.*

ADVERB **2** If an amount of something goes **up**, it increases. *The price of butter has gone **up**.*

a
b
c
d
e
f
g
h
i
j
k
l
m
n
o
p
q
r
s
t
u
v
w
x
y
z

235

upload **uploads, uploading, uploaded**
VERB

When you **upload** a computer file, you move it from your own computer to the Internet.

upper-case ADJECTIVE

Upper-case letters are capital letters. See **lower-case**

upright ADJECTIVE

If you are **upright**, you are standing up straight.

uproar **uproars** NOUN

An **uproar** is a lot of noise and shouting.

upset **upsets, upsetting, upset**
VERB **1** If someone **upsets** something, they turn it over by accident. *He **upset** a tin of paint on the carpet.*

ADJECTIVE **2** If you are **upset**, you are unhappy or disappointed.

upside down ADJECTIVE

Something that is **upside down** has been turned so that the part that should be at the top is at the bottom.

upstairs

ADVERB **1** If you go **upstairs** in a building, you go up to a higher floor.

ADVERB **2** Someone or something that is **upstairs** is on a higher floor than you.

up-to-date ADJECTIVE

Something that is **up-to-date** is new or modern.

upwards ADVERB

If something moves **upwards** it is going towards a higher place.

urgent ADJECTIVE

Something that is **urgent** needs to be done at once.

us PRONOUN

A speaker or writer uses **us** to mean himself or herself and one or more other people.

use **uses, using, used** VERB

If you **use** something, you do something with it that helps you.

used VERB

Something that **used** to be done was done in the past.

used to PHRASE If you are **used to** something, you are familiar with it and have often experienced it.

useful ADJECTIVE

If something is **useful**, it helps you in some way.

useless ADJECTIVE

If something is **useless**, you cannot use it.

user-friendly ADJECTIVE

If you describe a machine or system as **user-friendly**, you mean that it is well designed and easy to use.

usual ADJECTIVE

Something that is **usual** happens, or is done or used, most often.

usually ADVERB

If something **usually** happens, it happens most often.

A B C D E F G H I J K L M N O P Q R S T U V W X Y Z

Vv

vacant ADJECTIVE
Somewhere that is **vacant** has nobody in it.

vaccination **vaccinations** NOUN
A **vaccination** is an injection that stops you getting an illness.

vacuum cleaner **vacuum cleaners** NOUN
A **vacuum cleaner** is an electric machine which cleans by sucking up dirt.

vague **vaguer, vaguest** ADJECTIVE
Things that are **vague** are not definite or clear. *He had a **vague** feeling he should be doing something.*

vain ADJECTIVE
A **vain** person is too proud of how they look or what they can do.

valley **valleys** NOUN
A **valley** is a low piece of land between hills. Valleys often have rivers flowing through them.

valuable
ADJECTIVE **1** Things that are **valuable** are worth a lot of money.
ADJECTIVE **2** Help or advice that is **valuable** is very useful.

value
NOUN **1** The **value** of something is its importance or usefulness.
NOUN **2** The **value** of something such as jewellery is the amount of money that it is worth.

vampire **vampires** NOUN
In horror stories, **vampires** are creatures that suck the blood of living people.

van **vans** NOUN
A **van** is a vehicle larger than a car but smaller than a lorry. Vans are used for carrying goods.

vandal **vandals** NOUN
A **vandal** is someone who damages something useful or beautiful on purpose and for no good reason.

vanilla NOUN
Vanilla is a flavouring for food. It comes from the pods of a tropical plant.

vanish **vanishes, vanishing, vanished** VERB
If something **vanishes**, it disappears suddenly.

vapour **vapours** NOUN
Vapour is a mass of tiny drops of water or other liquids in the air, which appear as clouds, mist or fumes.

variety **variety** NOUN
A **variety** of things is lots of different types.

various ADJECTIVE
You say **various** to mean several different things of one kind. *There were **various** questions she wanted to ask.*

vase **vases** NOUN
A **vase** is a kind of jar used as an ornament, or to hold cut flowers.

a
b
c
d
e
f
g
h
i
j
k
l
m
n
o
p
q
r
s
t
u
v
w
x
y
z

A
B
C
D
E
F
G
H
I
J
K
L
M
N
O
P
Q
R
S
T
U
V
W
X
Y
Z

vast ADJECTIVE
Something that is **vast** is extremely large.

vegetable
vegetables NOUN
Vegetables are plants, or parts of plants such as leaves, that can be eaten.
See Vegetables on page 260

vegetarian **vegetarians** NOUN
A **vegetarian** is a person who does not eat meat or fish.

vehicle **vehicles** NOUN
A **vehicle** is a machine such as a car or bus that carries people or things from place to place.

veil **veils** NOUN
A **veil** is a piece of thin soft cloth that some women wear over their face or head.

vein **veins** NOUN
A **vein** is a tube inside the body which carries blood to the heart.

velvet NOUN
Velvet is a material which has soft short threads on one side.

verb **verbs** NOUN
In grammar, a **verb** is a word that expresses actions and states, for example "take" and "run".
See Verb on page 269

verdict **verdicts** NOUN
In a law court, a **verdict** is whether a prisoner is guilty or not guilty.

verse **verses**
NOUN **1 Verse** is another word for poetry.
NOUN **2** A **verse** is one of the parts that a poem or song is divided into.

version **versions** NOUN
A **version** of something is a form of it in which some details are different from earlier or later forms. *This is a different **version** of my story.*

vertical ADJECTIVE
Something that is **vertical** stands straight up from a flat surface.
See **horizontal**

very ADVERB
Very is used before words to make them stronger. *He had **very** bad dreams.*

vessel **vessels** NOUN
A **vessel** is a ship or boat.

vest **vests** NOUN
A **vest** is a piece of underwear for the top half of the body.

vet **vets** NOUN
A **vet** is a person whose job is to look after sick and injured animals. Vet is an abbreviation of **veterinary surgeon**.

via
PREPOSITION
If you go **via** a particular place, you go through it to get to somewhere else. *We go to school **via** the park.*

viaduct **viaducts** NOUN
A **viaduct** is a long high bridge that carries a road or railway across a valley.

vibrate **vibrates, vibrating, vibrated** VERB
If something **vibrates**, it shakes with a very slight, very quick movement.

vicious ADJECTIVE
Someone or something that is **vicious** is cruel and violent.

victim **victims** NOUN
A **victim** is someone who has been harmed or injured by someone or something.

victory **victories** NOUN
A **victory** is a success in a battle or competition.

video **videos, videoing, videoed** NOUN
A **video** is a recorded film that you can watch on a computer or television set.

video game **video games** NOUN
A **video game** is a game that can be played on the screen of a computer or television.

view **views** NOUN
The **view** from a window or a high place is everything that can be seen from there.

village **villages** NOUN
A **village** is a small group of houses and other buildings in a country area.

vine **vines** NOUN
A **vine** is a climbing plant that produces grapes.

vinegar NOUN
Vinegar is a sharp-tasting liquid that is used to add taste to some foods, and is also used for pickling.

violence NOUN
Violence is behaviour that is meant to hurt or kill people.

violent
ADJECTIVE **1** Someone who is **violent** uses force to hurt or kill people.
ADJECTIVE **2** Something that is **violent** happens suddenly and with great force. *A **violent** earthquake shook the city.*
violently ADVERB

violet **violets** NOUN
A **violet** is a small plant with purple or white flowers.

violin **violins** NOUN
A **violin** is a musical instrument with four strings. It is held under the chin and played with a bow.

virtual ADJECTIVE
Virtual means something that is very like a real thing but is not actually the same. *What he said was a **virtual** lie.*

virtual reality NOUN
Virtual reality is an image created by a computer that looks real to the person using it.

virus **viruses**
NOUN **1** A **virus** is a tiny germ which you cannot see without a microscope. Viruses can cause diseases.
NOUN **2** A disease caused by a virus can also be called a **virus**.

visible ADJECTIVE
Something that is **visible** can be seen.
visibly ADVERB

vision **visions**
NOUN **1** **Vision** is the ability to see clearly. *Your **vision** will be better if you wear glasses.*
NOUN **2** A **vision** is a picture in your mind.

visit **visits, visiting, visited** VERB
If you **visit** a person or a place, you go to see them.

visitor **visitors** NOUN
A **visitor** is someone who is visiting a person or place.

vital ADJECTIVE
If something is **vital** when you are doing something, you will not succeed without it. *It is **vital** to get the measurements exactly right.*

vitamin **vitamins** NOUN
A **vitamin** is one of the substances which you need to stay healthy. There are vitamins in many kinds of food.

a
b
c
d
e
f
g
h
i
j
k
l
m
n
o
p
q
r
s
t
u
v
w
x
y
z

vivid

ADJECTIVE **1** A **vivid** colour is very bright.

ADJECTIVE **2** Memories or descriptions that are **vivid** are clear and remain firmly fixed in your mind.

vividly ADVERB

vixen **vixens** NOUN

A **vixen** is a female fox.

vocabulary NOUN

Someone's **vocabulary** is the total number of words in a language that they know.

voice **voices**

NOUN **1** Someone's **voice** is the sound they make when they speak or sing.

NOUN **2** In grammar, the active **voice** and the passive voice refer to the relation between a verb and its subject. For example, the sentence "Brian hit the ball" is in the active voice, and "The ball was hit by Brian" is in the passive voice.

See **active**

volcano **volcanoes** NOUN

A **volcano** is a mountain with a hole called a crater in the top. Sometimes hot melted rock, gas, steam and ash burst from the crater.

volume **volumes**

NOUN **1** A **volume** is a book.

NOUN **2** The **volume** of something is the amount of space that it takes up.

NOUN **3** The **volume** of something, such as a radio or television, is how loud or quiet its sound is. *He played his radio at full **volume**.*

voluntary

ADJECTIVE **1 Voluntary** actions are ones that you offer to do, rather than being asked to or made to.

ADJECTIVE **2 Voluntary** work is done by people who are not paid for what they do.

voluntarily ADVERB

volunteer **volunteers, volunteering, volunteered**

VERB **1** If you **volunteer** to do something, you offer to do it without expecting any reward.

NOUN **2** A **volunteer** is someone who does work for which they are not paid.

vote **votes, voting, voted**

VERB **1** If you **vote**, you make a choice, usually by raising your hand or writing on a piece of paper. *We **voted** for Tim as group leader.*

VERB **2** If you **vote** that a particular thing should happen, that is what you suggest. *I **vote** we all go swimming.*

voucher **vouchers** NOUN

A **voucher** is a ticket or piece of paper that can be used instead of money.

vowel **vowels** NOUN

In the English language, the letters a, e, i, o and u are **vowels**.

See **consonant**

voyage **voyages** NOUN

A **voyage** is a long journey on a ship or in a spacecraft.

vulture **vultures** NOUN

A **vulture** is a large bird which feeds on dead animals. Vultures live in hot countries.

A B C D E F G H I J K L M N O P Q R S T U V W X Y Z

Ww

wade wades, wading, waded VERB
To **wade** means to walk through fairly shallow water.

wafer wafers NOUN
A **wafer** is a thin crisp biscuit.

wag wags, wagging, wagged VERB
When a dog **wags** its tail, it waves it from side to side because it is happy.

wagon wagons
NOUN **1** A **wagon** is a strong cart for carrying heavy loads. Wagons are usually pulled by a horse or tractor.
VERB **2** A **wagon** is also a railway truck.

wail wails, wailing, wailed VERB
If someone **wails**, they make a long crying noise.

waist waists NOUN
Your **waist** is the narrow middle part of your body, just below your chest.

wait waits, waiting, waited VERB
If you **wait**, you spend time before something happens.

wake wakes, waking, woke, woken VERB
When you **wake**, you stop sleeping.

walk walks, walking, walked VERB
When you **walk**, you move along by putting one foot in front of the other.

wall walls
NOUN **1** A **wall** is one of the vertical sides of a building or a room.
NOUN **2** A **wall** can also be used to divide or go round an area of land.

wallet wallets NOUN
A **wallet** is a small flat case that fits in a pocket. It is used to hold things such as paper money and credit cards.

wallpaper wallpapers NOUN
Wallpaper is thick coloured or patterned paper that is used for covering and decorating the walls of a room.

walnut walnuts NOUN
A **walnut** is a nut with a wrinkled shape and a light brown shell.

walrus walruses NOUN
A **walrus** is a mammal that lives in the sea and looks like a large seal. It has coarse whiskers and two long tusks.

wand wands NOUN
A **wand** is a long thin rod that magicians wave when they are performing tricks and magic.

wander wanders, wandering, wandered VERB
If you **wander**, you walk around without going in any particular direction.

want wants, wanting, wanted VERB
If you **want** something, you wish for it or need it.

war wars NOUN
A **war** is a period of fighting between countries.

wardrobe wardrobes NOUN
A **wardrobe** is a tall cupboard where you can hang your clothes.

warehouse warehouses NOUN
A **warehouse** is a large building which is used to store things.

warm warmer, warmest
ADJECTIVE **1** Something that is **warm** has some heat but not enough to be hot.
ADJECTIVE **2** Clothes and blankets that are **warm** are made of a material that stops you feeling cold.

A
B
C
D
E
F
G
H
I
J
K
L
M
N
O
P
Q
R
S
T
U
V
W
X
Y
Z

warmth NOUN

Warmth is a comfortable amount of heat.

warn warns, warning, warned VERB

If you **warn** someone, you tell them about a danger or problem that they might meet.

warning warnings NOUN

A **warning** is something that tells you about a possible problem or danger.

warren warrens NOUN

A **warren** is a group of holes in the ground which rabbits live in. The holes are connected by tunnels.

wary warier, wariest ADJECTIVE

If you are **wary** about something, you are careful because you are not sure about it.
warily ADVERB

was VERB

Was is a past tense form of **be**. It **was** my birthday yesterday.
See **be**

wash washes, washing, washed VERB

If you **wash** something, you clean it with soap and water.

washable ADJECTIVE

Clothes or materials that are **washable** can be washed in water without being damaged.

washing NOUN

Washing is clothes, towels and bedding that need to be washed.

washing machine washing machines NOUN

A **washing machine** is a machine for washing clothes in.

washing-up NOUN

If you do the **washing-up**, you wash things such as plates, pans and knives after a meal.

wasp wasps NOUN

A **wasp** is a flying insect with yellow and black stripes across its body. Wasps can sting.

waste wastes, wasting, wasted

VERB **1** If you **waste** something, such as time or money, you use too much of it on something that is not important.
NOUN **2 Waste** is material that is no longer wanted. This is often because the useful part of it has been taken out.

watch watches, watching, watched

NOUN **1** A **watch** is a small clock that you can wear on your wrist.
VERB **2** If you **watch** something, you look at it carefully to see what happens.

water waters, watering, watered

NOUN **1 Water** is a clear liquid that all living things need in order to live.
VERB **2** If you **water** a plant or animal, you give it water to drink.

waterfall waterfalls NOUN

A **waterfall** is water that flows over the edge of a cliff to the ground below.

waterlogged ADJECTIVE

Land that is **waterlogged** is so wet the soil cannot contain any more water.

waterproof ADJECTIVE

A material that is **waterproof** does not let water pass through it.

watertight ADJECTIVE

Something that is **watertight** is closed so tightly that it does not allow water to pass through.

wave waves, waving, waved

VERB **1** If you **wave**, you move your hand in the air, to say hello or goodbye.

VERB **2** If something **waves**, it moves gently up and down or from side to side. *The flags waved in the wind.*

NOUN **3** A **wave** is a raised line of water on the surface of the sea caused by wind or tides.

NOUN **4** A **wave** is also a gentle curving shape in someone's hair.

wax NOUN

Wax is a solid, slightly shiny substance, made of fat or oil. It is used to make candles and polish.

way ways

NOUN **1** A **way** of doing something is how it can be done.

NOUN **2** The **way** to a particular place is the direction you have to go to get there.

weak weaker, weakest

ADJECTIVE **1** People or animals that are **weak** do not have much strength or energy.

ADJECTIVE **2** If an object or part of an object is **weak**, it could break easily.

ADJECTIVE **3** Drinks, such as tea or coffee, that are **weak** do not have a strong taste.

wealthy wealthier, wealthiest ADJECTIVE

Someone who is **wealthy** has a lot of money.

weapon weapons NOUN

A **weapon** is an object such as a gun or missile which is used to hurt or kill people in a fight or war.

wear wears, wearing, wore, worn

VERB **1** When you **wear** things, such as clothes, you have them on your body.

VERB **2** When something **wears out**, it has been used so much that it cannot be used any more.

weary wearier, weariest ADJECTIVE

If you are **weary**, you are tired.

wearily ADVERB

weather NOUN

The **weather** is what it is like outside, for example raining, sunny or windy.

See Weather and seasons on page 263

weave weaves, weaving, wove, woven

VERB

When someone **weaves** cloth, they make it by crossing threads over and under each other, using a machine called a loom.

web webs

NOUN **1** A **web** is a fine net made by a spider to catch flies.

NOUN **2** The **web** is short for the **world wide web**.

webbed ADJECTIVE

Webbed feet have the toes connected by a piece of skin.

webcam webcams NOUN

A **webcam** is a camera that takes pictures which can be viewed on a website.

website websites NOUN

A **website** is a group of pages on the Internet which contain information about a particular subject.

a
b
c
d
e
f
g
h
i
j
k
l
m
n
o
p
q
r
s
t
u
v
w
x
y
z

wedding **weddings** NOUN
A **wedding** is when two people get married.

Wednesday **Wednesdays** NOUN
Wednesday is the day between Tuesday and Thursday.

weed **weeds** NOUN
A **weed** is any wild plant that grows where it is not wanted. Weeds grow strongly and stop other plants growing properly.

week **weeks** NOUN
A **week** is a period of seven days.

weekend **weekends** NOUN
A **weekend** is Saturday and Sunday.

weekly ADJECTIVE
Something that is **weekly** happens or appears once every week.

weep **weeps, weeping, wept** VERB
If someone **weeps**, they cry.

weigh **weighs, weighing, weighed**
VERB **1** If something **weighs** a particular amount, that is how heavy it is.
VERB **2** If you **weigh** something, you use scales to measure how heavy it is.

weight NOUN
The **weight** of something is its heaviness. Weight and mass are connected. Weight is usually measured in grams and kilograms.
See **mass**

weird **weirder, weirdest** ADJECTIVE
Something that is **weird** seems strange and peculiar.

welcome **welcomes, welcoming, welcomed** VERB
If you **welcome** someone, you speak to them in a friendly way when they arrive.

well **better, best; wells**
ADJECTIVE **1** If you are **well**, you are healthy.
ADVERB **2** If you do something **well**, you do it to a high standard.

NOUN **3** A **well** is a deep hole in the ground that has been dug to reach water or oil.

went VERB
Went is the past tense of **go**.

wept VERB
Wept is the past tense of **weep**.

were VERB
Were is a past tense form of **be**.
*They **were** at home yesterday.*
See **be**

west NOUN
The **west** is one of the four main points of the compass. It is the direction in which you look to see the sun set.
See **compass point**
western ADJECTIVE

wet **wetter, wettest**
ADJECTIVE **1** If something is **wet**, it is covered in water or some other liquid.
ADJECTIVE **2** If the weather is **wet**, it is raining.
ADJECTIVE **3** If something such as ink or cement is **wet**, it has not yet dried.

whale **whales** NOUN
A **whale** is a huge mammal that lives in the sea. Whales breathe through an opening in the top of their head.

what
ADJECTIVE OR PRONOUN **1** **What** is used in questions. *What time is it? What is your name?*
PRONOUN **2** You can use **what** to refer to information about something. *I don't know **what** you mean.*
what about PHRASE You say **what about** at the beginning of a question when you are

making a suggestion or offer. *What about a sandwich?*

wheat NOUN

Wheat is a cereal plant grown for its grain, which is used to make flour.

wheel wheels NOUN

A **wheel** is a circular object which turns round on a rod fixed to its centre. Wheels are fitted under things such as cars, bicycles and prams so that they can move along.

wheelbarrow wheelbarrows NOUN

A **wheelbarrow** is a small cart with a single wheel at the front.

wheelchair wheelchairs NOUN

A **wheelchair** is a chair with large wheels for use by people who find walking difficult or impossible.

when

ADVERB **1** You use **when** to ask what time something happened or will happen. *When are you leaving?*
CONJUNCTION **2** You use **when** to refer to a certain time. *I met him **when** we were at school together.*

where

ADVERB **1** You use **where** to ask questions about place. *Where is my book?*
CONJUNCTION **2** You use **where** to talk about the place in which something is situated or happening. *I don't know **where** we are.*

whether CONJUNCTION

You can use **whether** instead of **if**. *I don't know **whether** I can go.*

which

ADJECTIVE **1** You use **which** to ask for information about something when there are two or more possibilities. *Which room are you in?*
PRONOUN **2** You also use **which** when you are going to say more about something you have already mentioned. *We have a car **which** is dropping to bits.*

while

CONJUNCTION **1** If something happens **while** something else is happening, the two things happen at the same time.

NOUN **2** A **while** is a period of time. *She had to wait a little **while**.*

whimper whimpers, whimpering, whimpered VERB

When children or animals **whimper**, they make soft unhappy sounds, as if they are about to cry.

whine whines, whining, whined VERB

To **whine** is to make a long high-pitched noise because you are unhappy about something.

whip whips, whipping, whipped VERB

If you **whip** cream or eggs, you beat them until they are thick and frothy or stiff.

whirl whirls, whirling, whirled VERB

When something **whirls**, it turns round very fast.

whirlpool whirlpools NOUN

A **whirlpool** is a small place in a river or the sea where the water is moving quickly round and round, so that anything floating near it is pulled into its centre.

whirlwind whirlwinds NOUN

A **whirlwind** is a tall column of air which spins round and round very quickly.

whirr whirrs, whirring, whirred VERB

When something like a machine **whirrs**, it makes a series of low sounds so fast that it seems like one sound.

whisk whisks, whisking, whisked VERB

If you **whisk** something like cream, you stir it very fast.

whisker whiskers NOUN

The **whiskers** of an animal such as a cat or mouse are the long stiff hairs near its mouth.

whisper whispers, whispering, whispered VERB

When you **whisper**, you talk very quietly, using your breath and not your voice.

whistle whistles, whistling, whistled

NOUN **1** A **whistle** is a small metal tube which makes a loud sound when you blow it.

VERB **2** When you **whistle**, you make a loud high noise by using a whistle or by forcing your breath out between your lips.

white whiter, whitest; whites

ADJECTIVE **1** Something that is **white** is the colour of milk.

See Colours and shapes on page 266

ADJECTIVE **2** If someone goes **white**, their face becomes very pale because they are afraid, shocked or ill.

NOUN **3** The **white** of an egg is the transparent liquid surrounding the yolk.

whiteboard whiteboards NOUN

A **whiteboard** is a shiny white board on which people draw or write using special pens.

who

PRONOUN **1** You use **who** when you are asking about someone. *Who told you?*

PRONOUN **2** You use **who** at the beginning of a clause when you want to say more about someone you have just mentioned. *I've got a brother who wants to be a vet.*

whole wholes

NOUN **1** The **whole** of something is all of it. *It was the only pair in the whole of the country.*

ADJECTIVE **2** You use **whole** to describe all of something. *Take the whole cake.*

ADJECTIVE **3** **Whole** means in one piece.

whose

PRONOUN **1** You use **whose** to ask who something belongs to. *Whose book is this?*

PRONOUN **2** You use **whose** in front of information relating to a person or thing you have just mentioned. *That's the girl whose mother is a lawyer.*

why

ADVERB **1** You use **why** in questions when you ask about the reason for something. *Why did you do that?*

ADVERB **2** You also use **why** to talk about the reasons for something. *She wondered why he was there.*

wicked ADJECTIVE

Someone or something **wicked** is very bad.

wide wider, widest

ADJECTIVE **1** Something that is **wide** measures a lot from one side to the other.

ADVERB **2** If you open something **wide**, you open it a long way.

widow widows NOUN

A **widow** is a woman whose husband has died.

See **widower**

widower widowers NOUN

A **widower** is a man whose wife has died.
See **widow**

width widths NOUN

The **width** of something is the distance from one side to the other.

wife wives NOUN

A man's **wife** is the woman he is married to.

wig wigs NOUN

A **wig** is a false head of hair. People wear wigs because they are bald, or to cover their own hair.

wild wilder, wildest

ADJECTIVE **1** **Wild** animals, birds and plants live in natural surroundings and are not looked after by people.

ADJECTIVE **2** **Wild** behaviour is excited and not controlled.

wildlife NOUN
Wildlife means wild animals and plants.

will
VERB **1** You use **will** to form the future tense. *Robin **will** be quite annoyed.*
VERB **2** You use **will** when asking or telling someone to do something. ***Will** you do me a favour?*

willing
ADJECTIVE **1** If you are **willing** to do something, you are ready and happy to do it if someone wants you to.
ADJECTIVE **2** A **willing** person is someone who does things cheerfully.

willow **willows** NOUN
A **willow** is a tree with long thin branches and narrow leaves that likes to grow near water.

win **wins, winning, won**
VERB **1** If you **win** a race or game, you do better than the others taking part.
VERB **2** If you **win** a prize, you get it as a reward for doing something well.

wind **winds, winding, wound**
(*rhymes with* **tinned**) NOUN **1** A **wind** is a current of air that moves across the earth's surface.
(*rhymes with* **mind**) VERB **2** If a road or river **winds**, it has lots of bends in it.
VERB **3** When you **wind** something round something else, you wrap it round several times.

windmill **windmills** NOUN
A **windmill** is a building with large sails on the outside, which turn as the wind blows. This works a machine that grinds corn to make flour.

window **windows**
NOUN
A **window** is a space in a wall or vehicle. It has glass in it so that light can come in and you can see through.

windscreen **windscreens** NOUN
The **windscreen** of a vehicle is the glass window at the front.

windy **windier, windiest** ADJECTIVE
If it is **windy**, the wind is blowing hard.

wine **wines** NOUN
Wine is a strong drink usually made from the juice of grapes.

wing **wings**
NOUN **1** The **wings** of a bird or insect are the two limbs on its body that it uses for flying.
NOUN **2** The **wings** of an aeroplane are the long flat parts sticking out of its sides, which support it in the air.

wink **winks, winking, winked** VERB
When you **wink**, you close one eye for a moment. *She **winked** to show that she was joking.*

winner **winners** NOUN
If someone or something wins a prize, race or competition, they are the **winner**.

winter **winters** NOUN
Winter is the season between autumn and spring.

wipe **wipes, wiping, wiped** VERB
If you **wipe** something, you rub its surface lightly to remove dirt or liquid.

wire **wires** NOUN
Wire is a long, thin, flexible piece of metal which can be used to make or fasten things or to carry an electric current.

wireless ADJECTIVE
Wireless technology uses radio waves rather than electricity and therefore does not require any wires.

a
b
c
d
e
f
g
h
i
j
k
l
m
n
o
p
q
r
s
t
u
v
w
x
y
z

A
B
C
D
E
F
G
H
I
J
K
L
M
N
O
P
Q
R
S
T
U
V
W
X
Y
Z

wise **wiser, wisest** ADJECTIVE
Someone who is **wise** can use their experience and knowledge to make sensible decisions.
wisdom NOUN

wish **wishes, wishing, wished**
VERB **1** If you **wish** that something would happen, you would like it to happen.
NOUN **2** A **wish** is the act of wishing for something you would like to happen.

witch **witches** NOUN
In fairy stories, a **witch** is a woman who has magic powers.
See **wizard**

with
PREPOSITION **1** If you are **with** someone, you are in their company. *I was there **with** Mum and Dad.*
PREPOSITION **2** **With** can mean using or having. *She worked **with** a big brush.*

wither **withers, withering, withered** VERB
If a plant **withers**, it shrivels up and dies.

within
PREPOSITION **1** **Within** means not going outside certain limits. *Stay **within** the school grounds.*
PREPOSITION **2** **Within** can also mean before a period of time has passed. *You must write back **within** ten days.*

without
PREPOSITION **1** **Without** means not having or using. *You can't get in **without** a key.*
PREPOSITION **2** **Without** can mean not in someone's company. *He went **without** me.*
PREPOSITION **3** **Without** can also mean that something does not happen. *She rang three times **without** an answer.*

witness **witnesses, witnessing, witnessed**
NOUN **1** A **witness** is someone who has seen an event such as an accident and can describe what happened.
VERB **2** If you **witness** an event, you see it happen.

wizard **wizards** NOUN
In fairy stories, a **wizard** is a man who has magic powers.
See **witch**

wobble **wobbles, wobbling, wobbled** VERB
If something **wobbles**, it makes small movements from side to side.

woke VERB
Woke is the past tense of **wake**.

woken VERB
Woken is the past participle of **wake**.

wolf **wolves** NOUN
A **wolf** is a wild animal that looks like a large dog. Wolves live in a group called a pack.

woman **women** NOUN
A **woman** is an adult female human being.
See **man**

won VERB
Won is the past tense of **win**.

wonder **wonders, wondering, wondered**
VERB **1** If you **wonder** about something, you wish you knew more about it.
VERB **2** If you **wonder** what to do about something, you are not sure what to do about it.
NOUN **3** **Wonder** is a feeling of great and pleasant surprise.

wonderful ADJECTIVE
If something is **wonderful**, it makes you feel very happy.

won't VERB
Won't is a contraction of **will not**.

wood **woods**
NOUN **1** **Wood** is the substance which forms the trunks and branches of trees.
NOUN **2** A **wood** is a large area of trees growing near each other.

wooden ADJECTIVE
Something that is **wooden** is made of wood.

woodpecker **woodpeckers** NOUN
A **woodpecker** is a bird with a long sharp beak. It drills holes in trees to find insects.

woodwork
NOUN **1** The **woodwork** in a house is all the parts that are made of wood, such as the doors and window frames.
NOUN **2** **Woodwork** is making things out of wood.

woof **woofs** NOUN
Woof is the noise that a dog makes when it barks.

wool
NOUN **1** **Wool** is the hair that grows on sheep and on some other animals.
NOUN **2** **Wool** is also the yarn spun from the wool of animals which is used to knit, weave, and make things like clothes, blankets and carpets.

woollen ADJECTIVE
Something that is **woollen** is made from wool.

woolly **woollier, woolliest** ADJECTIVE
Something that is **woolly** is made of wool, or looks like wool.

word **words** NOUN
A **word** is a set of sounds or letters that has a meaning. A word can be written or spoken. When it is written, there are no spaces between the letters.

wore VERB
Wore is the past tense of **wear**.

work **works, working, worked**
VERB **1** When you **work**, you spend time and energy doing something useful.
VERB **2** People who **work** have a job that they are paid to do.
VERB **3** If something **works**, it does what it is supposed to do.

work out **works out, working out, worked out**

VERB **1** If you **work out** the answer to a problem, you find the answer.
VERB **2** If you **work out**, you do exercises to make your body fit and strong.

world **worlds** NOUN
The **world** is the planet we live on.

world wide web NOUN
The **world wide web** is a very large number of websites all joined together. You can use it to search for information.

worm **worms** NOUN
A **worm** is a small animal with a long thin body. Worms have no bones and no legs. They live in the soil.

worn
VERB **1** **Worn** is the past participle of **wear**.
ADJECTIVE **2** Something that is **worn** is damaged or thin because it is old and has been used a lot.

worry **worries, worrying, worried** VERB
If you **worry**, you keep thinking about problems or about unpleasant things that might happen.

worse
ADJECTIVE **1** **Worse** is the comparative form of **bad**.
ADJECTIVE **2** If someone who is ill gets **worse**, they are more ill than before.

worship **worships, worshipping, worshipped** VERB
If you **worship** a god, you show your respect by praying and singing hymns.

worst ADJECTIVE
Worst is the superlative form of **bad**.

worth
ADJECTIVE **1** If something is **worth** a particular amount of money, it could be sold for that amount.
ADJECTIVE **2** If something is **worth** doing, it is enjoyable or useful. *That film is **worth** seeing.*

a
b
c
d
e
f
g
h
i
j
k
l
m
n
o
p
q
r
s
t
u
v
w
x
y
z

A
B
C
D
E
F
G
H
I
J
K
L
M
N
O
P
Q
R
S
T
U
V
W
X
Y
Z

250

would

VERB **1** You use **would** to say what someone thought was going to happen. *We were sure it would rain.*

VERB **2** You also use **would** to say you want something to happen. *I would like to know how they do that.*

wound wounds

(*rhymes with* **round**) VERB **1** **Wound** is the past tense of **wind**.

(*said* **woond**) NOUN **2** A **wound** is an injury to your body, especially a cut in your skin.

wove VERB

Wove is the past tense of **weave**.

woven VERB

Woven is the past participle of **weave**.

wrap wraps, wrapping, wrapped VERB

When you **wrap** something, you cover it tightly with something like paper.

wrapping wrappings NOUN

Wrapping is the material used to cover and protect something.

wreath wreaths NOUN

A **wreath** is an arrangement of flowers and leaves, often in the shape of a circle.

wreck wrecks, wrecking, wrecked

VERB **1** If someone or something **wrecks** something, they destroy it completely.

VERB **2** If a ship is **wrecked**, it is so badly damaged that it can no longer sail.

NOUN **3** A **wreck** is a vehicle that has been badly damaged in an accident.

wren wrens NOUN

A **wren** is a tiny brown bird.

wrestle wrestles, wrestling, wrestled

VERB

If you **wrestle** with someone, you fight them by holding or throwing them, but not hitting them.

wriggle wriggles, wriggling, wriggled

VERB

When you **wriggle**, you twist and turn your body with quick movements.

wring wrings, wringing, wrung VERB

If you **wring** a wet piece of cloth, you squeeze the water out of it by twisting it.

wrinkle wrinkles

NOUN **1** A **wrinkle** is a line in someone's skin, especially on their face, that forms as they grow old.

NOUN **2** A **wrinkle** is also a raised fold in something like cloth or thin paper.

wrinkled ADJECTIVE

If something is **wrinkled**, it has folds or lines in it.

wrist wrists NOUN

Your **wrist** is the part of your body between your hand and your arm, which bends when you move your hand.

write writes, writing, wrote, written

VERB **1** When you **write**, you use a pen or pencil to make words, letters or numbers.

VERB **2** If you **write** something such as a poem or a story, you create it.

VERB **3** When you **write** to someone, you tell them about something in a letter.

writing

NOUN **1** **Writing** is something that has been written or printed.

NOUN **2** Your **writing** is the way you write with a pen or pencil.

written VERB

Written is the past participle of **write**.

wrong

ADJECTIVE **1** Something that is **wrong** is not correct.

ADJECTIVE **2** If there is something **wrong** with a machine, vehicle, or piece of equipment, it is not working properly.

ADJECTIVE **3** If a person does something **wrong**, they do something bad.

wrote VERB

Wrote is the past tense of **write**.

wrung VERB

Wrung is the past tense of **wring**.

Xx

X-ray **X-rays** NOUN
An **X-ray** is a ray that can pass through some solid materials. X-rays are used by doctors to examine bones or organs inside people's bodies.

xylophone **xylophones** NOUN
A **xylophone** is a musical instrument made of wooden bars of different lengths which are arranged in a row. You play a xylophone by hitting the bars with special hammers.

Yy

yacht **yachts** NOUN
A **yacht** is a large boat with sails or a motor. Yachts are used for racing or for pleasure trips.

yam **yams** NOUN
A **yam** is a root vegetable which grows in tropical regions.

yard **yards**
NOUN **1** A **yard** is a unit of length equal to just under one metre.
NOUN **2** A **yard** is also an enclosed area that is usually next to a building.

yarn **yarns** NOUN
Yarn is thread made from something such as wool or cotton. It is used for knitting or making cloth.

yawn **yawns, yawning, yawned** VERB
When you **yawn**, you open your mouth wide and take in more air than usual. You often yawn when you are tired or bored.

year **years** NOUN
A **year** is a period of time. It is equal to 12 months, or 52 weeks, or 365 days.

yeast NOUN
Yeast is a kind of fungus that is used to make bread rise. It is also used in making drinks such as beer.

a b c d e f g h i j k l m n o p q r s t u v w x y z

251

A
B
C
D
E
F
G
H
I
J
K
L
M
N
O
P
Q
R
S
T
U
V
W
X
Y
Z

yell **yells, yelling, yelled** VERB
If you **yell**, you shout loudly. People sometimes yell if they are excited, angry, or in pain.

yellow ADJECTIVE
Something that is **yellow** is the colour of lemons or egg yolks.
See Colours and shapes on page 266

yelp **yelps, yelping, yelped** VERB
If people or animals **yelp**, they give a sudden short cry. This is often because they are frightened or in pain.

yes INTERJECTION
You say **yes** to agree with someone, to say that something is true, or to accept something.

yesterday ADVERB
Yesterday is the day before today.

yet
ADVERB **1** You say **yet** when you mean up till now. *She hasn't come **yet**.*
ADVERB **2** If something should not be done **yet**, it should be done later. *Don't switch it off **yet**.*
CONJUNCTION **3** You can use **yet** to introduce something which is rather surprising. *He doesn't like maths, **yet** he always does well.*

yew **yews** NOUN
A **yew** is an evergreen tree with thin, dark green leaves. Some yew trees have red berries.

yogurt **yogurts**; also spelt **yoghurt** NOUN
Yogurt is a slightly sour, thick liquid food made from milk.
See Other foods on page 261

yolk **yolks** NOUN
A **yolk** is the yellow part in the middle of an egg.

you PRONOUN
You means the person or people that someone is talking or writing to. *Can I help **you**?*

young **younger, youngest**
ADJECTIVE **1** A **young** person, animal or plant has not been alive for very long.
NOUN **2** The **young** of an animal are its babies.

your ADJECTIVE
Your means belonging or relating to the person or group of people that someone is speaking to.
*****Your** teacher seems nice.*

yourself **yourselves** PRONOUN
If you do something **yourself**, no one else does it. *If you do that, you'll hurt **yourself**.*
by yourself PHRASE If you are **by yourself**, you are on your own. *What are you doing here all **by yourself**?*

youth **youths**
NOUN **1** A **youth** is a boy or young man.
NOUN **2** Your **youth** is the time in your life when you are young.

yo-yo **yo-yos** NOUN
A **yo-yo** is a round wooden or plastic toy attached to a piece of string. You play by making the yo-yo rise and fall on the string.

Zz

zap zaps, zapping, zapped
VERB **1** If you **zap** something or somebody in a computer game, you get rid of them.
VERB **2** To **zap** also means to keep changing channels on the television.

zebra zebras NOUN
A **zebra** is a type of African wild horse with black and white stripes over its body.

zebra crossing zebra crossings NOUN
A **zebra crossing** is a place where you can cross the road safely. The road is marked with black and white stripes.

zero zeros
NOUN **1** **Zero** is the number 0.
NOUN **2** **Zero** is also the freezing point of water, 0°C.

zigzag zigzags NOUN
A **zigzag** is a line which keeps changing direction sharply.

zip zips NOUN
A **zip** is a long narrow fastener with two rows of teeth that are closed or opened by a small clip pulled between them.

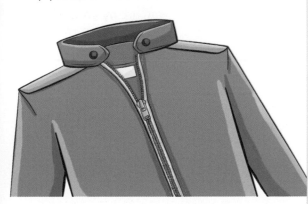

zone zones NOUN
A **zone** is an area of land or sea that is considered to be different from the areas around it. *My dad wants to turn the garden into a cat-free* **zone**.

zoo zoos NOUN
A **zoo** is a park where wild animals are kept so that people can look at them or study them.

zoom zooms, zooming, zoomed
VERB **1** To **zoom** somewhere means to go there very quickly.
VERB **2** If a camera **zooms** in on a person or thing being photographed, it gives a close-up picture of them.

a
b
c
d
e
f
g
h
i
j
k
l
m
n
o
p
q
r
s
t
u
v
w
x
y
z

Word Wizard

The body

head

shoulder

wrist

arm

chest

calf

stomach

hip

thigh

foot

bottom

waist

leg

knee

back

The face

head

elbow

hand

eyebrow

eyelash

eye

nose

ear

mouth

lip

tooth

neck

Clothes

shirt

tie

waistcoat

jacket

suit

trousers

shoes

cardigan

blouse

skirt

jumper

shorts

trainers

socks

hat

gloves

scarf

jeans

sweatshirt

dress

jacket

T-shirt

coat

nightdress

pyjamas

slippers

Family

Kate's grandfather

Kate's grandmother

Kate's father

Kate's mother

Kate's uncle

Kate's aunt

Kate's cousin

Kate   **Rob**

Rob's wife

Kate's husband

Kate's sister   Kate's brother-in-law

Kate's sister-in-law   Kate's brother

Kate's niece

Kate's son

Kate's daughter

Kate's nephew

Feelings

angry

bored

happy

frightened

excited

sad

surprised

tired

shocked

confused

259

Food and drink

Fruit

apple

banana

cherries

grapes

mango

pineapple

peach

pear

melon

plum

raspberry

strawberry

grapefruit

lemon

lime

orange

Vegetables

beans

broccoli

cabbage

carrot

garlic

cauliflower

leek

chilli pepper

cucumber

mushrooms

onion

pepper

lettuce

spring onions

potato

tomato

Other foods

biscuit

cheese

crisps

chips

egg

ice cream

jam

pasta

salt and pepper

cake

salad

sandwich

soup

rice

cereal

yogurt

butter   bread

Drinks

coffee

orange juice

milk

tea

School and study

- projector
- notice board
- interactive whiteboard
- teacher
- timetable
- globe
- computer
- books
- textbook
- chair
- exercise book
- desk
- student/pupil

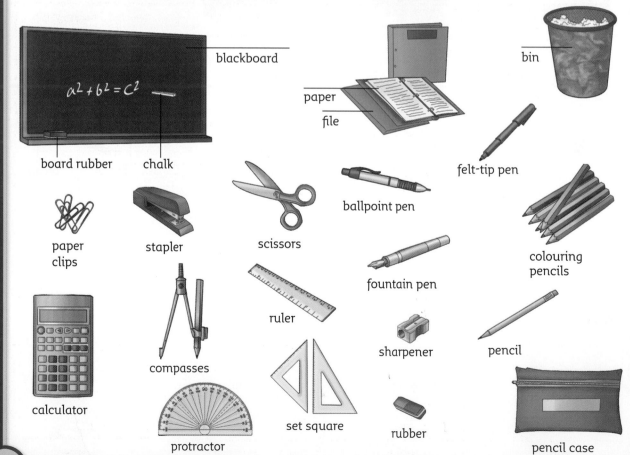

- blackboard
- bin
- paper
- file
- board rubber
- chalk
- felt-tip pen
- paper clips
- stapler
- scissors
- ballpoint pen
- colouring pencils
- fountain pen
- calculator
- compasses
- ruler
- sharpener
- pencil
- protractor
- set square
- rubber
- pencil case

$$a^2 + b^2 = c^2$$

Weather

It's rainy

It's sunny

It's cloudy

It's windy

It's foggy

It's snowy

It's stormy

It's icy

flood

lightning

rainbow

Seasons

spring

summer

autumn

winter

Insects

ant

bee

beetle

fly

butterfly

dragonfly

grasshopper

ladybird

mosquito

Amphibians

frog

toad

newt

Reptiles

alligator

crocodile

lizard

snake

tortoise

turtle

Young animals

bear and **cub**

cat and **kitten**

deer and **fawn**

goat and **kid**

goose and **gosling**

hare and **leveret**

horse and **foal**

kangaroo and **joey**

pig and **piglet**

rabbit and **kitten**

seal and **calf**
or **pup**

sheep and **lamb**

tiger and **cub**

swan and **cygnet**

whale and **calf**

More young animals

bird and **chick**
chicken and **chick**
cow and **calf**
dog and **puppy**
duck and **duckling**
elephant and **calf**
fox and **cub**
lion and **cub**
wolf and **cub**

Colours and shapes

black

oval

grey

circle

green

star

yellow

square

white

rectangle

blue

pentagon

brown

hexagon

purple

heptagon

red

octagon

pink

quadrilaterals

orange

diamond *or* rhombus

maroon

triangle

lilac

equilateral triangle

turquoise

isosceles triangle

indigo

kite

beige

oblong

navy

semicircle

Solid shapes (3D)

cube

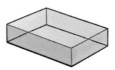

cuboid

square pyramid

regular tetrahedron *or* triangular pyramid

cone

sphere

hemisphere

cylinder

Words we use a lot

a	began	for	home	must	said	this	when
about	being	from	how	my	saw	three	where
after	but	get	I	name	say	to	which
again	by	go	if	next	seen	too	who
all	came	goes	in	no	she	took	why
along	can	going	is	not	should	two	will
am	can't	got	it	now	so	up	with
an	come	had	its	of	some	upon	woman
and	coming	hadn't	it's	off	suddenly	us	would
another	could	has	just	okay	take	very	wouldn't
are	couldn't	hasn't	last	on	than	want	yes
aren't	did	have	made	once	that	was	you
as	didn't	haven't	make	one	the	wasn't	your
at	do	he	man	or	their	way	
away	does	heard	many	our	them	we	
back	doesn't	her	may	out	then	went	
be	don't	here	me	over	there	were	
because	every	him	more	people	these	weren't	
been	first	his	much	put	they	what	

Silent letters

Each of these words has a silent letter. Can you think of any other words like these?

clim<u>b</u>	<u>k</u>nit
colum<u>n</u>	<u>k</u>nock
com<u>b</u>	<u>k</u>not
dou<u>b</u>t	<u>k</u>now
<u>g</u>host	lam<u>b</u>
<u>g</u>nat	s<u>c</u>issors
<u>g</u>naw	s<u>w</u>ord
<u>h</u>our	<u>w</u>rap
<u>k</u>nee	<u>w</u>riggle
<u>k</u>nife	<u>w</u>rite

Confusable words

These words have different meanings but are easy to mix up.

its (belongs to it)	The dog wagged <u>its</u> tail.
it's (it is)	<u>It's</u> not funny.
loose	My tooth's <u>loose</u>.
lose	Don't <u>lose</u> your pen.
passed	I <u>passed</u> my test.
past	It's ten <u>past</u> three.
their (belongs to them)	The girls counted <u>their</u> money.
they're (they are)	<u>They're</u> going to the shop.
there	<u>There</u> are 26 chairs in this room.
	Put your bag down <u>there</u>.
than	I am shorter <u>than</u> you.
then (at that time)	<u>Then</u> I heard footsteps.
too	Can I come <u>too</u>? This is <u>too</u> hard.
two	I'd like <u>two</u> cakes.
to	I want <u>to</u> swim. Let's go <u>to</u> the beach.
whose (belongs to whom)	<u>Whose</u> bag is this?
who's (who is or who has)	<u>Who's</u> that?
	I know <u>who's</u> been sending you notes.

Parts of speech

Noun

A **noun** is a person, place, thing or idea. There are different types of noun.

A noun can be **singular**, which means one ...

cat

... or **plural**, which means more than one.

cats

Common nouns name people, places, things, or ideas in general. For example, "boy", "dog", "school", "computer" and "happiness" are common nouns.

Proper nouns are the names of particular people, places or things. They start with a capital letter. For example, "Ben", "France" and "Buckingham Palace" are proper nouns.

Collective nouns

A **collective noun** names a group of things.

a **bunch** of grapes

a **clutch** of eggs

a **flock** of sheep

a **pack** of wolves

a **litter** of puppies

a **herd** of cows

a **pride** of lions

a **school** of dolphins

a **shoal** of fish

a **swarm** of bees

Pronoun

A **pronoun** is used to replace a noun.

I	me	my	mine	myself
you	you	your	yours	yourself, yourselves
he, she, it	him, her, it	his, her, its	his, hers, its	himself, herself, itself
we	us	our	ours	ourselves
they	them	their	theirs	themselves

Personal pronouns are used for a person or thing that has already been named, for example "me", "her", "you", "it".
John jumped for the ball. He caught it!

Possessive pronouns show that a noun belongs to a person or thing that has already been named, for example, "my", "their", "his", "our".
The bird flapped its wings.

Adjective

An **adjective** describes a noun. For example, "tall", "happy" and "lucky" are all adjectives.

Some adjectives have a **comparative** and a **superlative** form. In most cases, these forms are made by adding **-er** or **-est** to the adjective.

adjective	comparative (more)	superlative (most)
tall	taller	tallest
hot	hotter	hottest
good	better	best
lucky	luckier	luckiest

Verb

A **verb** is an action word. It tells you what people and things do. For example, "sleep", "think" and "play" are all verbs.

Verbs have different forms called **tenses**. A tense shows whether you are talking about the past, present or future.

past	present	future
I played	*I play*	*I will play*
	I am playing	

Adverb

An **adverb** tells you more about a verb. For example, "shyly", "brightly" and "happily" are all adverbs. Many adverbs end in the suffix **-ly**.

How did Mary and Brian talk?
They talked loudly.

Other adverbs tell you where, when, or how often something happens.

where: outside, inside, here, there
when: today, soon, immediately
how often: never, frequently, often, always

Punctuation

ABC	A **capital letter** is used at the beginning of a sentence and for proper nouns.	*My brother Jim lives in New Zealand.*
.	You put a **full stop** at the end of a sentence.	*This is a sentence.*
?	You put a **question mark** at the end of a question.	*Can you come to my party?*
,	You use a **comma** to separate parts of a sentence or items on a list.	*She brought sandwiches, crisps, apples and juice to the picnic.*
!	You use an **exclamation mark** at the end of a sentence to show a strong feeling.	*Wow!*
'	An **apostrophe** is used in contractions and to show belonging.	*I didn't mean to break my brother's toy.*
" " ' '	**Speech marks** show where speech begins and ends.	*"I like your hair," she said.*
-	You use a **hyphen** to join together words or parts of words.	*I'm left-handed.*
( )	**Brackets** are used to show that something is not part of the main text.	*My cousin (the one from America) is coming to stay.*
–	A **dash** can be used instead of brackets, or to show a change of subject.	*My best friend – besides you – is George.*
:	You can use a **colon** for several things, for example in front of a list.	*You will need the following: strong walking boots, a map and a compass.*
;	A **semicolon** is used to separate different parts of a sentence or list, or to show a pause.	*The pizza choices are: cheese; onions, peppers and mushrooms; ham and pineapple; pepperoni; or sausage.*

Prefixes

A **prefix** is a group of letters added to the beginning of a word to make a new word.

prefix	meaning	example	prefix	meaning	example
anti-	opposite of, against	anticlockwise	**over-**	too much	oversleep
			poly-	many	polygon
co-	together	copilot	**pre-**	before	prehistoric
de-	take away	decode	**re-**	again	rearrange
dis-	opposite of	disappear	**semi-**	half	semicircle
ex-	former	ex-husband	**sub-**	under, part of	subheading
micro-	very small	microscope	**super-**	larger, more than	supersonic
mid-	middle	midnight			
mini-	smaller	minibus	**un-**	not	unlucky
mis-	wrong	misspell	**under-**	under or not enough	underground
non-	not	non-fiction			

Suffixes

A **suffix** is a letter or group of letters added to the end of a word to make a new word.

Some suffixes can change nouns into other nouns:

-hood	child	→	child**hood**		
-ist	art	→	art**ist**	science →	scient**ist**
-ship	friend	→	friend**ship**		

Some suffixes can change nouns into other nouns:

-ess	lion	→	lion**ess**	prince →	princ**ess**

Some suffixes can form a diminutive (a small word):

-ette	disk	→	disk**ette**

Some suffixes can change nouns or verbs into adjectives:

-able	comfort	→	comfort**able**	enjoy →	enjoy**able**
-al	music	→	music**al**		
-ary	imagine	→	imagin**ary**		
-ful	help	→	help**ful**		
-ible	sense	→	sens**ible**		
-ic	angel	→	angel**ic**	drama →	dramat**ic**
-ish	child	→	child**ish**		
-ive	act	→	act**ive**	persuade →	persuas**ive**
-less	care	→	care**less**		
-like	life	→	life**like**		
-ous	poison	→	poison**ous**		
-worthy	trust	→	trust**worthy**		
-y	health	→	health**y**		

Some suffixes can change adjectives into adverbs:

-ally	automatic	→	automatic**ally**		
-ly	slow	→	slow**ly**	happy →	happi**ly**

Some suffixes can change verbs or adjectives into nouns:

-ment	advertise	→	advertise**ment**	enjoy →	enjoy**ment**
-ness	ill	→	ill**ness**	happy →	happi**ness**
-sion	divide	→	divi**sion**		
-tion	add	→	addi**tion**	invite →	invita**tion**

Some suffixes can change nouns into verbs:

-ate	illustration	→	illustr**ate**

Synonyms

Synonyms are words that have the same, or almost the same, meaning. Here are some useful synonyms for everyday words:

angry
furious, mad, annoyed, outraged, indignant

bad
a bad person – wicked, nasty
a bad child – naughty, spiteful, defiant
bad food – rotten, decayed
a bad pain – severe
bad news – distressing, grave, terrible

big
huge, large, enormous, gigantic, vast, colossal

good
a good dog – well-behaved
a good painting – fine
a good film – enjoyable
a good worker – able, clever

happy
cheerful, content, delighted, glad, pleased, thrilled

kind
kind of person or thing – type, class, group

level
grade, position, stage

lots or **a lot**
plenty, a great deal, heaps, loads, many, a large amount, masses, piles

lovely
a lovely day – pleasant, glorious, sunny, splendid
a lovely meal – tasty, scrumptious, delicious
a lovely person – warm, kind, helpful, friendly
a lovely time – enjoyable, great, fantastic, wonderful, fabulous

nasty
a nasty person – unkind, rude, unpleasant
a nasty taste – horrible, foul, disgusting, awful

nice
nice food – delicious
a nice person – kind, helpful, pleasant
a nice view – lovely

rough
a rough road – bumpy, stony
a rough sea – choppy, stormy

small
a small problem – unimportant, trivial
a small child – little, tiny, young
a small room – cramped, cosy, modest

What else can you say?

The word "said" is useful, but here are some more interesting words that you can use to describe speech:

answer
reply, respond, retort, admit, agree

ask
enquire, demand, beg, query, wonder

said
announced, whispered, shouted, stammered, mumbled, yelled, shrieked, screamed, cried, murmured, remarked, declared, groaned, snarled, whimpered, admitted

Antonyms

Antonyms are words that have the opposite meaning.

cold   hot

for   against

exact   approximate

on   off

left   right

old   young

wide   narrow

up   down

before   after

old   new

digital   analogue

right   wrong

exciting   boring

to   from

gentle   rough

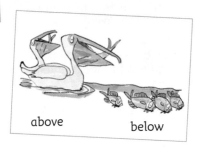

above   below

formal   informal

empty   full

under   over

deep   shallow

fiction   non-fiction

with   without

rough   smooth

in   out

sink   float

short   long

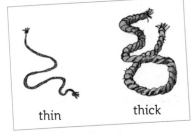

thin   thick

thin   fat

light   dark

closed   open

happy   sad

short   tall

ascend   descend

beginning   end

hollow   solid

Where words come from

Days of the week

Most of the days of the week were named by the Saxons. The Saxons came from Denmark and Germany to live in Britain over 1500 years ago.

Sunday is named after the **sun**.

Monday is named after the **moon**.

Tuesday is named after **Tiu**, the Saxon god of war and of the sky.

Wednesday is named after **Woden**, leader of the Viking gods.

Thursday is named after **Thor**, the Saxon god of thunder and lightning.

Friday was named after **Frigga**. She was goddess of love, and sat on a throne beside her husband, Woden.

Saturday is named after **Saturn**, the Roman god of farmers and farming.

Months of the year

The months of the year were given their names by the Romans.

January is named after **Janus**, the Roman god of doorways and beginnings.

February is named after **Februa**, a Roman festival when people were purified.

March is named after **Mars**, the Roman god of war.

April's name comes from the Latin word **aperire**, meaning "to open". Spring is when the year "opens".

May is named after **Maiestas**, Roman goddess of honour and reverence.

June is named after the Roman goddess **Juno**, queen of heaven.

July was named after **Julius Caesar**, army general and ruler of Ancient Rome.

August was named after the Roman emperor **Augustus**.

September comes from the Latin word **septem**, meaning "seven". The Roman year used to begin in March, so September was their seventh month.

October comes from the Latin word **octo**, meaning "eight". October was once the eighth month.

November comes from the Latin word **novem**, meaning "nine". November was once the ninth month.

December comes from the Latin word **decem**, meaning "ten". December was once the tenth month.

Words from the world

Lots of the words we use in the English language today come from other parts of the world. Here are some examples:

alphabet

This word comes from Greece. **Alpha** was the first letter of the Greek alphabet, and **beta** was the second. The two words together give us alphabet.

amphibian

This is another word from Greece. It comes from the Greek word **amphibios**, which means "living a double life". Amphibians are animals that can live on land or in water – so they live a double life!

bungalow

This word, which means "a low house", comes from India. The Hindi word for house is **bangla**.

bus

This word comes from Italy. It is short for **omnibus**, the Latin word for "everybody". Buses carry lots of people.

dandelion

This word comes from the French words **dent de lion**, meaning "a lion's tooth". This is because people thought the petals of the dandelion looked like a lion's teeth!

fete

This is another French word. It means "feast" in French. In English it means an outdoor event with competitions and stalls which sell things.

jungle

Jungle is a word from India. The Hindi word for jungle is **jangal**.

muscle

This word comes from the Latin word **musculus**, meaning "little mouse", because people thought muscles looked like mice beneath the skin!

porcupine

This comes from the Old French words **porc-espin**, meaning "pig with spines".

pyjamas

This word comes from Iran (which used to be called Persia). In Persia, **pay jama** meant "leg clothes".

Top tips for tricky words

Sometimes thinking of a silly phrase or sentence can help you remember how to spell tricky words. Here are some examples:

beautiful
Big elephants are useful.

qu words (q is always followed by u)
The Queen always carries an umbrella.

See how many of these you can remember. Then see if you can think up some of your own!

all right
It's either all right or all wrong.

believe
Believe has a lie in it.

hear
You hear with your ear.

February
You say "br" in February because it's cold.

different
One thing differs from another.

piece
Have a piece of pie.

friend
I'm seeing my friend on Friday, which comes at the end of the week.

library
Look into books. Reach and read yours.

necessary
Necessary has one collar and two socks (one **c** and two **s**'s!).

because
Ben eats cake and uses six eggs.

receive
R-e-c-e is very easy.

separate
Separate has a rat in it.

there
There is a place like here.

weather
We eat in all kinds of weather.

whose
Whose hose is that?

Sound it out!

Another good way to remember the spelling of some words is to sound out their different parts. Try these!

answer
ans-wer

cupboard
cup-board

Wednesday
Wed-nes-day

together
to-get-her

Top tips for learning to spell a tricky word

- **Look** at the word in the dictionary and point to it.

- **Say** the word out loud, then spell it out.

- **Cover** the word up, remembering what it looks like.

- **Write** the word down on a piece of paper and say it out loud again.

- **Check** your spelling against the dictionary.

- If you got it wrong, cover the page again and **try again!**

Tricky words to learn

The words on this list are tricky, so learn all of them to be a top speller!

address	definite	remember
among	does	rhyme
autumn	everybody	scissors
awful	exciting	sentence
beginning	exercise	straight
breakfast	guess	through
build	interest	trouble
careful	necessary	until
certain	people	usually
course	really	whole

Plurals

A plural word is what we use when there is more than one of something. It is often made by adding **s** to a word, like this:

singular **day**
plural **days**

Sometimes plurals are made by taking away the **y** at the end of the word and adding **ies**, like this:

singular **pony**
plural **ponies**

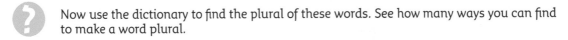 Now use the dictionary to find the plural of these words. See how many ways you can find to make a word plural.

horse	**volcano**
thief	**child**
party	**fly**
class	**monkey**
torch	**woman**

Measures

Length
millimetre (mm)
centimetre (cm)
metre (m)
kilometre (km)
mile

Mass or weight
gram (g)
half-kilogram
kilogram (kg)

Capacity
millilitre (ml)
half-litre
litre (l)
pint (pt)

Numbers

0 zero	30 thirty	1st first
1 one	31 thirty-one	2nd second
2 two	40 forty	3rd third
3 three	41 forty-one	4th fourth
4 four	50 fifty	5th fifth
5 five	51 fifty-one	6th sixth
6 six	60 sixty	7th seventh
7 seven	61 sixty-one	8th eighth
8 eight	70 seventy	9th ninth
9 nine	71 seventy-one	10th tenth
10 ten	80 eighty	11th eleventh
11 eleven	81 eighty-one	12th twelfth
12 twelve	90 ninety	13th thirteenth
13 thirteen	91 ninety-one	14th fourteenth
14 fourteen	100 one hundred	15th fifteenth
15 fifteen	101 one hundred and one	16th sixteenth
16 sixteen	150 one hundred and fifty	17th seventeenth
17 seventeen	200 two hundred	18th eighteenth
18 eighteen	1000 one thousand	19th nineteenth
19 nineteen	10 000 ten thousand	20th twentieth
20 twenty	100 000 one hundred thousand	21st twenty-first
21 twenty-one	1 000 000 one million	

Fractions

$\frac{1}{4}$ quarter

$\frac{1}{2}$ half

$\frac{1}{6}$ sixth

$\frac{1}{5}$ fifth

$\frac{1}{8}$ eighth

$\frac{1}{3}$ third

$\frac{1}{10}$ tenth

Time

9:50 a.m.

10 minutes to 10

7:25 p.m.

25 minutes past 7

Telling time

a.m.

p.m.

o'clock

half past

quarter past

quarter to

analogue

digital

clock

watch

timer

More time words

yesterday
today
tomorrow

calendar
date
weekend
holiday
birthday

second
minute
hour
day
week
fortnight
month
year
leap year
decade
century
millennium

dawn
morning
midday
noon
afternoon
dusk
evening
night
midnight

bedtime
daytime
dinnertime
playtime

Months
January
February
March
April
May
June
July
August
September
October
November
December

How often?
never
once
twice
sometimes
often
usually
always

Days
Monday
Tuesday
Wednesday
Thursday
Friday
Saturday
Sunday

Seasons
spring
summer
autumn
winter

Picture Credits